THE INVINCIBLE

IRON MAN

DRAGON SEED SAGA

THE INVINCIBLE
IRON MAN
DRAGON SEED SAGA

Writer: John Byrne
Pencilers: Paul Ryan & M.D. Bright
Inker: Bob Wiacek
Letterers: Michael Heisler & Phil Felix
Colorist: Paul Becton
Editor: Nelson Yomtov

Collection Editor: Mark D. Beazley
Editorial Assistant: Alex Starbuck
Assistant Editors: Cory Levine & John Denning
Editor, Special Projects: Jennifer Grünwald
Senior Editor, Special Projects: Jeff Youngquist
Senior Vice President of Sales: David Gabriel
Production: Jerron Quality Color
Research: Chad Anderson
Vice President of Creative: Tom Marvelli

Editor in Chief: Joe Quesada
Publisher: Dan Buckley

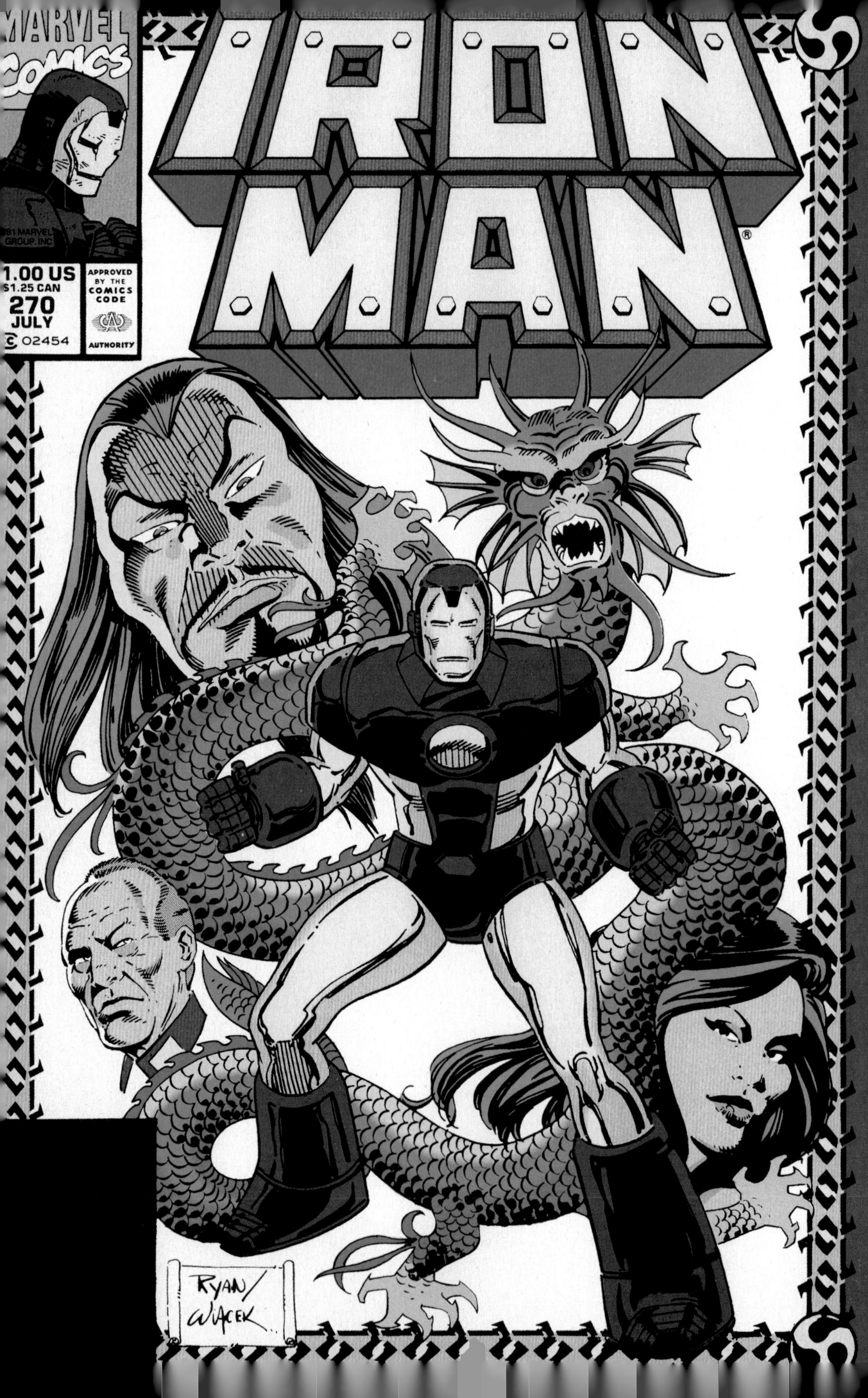
MARVEL COMICS
IRON MAN
$1.00 US
$1.25 CAN
270
JULY
02454
APPROVED BY THE COMICS CODE AUTHORITY
RYAN/
WIACEK

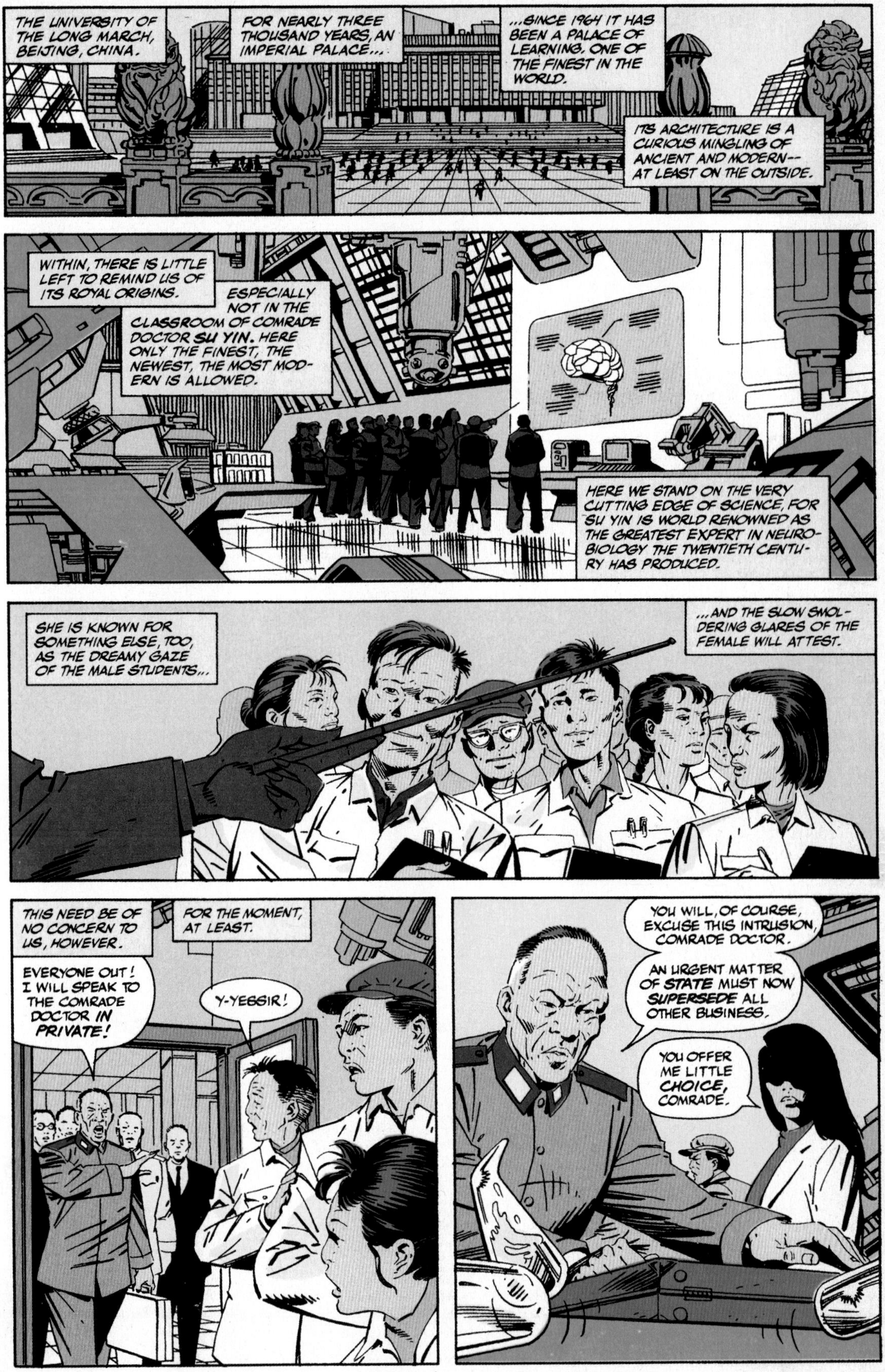
THE UNIVERSITY OF THE LONG MARCH, BEIJING, CHINA.
FOR NEARLY THREE THOUSAND YEARS, AN IMPERIAL PALACE...
...SINCE 1964 IT HAS BEEN A PALACE OF LEARNING. ONE OF THE FINEST IN THE WORLD.
ITS ARCHITECTURE IS A CURIOUS MINGLING OF ANCIENT AND MODERN-- AT LEAST ON THE OUTSIDE.
WITHIN, THERE IS LITTLE LEFT TO REMIND US OF ITS ROYAL ORIGINS.
ESPECIALLY NOT IN THE CLASSROOM OF COMRADE DOCTOR SU YIN. HERE ONLY THE FINEST, THE NEWEST, THE MOST MODERN IS ALLOWED.
HERE WE STAND ON THE VERY CUTTING EDGE OF SCIENCE, FOR SU YIN IS WORLD RENOWNED AS THE GREATEST EXPERT IN NEUROBIOLOGY THE TWENTIETH CENTURY HAS PRODUCED.
SHE IS KNOWN FOR SOMETHING ELSE, TOO, AS THE DREAMY GAZE OF THE MALE STUDENTS...
...AND THE SLOW SMOLDERING GLARES OF THE FEMALE WILL ATTEST.
THIS NEED BE OF NO CONCERN TO US, HOWEVER.
FOR THE MOMENT, AT LEAST.
EVERYONE OUT! I WILL SPEAK TO THE COMRADE DOCTOR IN PRIVATE!
Y-YESSIR!
YOU WILL, OF COURSE, EXCUSE THIS INTRUSION, COMRADE DOCTOR.
AN URGENT MATTER OF STATE MUST NOW SUPERSEDE ALL OTHER BUSINESS.
YOU OFFER ME LITTLE CHOICE, COMRADE.

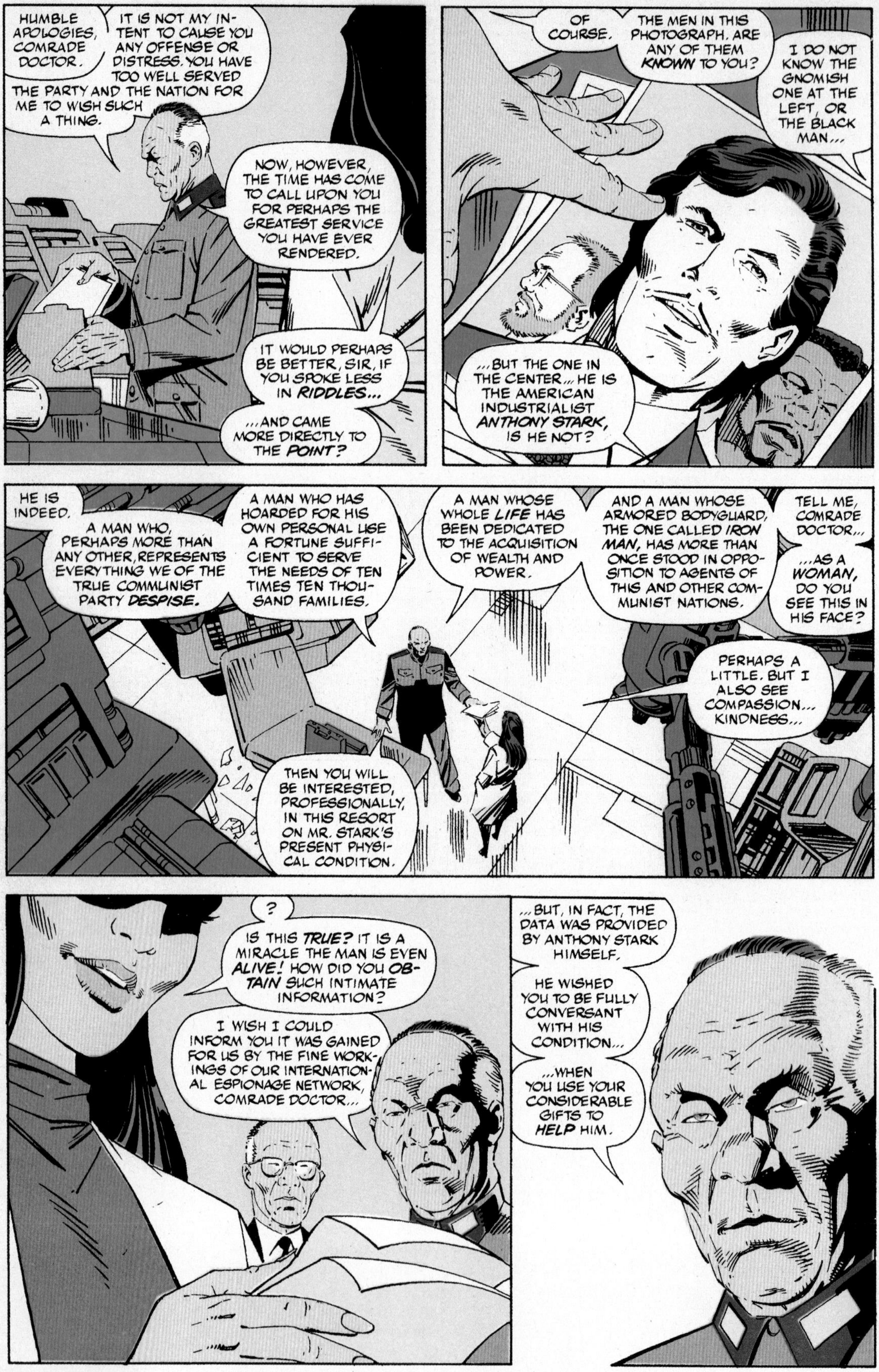
HUMBLE APOLOGIES, COMRADE DOCTOR.
IT IS NOT MY INTENT TO CAUSE YOU ANY OFFENSE OR DISTRESS. YOU HAVE TOO WELL SERVED THE PARTY AND THE NATION FOR ME TO WISH SUCH A THING.
NOW, HOWEVER, THE TIME HAS COME TO CALL UPON YOU FOR PERHAPS THE GREATEST SERVICE YOU HAVE EVER RENDERED.
IT WOULD PERHAPS BE BETTER, SIR, IF YOU SPOKE LESS IN RIDDLES...
...AND CAME MORE DIRECTLY TO THE POINT?
OF COURSE.
THE MEN IN THIS PHOTOGRAPH. ARE ANY OF THEM KNOWN TO YOU?
I DO NOT KNOW THE GNOMISH ONE AT THE LEFT, OR THE BLACK MAN...
...BUT THE ONE IN THE CENTER... HE IS THE AMERICAN INDUSTRIALIST ANTHONY STARK, IS HE NOT?
HE IS INDEED.
A MAN WHO, PERHAPS MORE THAN ANY OTHER, REPRESENTS EVERYTHING WE OF THE TRUE COMMUNIST PARTY DESPISE.
A MAN WHO HAS HOARDED FOR HIS OWN PERSONAL USE A FORTUNE SUFFICIENT TO SERVE THE NEEDS OF TEN TIMES TEN THOUSAND FAMILIES.
A MAN WHOSE WHOLE LIFE HAS BEEN DEDICATED TO THE ACQUISITION OF WEALTH AND POWER.
AND A MAN WHOSE ARMORED BODYGUARD, THE ONE CALLED IRON MAN, HAS MORE THAN ONCE STOOD IN OPPOSITION TO AGENTS OF THIS AND OTHER COMMUNIST NATIONS.
TELL ME, COMRADE DOCTOR...
...AS A WOMAN, DO YOU SEE THIS IN HIS FACE?
PERHAPS A LITTLE. BUT I ALSO SEE COMPASSION... KINDNESS...
THEN YOU WILL BE INTERESTED, PROFESSIONALLY, IN THIS RESORT ON MR. STARK'S PRESENT PHYSICAL CONDITION.
?
IS THIS TRUE? IT IS A MIRACLE THE MAN IS EVEN ALIVE! HOW DID YOU OBTAIN SUCH INTIMATE INFORMATION?
I WISH I COULD INFORM YOU IT WAS GAINED FOR US BY THE FINE WORKINGS OF OUR INTERNATIONAL ESPIONAGE NETWORK, COMRADE DOCTOR...
...BUT, IN FACT, THE DATA WAS PROVIDED BY ANTHONY STARK HIMSELF.
HE WISHED YOU TO BE FULLY CONVERSANT WITH HIS CONDITION...
...WHEN YOU USE YOUR CONSIDERABLE GIFTS TO HELP HIM.

WHEN MULTI-BILLIONAIRE INDUSTRIALIST **TONY STARK**, INVENTOR EXTRAORDINAIRE, DONS HIS SOLAR-CHARGED, STEEL-MESH ARMOR, HE BECOMES A HIGH-TECH WARRIOR—THE WORLD'S GREATEST HUMAN FIGHTING MACHINE!

Stan Lee PRESENTS: THE INVINCIBLE IRON MAN™

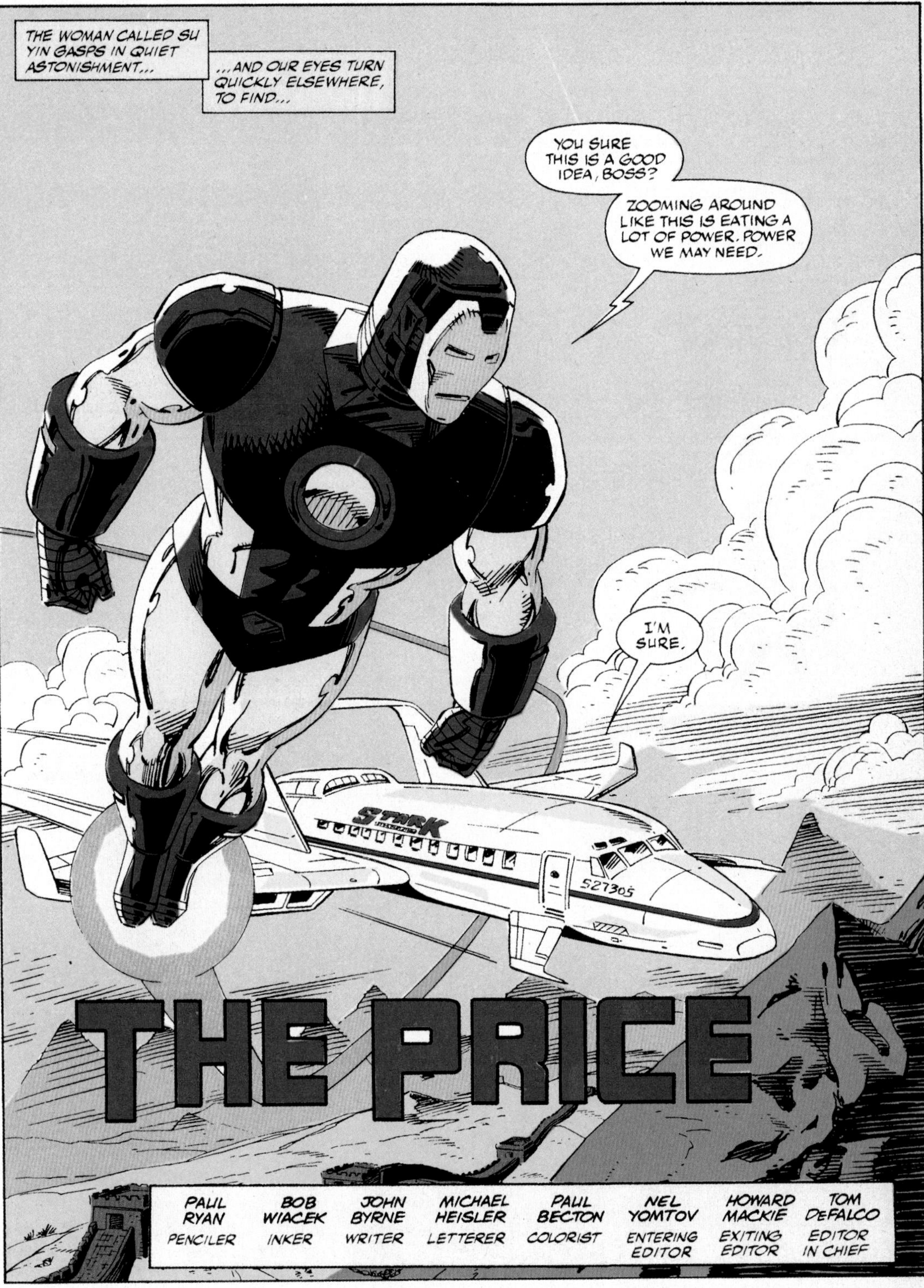

THE WOMAN CALLED SU YIN GASPS IN QUIET ASTONISHMENT...
...AND OUR EYES TURN QUICKLY ELSEWHERE, TO FIND...
YOU SURE THIS IS A GOOD IDEA, BOSS?
ZOOMING AROUND LIKE THIS IS EATING A LOT OF POWER. POWER WE MAY NEED.
I'M SURE.
STARK
S27305
THE PRICE
PAUL RYAN PENCILER
BOB WIACEK INKER
JOHN BYRNE WRITER
MICHAEL HEISLER LETTERER
PAUL BECTON COLORIST
NEL YOMTOV ENTERING EDITOR
HOWARD MACKIE EXITING EDITOR
TOM DEFALCO EDITOR IN CHIEF

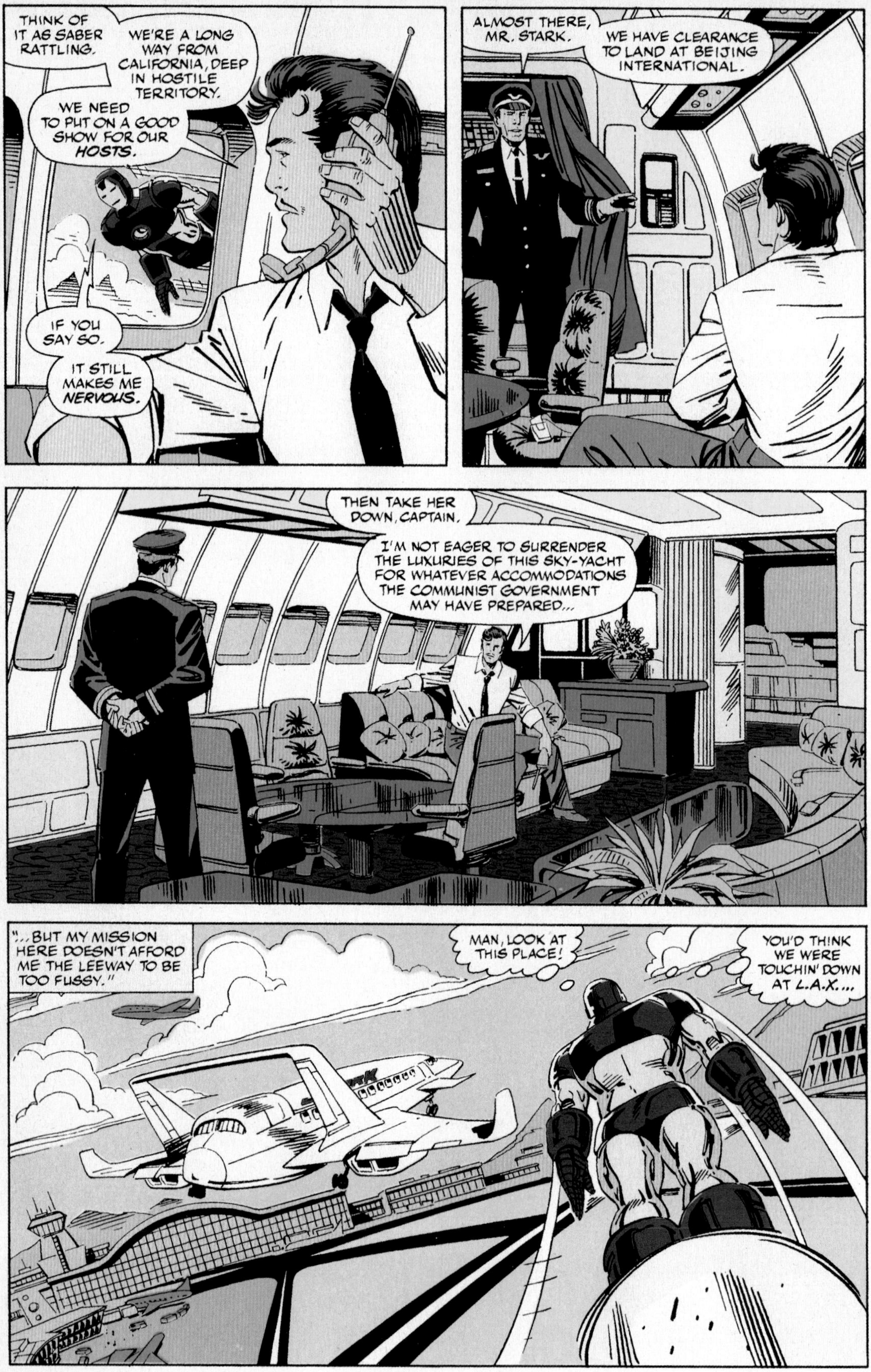
THINK OF IT AS SABER RATTLING.
WE'RE A LONG WAY FROM CALIFORNIA, DEEP IN HOSTILE TERRITORY.
WE NEED TO PUT ON A GOOD SHOW FOR OUR HOSTS.
IF YOU SAY SO.
IT STILL MAKES ME NERVOUS.
ALMOST THERE, MR. STARK.
WE HAVE CLEARANCE TO LAND AT BEIJING INTERNATIONAL.
THEN TAKE HER DOWN, CAPTAIN.
I'M NOT EAGER TO SURRENDER THE LUXURIES OF THIS SKY-YACHT FOR WHATEVER ACCOMMODATIONS THE COMMUNIST GOVERNMENT MAY HAVE PREPARED...
"...BUT MY MISSION HERE DOESN'T AFFORD ME THE LEEWAY TO BE TOO FUSSY."
MAN, LOOK AT THIS PLACE!
YOU'D THINK WE WERE TOUCHIN' DOWN AT L.A.X....

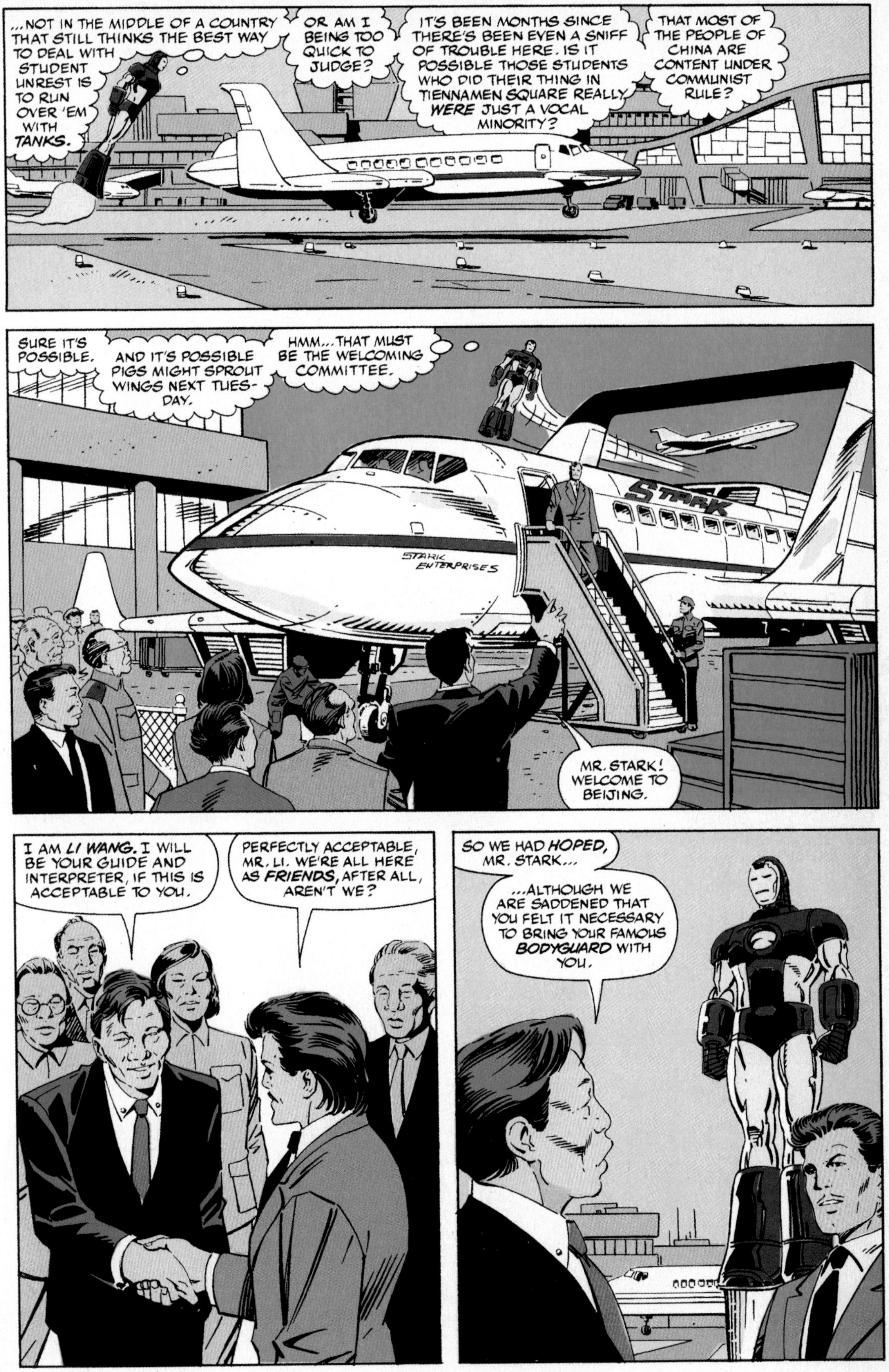
...NOT IN THE MIDDLE OF A COUNTRY THAT STILL THINKS THE BEST WAY TO DEAL WITH STUDENT UNREST IS TO RUN OVER 'EM WITH TANKS.
OR AM I BEING TOO QUICK TO JUDGE?
IT'S BEEN MONTHS SINCE THERE'S BEEN EVEN A SNIFF OF TROUBLE HERE. IS IT POSSIBLE THOSE STUDENTS WHO DID THEIR THING IN TIENNAMEN SQUARE REALLY WERE JUST A VOCAL MINORITY?
THAT MOST OF THE PEOPLE OF CHINA ARE CONTENT UNDER COMMUNIST RULE?
SURE IT'S POSSIBLE.
AND IT'S POSSIBLE PIGS MIGHT SPROUT WINGS NEXT TUES-DAY.
HMM... THAT MUST BE THE WELCOMING COMMITTEE.
STARK
STARK ENTERPRISES
MR. STARK! WELCOME TO BEIJING.
I AM LI WANG. I WILL BE YOUR GUIDE AND INTERPRETER, IF THIS IS ACCEPTABLE TO YOU.
PERFECTLY ACCEPTABLE, MR. LI. WE'RE ALL HERE AS FRIENDS, AFTER ALL, AREN'T WE?
SO WE HAD HOPED, MR. STARK...
...ALTHOUGH WE ARE SADDENED THAT YOU FELT IT NECESSARY TO BRING YOUR FAMOUS BODYGUARD WITH YOU.

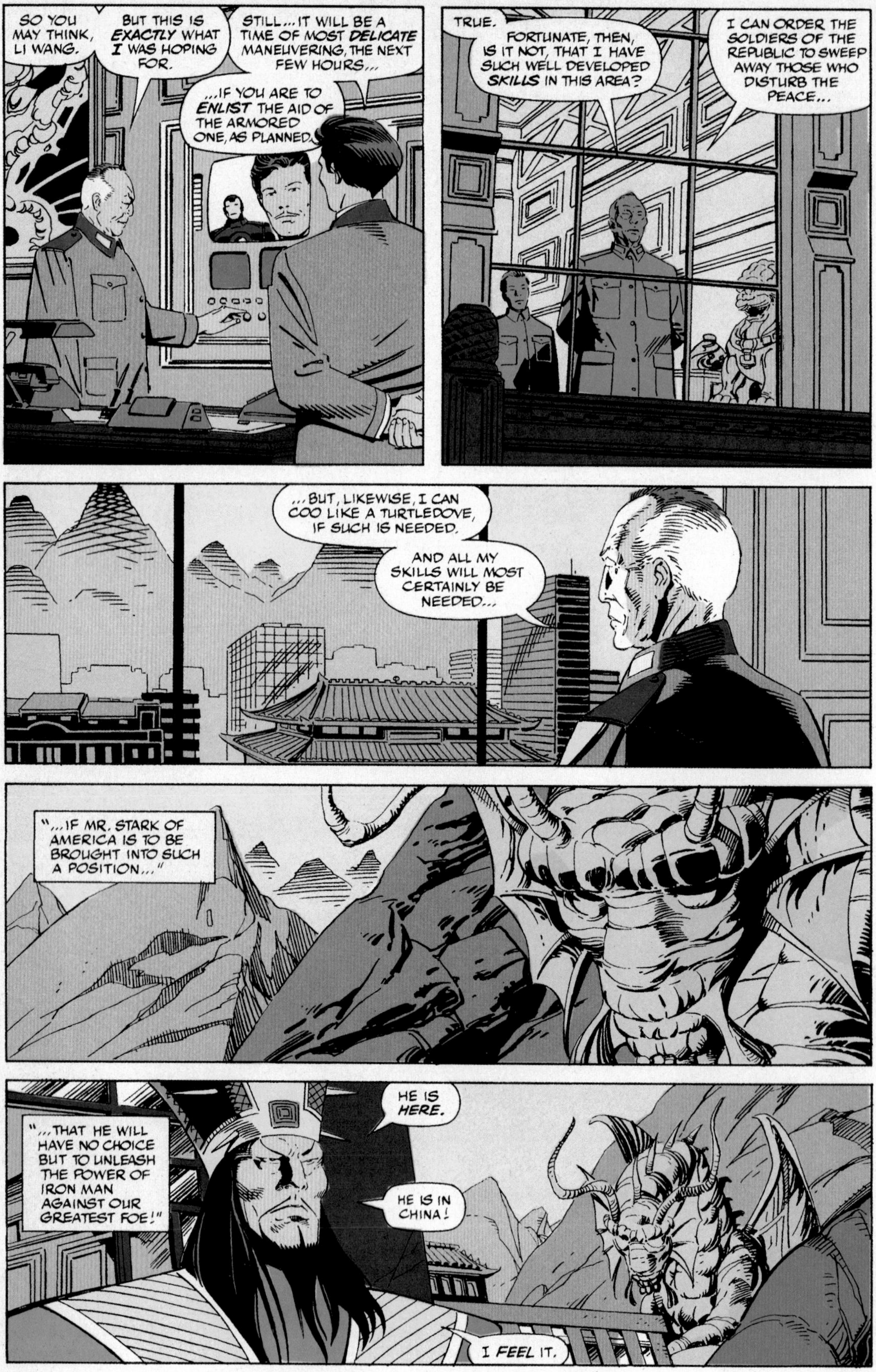
SO YOU MAY THINK, LI WANG.
BUT THIS IS EXACTLY WHAT I WAS HOPING FOR.
STILL... IT WILL BE A TIME OF MOST DELICATE MANEUVERING, THE NEXT FEW HOURS...
...IF YOU ARE TO ENLIST THE AID OF THE ARMORED ONE, AS PLANNED.
TRUE.
FORTUNATE, THEN, IS IT NOT, THAT I HAVE SUCH WELL DEVELOPED SKILLS IN THIS AREA?
I CAN ORDER THE SOLDIERS OF THE REPUBLIC TO SWEEP AWAY THOSE WHO DISTURB THE PEACE...
...BUT, LIKEWISE, I CAN COO LIKE A TURTLEDOVE, IF SUCH IS NEEDED.
AND ALL MY SKILLS WILL MOST CERTAINLY BE NEEDED...
"...IF MR. STARK OF AMERICA IS TO BE BROUGHT INTO SUCH A POSITION..."
"...THAT HE WILL HAVE NO CHOICE BUT TO UNLEASH THE POWER OF IRON MAN AGAINST OUR GREATEST FOE!"
HE IS HERE.
HE IS IN CHINA!
I FEEL IT.

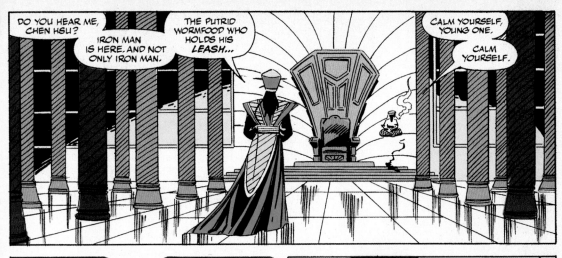

DO YOU HEAR ME, CHEN HSU?

IRON MAN IS HERE. AND NOT ONLY IRON MAN.

THE PUTRID WORMFOOD WHO HOLDS HIS *LEASH*...

CALM YOURSELF, YOUNG ONE.

CALM YOURSELF.

THE MOMENT YOU HAVE *LONGED* FOR DRAWS CLOSE TO HAND. BUT YOU MUST NOT LET THE *HATRED* YOU BEAR...

...POISON YOUR WITS AND DIVERT YOUR POWER. THE TIME OF *PURGING* IS NEAR.

THAT DONE, THE MATTER WHICH IS OUR *TRUE* CONCERN CAN BE TURNED TO.

"TRUE CONCERN?"

ALWAYS YOUR WORDS ARE LIKE CHINESE BOXES, CHEN HSU.

WITH EACH DAY I THINK I HAVE COME TO UNDERSTAND YOU AT LAST.

AND WITH EACH DAY YOU REVEAL I HAVE NOT UNDERSTOOD YOU AT ALL.

WHAT IS THIS "TRUE CONCERN" OF WHICH YOU SPEAK?

ALL IN GOOD TIME, YOUNG ONE. ALL IN GOOD TIME.

TAKE SOLACE IN THE KNOWLEDGE THAT THE HOUR OF AWAKENING IS NIGH. BEFORE THIS WEEK IS OUT, YOU WILL RULE NOT MERELY ONE-THIRD OF CHINA, AS YOU DO NOW...

...BUT ALL THE WORLD!

AND AS THESE WORDS ARE SPOKEN...

...THROUGH THE STREETS-- THE NOW PEACEFUL STREETS OF CHINA'S CAPITAL...

...WINDS A CARAVAN OF LIMOUSINES THAT STAND IN STARK CONTRAST TO THE SIMPLE BICYCLES THAT PROVIDE TRANSPORT FOR MOST OF THE POPULATION.

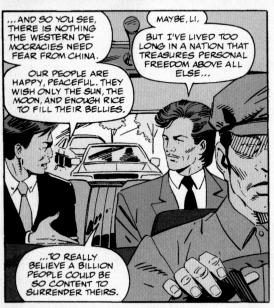

...AND SO YOU SEE, THERE IS NOTHING THE WESTERN DEMOCRACIES NEED FEAR FROM CHINA.

OUR PEOPLE ARE HAPPY, PEACEFUL. THEY WISH ONLY THE SUN, THE MOON, AND ENOUGH RICE TO FILL THEIR BELLIES.

MAYBE, LI.

BUT I'VE LIVED TOO LONG IN A NATION THAT TREASURES PERSONAL FREEDOM ABOVE ALL ELSE...

...TO REALLY BELIEVE A BILLION PEOPLE COULD BE SO CONTENT TO SURRENDER THEIRS.

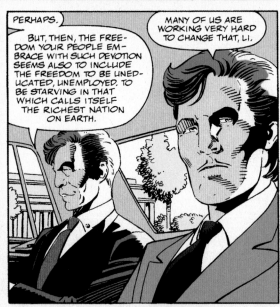

PERHAPS.

BUT, THEN, THE FREEDOM YOUR PEOPLE EMBRACE WITH SUCH DEVOTION SEEMS ALSO TO INCLUDE THE FREEDOM TO BE UNEDUCATED, UNEMPLOYED. TO BE STARVING IN THAT WHICH CALLS ITSELF THE RICHEST NATION ON EARTH.

MANY OF US ARE WORKING VERY HARD TO CHANGE THAT, LI.

SO YOU SAY, YET THIS GREAT EFFORT ON YOUR PART...

...HAS NOT CREATED SUFFICIENT *GRATITUDE* IN THOSE BELOW YOU THAT YOU HAVE BEEN ABLE TO *RETIRE* YOUR FAMOUS BODYGUARD.

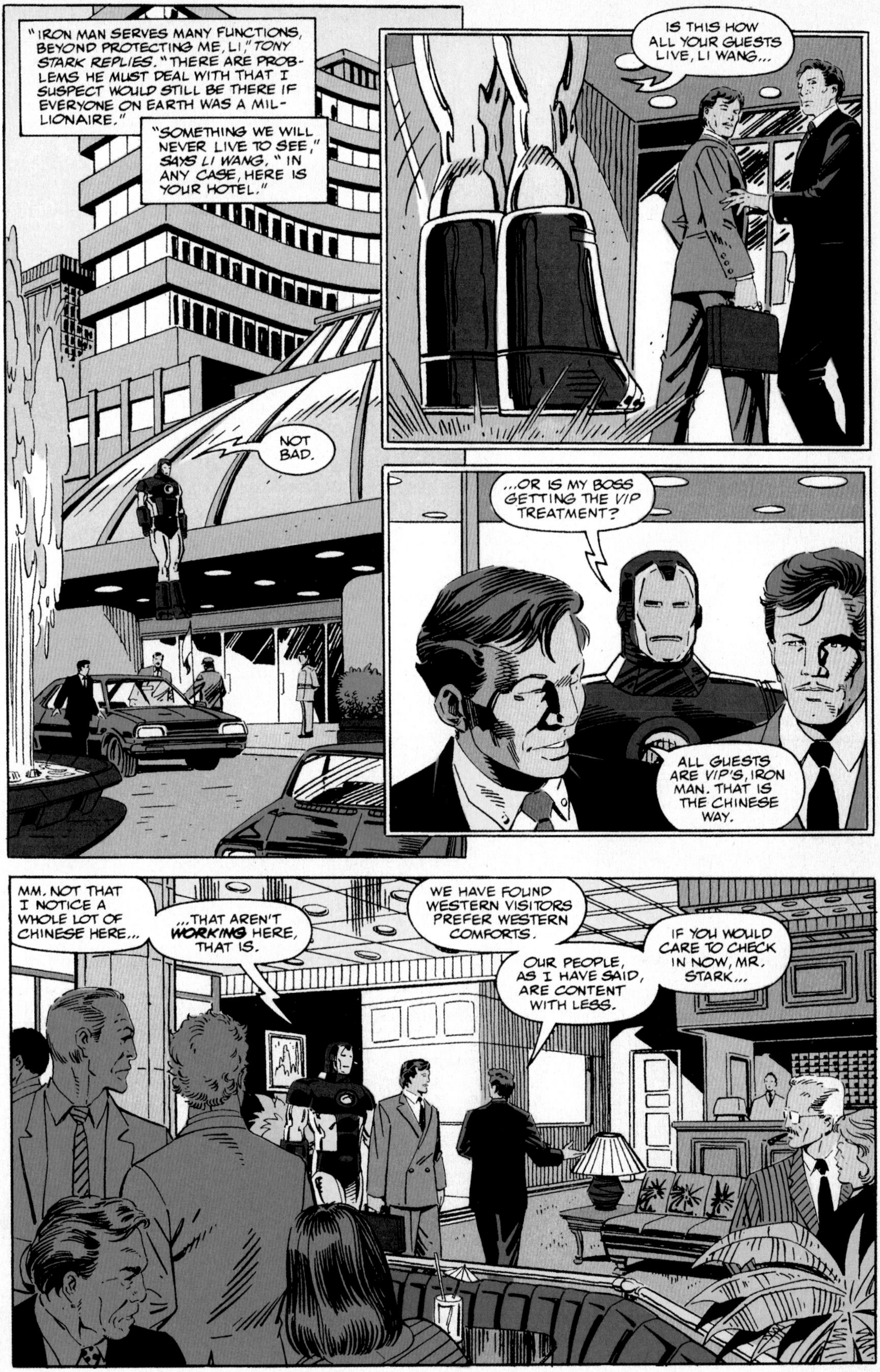
"IRON MAN SERVES MANY FUNCTIONS, BEYOND PROTECTING ME, LI," TONY STARK REPLIES. "THERE ARE PROBLEMS HE MUST DEAL WITH THAT I SUSPECT WOULD STILL BE THERE IF EVERYONE ON EARTH WAS A MILLIONAIRE."
"SOMETHING WE WILL NEVER LIVE TO SEE," SAYS LI WANG. "IN ANY CASE, HERE IS YOUR HOTEL."
NOT BAD.
IS THIS HOW ALL YOUR GUESTS LIVE, LI WANG...
...OR IS MY BOSS GETTING THE VIP TREATMENT?
ALL GUESTS ARE VIP'S, IRON MAN. THAT IS THE CHINESE WAY.
MM. NOT THAT I NOTICE A WHOLE LOT OF CHINESE HERE...
...THAT AREN'T WORKING HERE, THAT IS.
WE HAVE FOUND WESTERN VISITORS PREFER WESTERN COMFORTS.
OUR PEOPLE, AS I HAVE SAID, ARE CONTENT WITH LESS.
IF YOU WOULD CARE TO CHECK IN NOW, MR. STARK...

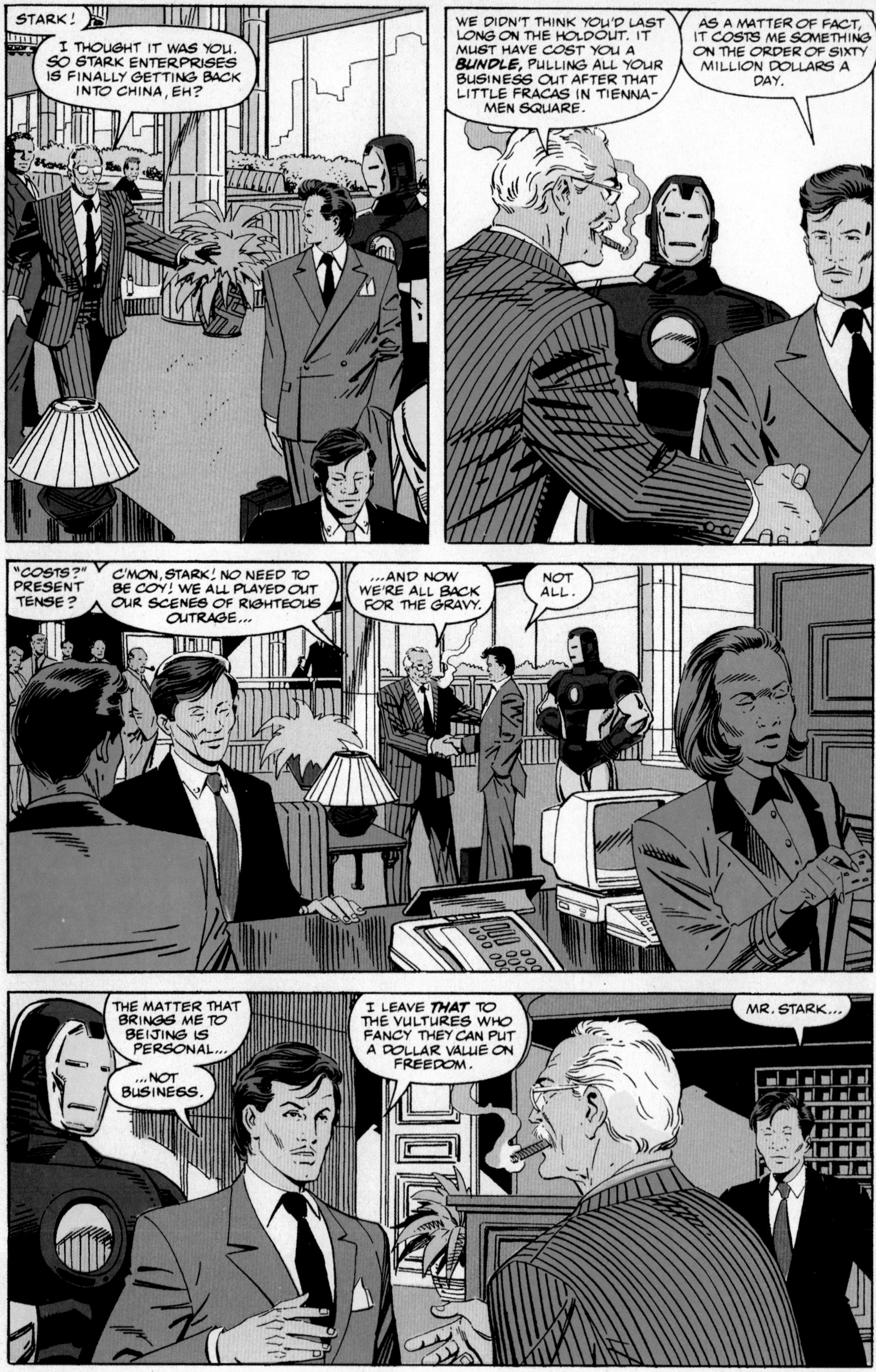
STARK!
I THOUGHT IT WAS YOU. SO STARK ENTERPRISES IS FINALLY GETTING BACK INTO CHINA, EH?
WE DIDN'T THINK YOU'D LAST LONG ON THE HOLDOUT. IT MUST HAVE COST YOU A BUNDLE, PULLING ALL YOUR BUSINESS OUT AFTER THAT LITTLE FRACAS IN TIENNAMEN SQUARE.
AS A MATTER OF FACT, IT COSTS ME SOMETHING ON THE ORDER OF SIXTY MILLION DOLLARS A DAY.
"COSTS?" PRESENT TENSE?
C'MON, STARK! NO NEED TO BE COY! WE ALL PLAYED OUT OUR SCENES OF RIGHTEOUS OUTRAGE...
...AND NOW WE'RE ALL BACK FOR THE GRAVY.
NOT ALL.
THE MATTER THAT BRINGS ME TO BEIJING IS PERSONAL...
...NOT BUSINESS.
I LEAVE THAT TO THE VULTURES WHO FANCY THEY CAN PUT A DOLLAR VALUE ON FREEDOM.
MR. STARK...

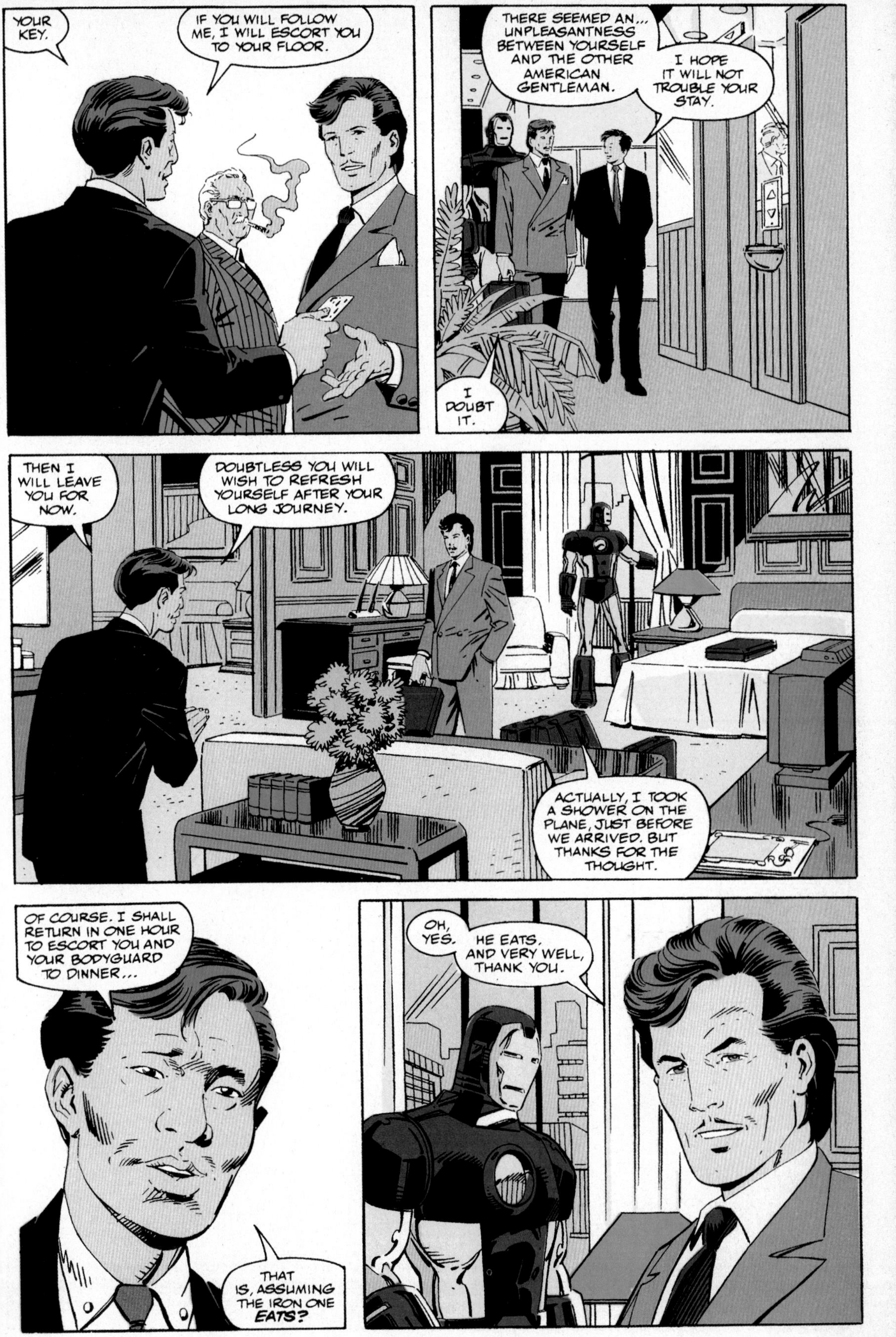
YOUR KEY.
IF YOU WILL FOLLOW ME, I WILL ESCORT YOU TO YOUR FLOOR.
THERE SEEMED AN... UNPLEASANTNESS BETWEEN YOURSELF AND THE OTHER AMERICAN GENTLEMAN.
I HOPE IT WILL NOT TROUBLE YOUR STAY.
I DOUBT IT.
THEN I WILL LEAVE YOU FOR NOW.
DOUBTLESS YOU WILL WISH TO REFRESH YOURSELF AFTER YOUR LONG JOURNEY.
ACTUALLY, I TOOK A SHOWER ON THE PLANE, JUST BEFORE WE ARRIVED. BUT THANKS FOR THE THOUGHT.
OF COURSE. I SHALL RETURN IN ONE HOUR TO ESCORT YOU AND YOUR BODYGUARD TO DINNER...
THAT IS, ASSUMING THE IRON ONE *EATS?*
OH, YES.
HE EATS. AND VERY WELL, THANK YOU.

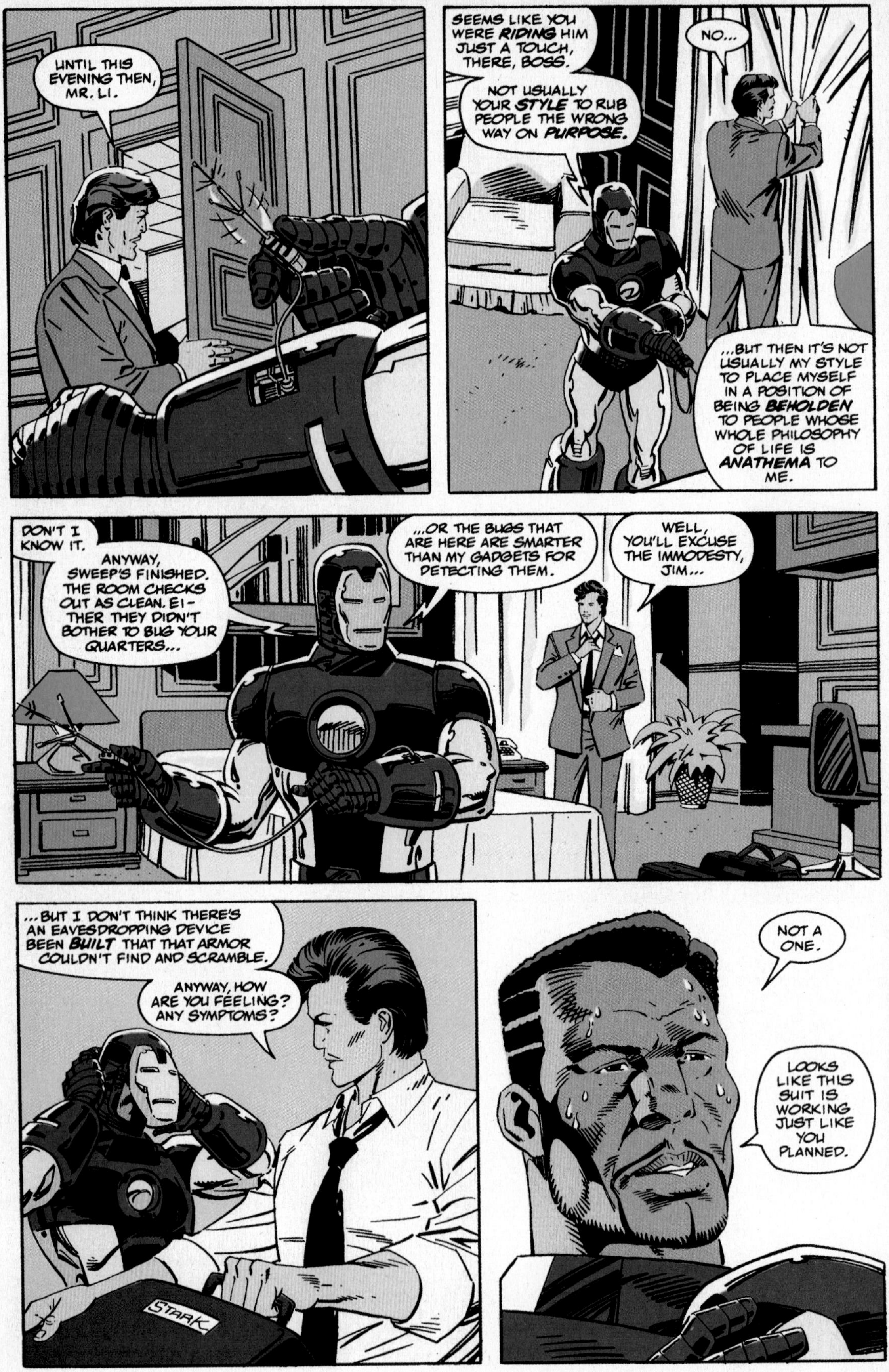

UNTIL THIS EVENING THEN, MR. LI.
SEEMS LIKE YOU WERE RIDING HIM JUST A TOUCH, THERE, BOSS.
NOT USUALLY YOUR STYLE TO RUB PEOPLE THE WRONG WAY ON PURPOSE.
NO...
...BUT THEN IT'S NOT USUALLY MY STYLE TO PLACE MYSELF IN A POSITION OF BEING BEHOLDEN TO PEOPLE WHOSE WHOLE PHILOSOPHY OF LIFE IS ANATHEMA TO ME.
DON'T I KNOW IT.
ANYWAY, SWEEP'S FINISHED. THE ROOM CHECKS OUT AS CLEAN. EI-THER THEY DIDN'T BOTHER TO BUG YOUR QUARTERS...
...OR THE BUGS THAT ARE HERE ARE SMARTER THAN MY GADGETS FOR DETECTING THEM.
WELL, YOU'LL EXCUSE THE IMMODESTY, JIM...
...BUT I DON'T THINK THERE'S AN EAVESDROPPING DEVICE BEEN BUILT THAT THAT ARMOR COULDN'T FIND AND SCRAMBLE.
ANYWAY, HOW ARE YOU FEELING? ANY SYMPTOMS?
STARK
NOT A ONE.
LOOKS LIKE THIS SUIT IS WORKING JUST LIKE YOU PLANNED.

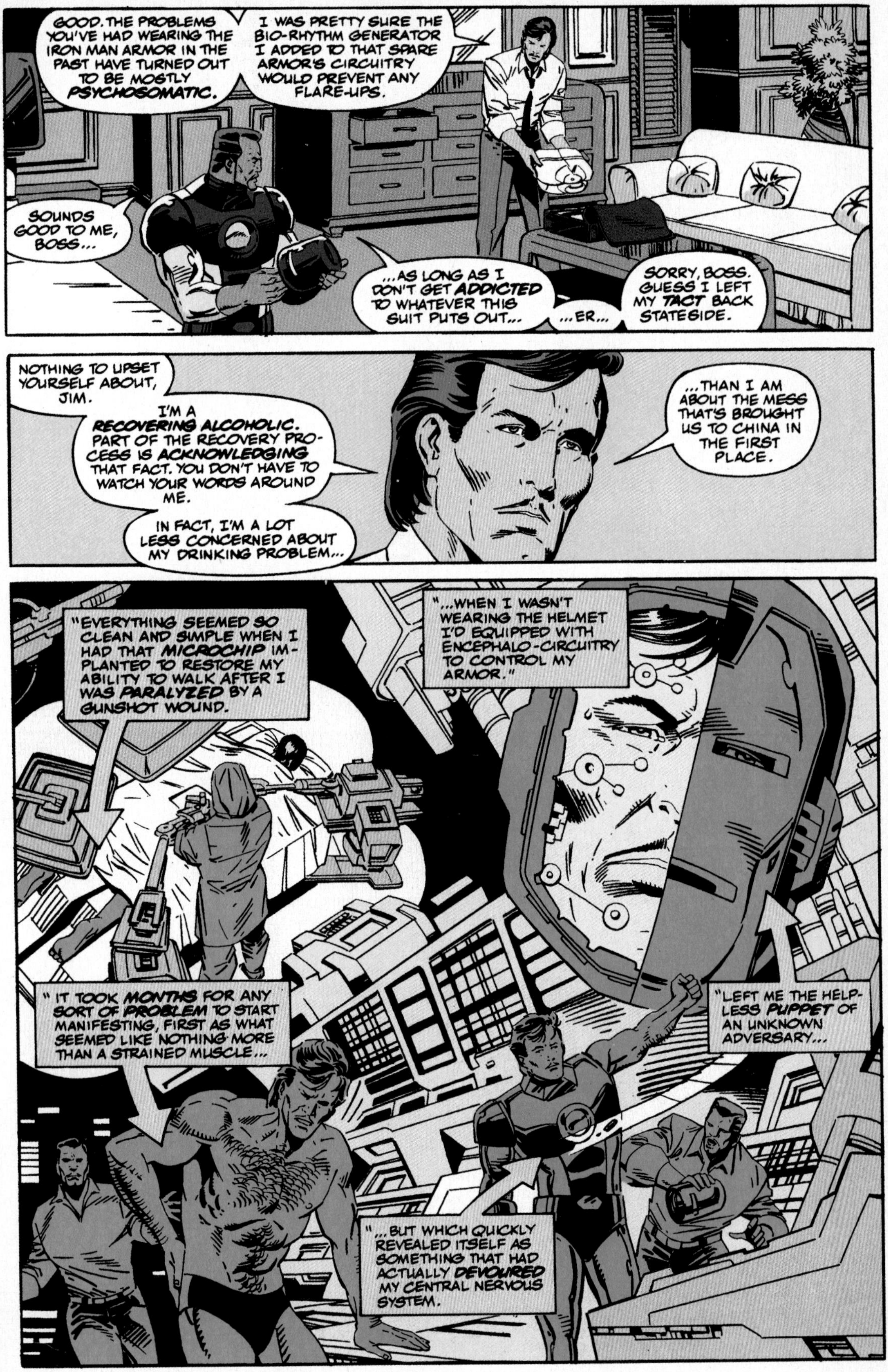
GOOD. THE PROBLEMS YOU'VE HAD WEARING THE IRON MAN ARMOR IN THE PAST HAVE TURNED OUT TO BE MOSTLY PSYCHOSOMATIC.
I WAS PRETTY SURE THE BIO-RHYTHM GENERATOR I ADDED TO THAT SPARE ARMOR'S CIRCUITRY WOULD PREVENT ANY FLARE-UPS.
SOUNDS GOOD TO ME, BOSS...
...AS LONG AS I DON'T GET ADDICTED TO WHATEVER THIS SUIT PUTS OUT...
...ER...
SORRY, BOSS. GUESS I LEFT MY TACT BACK STATESIDE.
NOTHING TO UPSET YOURSELF ABOUT, JIM.
I'M A RECOVERING ALCOHOLIC. PART OF THE RECOVERY PROCESS IS ACKNOWLEDGING THAT FACT. YOU DON'T HAVE TO WATCH YOUR WORDS AROUND ME.
IN FACT, I'M A LOT LESS CONCERNED ABOUT MY DRINKING PROBLEM...
...THAN I AM ABOUT THE MESS THAT'S BROUGHT US TO CHINA IN THE FIRST PLACE.
"EVERYTHING SEEMED SO CLEAN AND SIMPLE WHEN I HAD THAT MICROCHIP IMPLANTED TO RESTORE MY ABILITY TO WALK AFTER I WAS PARALYZED BY A GUNSHOT WOUND.
"...WHEN I WASN'T WEARING THE HELMET I'D EQUIPPED WITH ENCEPHALO-CIRCUITRY TO CONTROL MY ARMOR."
" IT TOOK MONTHS FOR ANY SORT OF PROBLEM TO START MANIFESTING, FIRST AS WHAT SEEMED LIKE NOTHING MORE THAN A STRAINED MUSCLE...
"LEFT ME THE HELPLESS PUPPET OF AN UNKNOWN ADVERSARY...
"...BUT WHICH QUICKLY REVEALED ITSELF AS SOMETHING THAT HAD ACTUALLY DEVOURED MY CENTRAL NERVOUS SYSTEM.

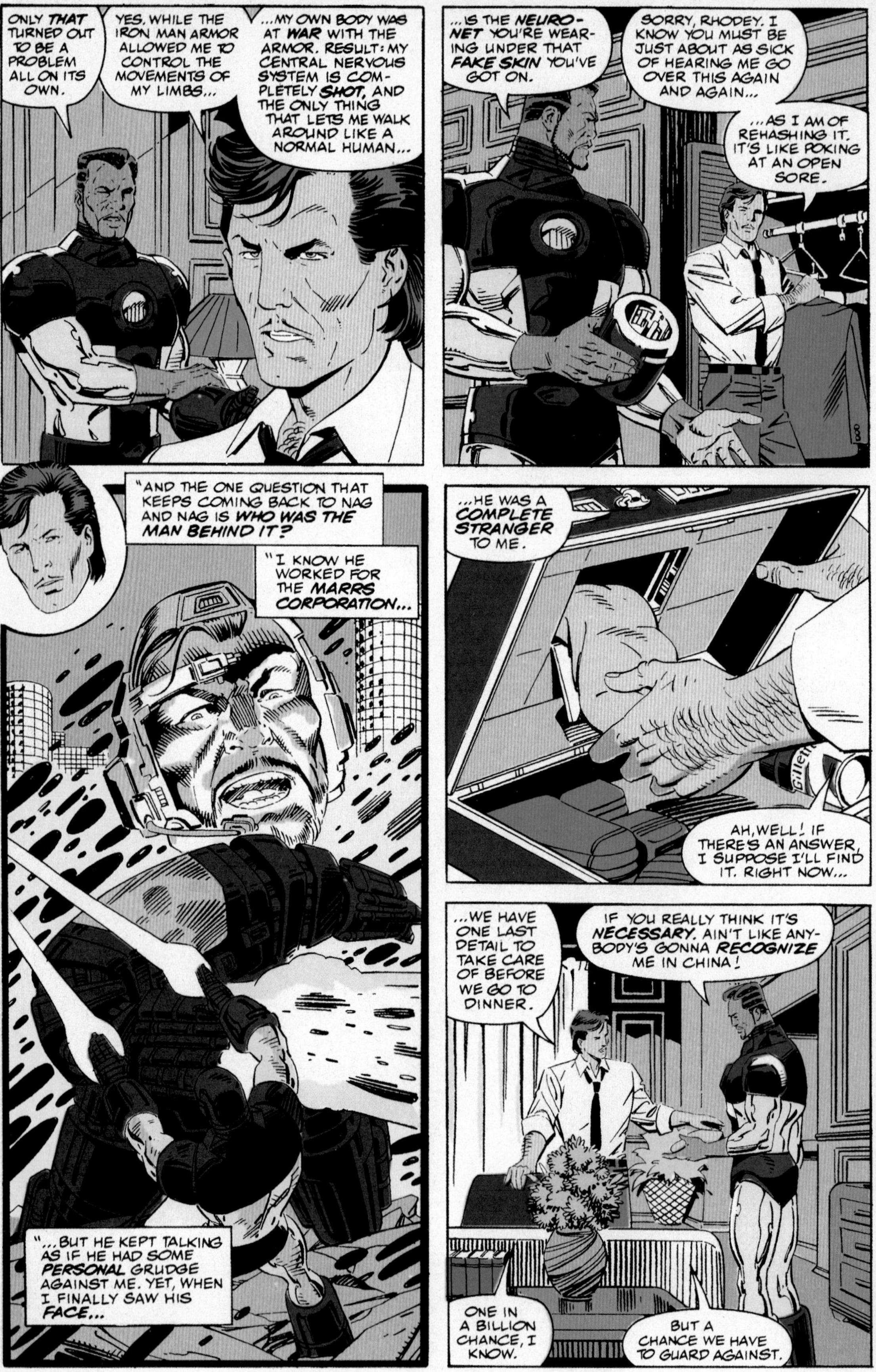
ONLY THAT TURNED OUT TO BE A PROBLEM ALL ON ITS OWN.
YES. WHILE THE IRON MAN ARMOR ALLOWED ME TO CONTROL THE MOVEMENTS OF MY LIMBS...
...MY OWN BODY WAS AT WAR WITH THE ARMOR. RESULT: MY CENTRAL NERVOUS SYSTEM IS COMPLETELY SHOT, AND THE ONLY THING THAT LETS ME WALK AROUND LIKE A NORMAL HUMAN...
...IS THE NEURO-NET YOU'RE WEARING UNDER THAT FAKE SKIN YOU'VE GOT ON.
SORRY, RHODEY. I KNOW YOU MUST BE JUST ABOUT AS SICK OF HEARING ME GO OVER THIS AGAIN AND AGAIN...
...AS I AM OF REHASHING IT. IT'S LIKE POKING AT AN OPEN SORE.
"AND THE ONE QUESTION THAT KEEPS COMING BACK TO NAG AND NAG IS WHO WAS THE MAN BEHIND IT?
"I KNOW HE WORKED FOR THE MARRS CORPORATION...
"...BUT HE KEPT TALKING AS IF HE HAD SOME PERSONAL GRUDGE AGAINST ME. YET, WHEN I FINALLY SAW HIS FACE...
...HE WAS A COMPLETE STRANGER TO ME.
AH, WELL! IF THERE'S AN ANSWER, I SUPPOSE I'LL FIND IT. RIGHT NOW...
...WE HAVE ONE LAST DETAIL TO TAKE CARE OF BEFORE WE GO TO DINNER.
IF YOU REALLY THINK IT'S NECESSARY. AIN'T LIKE ANY-BODY'S GONNA RECOGNIZE ME IN CHINA!
ONE IN A BILLION CHANCE, I KNOW.
BUT A CHANCE WE HAVE TO GUARD AGAINST.

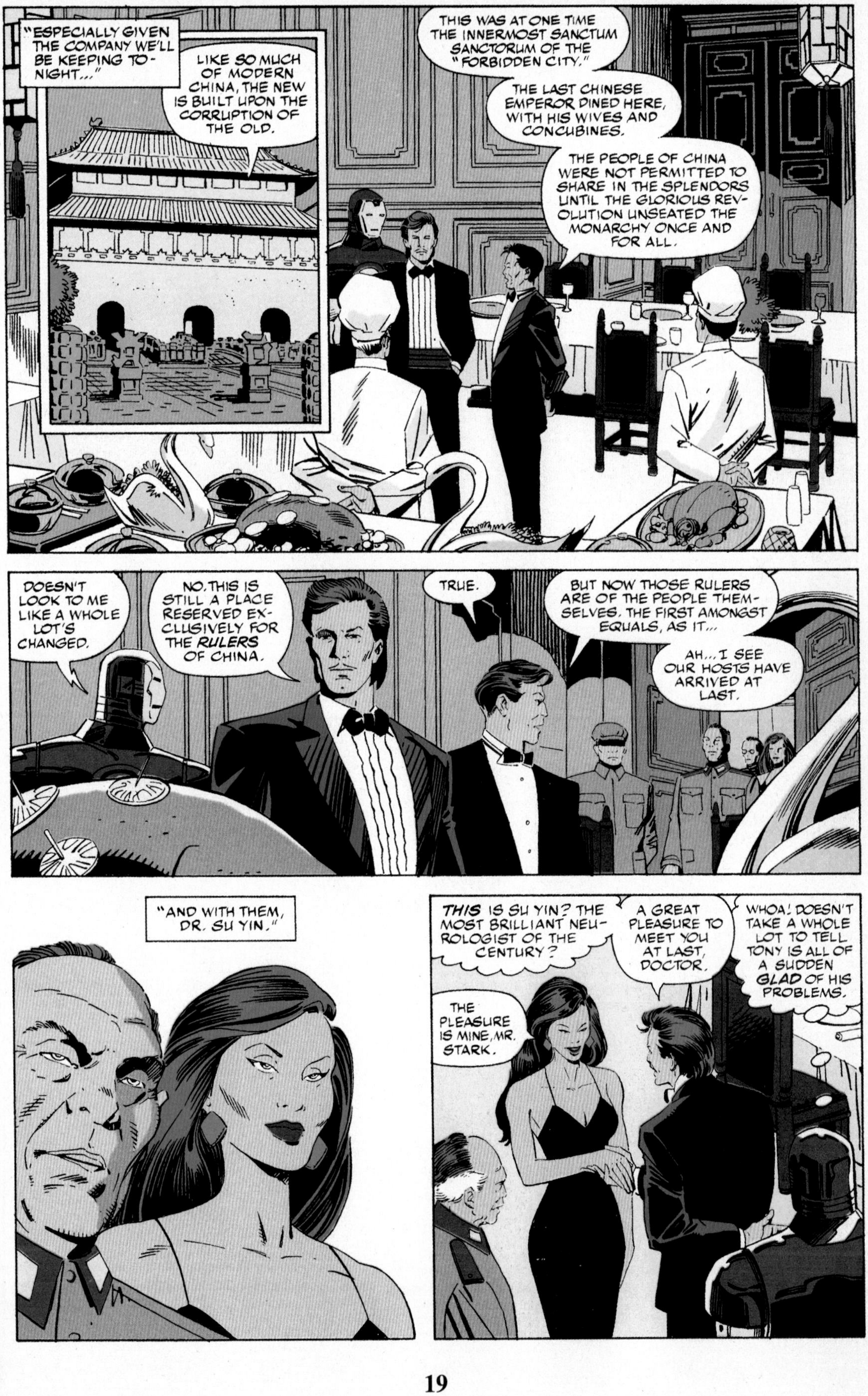
"ESPECIALLY GIVEN THE COMPANY WE'LL BE KEEPING TO-NIGHT..."
LIKE SO MUCH OF MODERN CHINA, THE NEW IS BUILT UPON THE CORRUPTION OF THE OLD.
THIS WAS AT ONE TIME THE INNERMOST SANCTUM SANCTORUM OF THE "FORBIDDEN CITY."
THE LAST CHINESE EMPEROR DINED HERE, WITH HIS WIVES AND CONCUBINES.
THE PEOPLE OF CHINA WERE NOT PERMITTED TO SHARE IN THE SPLENDORS UNTIL THE GLORIOUS REV-OLUTION UNSEATED THE MONARCHY ONCE AND FOR ALL.
DOESN'T LOOK TO ME LIKE A WHOLE LOT'S CHANGED.
NO. THIS IS STILL A PLACE RESERVED EX-CLUSIVELY FOR THE *RULERS* OF CHINA.
TRUE.
BUT NOW THOSE RULERS ARE OF THE PEOPLE THEM-SELVES. THE FIRST AMONGST EQUALS, AS IT...
AH... I SEE OUR HOSTS HAVE ARRIVED AT LAST.
"AND WITH THEM, DR. SU YIN."
THIS IS SU YIN? THE MOST BRILLIANT NEU-ROLOGIST OF THE CENTURY?
A GREAT PLEASURE TO MEET YOU AT LAST, DOCTOR.
WHOA! DOESN'T TAKE A WHOLE LOT TO TELL TONY IS ALL OF A SUDDEN *GLAD* OF HIS PROBLEMS.
THE PLEASURE IS MINE, MR. STARK.

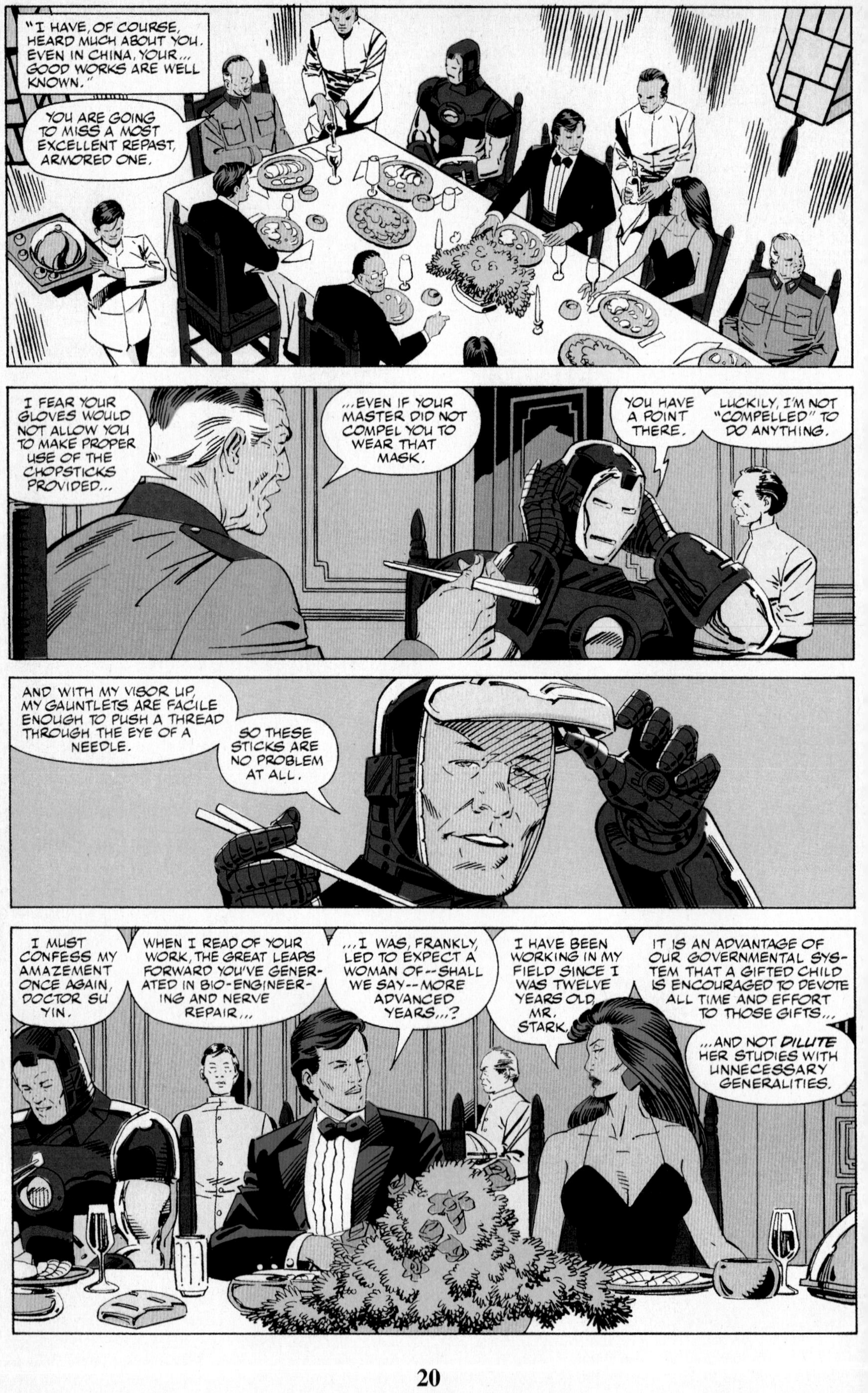
"I HAVE, OF COURSE, HEARD MUCH ABOUT YOU. EVEN IN CHINA, YOUR... GOOD WORKS ARE WELL KNOWN."
YOU ARE GOING TO MISS A MOST EXCELLENT REPAST, ARMORED ONE.
I FEAR YOUR GLOVES WOULD NOT ALLOW YOU TO MAKE PROPER USE OF THE CHOPSTICKS PROVIDED...
...EVEN IF YOUR MASTER DID NOT COMPEL YOU TO WEAR THAT MASK.
YOU HAVE A POINT THERE.
LUCKILY, I'M NOT "COMPELLED" TO DO ANYTHING.
AND WITH MY VISOR UP, MY GAUNTLETS ARE FACILE ENOUGH TO PUSH A THREAD THROUGH THE EYE OF A NEEDLE.
SO THESE STICKS ARE NO PROBLEM AT ALL.
I MUST CONFESS MY AMAZEMENT ONCE AGAIN, DOCTOR SU YIN.
WHEN I READ OF YOUR WORK, THE GREAT LEAPS FORWARD YOU'VE GENERATED IN BIO-ENGINEERING AND NERVE REPAIR...
...I WAS, FRANKLY, LED TO EXPECT A WOMAN OF--SHALL WE SAY--MORE ADVANCED YEARS...?
I HAVE BEEN WORKING IN MY FIELD SINCE I WAS TWELVE YEARS OLD, MR. STARK.
IT IS AN ADVANTAGE OF OUR GOVERNMENTAL SYSTEM THAT A GIFTED CHILD IS ENCOURAGED TO DEVOTE ALL TIME AND EFFORT TO THOSE GIFTS...
...AND NOT *DILUTE* HER STUDIES WITH UNNECESSARY GENERALITIES.

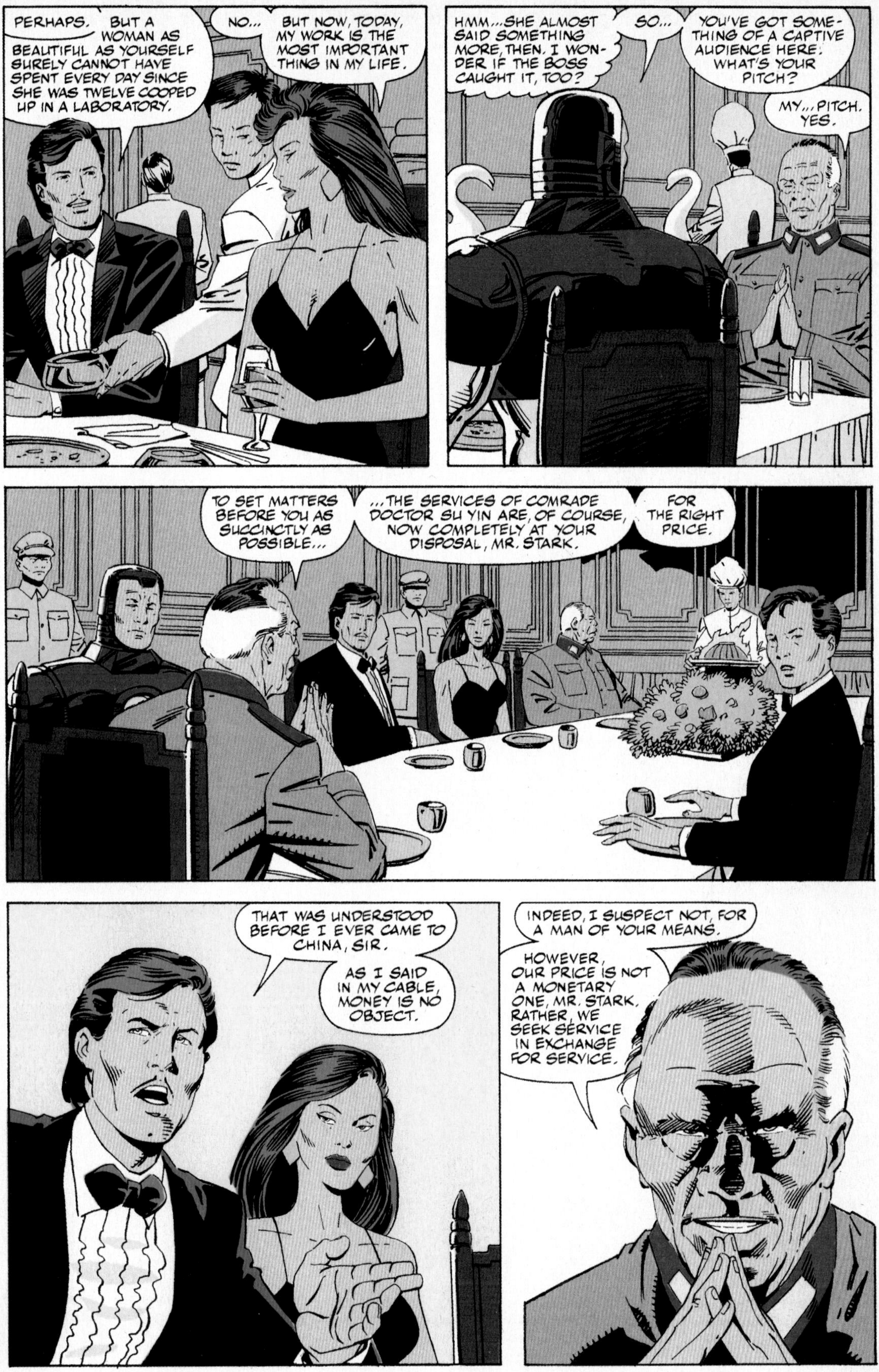
PERHAPS. BUT A WOMAN AS BEAUTIFUL AS YOURSELF SURELY CANNOT HAVE SPENT EVERY DAY SINCE SHE WAS TWELVE COOPED UP IN A LABORATORY.
NO...
BUT NOW, TODAY, MY WORK IS THE MOST IMPORTANT THING IN MY LIFE.
HMM...SHE ALMOST SAID SOMETHING MORE, THEN. I WONDER IF THE BOSS CAUGHT IT, TOO?
SO...
YOU'VE GOT SOMETHING OF A CAPTIVE AUDIENCE HERE. WHAT'S YOUR PITCH?
MY... PITCH. YES.
TO SET MATTERS BEFORE YOU AS SUCCINCTLY AS POSSIBLE...
...THE SERVICES OF COMRADE DOCTOR SU YIN ARE, OF COURSE, NOW COMPLETELY AT YOUR DISPOSAL, MR. STARK.
FOR THE RIGHT PRICE.
THAT WAS UNDERSTOOD BEFORE I EVER CAME TO CHINA, SIR.
AS I SAID IN MY CABLE, MONEY IS NO OBJECT.
INDEED, I SUSPECT NOT, FOR A MAN OF YOUR MEANS.
HOWEVER, OUR PRICE IS NOT A MONETARY ONE, MR. STARK. RATHER, WE SEEK SERVICE IN EXCHANGE FOR SERVICE.

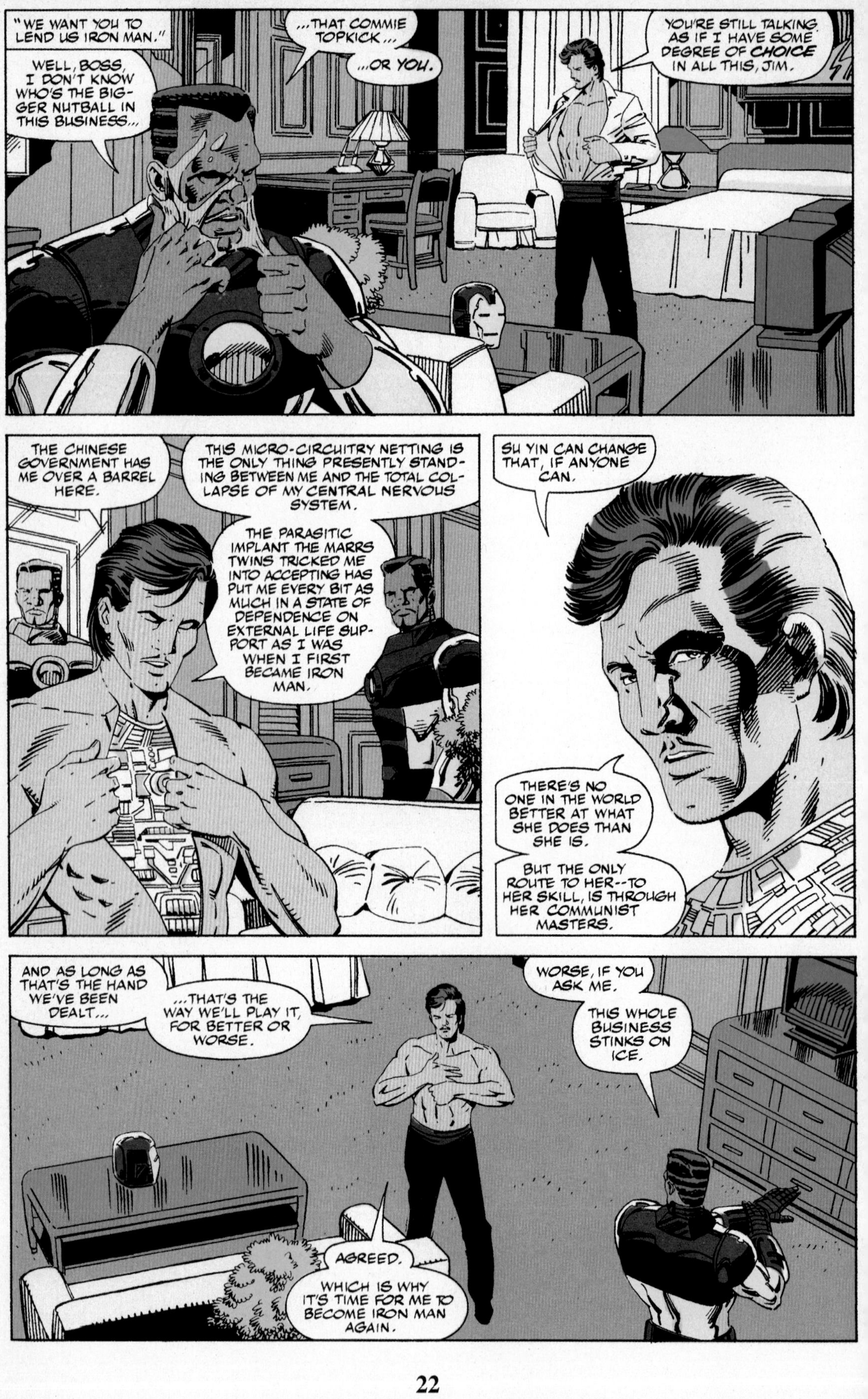
"WE WANT YOU TO LEND US IRON MAN."
WELL, BOSS, I DON'T KNOW WHO'S THE BIGGER NUTBALL IN THIS BUSINESS...
...THAT COMMIE TOPKICK...
...OR YOU.
YOU'RE STILL TALKING AS IF I HAVE SOME DEGREE OF CHOICE IN ALL THIS, JIM.
THE CHINESE GOVERNMENT HAS ME OVER A BARREL HERE.
THIS MICRO-CIRCUITRY NETTING IS THE ONLY THING PRESENTLY STANDING BETWEEN ME AND THE TOTAL COLLAPSE OF MY CENTRAL NERVOUS SYSTEM.
THE PARASITIC IMPLANT THE MARRS TWINS TRICKED ME INTO ACCEPTING HAS PUT ME EVERY BIT AS MUCH IN A STATE OF DEPENDENCE ON EXTERNAL LIFE SUPPORT AS I WAS WHEN I FIRST BECAME IRON MAN.
SU YIN CAN CHANGE THAT, IF ANYONE CAN.
THERE'S NO ONE IN THE WORLD BETTER AT WHAT SHE DOES THAN SHE IS.
BUT THE ONLY ROUTE TO HER--TO HER SKILL, IS THROUGH HER COMMUNIST MASTERS.
AND AS LONG AS THAT'S THE HAND WE'VE BEEN DEALT...
...THAT'S THE WAY WE'LL PLAY IT, FOR BETTER OR WORSE.
WORSE, IF YOU ASK ME.
THIS WHOLE BUSINESS STINKS ON ICE.
AGREED.
WHICH IS WHY IT'S TIME FOR ME TO BECOME IRON MAN AGAIN.

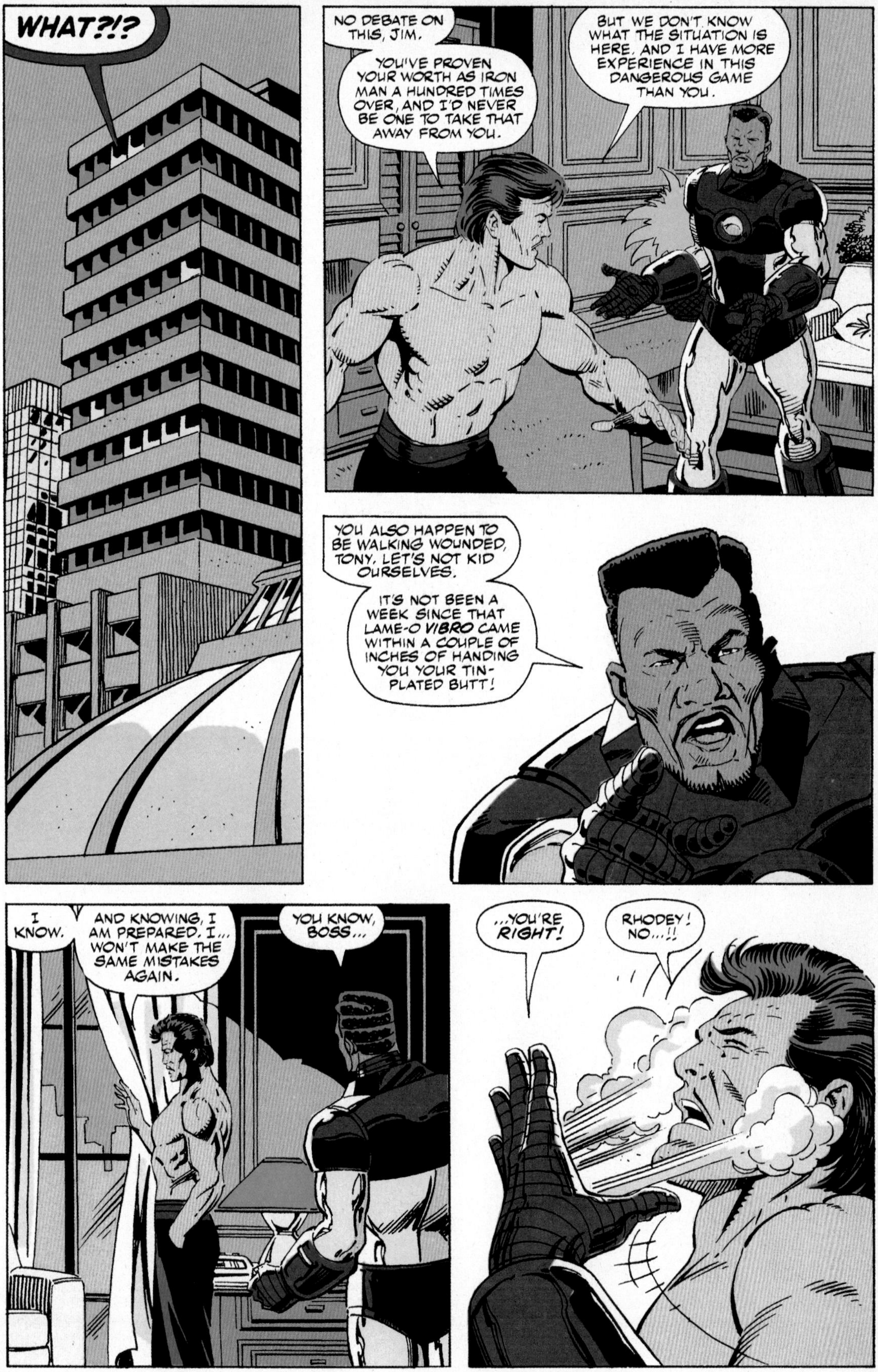
WHAT?!?
NO DEBATE ON THIS, JIM.
YOU'VE PROVEN YOUR WORTH AS IRON MAN A HUNDRED TIMES OVER, AND I'D NEVER BE ONE TO TAKE THAT AWAY FROM YOU.
BUT WE DON'T KNOW WHAT THE SITUATION IS HERE, AND I HAVE MORE EXPERIENCE IN THIS DANGEROUS GAME THAN YOU.
YOU ALSO HAPPEN TO BE WALKING WOUNDED, TONY. LET'S NOT KID OURSELVES.
IT'S NOT BEEN A WEEK SINCE THAT LAME-O VIBRO CAME WITHIN A COUPLE OF INCHES OF HANDING YOU YOUR TIN-PLATED BUTT!
I KNOW.
AND KNOWING, I AM PREPARED. I... WON'T MAKE THE SAME MISTAKES AGAIN.
YOU KNOW, BOSS...
...YOU'RE RIGHT!
RHODEY! NO...!!

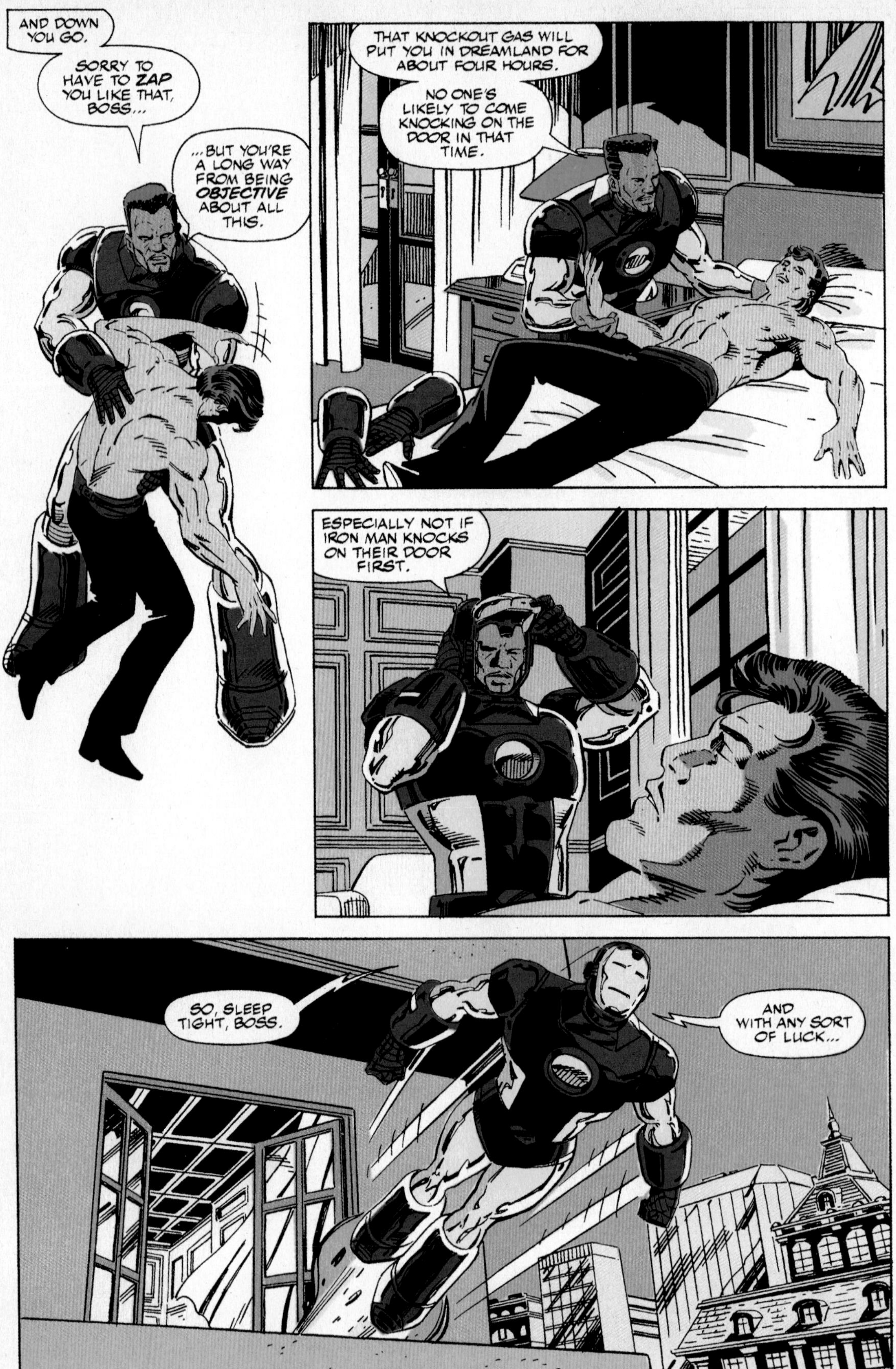
AND DOWN YOU GO.
SORRY TO HAVE TO ZAP YOU LIKE THAT, BOSS...
...BUT YOU'RE A LONG WAY FROM BEING OBJECTIVE ABOUT ALL THIS.
THAT KNOCKOUT GAS WILL PUT YOU IN DREAMLAND FOR ABOUT FOUR HOURS.
NO ONE'S LIKELY TO COME KNOCKING ON THE DOOR IN THAT TIME.
ESPECIALLY NOT IF IRON MAN KNOCKS ON THEIR DOOR FIRST.
SO, SLEEP TIGHT, BOSS.
AND WITH ANY SORT OF LUCK...

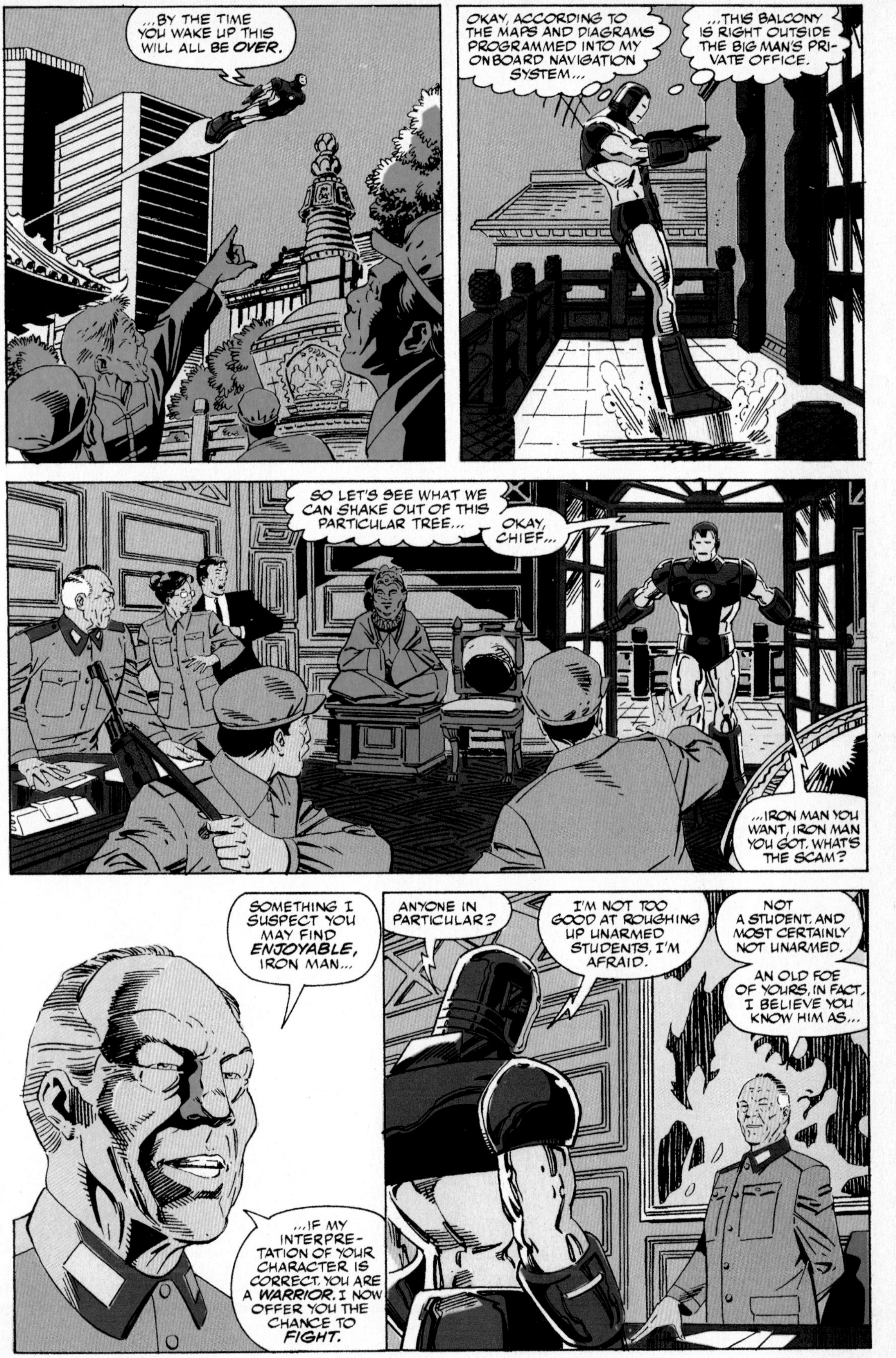
...BY THE TIME YOU WAKE UP THIS WILL ALL BE OVER.
OKAY, ACCORDING TO THE MAPS AND DIAGRAMS PROGRAMMED INTO MY ONBOARD NAVIGATION SYSTEM...
...THIS BALCONY IS RIGHT OUTSIDE THE BIG MAN'S PRIVATE OFFICE.
SO LET'S SEE WHAT WE CAN SHAKE OUT OF THIS PARTICULAR TREE...
OKAY, CHIEF...
...IRON MAN YOU WANT, IRON MAN YOU GOT. WHAT'S THE SCAM?
SOMETHING I SUSPECT YOU MAY FIND ENJOYABLE, IRON MAN...
...IF MY INTERPRETATION OF YOUR CHARACTER IS CORRECT. YOU ARE A WARRIOR. I NOW OFFER YOU THE CHANCE TO FIGHT.
ANYONE IN PARTICULAR?
I'M NOT TOO GOOD AT ROUGHING UP UNARMED STUDENTS, I'M AFRAID.
NOT A STUDENT. AND MOST CERTAINLY NOT UNARMED.
AN OLD FOE OF YOURS, IN FACT. I BELIEVE YOU KNOW HIM AS...

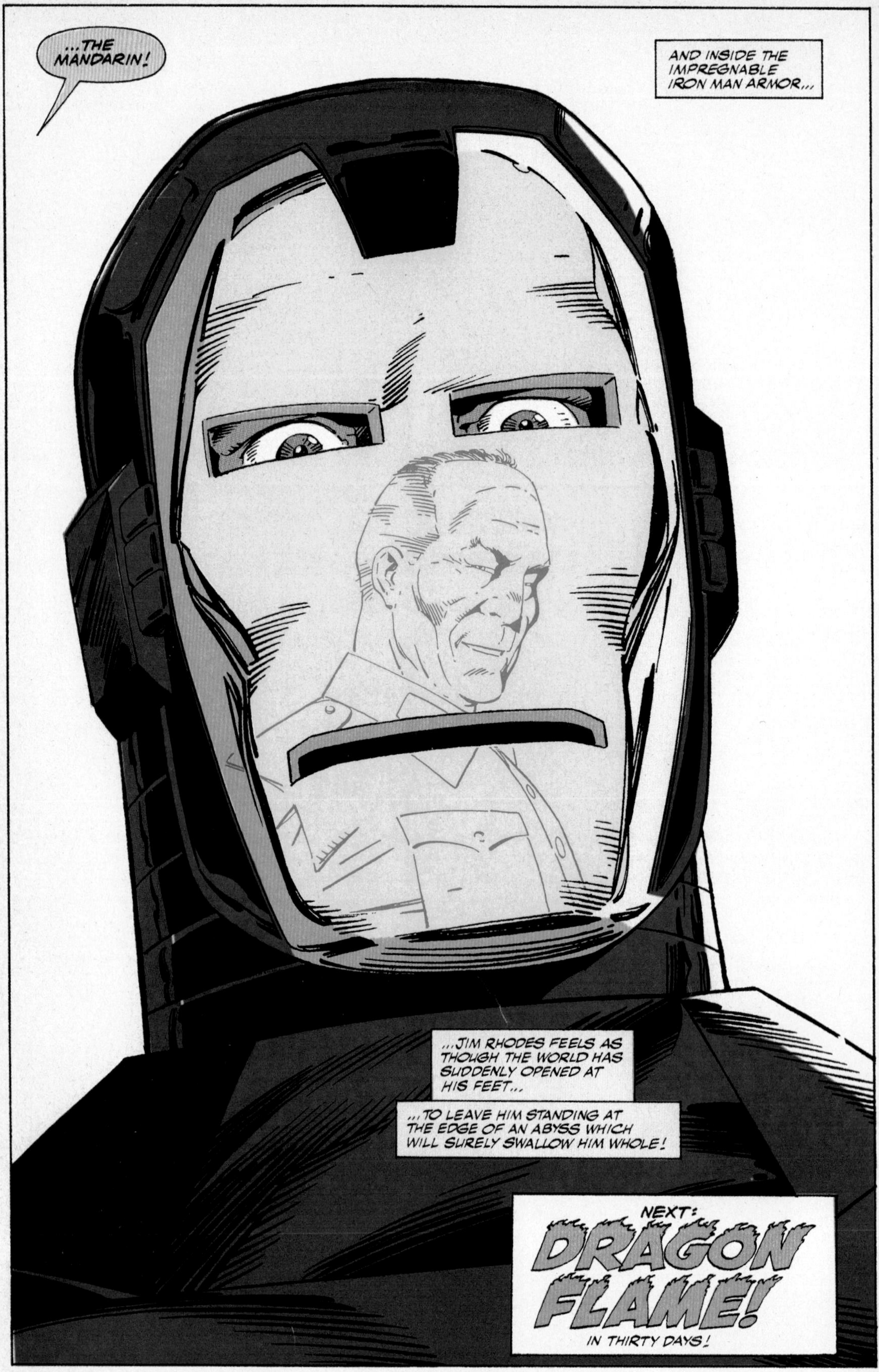
...THE MANDARIN!
AND INSIDE THE IMPREGNABLE IRON MAN ARMOR...
...JIM RHODES FEELS AS THOUGH THE WORLD HAS SUDDENLY OPENED AT HIS FEET...
...TO LEAVE HIM STANDING AT THE EDGE OF AN ABYSS WHICH WILL SURELY SWALLOW HIM WHOLE!
NEXT:
DRAGON FLAME!
IN THIRTY DAYS!

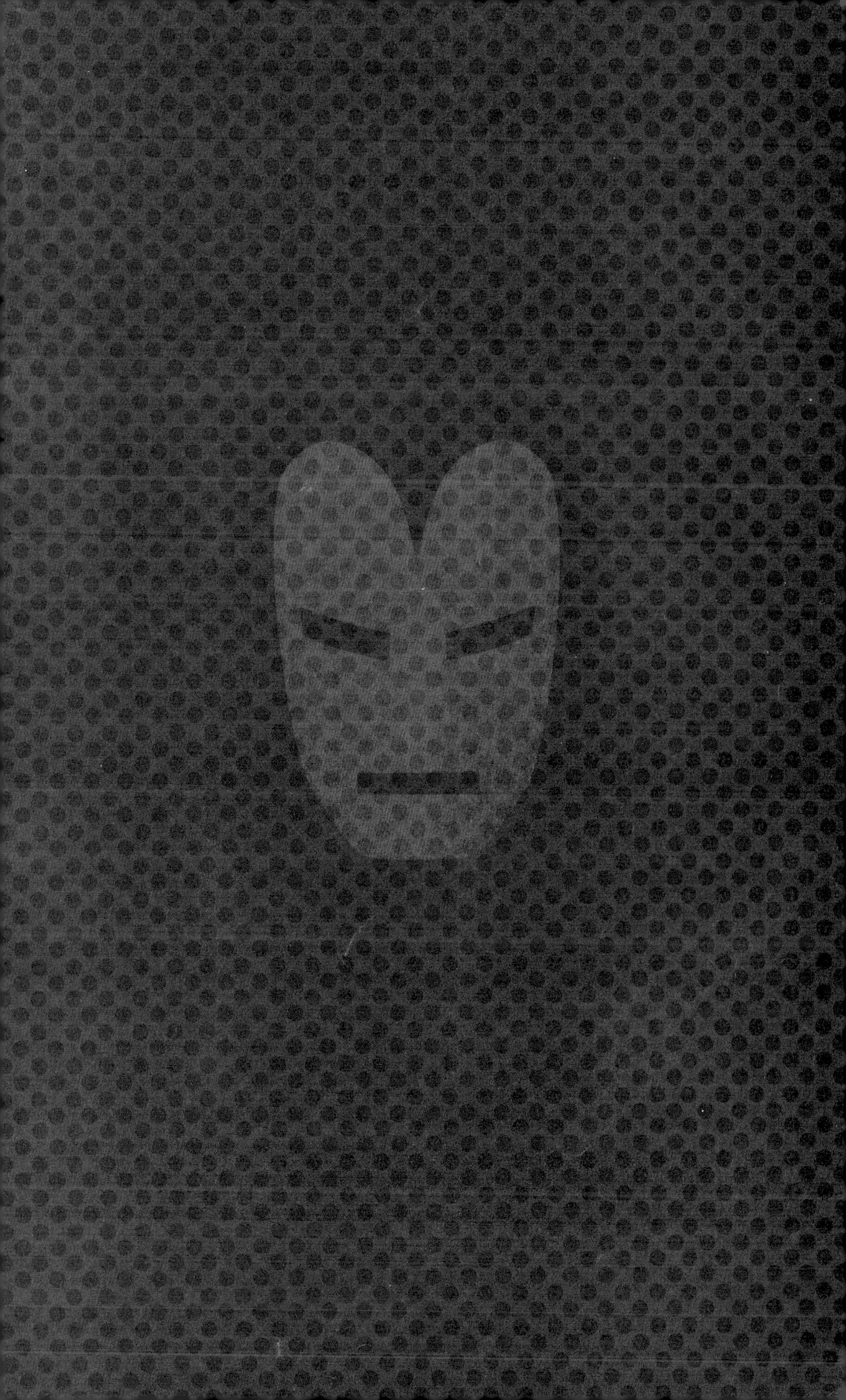

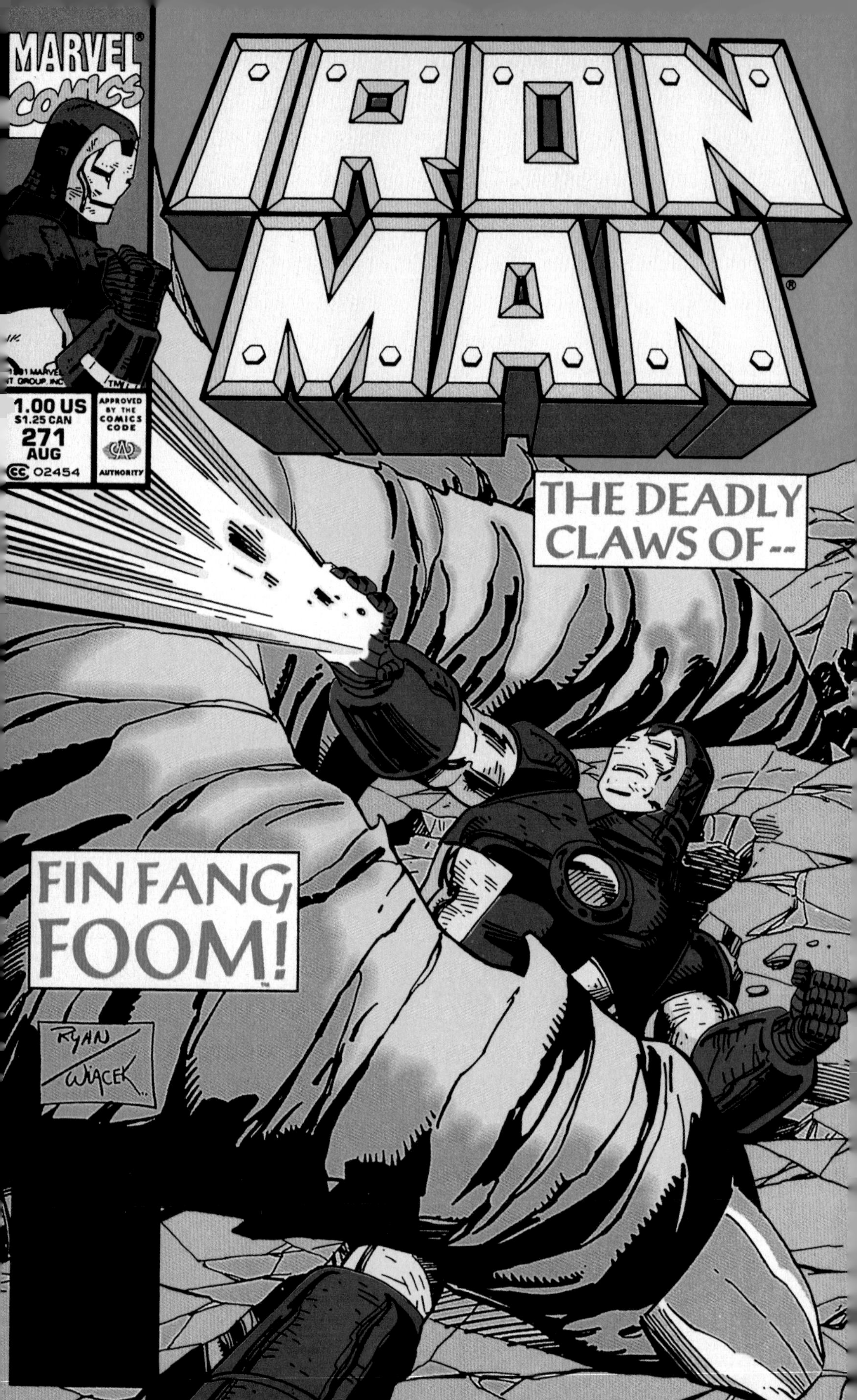
MARVEL COMICS
IRON MAN
1.00 US
$1.25 CAN
271
AUG
02454
APPROVED BY THE COMICS CODE AUTHORITY
THE DEADLY CLAWS OF--
FIN FANG FOOM!
RYAN
WIACEK

WHEN MULTI-BILLIONAIRE INDUSTRIALIST **TONY STARK**, INVENTOR EXTRAORDINAIRE, DONS HIS SOLAR-CHARGED, STEEL-MESH ARMOR, HE BECOMES A HIGH-TECH WARRIOR—THE WORLD'S GREATEST HUMAN FIGHTING MACHINE! STAN LEE PRESENTS . . .

THE INVINCIBLE **IRON MAN!**

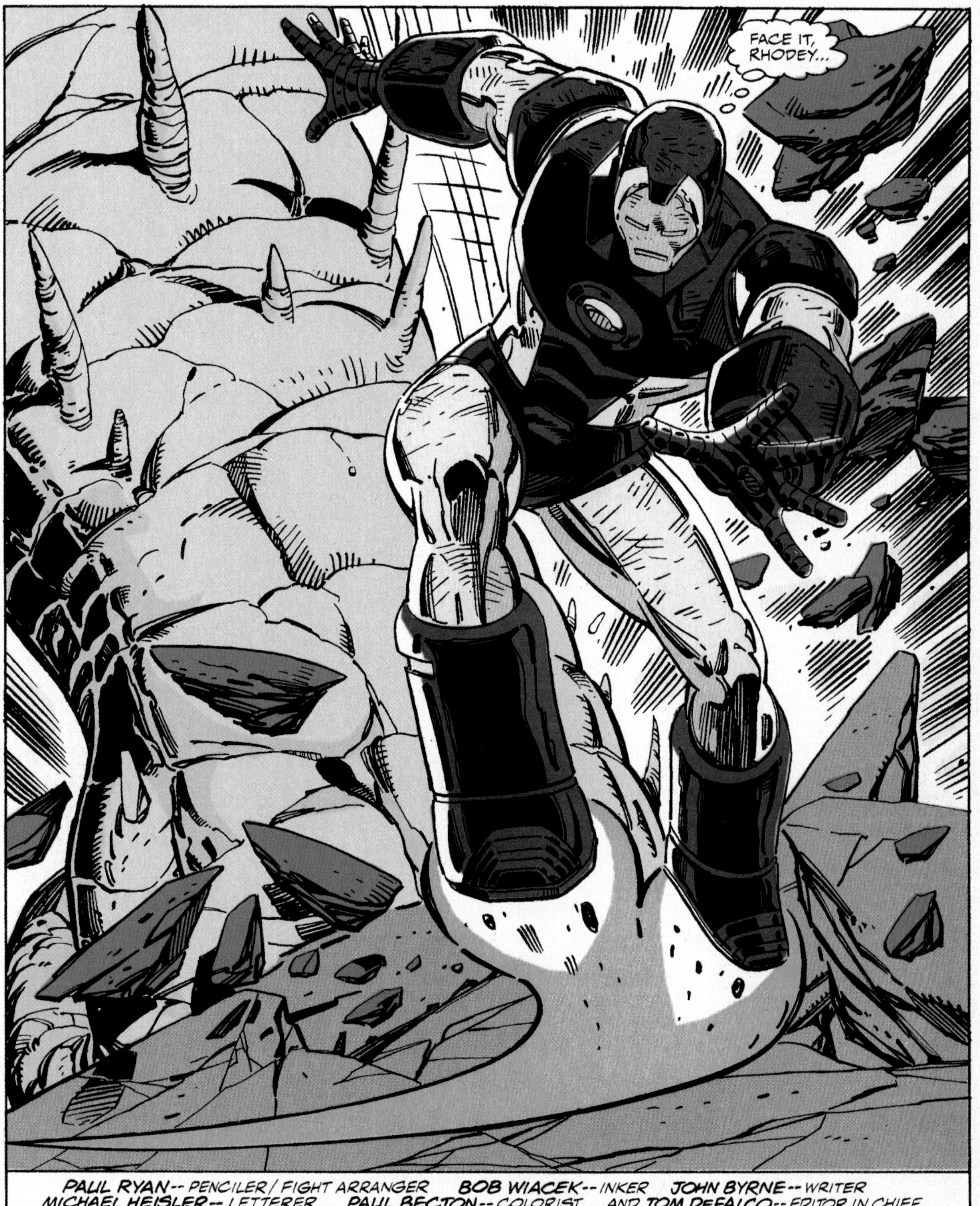

FACE IT, RHODEY...

PAUL RYAN-- PENCILER / FIGHT ARRANGER **BOB WIACEK**-- INKER **JOHN BYRNE**-- WRITER
MICHAEL HEISLER-- LETTERER **PAUL BECTON**-- COLORIST AND **TOM DEFALCO**-- EDITOR IN CHIEF
WELCOME ABOARD **NELSON YOMTOV**-- EDITOR

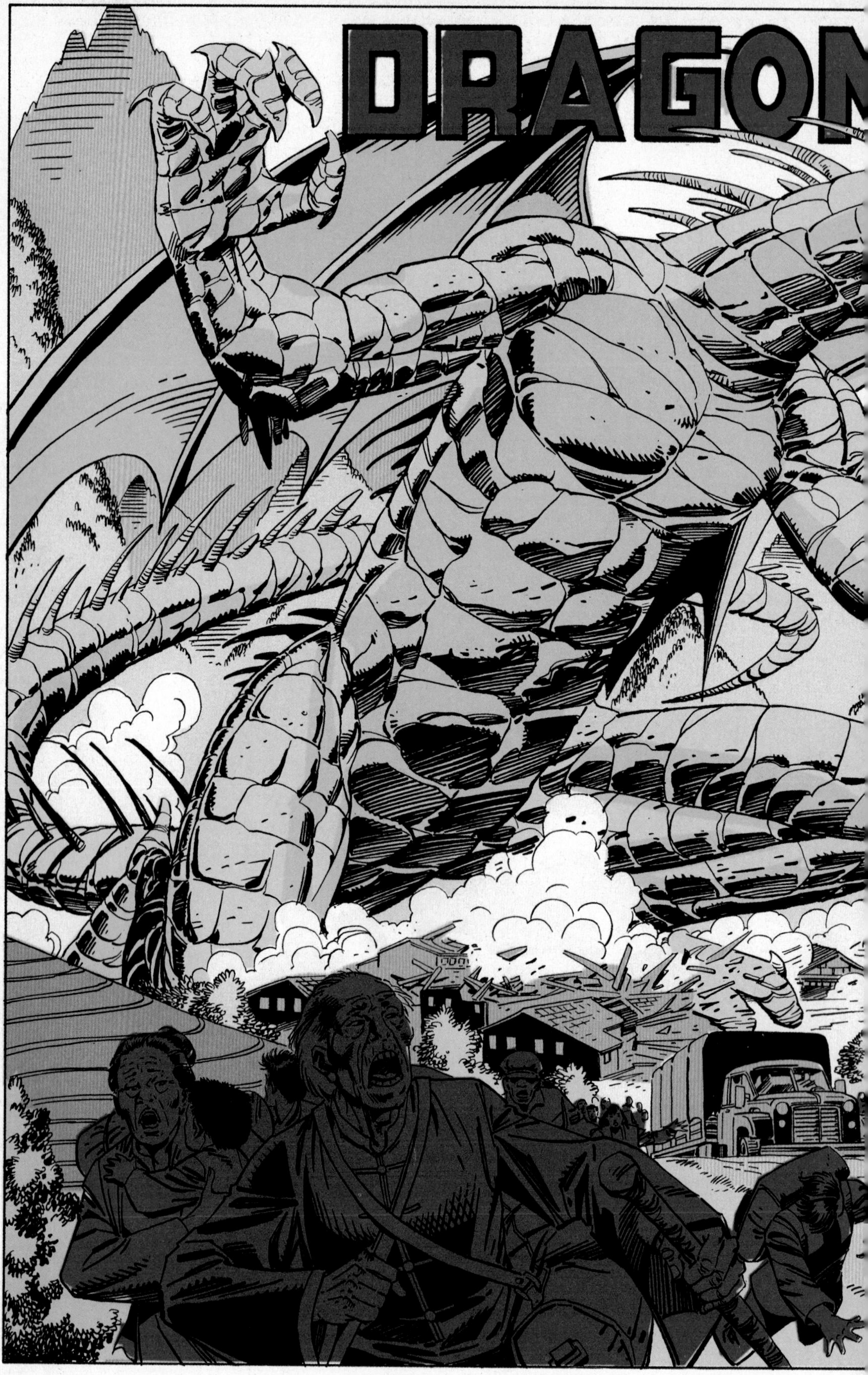
DRAGON

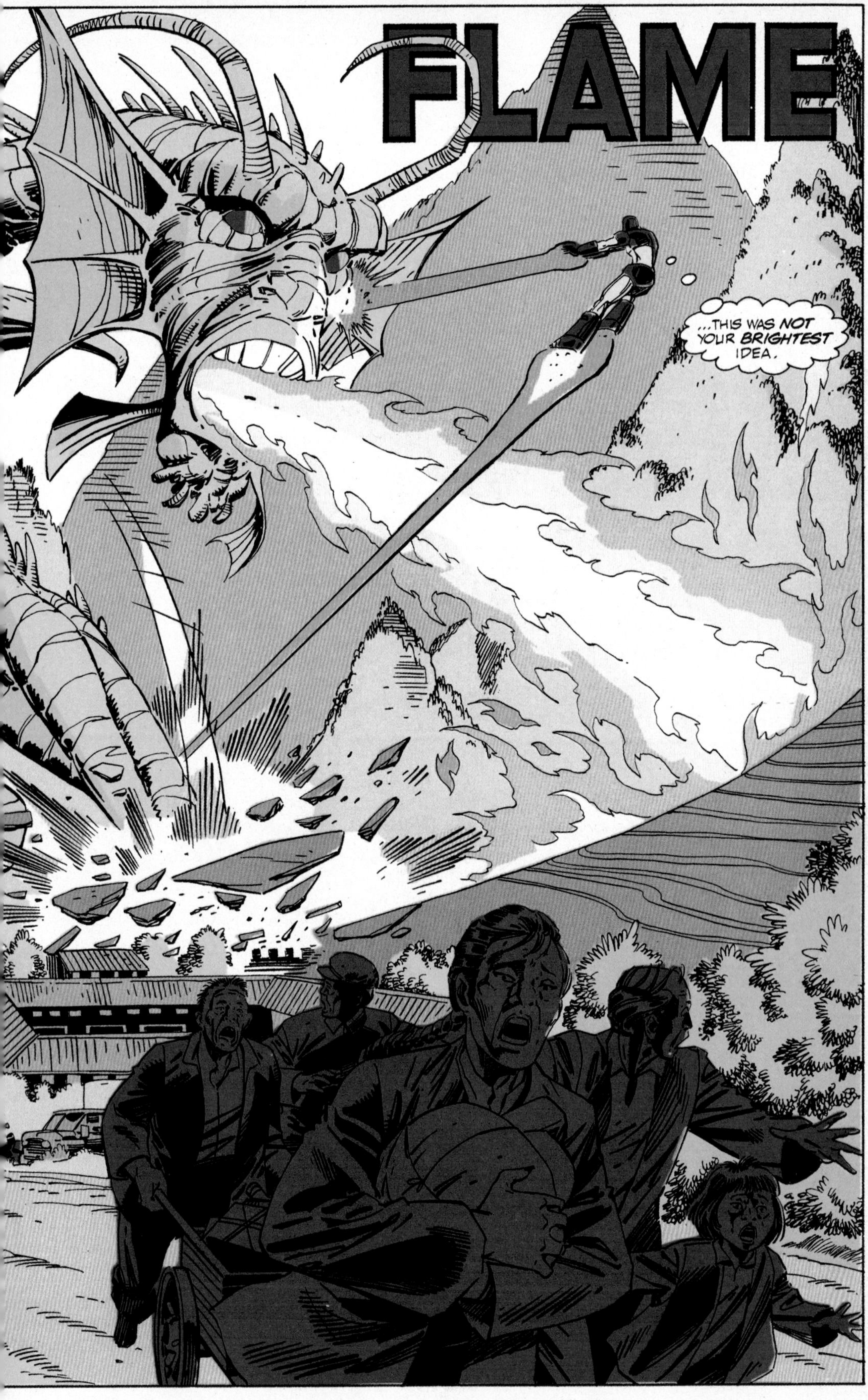
FLAME
...THIS WAS NOT YOUR BRIGHTEST IDEA.

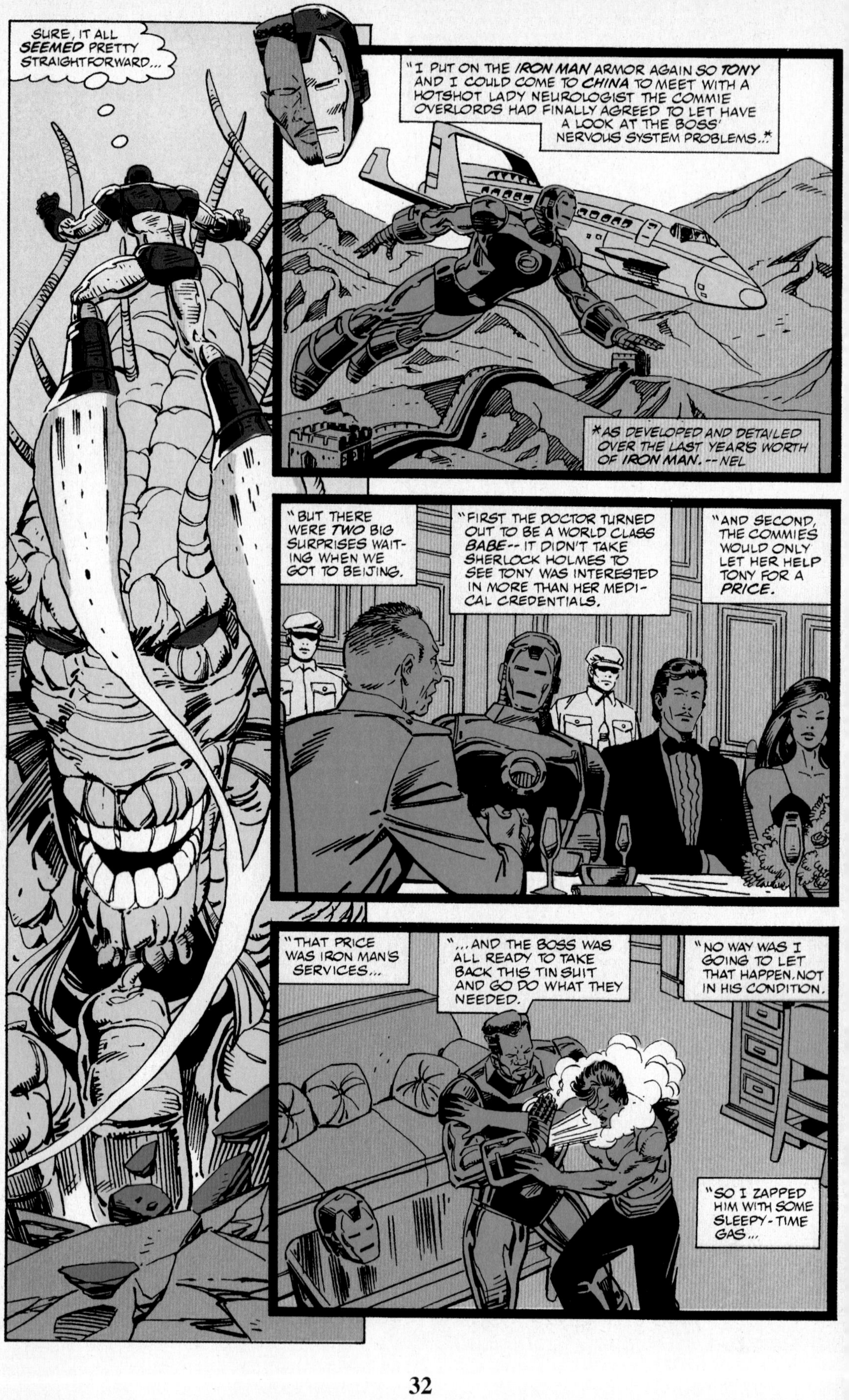
SURE, IT ALL SEEMED PRETTY STRAIGHTFORWARD...
"I PUT ON THE IRON MAN ARMOR AGAIN SO TONY AND I COULD COME TO CHINA TO MEET WITH A HOTSHOT LADY NEUROLOGIST THE COMMIE OVERLORDS HAD FINALLY AGREED TO LET HAVE A LOOK AT THE BOSS' NERVOUS SYSTEM PROBLEMS...*
*AS DEVELOPED AND DETAILED OVER THE LAST YEAR'S WORTH OF IRON MAN. --NEL
"BUT THERE WERE TWO BIG SURPRISES WAITING WHEN WE GOT TO BEIJING.
"FIRST THE DOCTOR TURNED OUT TO BE A WORLD CLASS BABE-- IT DIDN'T TAKE SHERLOCK HOLMES TO SEE TONY WAS INTERESTED IN MORE THAN HER MEDICAL CREDENTIALS.
"AND SECOND, THE COMMIES WOULD ONLY LET HER HELP TONY FOR A PRICE.
"THAT PRICE WAS IRON MAN'S SERVICES...
"...AND THE BOSS WAS ALL READY TO TAKE BACK THIS TIN SUIT AND GO DO WHAT THEY NEEDED.
"NO WAY WAS I GOING TO LET THAT HAPPEN. NOT IN HIS CONDITION.
"SO I ZAPPED HIM WITH SOME SLEEPY-TIME GAS...

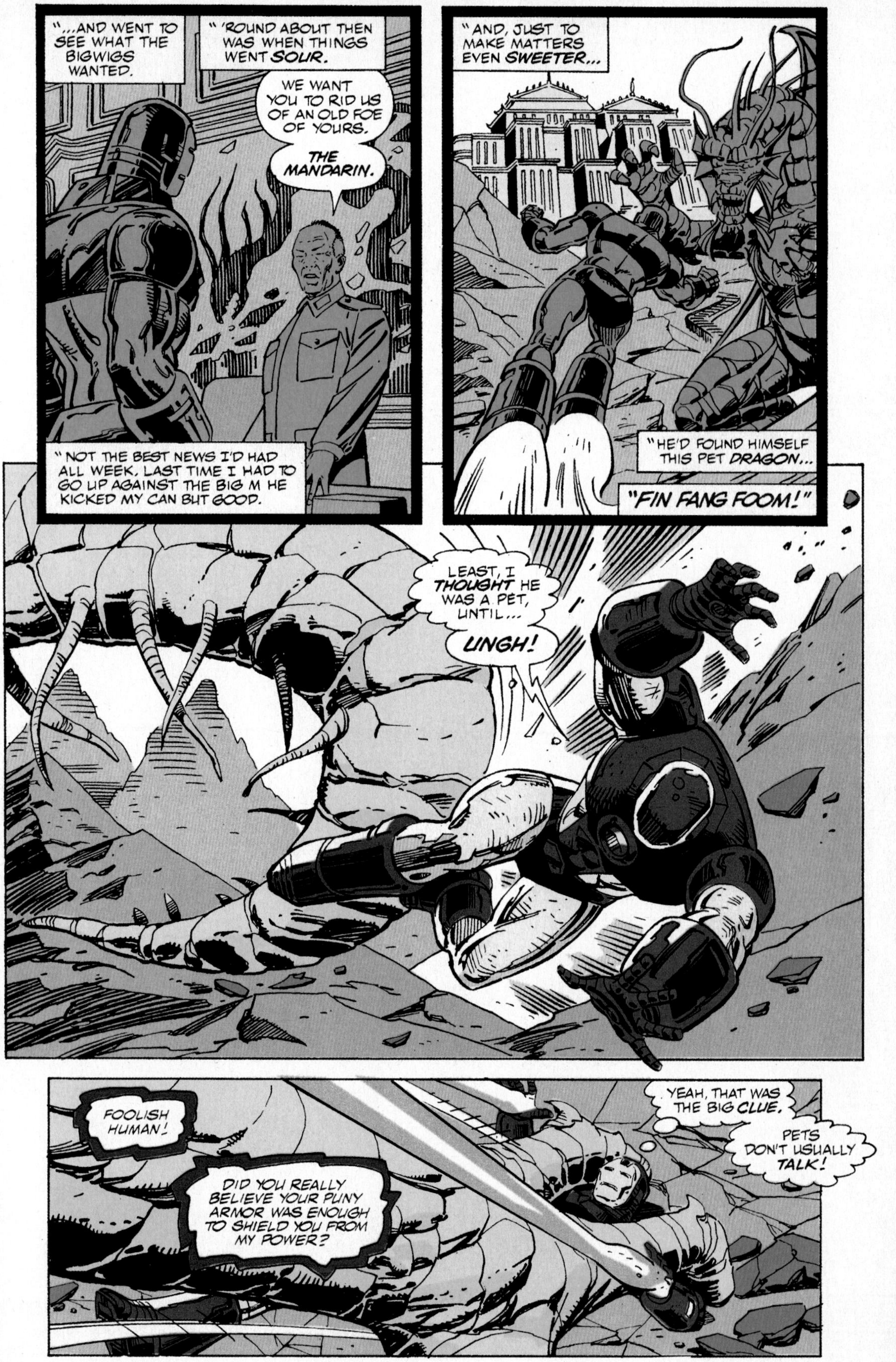
"...AND WENT TO SEE WHAT THE BIGWIGS WANTED.
"'ROUND ABOUT THEN WAS WHEN THINGS WENT SOUR.
WE WANT YOU TO RID US OF AN OLD FOE OF YOURS.
THE MANDARIN.
"NOT THE BEST NEWS I'D HAD ALL WEEK. LAST TIME I HAD TO GO UP AGAINST THE BIG M HE KICKED MY CAN BUT GOOD.
"AND, JUST TO MAKE MATTERS EVEN SWEETER...
"HE'D FOUND HIMSELF THIS PET DRAGON...
"FIN FANG FOOM!"
LEAST, I THOUGHT HE WAS A PET, UNTIL...
UNGH!
FOOLISH HUMAN!
DID YOU REALLY BELIEVE YOUR PUNY ARMOR WAS ENOUGH TO SHIELD YOU FROM MY POWER?
YEAH, THAT WAS THE BIG CLUE.
PETS DON'T USUALLY TALK!

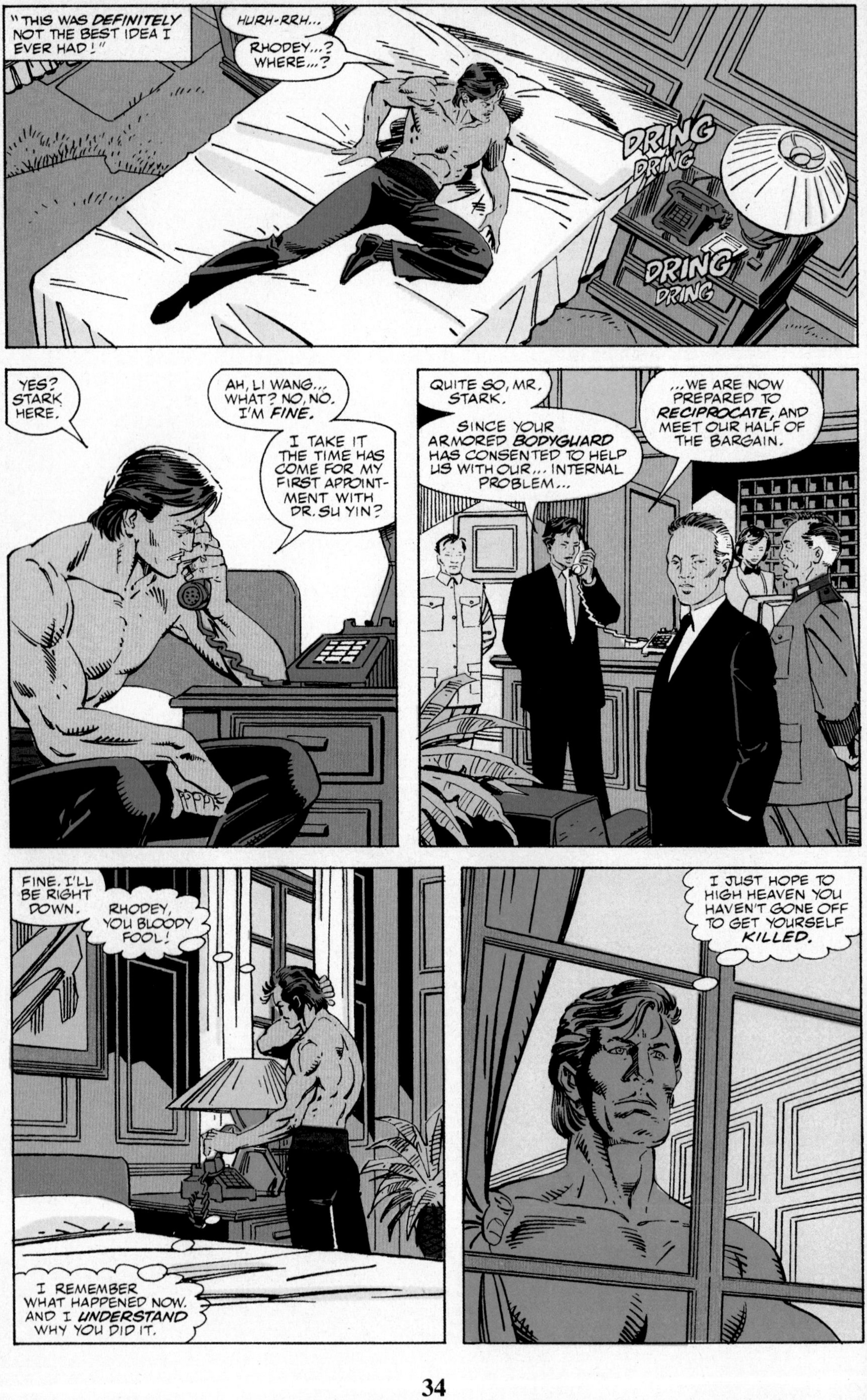
"THIS WAS DEFINITELY NOT THE BEST IDEA I EVER HAD!"
HURH-RRH...
RHODEY...? WHERE...?
DRING DRING
DRING DRING
YES? STARK HERE.
AH, LI WANG... WHAT? NO, NO. I'M FINE.
I TAKE IT THE TIME HAS COME FOR MY FIRST APPOINTMENT WITH DR. SU YIN?
QUITE SO, MR. STARK.
SINCE YOUR ARMORED BODYGUARD HAS CONSENTED TO HELP US WITH OUR... INTERNAL PROBLEM...
...WE ARE NOW PREPARED TO RECIPROCATE, AND MEET OUR HALF OF THE BARGAIN.
FINE. I'LL BE RIGHT DOWN.
RHODEY, YOU BLOODY FOOL!
I REMEMBER WHAT HAPPENED NOW. AND I UNDERSTAND WHY YOU DID IT.
I JUST HOPE TO HIGH HEAVEN YOU HAVEN'T GONE OFF TO GET YOURSELF KILLED.

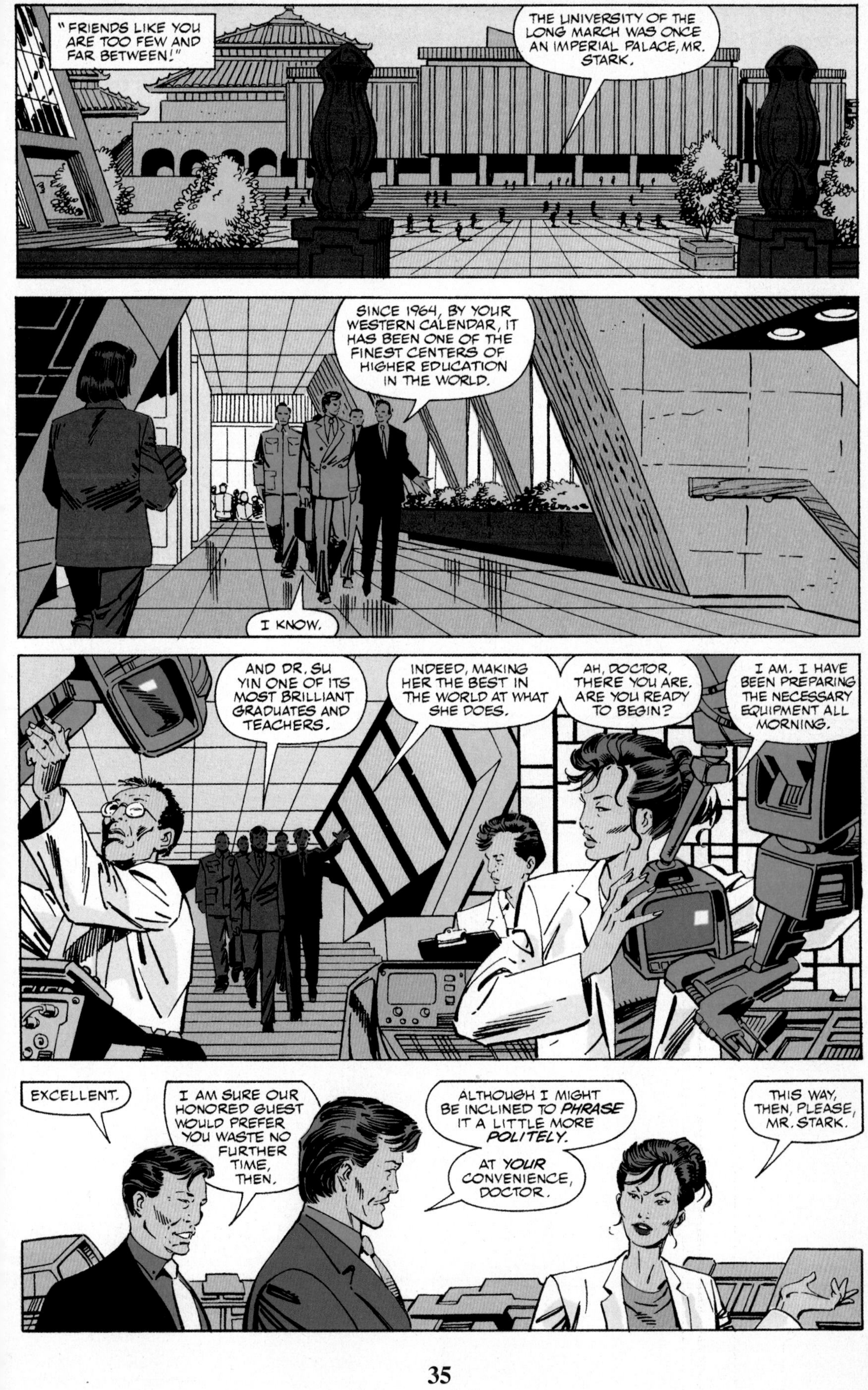
"FRIENDS LIKE YOU ARE TOO FEW AND FAR BETWEEN!"
THE UNIVERSITY OF THE LONG MARCH WAS ONCE AN IMPERIAL PALACE, MR. STARK.
SINCE 1964, BY YOUR WESTERN CALENDAR, IT HAS BEEN ONE OF THE FINEST CENTERS OF HIGHER EDUCATION IN THE WORLD.
I KNOW.
AND DR. SU YIN ONE OF ITS MOST BRILLIANT GRADUATES AND TEACHERS.
INDEED, MAKING HER THE BEST IN THE WORLD AT WHAT SHE DOES.
AH, DOCTOR, THERE YOU ARE. ARE YOU READY TO BEGIN?
I AM. I HAVE BEEN PREPARING THE NECESSARY EQUIPMENT ALL MORNING.
EXCELLENT.
I AM SURE OUR HONORED GUEST WOULD PREFER YOU WASTE NO FURTHER TIME, THEN.
ALTHOUGH I MIGHT BE INCLINED TO PHRASE IT A LITTLE MORE POLITELY.
AT YOUR CONVENIENCE, DOCTOR.
THIS WAY, THEN, PLEASE, MR. STARK.

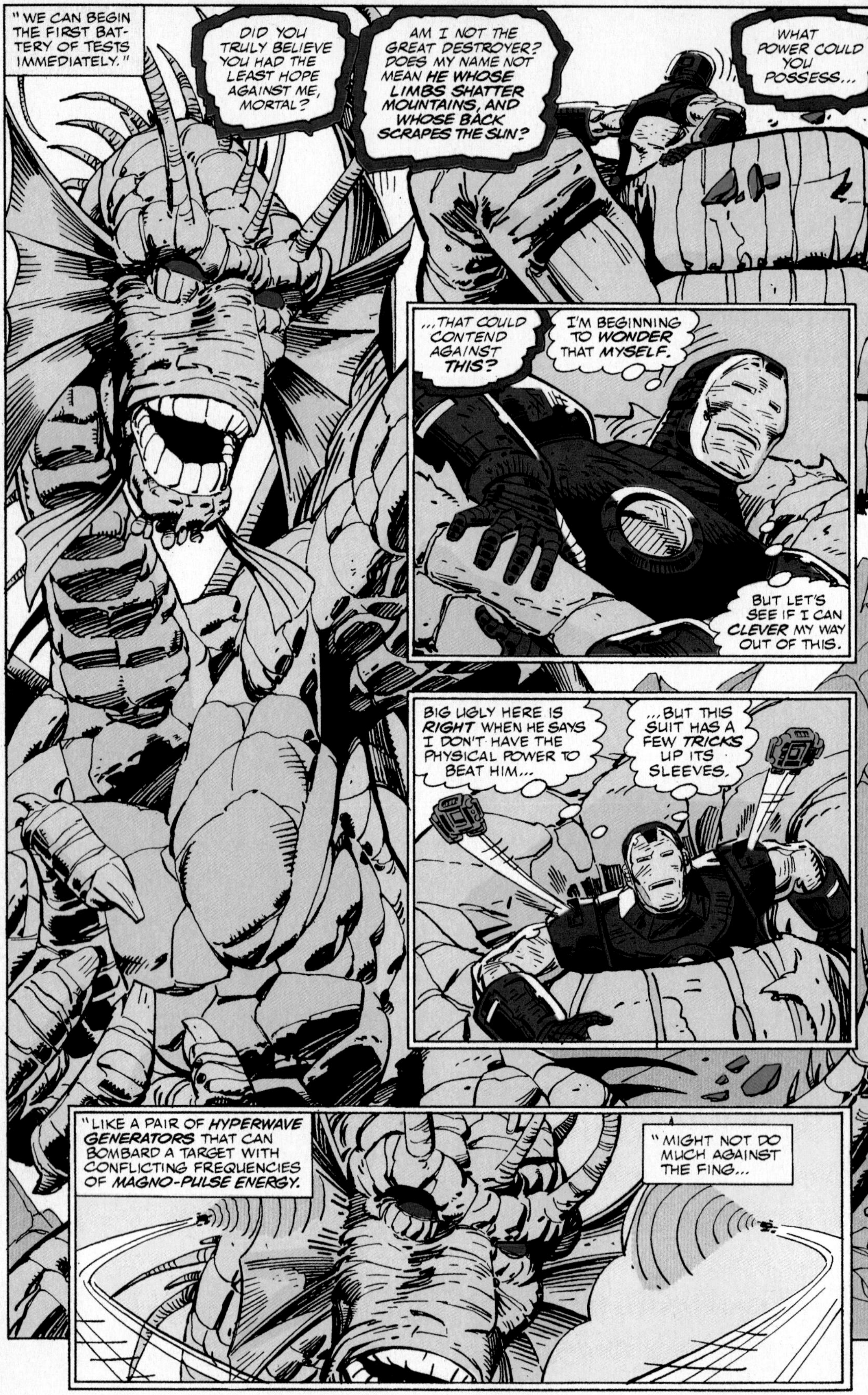
"WE CAN BEGIN THE FIRST BATTERY OF TESTS IMMEDIATELY."
DID YOU TRULY BELIEVE YOU HAD THE LEAST HOPE AGAINST ME, MORTAL?
AM I NOT THE GREAT DESTROYER? DOES MY NAME NOT MEAN HE WHOSE LIMBS SHATTER MOUNTAINS, AND WHOSE BACK SCRAPES THE SUN?
WHAT POWER COULD YOU POSSESS...
...THAT COULD CONTEND AGAINST THIS?
I'M BEGINNING TO WONDER THAT MYSELF.
BUT LET'S SEE IF I CAN CLEVER MY WAY OUT OF THIS.
BIG UGLY HERE IS RIGHT WHEN HE SAYS I DON'T HAVE THE PHYSICAL POWER TO BEAT HIM...
...BUT THIS SUIT HAS A FEW TRICKS UP ITS SLEEVES.
"LIKE A PAIR OF HYPERWAVE GENERATORS THAT CAN BOMBARD A TARGET WITH CONFLICTING FREQUENCIES OF MAGNO-PULSE ENERGY.
"MIGHT NOT DO MUCH AGAINST THE FING...

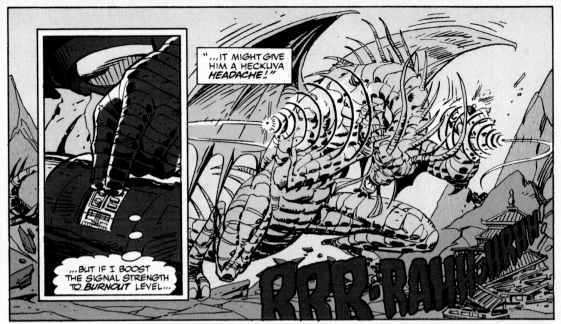

"...IT MIGHT GIVE HIM A HECKUVA *HEADACHE!*"

...BUT IF I BOOST THE SIGNAL STRENGTH TO *BURNOUT* LEVEL...

RRR-RAHH-HRHH!

WHOOPS...

TOSSED ME TOO FAST FOR MY BOOT JETS TO KICK IN.

BUT I CAN JUST *GRAB*...

DID IT!

BUT THIS HAS ONLY BOUGHT ME A SHORT *BREATHER.*

THOSE HYPERWAVE GENERATORS WON'T LAST MORE THAN ANOTHER THIRTY SECONDS AT MAXIMUM...

UH OH...

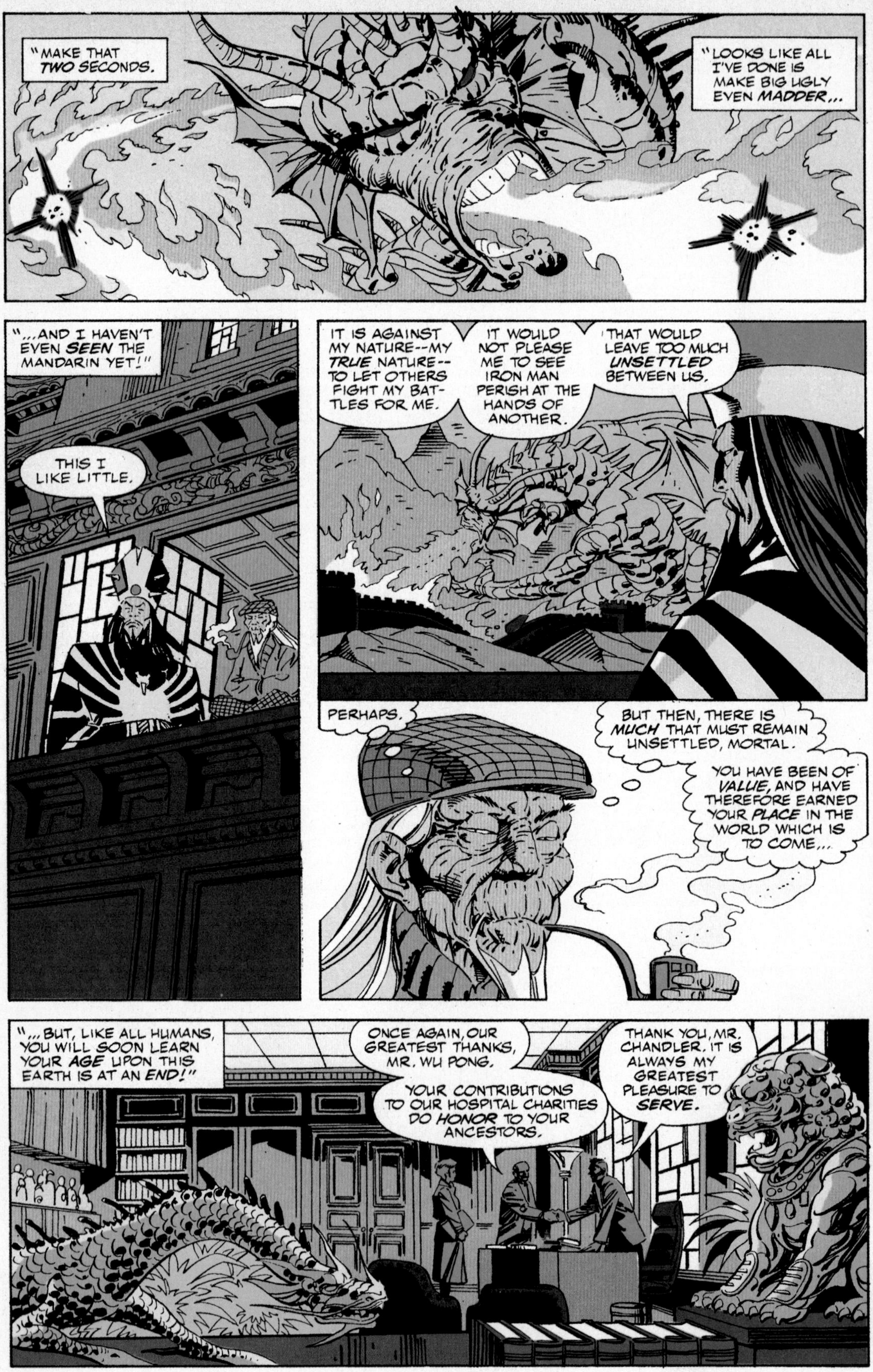
"MAKE THAT TWO SECONDS.
"LOOKS LIKE ALL I'VE DONE IS MAKE BIG UGLY EVEN MADDER...
"...AND I HAVEN'T EVEN SEEN THE MANDARIN YET!"
THIS I LIKE LITTLE.
IT IS AGAINST MY NATURE--MY TRUE NATURE-- TO LET OTHERS FIGHT MY BATTLES FOR ME.
IT WOULD NOT PLEASE ME TO SEE IRON MAN PERISH AT THE HANDS OF ANOTHER.
THAT WOULD LEAVE TOO MUCH UNSETTLED BETWEEN US.
PERHAPS.
BUT THEN, THERE IS MUCH THAT MUST REMAIN UNSETTLED, MORTAL.
YOU HAVE BEEN OF VALUE, AND HAVE THEREFORE EARNED YOUR PLACE IN THE WORLD WHICH IS TO COME...
"...BUT, LIKE ALL HUMANS, YOU WILL SOON LEARN YOUR AGE UPON THIS EARTH IS AT AN END!"
ONCE AGAIN, OUR GREATEST THANKS, MR. WU PONG.
YOUR CONTRIBUTIONS TO OUR HOSPITAL CHARITIES DO HONOR TO YOUR ANCESTORS.
THANK YOU, MR. CHANDLER. IT IS ALWAYS MY GREATEST PLEASURE TO SERVE.

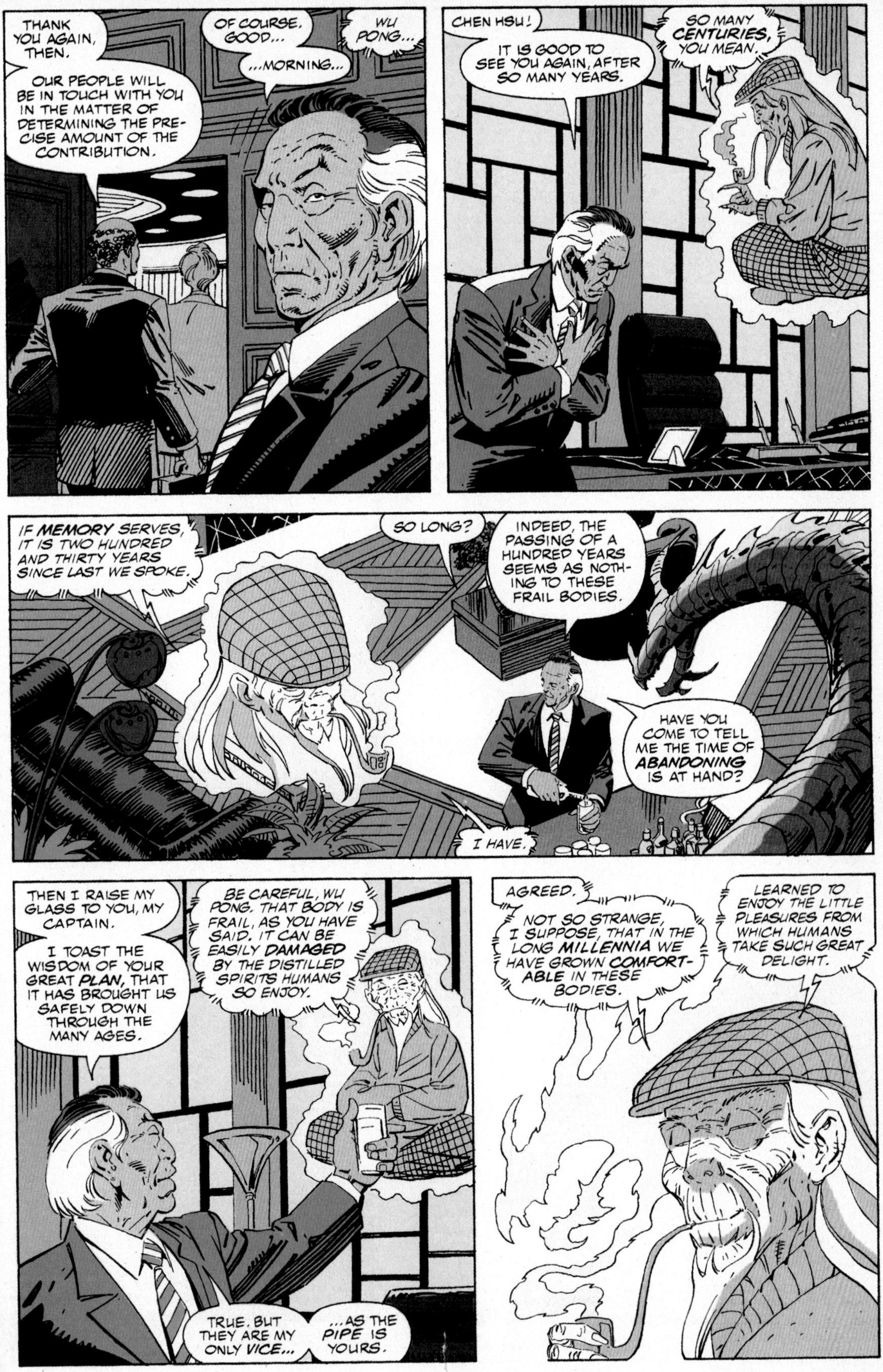
THANK YOU AGAIN, THEN.
OUR PEOPLE WILL BE IN TOUCH WITH YOU IN THE MATTER OF DETERMINING THE PRECISE AMOUNT OF THE CONTRIBUTION.
OF COURSE. GOOD...
...MORNING...
WU PONG...
CHEN HSU!
IT IS GOOD TO SEE YOU AGAIN, AFTER SO MANY YEARS.
SO MANY CENTURIES, YOU MEAN.
IF MEMORY SERVES, IT IS TWO HUNDRED AND THIRTY YEARS SINCE LAST WE SPOKE.
SO LONG?
INDEED, THE PASSING OF A HUNDRED YEARS SEEMS AS NOTHING TO THESE FRAIL BODIES.
HAVE YOU COME TO TELL ME THE TIME OF ABANDONING IS AT HAND?
I HAVE.
THEN I RAISE MY GLASS TO YOU, MY CAPTAIN.
I TOAST THE WISDOM OF YOUR GREAT PLAN, THAT IT HAS BROUGHT US SAFELY DOWN THROUGH THE MANY AGES.
BE CAREFUL, WU PONG. THAT BODY IS FRAIL, AS YOU HAVE SAID. IT CAN BE EASILY DAMAGED BY THE DISTILLED SPIRITS HUMANS SO ENJOY.
TRUE. BUT THEY ARE MY ONLY VICE...
...AS THE PIPE IS YOURS.
AGREED.
NOT SO STRANGE, I SUPPOSE, THAT IN THE LONG MILLENNIA WE HAVE GROWN COMFORTABLE IN THESE BODIES.
LEARNED TO ENJOY THE LITTLE PLEASURES FROM WHICH HUMANS TAKE SUCH GREAT DELIGHT.

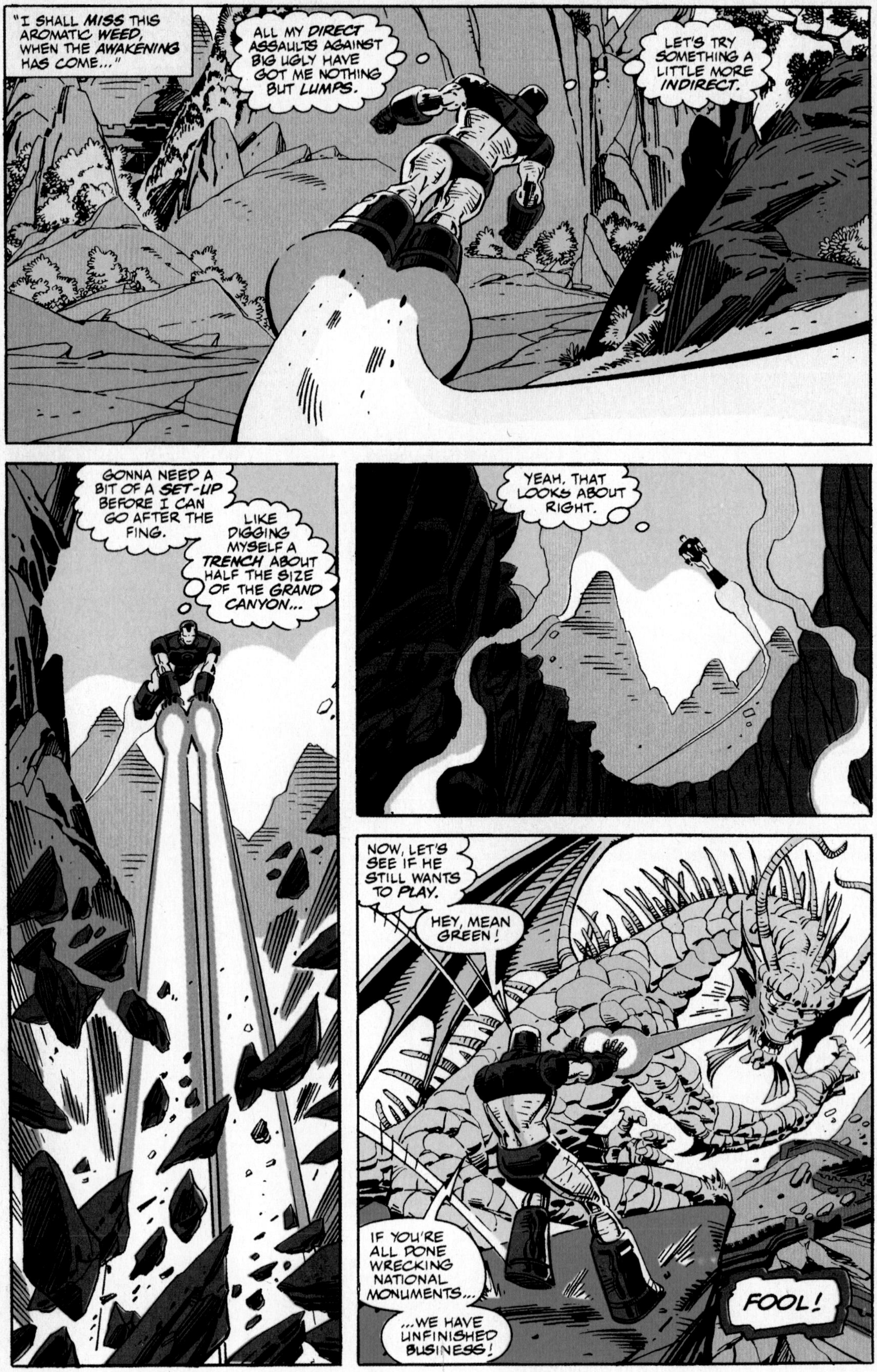
"I SHALL MISS THIS AROMATIC WEED, WHEN THE AWAKENING HAS COME..."
ALL MY DIRECT ASSAULTS AGAINST BIG UGLY HAVE GOT ME NOTHING BUT LUMPS.
LET'S TRY SOMETHING A LITTLE MORE INDIRECT.
GONNA NEED A BIT OF A SET-UP BEFORE I CAN GO AFTER THE FING.
LIKE DIGGING MYSELF A TRENCH ABOUT HALF THE SIZE OF THE GRAND CANYON...
YEAH, THAT LOOKS ABOUT RIGHT.
NOW, LET'S SEE IF HE STILL WANTS TO PLAY.
HEY, MEAN GREEN!
IF YOU'RE ALL DONE WRECKING NATIONAL MONUMENTS...
...WE HAVE UNFINISHED BUSINESS!
FOOL!

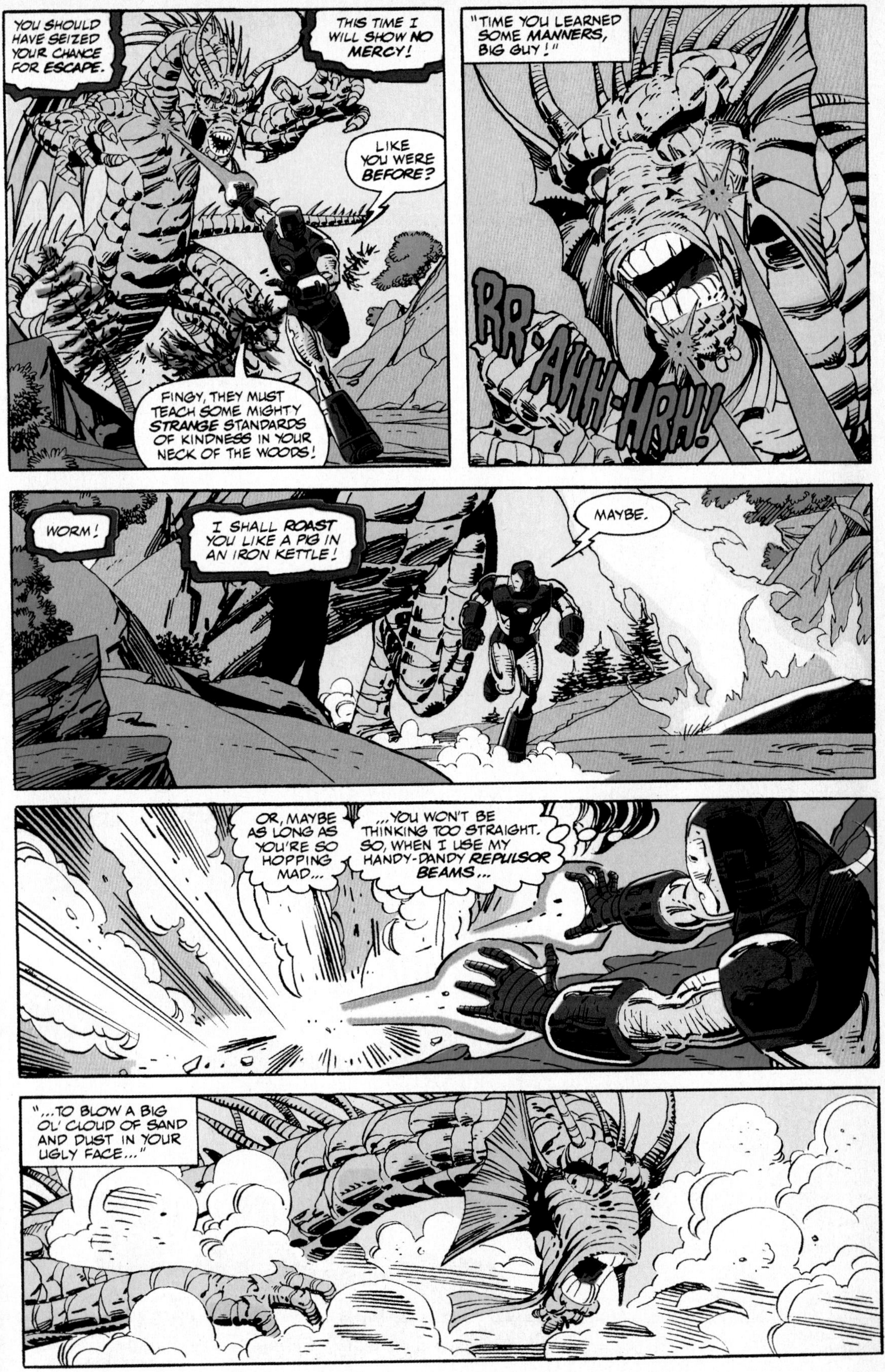
YOU SHOULD HAVE SEIZED YOUR CHANCE FOR ESCAPE.
THIS TIME I WILL SHOW NO MERCY!
LIKE YOU WERE BEFORE?
FINGY, THEY MUST TEACH SOME MIGHTY STRANGE STANDARDS OF KINDNESS IN YOUR NECK OF THE WOODS!
"TIME YOU LEARNED SOME MANNERS, BIG GUY!"
RR-AHH-HRH!
WORM!
I SHALL ROAST YOU LIKE A PIG IN AN IRON KETTLE!
MAYBE.
OR, MAYBE AS LONG AS YOU'RE SO HOPPING MAD...
...YOU WON'T BE THINKING TOO STRAIGHT. SO, WHEN I USE MY HANDY-DANDY REPULSOR BEAMS...
"...TO BLOW A BIG OL' CLOUD OF SAND AND DUST IN YOUR UGLY FACE..."

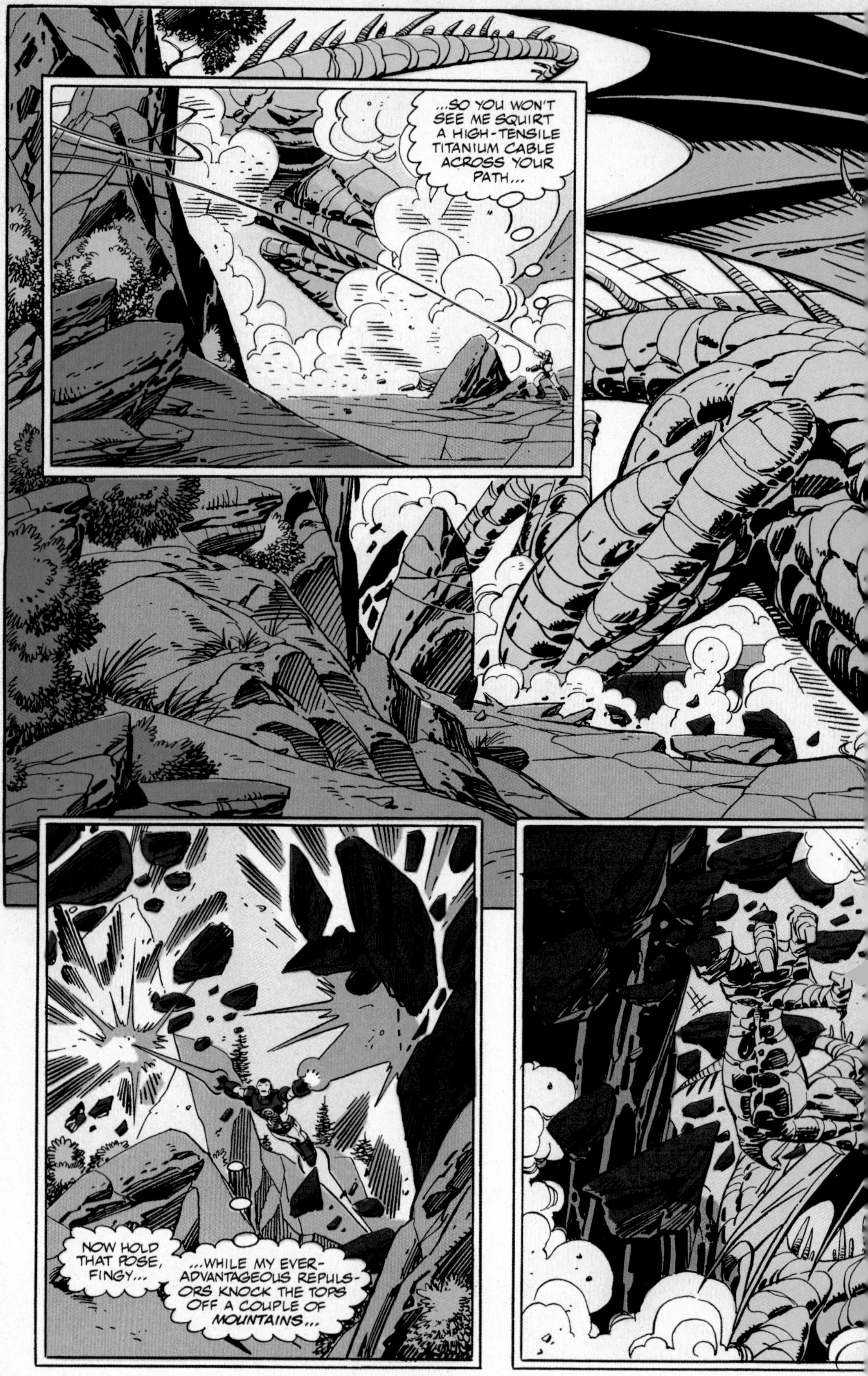
...SO YOU WON'T SEE ME SQUIRT A HIGH-TENSILE TITANIUM CABLE ACROSS YOUR PATH...
NOW HOLD THAT POSE, FINGY...
...WHILE MY EVER-ADVANTAGEOUS REPULS-ORS KNOCK THE TOPS OFF A COUPLE OF MOUNTAINS...

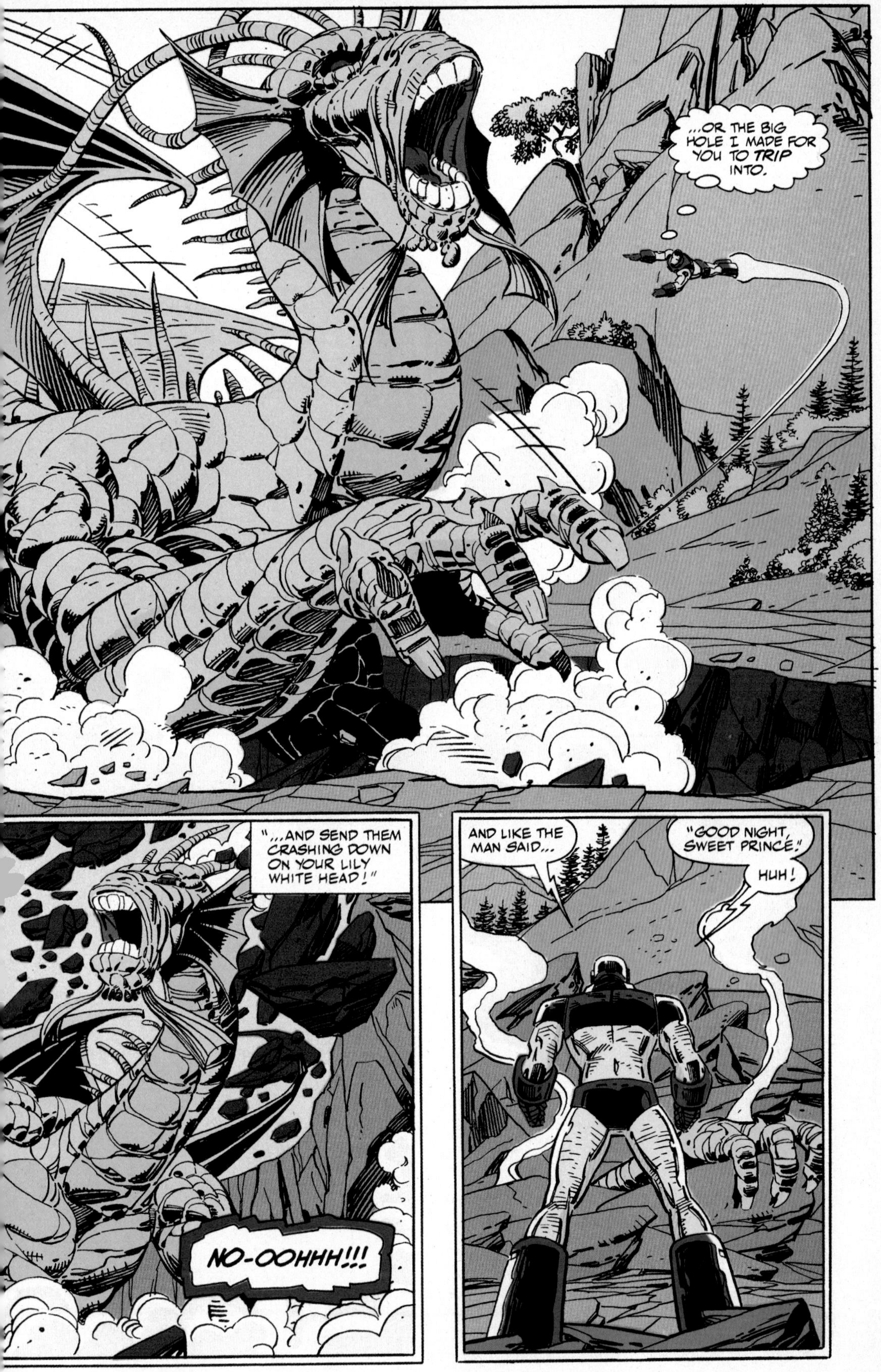
...OR THE BIG HOLE I MADE FOR YOU TO TRIP INTO.
"...AND SEND THEM CRASHING DOWN ON YOUR LILY WHITE HEAD!"
NO-OOHHH!!!
AND LIKE THE MAN SAID...
"GOOD NIGHT, SWEET PRINCE."
HUH!

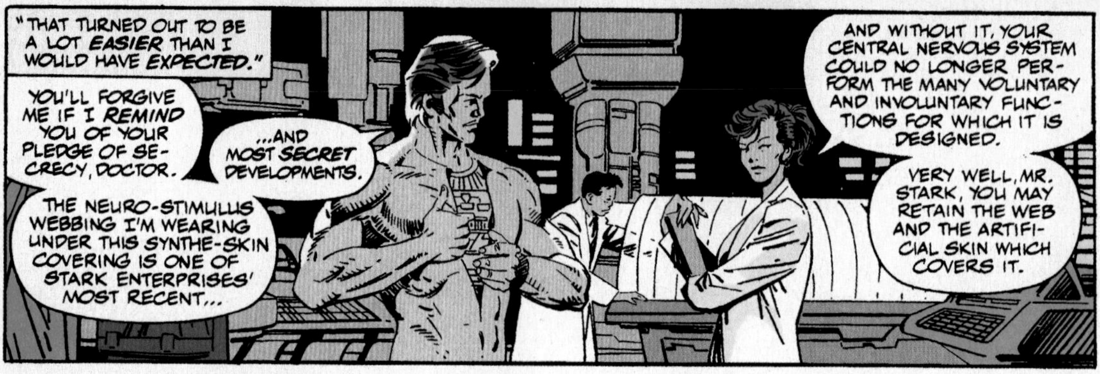
"THAT TURNED OUT TO BE A LOT EASIER THAN I WOULD HAVE EXPECTED."
YOU'LL FORGIVE ME IF I REMIND YOU OF YOUR PLEDGE OF SE-CRECY, DOCTOR.
THE NEURO-STIMULUS WEBBING I'M WEARING UNDER THIS SYNTHE-SKIN COVERING IS ONE OF STARK ENTERPRISES' MOST RECENT...
...AND MOST SECRET DEVELOPMENTS.
AND WITHOUT IT, YOUR CENTRAL NERVOUS SYSTEM COULD NO LONGER PER-FORM THE MANY VOLUNTARY AND INVOLUNTARY FUNC-TIONS FOR WHICH IT IS DESIGNED.
VERY WELL, MR. STARK, YOU MAY RETAIN THE WEB AND THE ARTIFI-CIAL SKIN WHICH COVERS IT.

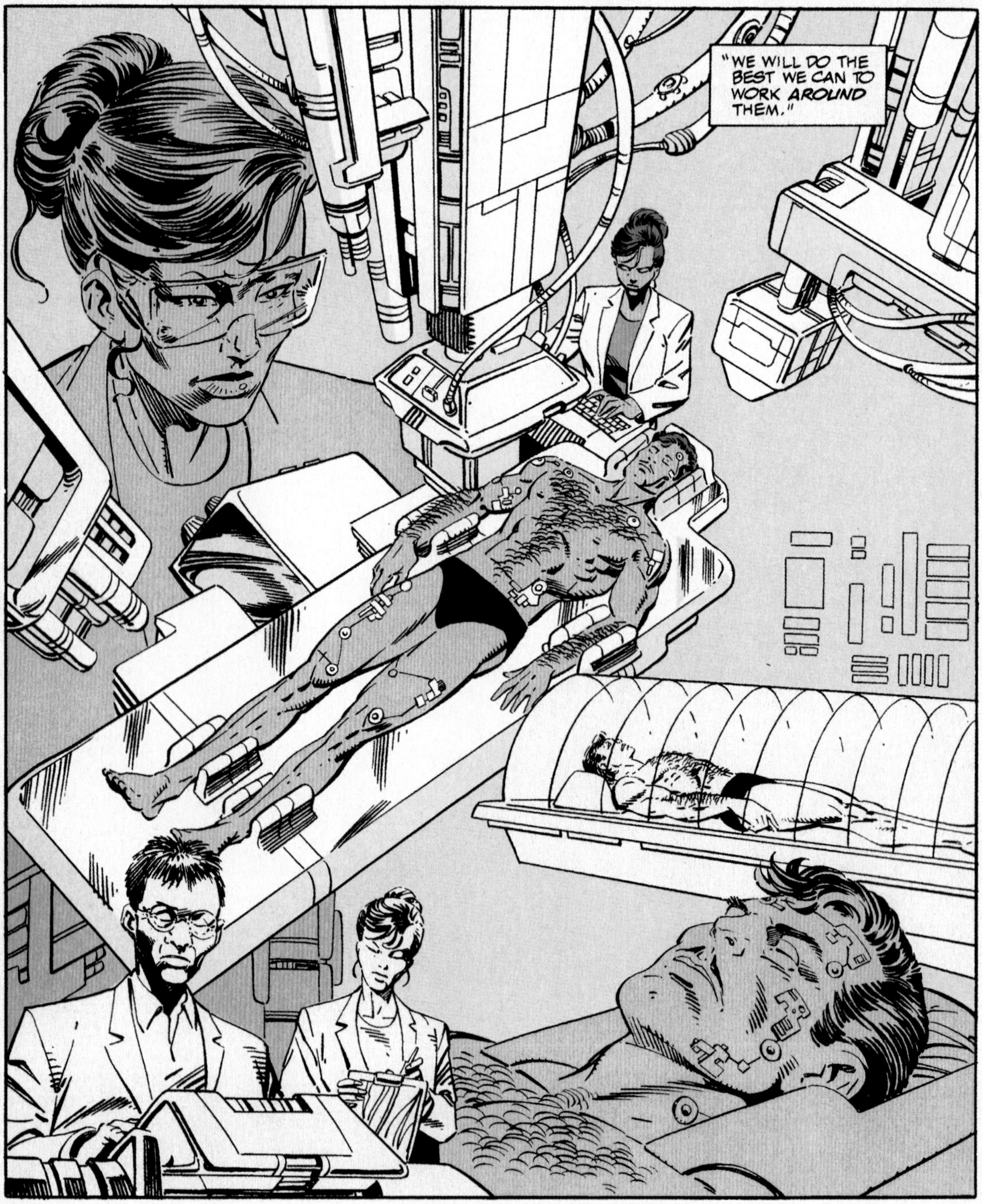
"WE WILL DO THE BEST WE CAN TO WORK AROUND THEM."

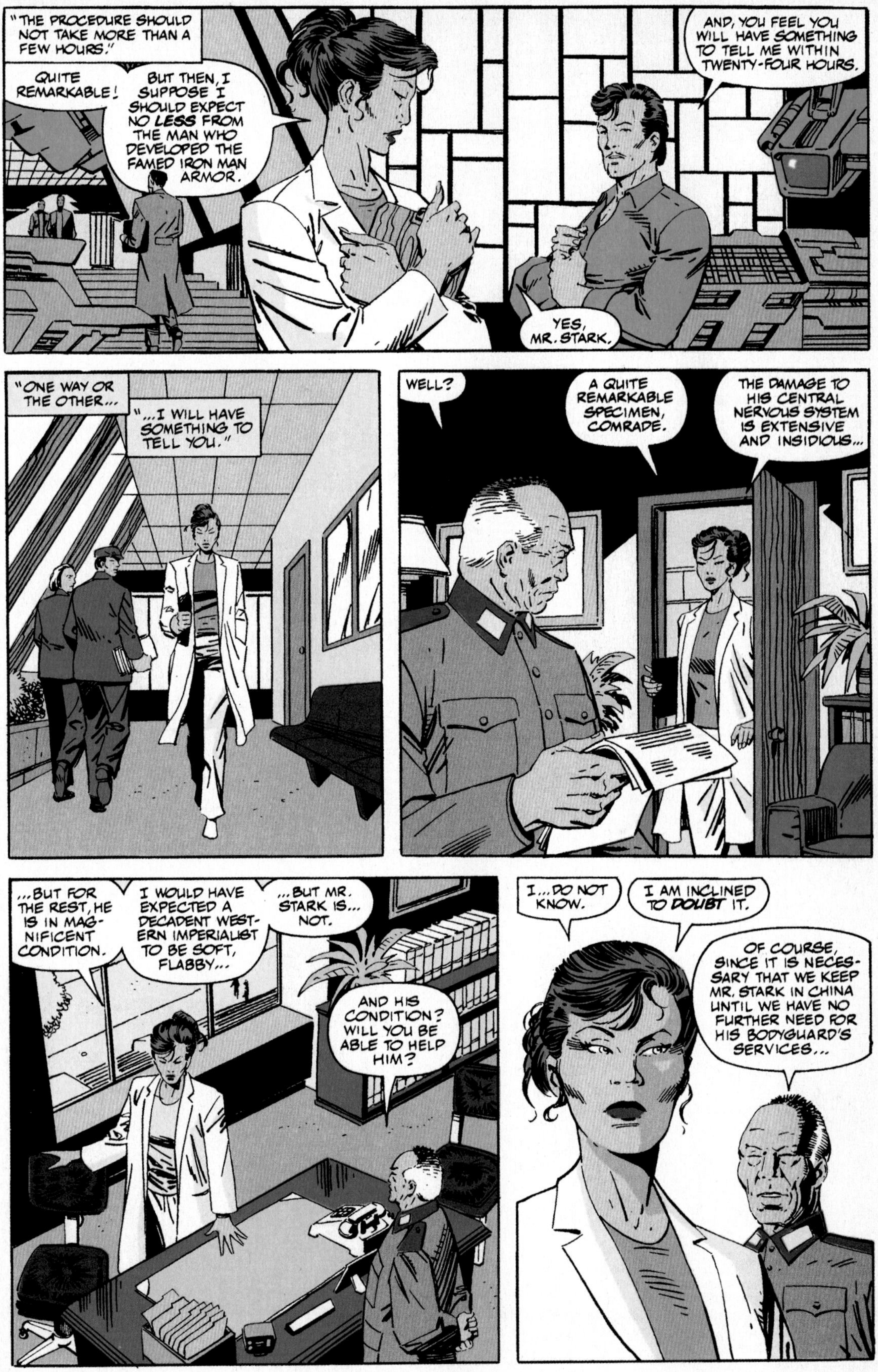
"THE PROCEDURE SHOULD NOT TAKE MORE THAN A FEW HOURS."
QUITE REMARKABLE!
BUT THEN, I SUPPOSE I SHOULD EXPECT NO LESS FROM THE MAN WHO DEVELOPED THE FAMED IRON MAN ARMOR.
AND, YOU FEEL YOU WILL HAVE SOMETHING TO TELL ME WITHIN TWENTY-FOUR HOURS.
YES, MR. STARK.
"ONE WAY OR THE OTHER...
"...I WILL HAVE SOMETHING TO TELL YOU."
WELL?
A QUITE REMARKABLE SPECIMEN, COMRADE.
THE DAMAGE TO HIS CENTRAL NERVOUS SYSTEM IS EXTENSIVE AND INSIDIOUS...
...BUT FOR THE REST, HE IS IN MAGNIFICENT CONDITION.
I WOULD HAVE EXPECTED A DECADENT WESTERN IMPERIALIST TO BE SOFT, FLABBY...
...BUT MR. STARK IS... NOT.
AND HIS CONDITION? WILL YOU BE ABLE TO HELP HIM?
I... DO NOT KNOW.
I AM INCLINED TO DOUBT IT.
OF COURSE, SINCE IT IS NECESSARY THAT WE KEEP MR. STARK IN CHINA UNTIL WE HAVE NO FURTHER NEED FOR HIS BODYGUARD'S SERVICES...

"YOU WILL NOT HESITATE TO *LIE* TO HIM."

ALEXI ALEXIVITCH...

NATALIE ALIANOVNA! SURELY IT HAS BEEN A THOUSAND YEARS! WHAT BRINGS YOU TO A PLACE LIKE THIS?*

* TRANSLATED FROM RUSSIAN. --NEL

I THINK YOU *CAN GUESS*, ALEXI ALEXIVITCH.

YOU KNOW THE *DATE*.

AH, YES. BUT, SURELY THIS IS NO MATTER FOR YOUR CONCERN? IT IS *YEARS* SINCE YOU HAVE BEEN WITH THE KGB.

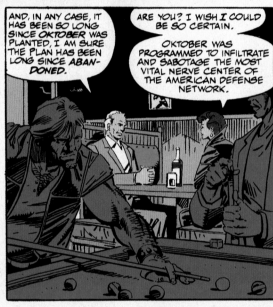

AND, IN ANY CASE, IT HAS BEEN SO LONG SINCE *OKTOBER* WAS PLANTED, I AM SURE THE PLAN HAS BEEN LONG SINCE *ABANDONED*.

ARE YOU? I WISH *I* COULD BE SO CERTAIN. OKTOBER WAS PROGRAMMED TO INFILTRATE AND SABOTAGE THE MOST VITAL NERVE CENTER OF THE AMERICAN DEFENSE NETWORK.

IF HE *IS* TRIGGERED NOW...IF HE PROCEEDS AS PROGRAMMED, ALL THE PEACE AND GOOD WILL OUR TWO COUNTRIES HAVE CREATED OVER THE PAST YEAR COULD BE *BLASTED* AWAY.

ATOMIZED IN A RAIN OF *NUCLEAR FIRE!*

TSK TSK! YOU HAVE LIVED TOO LONG IN THE SOFT DECADENCE OF THIS COUNTRY, NATASHA. IT HAS GIVEN YOU A PENCHANT FOR THE *MELODRAMATIC*.

OKTOBER IS NOTHING TO WORRY ABOUT. I AM *SURE* OF THIS.

THAT IS NOT GOOD ENOUGH.

NATASHA!

IF OKTOBER IS STILL IN AMERICA...IF HE IS STILL *ALIVE*...IF HE HAS BEEN *TRIGGERED*...

HE MUST BE *STOPPED*--NO MATTER *WHAT* THE COST!

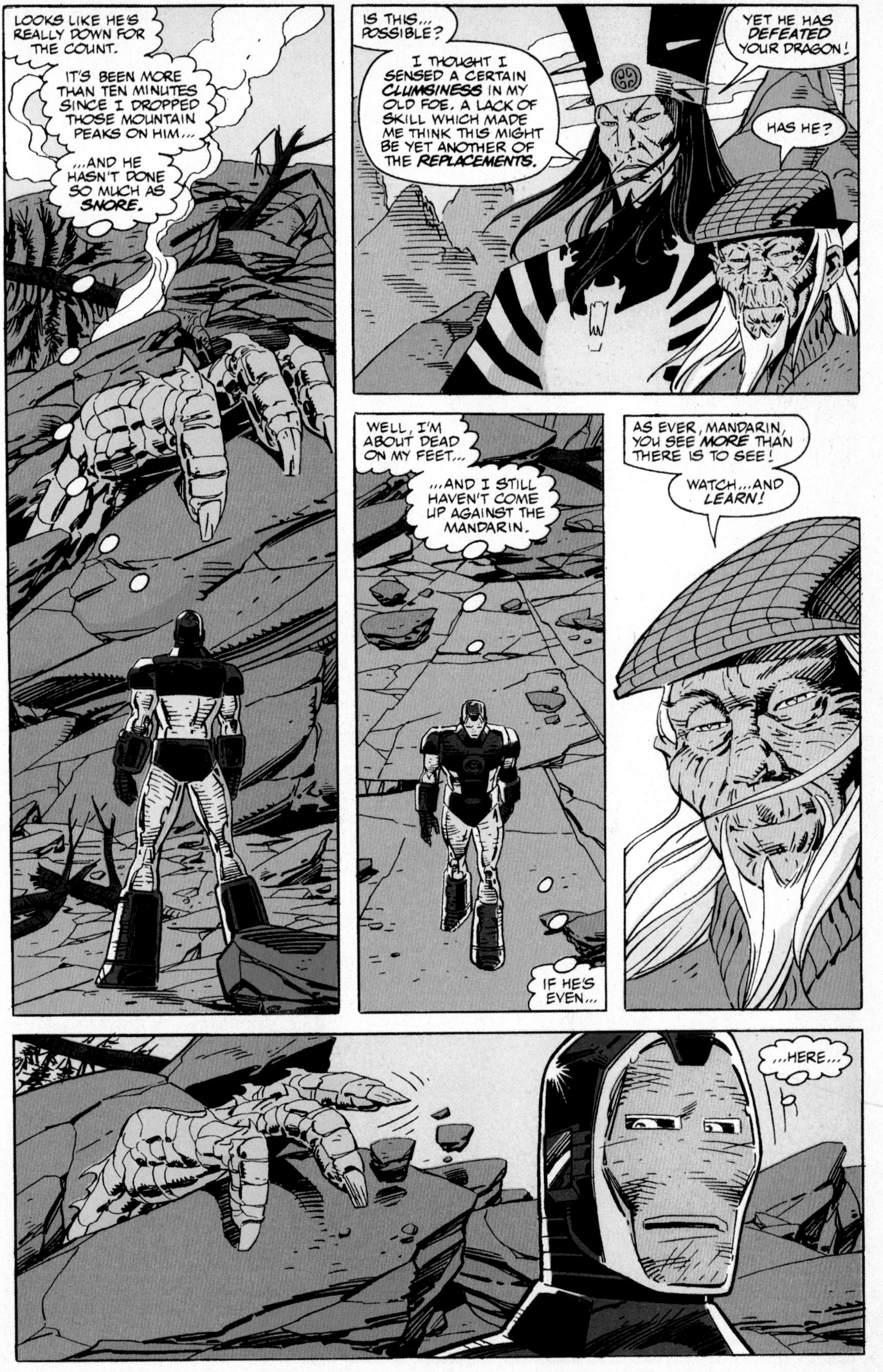
LOOKS LIKE HE'S REALLY DOWN FOR THE COUNT.
IT'S BEEN MORE THAN TEN MINUTES SINCE I DROPPED THOSE MOUNTAIN PEAKS ON HIM...
...AND HE HASN'T DONE SO MUCH AS SNORE.
IS THIS... POSSIBLE?
I THOUGHT I SENSED A CERTAIN CLUMSINESS IN MY OLD FOE. A LACK OF SKILL WHICH MADE ME THINK THIS MIGHT BE YET ANOTHER OF THE REPLACEMENTS.
YET HE HAS DEFEATED YOUR DRAGON!
HAS HE?
WELL, I'M ABOUT DEAD ON MY FEET...
...AND I STILL HAVEN'T COME UP AGAINST THE MANDARIN.
IF HE'S EVEN...
AS EVER, MANDARIN, YOU SEE MORE THAN THERE IS TO SEE!
WATCH...AND LEARN!
...HERE...

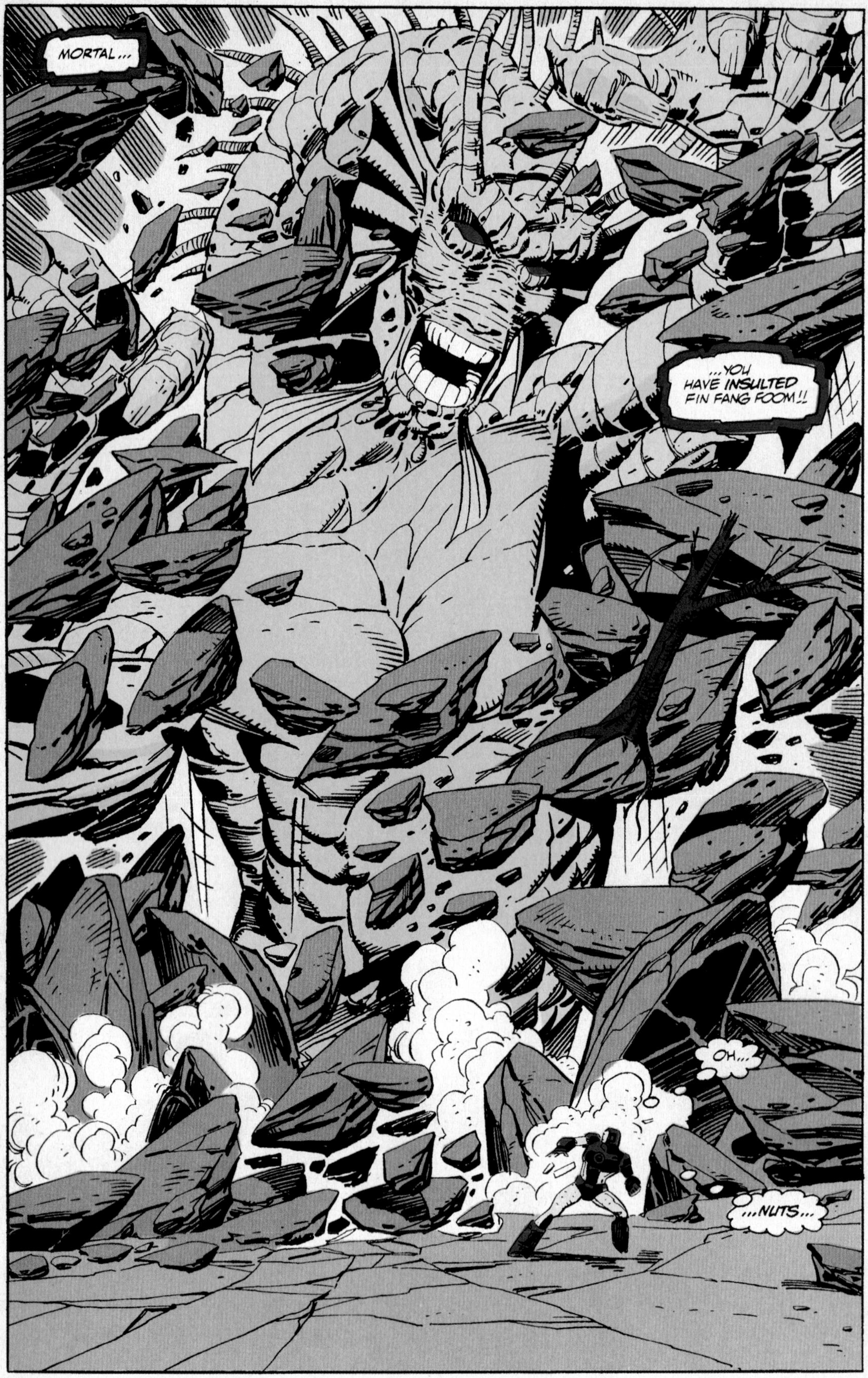
MORTAL...
...YOU HAVE INSULTED FIN FANG FOOM!!
OH...
...NUTS...

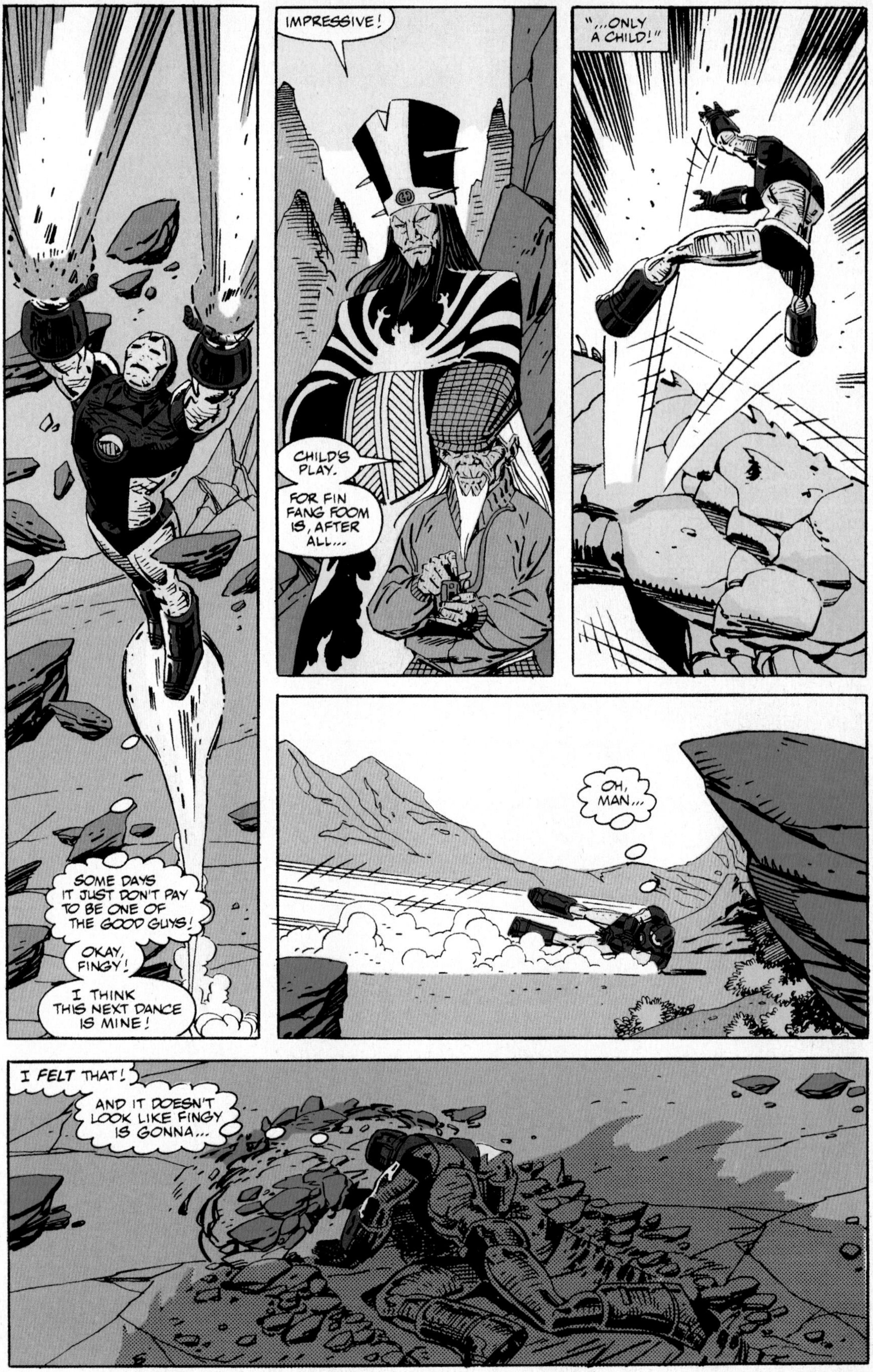
IMPRESSIVE!
CHILD'S PLAY.
FOR FIN FANG FOOM IS, AFTER ALL...
"...ONLY A CHILD!"
SOME DAYS IT JUST DON'T PAY TO BE ONE OF THE GOOD GUYS!
OKAY, FINGY!
I THINK THIS NEXT DANCE IS MINE!
OH, MAN...
I FELT THAT!
AND IT DOESN'T LOOK LIKE FINGY IS GONNA...

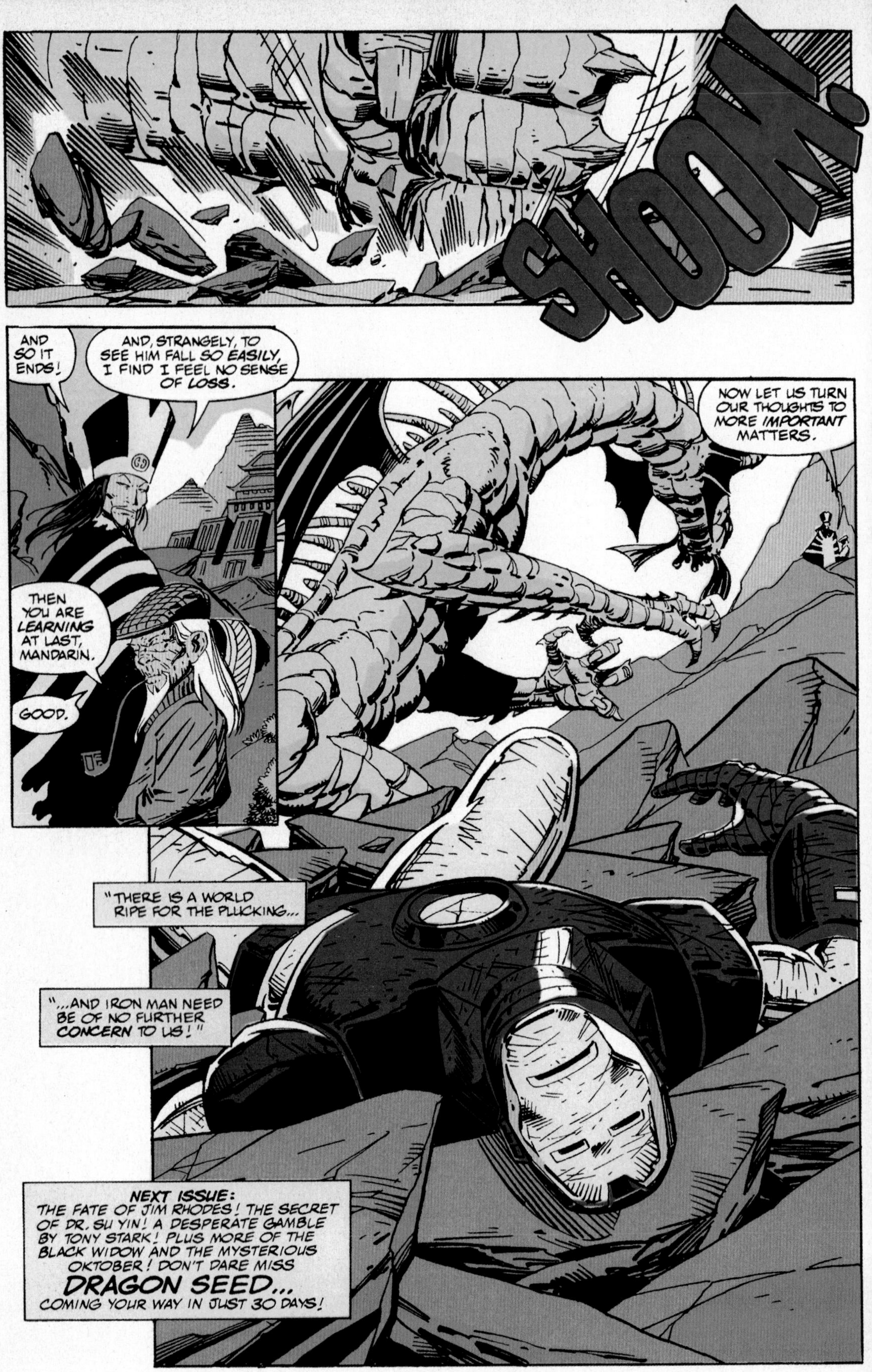
SHOOM!
AND SO IT ENDS!
AND, STRANGELY, TO SEE HIM FALL SO EASILY, I FIND I FEEL NO SENSE OF LOSS.
THEN YOU ARE LEARNING AT LAST, MANDARIN.
GOOD.
NOW LET US TURN OUR THOUGHTS TO MORE IMPORTANT MATTERS.
"THERE IS A WORLD RIPE FOR THE PLUCKING...
"...AND IRON MAN NEED BE OF NO FURTHER CONCERN TO US!"
NEXT ISSUE: THE FATE OF JIM RHODES! THE SECRET OF DR. SU YIN! A DESPERATE GAMBLE BY TONY STARK! PLUS MORE OF THE BLACK WIDOW AND THE MYSTERIOUS OKTOBER! DON'T DARE MISS DRAGON SEED... COMING YOUR WAY IN JUST 30 DAYS!

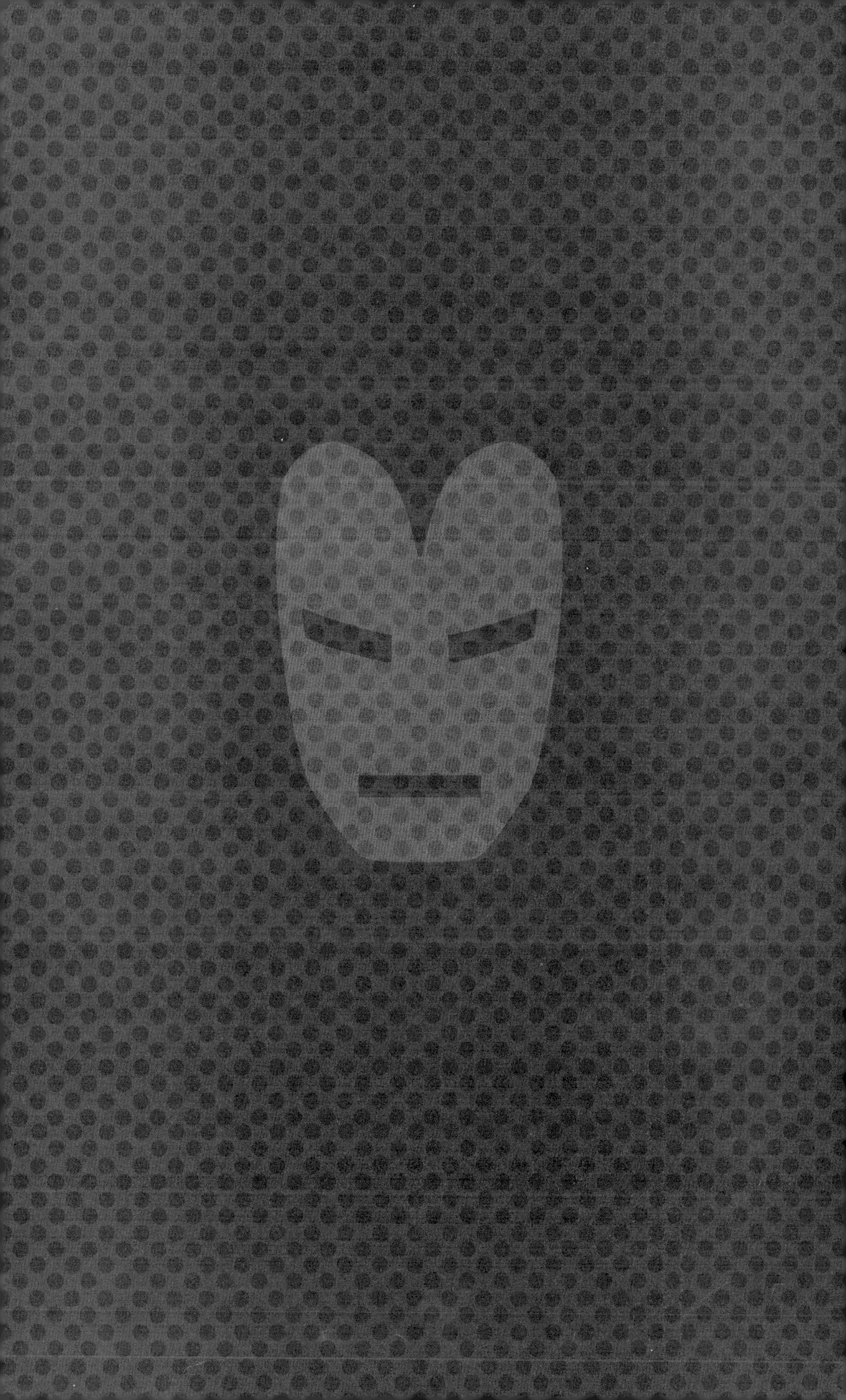

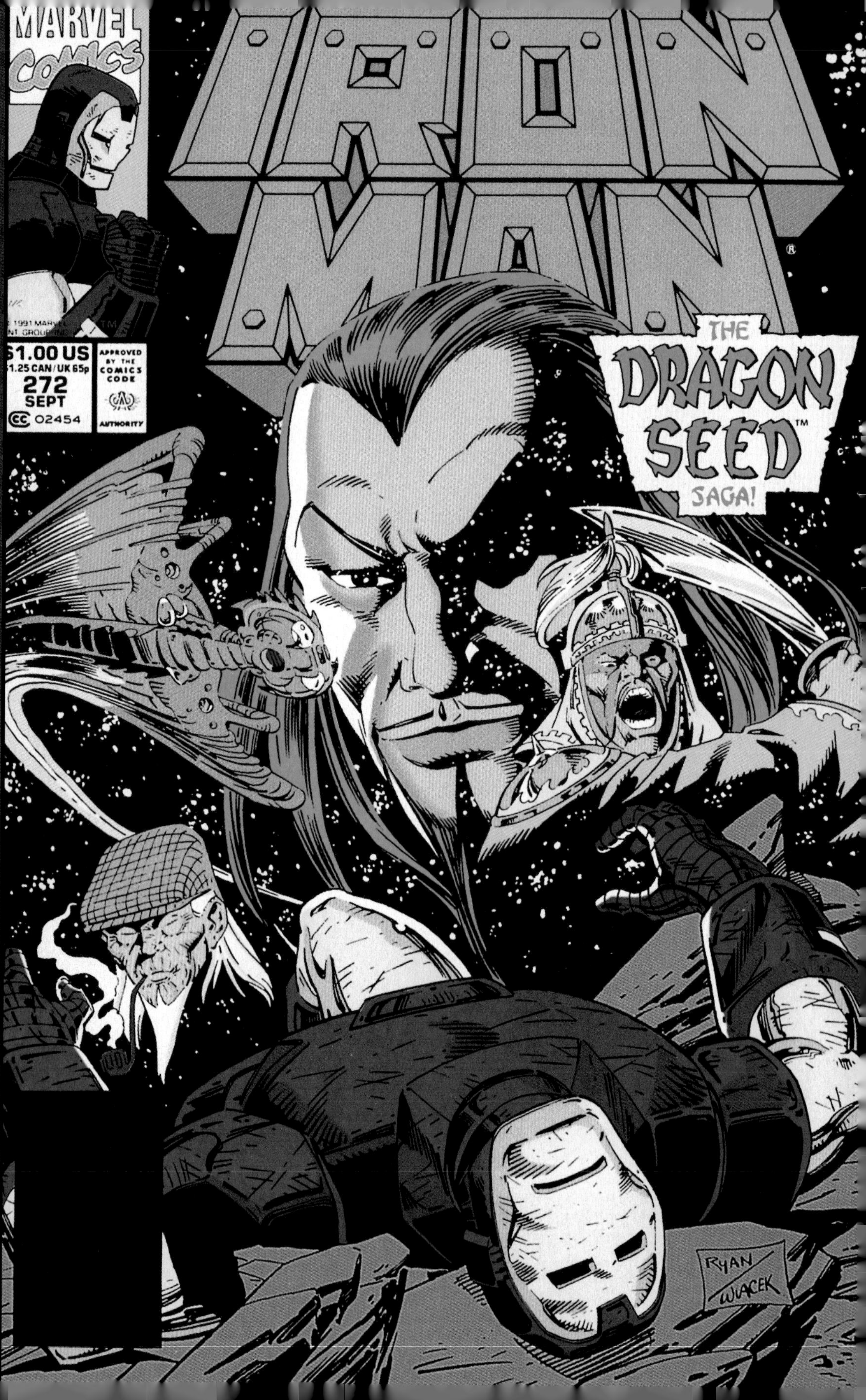
MARVEL COMICS
IRON MAN
$1.00 US
$1.25 CAN/UK 65p
272
SEPT
02454
APPROVED BY THE COMICS CODE AUTHORITY
THE DRAGON SEED™ SAGA!
RYAN WIACEK

WHEN MULTI-BILLIONAIRE INDUSTRIALIST TONY STARK, INVENTOR EXTRAORDINAIRE, DONS HIS SOLAR-CHARGED, STEEL-MESH ARMOR, HE BECOMES A HIGH-TECH WARRIOR—THE WORLD'S GREATEST HUMAN FIGHTING MACHINE! STAN LEE PRESENTS . . . THE INVINCIBLE IRON MAN!

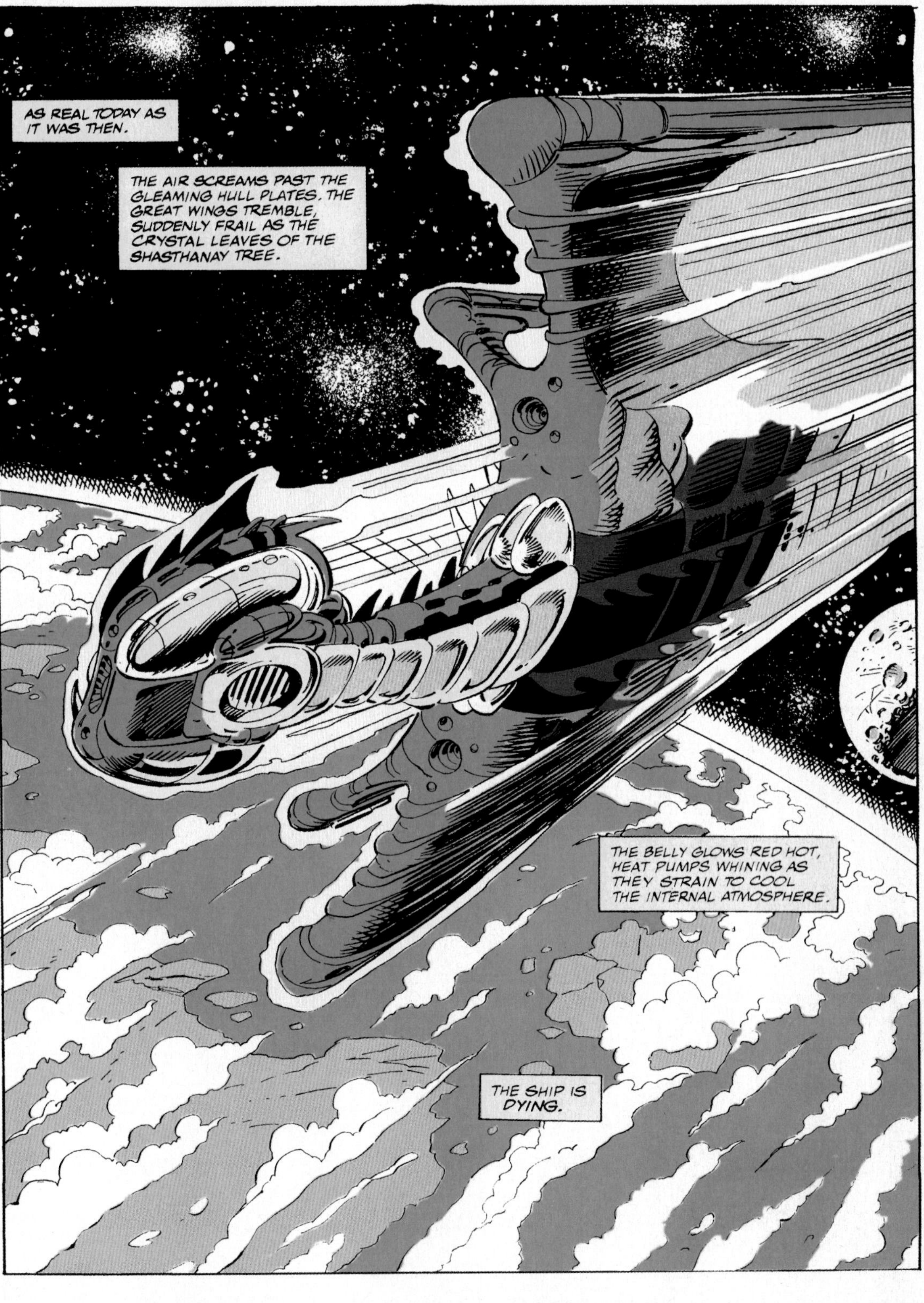
AS REAL TODAY AS IT WAS THEN.
THE AIR SCREAMS PAST THE GLEAMING HULL PLATES. THE GREAT WINGS TREMBLE, SUDDENLY FRAIL AS THE CRYSTAL LEAVES OF THE SHASTHANAY TREE.
THE BELLY GLOWS RED HOT, HEAT PUMPS WHINING AS THEY STRAIN TO COOL THE INTERNAL ATMOSPHERE.
THE SHIP IS DYING.

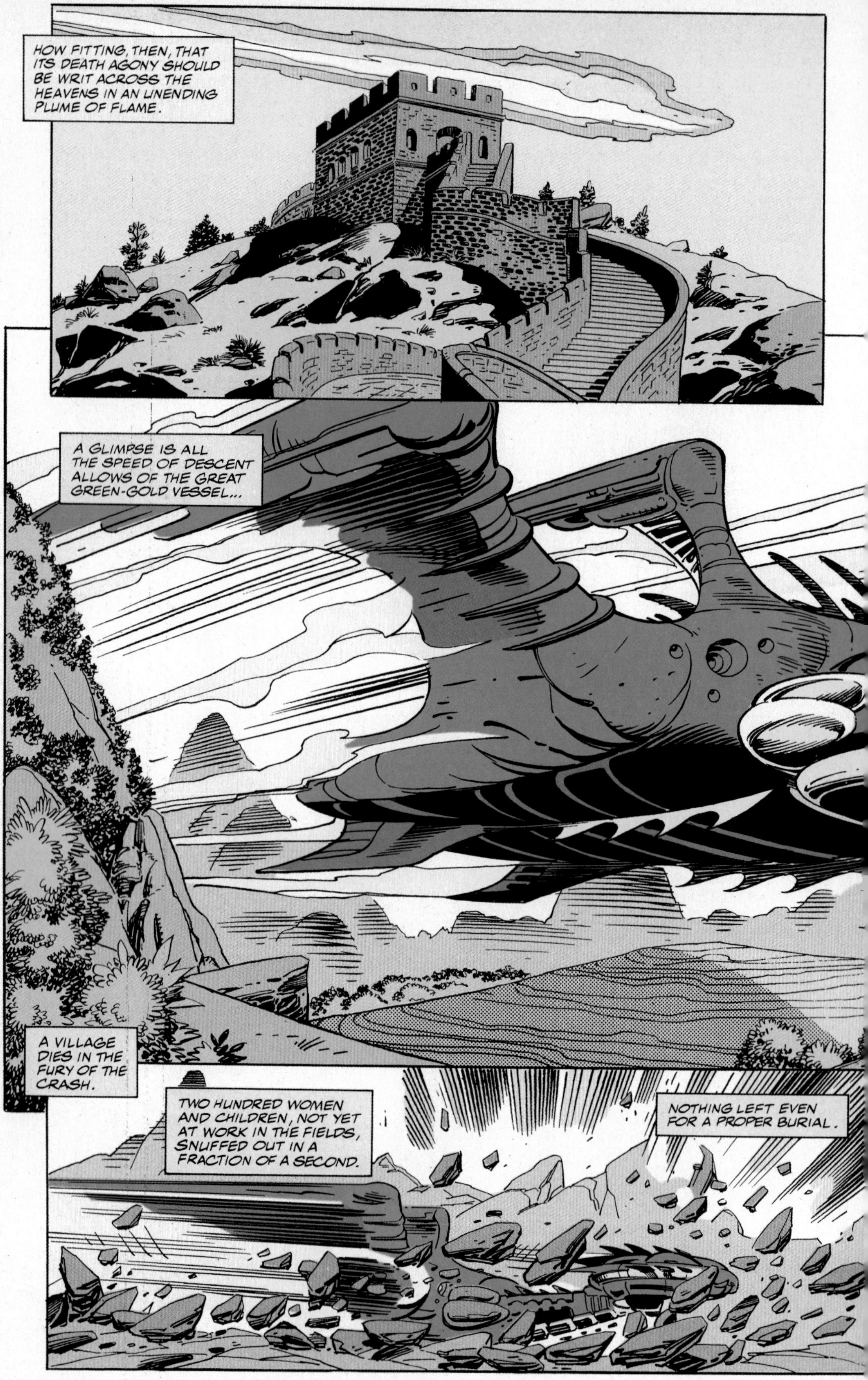
HOW FITTING, THEN, THAT ITS DEATH AGONY SHOULD BE WRIT ACROSS THE HEAVENS IN AN UNENDING PLUME OF FLAME.
A GLIMPSE IS ALL THE SPEED OF DESCENT ALLOWS OF THE GREAT GREEN-GOLD VESSEL...
A VILLAGE DIES IN THE FURY OF THE CRASH.
TWO HUNDRED WOMEN AND CHILDREN, NOT YET AT WORK IN THE FIELDS, SNUFFED OUT IN A FRACTION OF A SECOND.
NOTHING LEFT EVEN FOR A PROPER BURIAL.

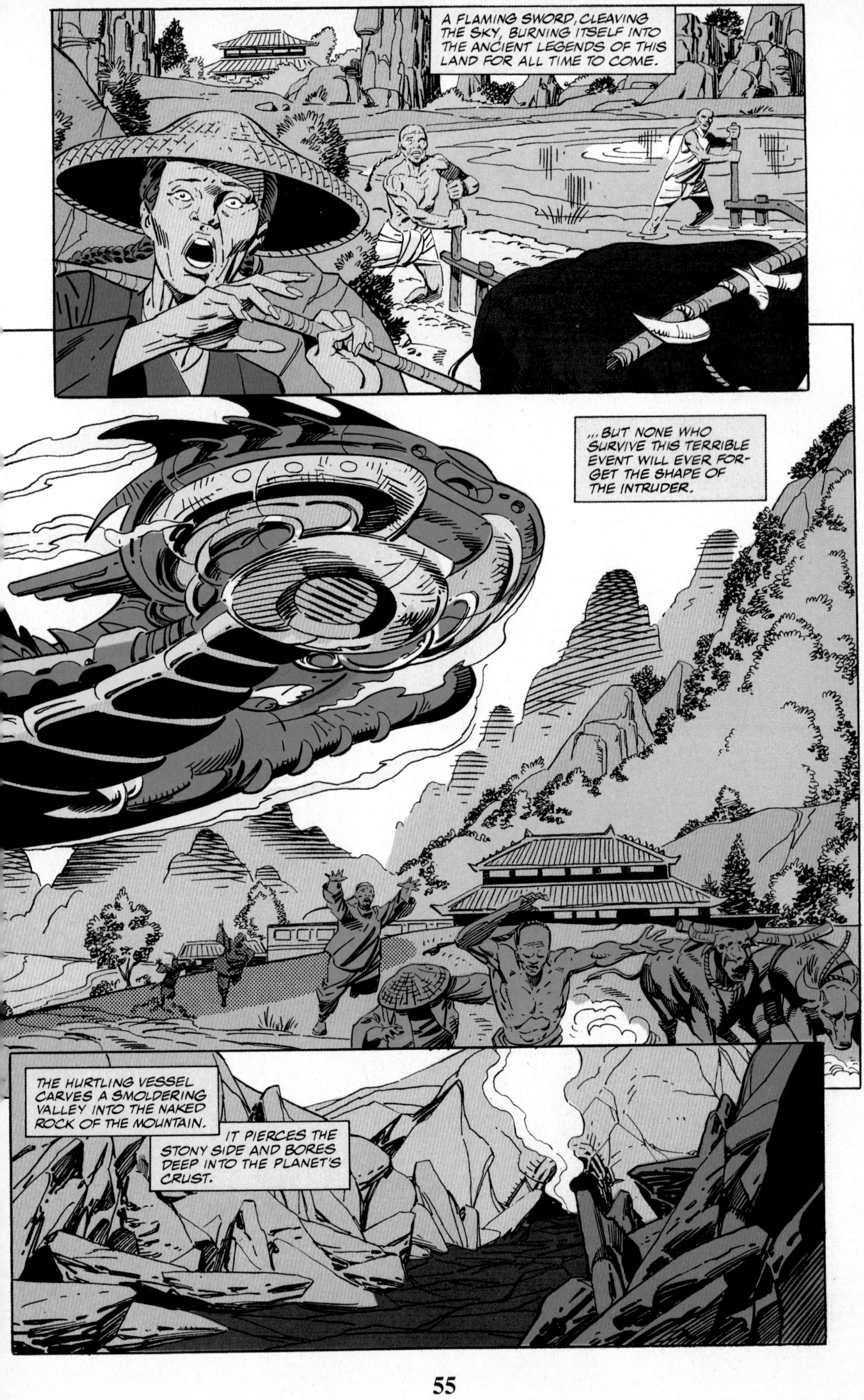
A FLAMING SWORD, CLEAVING THE SKY, BURNING ITSELF INTO THE ANCIENT LEGENDS OF THIS LAND FOR ALL TIME TO COME.
...BUT NONE WHO SURVIVE THIS TERRIBLE EVENT WILL EVER FOR-GET THE SHAPE OF THE INTRUDER.
THE HURTLING VESSEL CARVES A SMOLDERING VALLEY INTO THE NAKED ROCK OF THE MOUNTAIN.
IT PIERCES THE STONY SIDE AND BORES DEEP INTO THE PLANET'S CRUST.

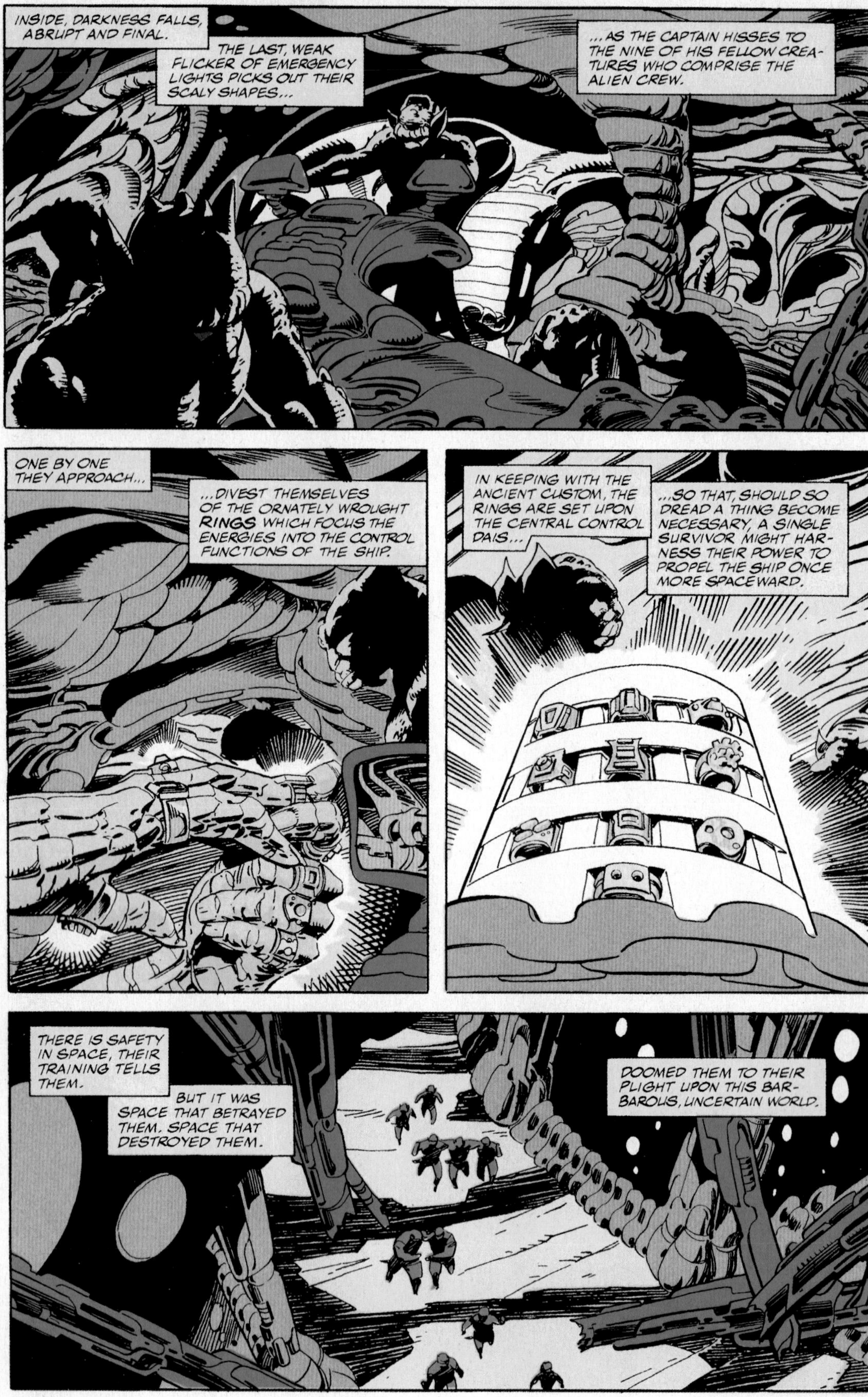
INSIDE, DARKNESS FALLS, ABRUPT AND FINAL.
THE LAST, WEAK FLICKER OF EMERGENCY LIGHTS PICKS OUT THEIR SCALY SHAPES...
...AS THE CAPTAIN HISSES TO THE NINE OF HIS FELLOW CREATURES WHO COMPRISE THE ALIEN CREW.
ONE BY ONE THEY APPROACH...
...DIVEST THEMSELVES OF THE ORNATELY WROUGHT RINGS WHICH FOCUS THE ENERGIES INTO THE CONTROL FUNCTIONS OF THE SHIP.
IN KEEPING WITH THE ANCIENT CUSTOM, THE RINGS ARE SET UPON THE CENTRAL CONTROL DAIS...
...SO THAT, SHOULD SO DREAD A THING BECOME NECESSARY, A SINGLE SURVIVOR MIGHT HARNESS THEIR POWER TO PROPEL THE SHIP ONCE MORE SPACEWARD.
THERE IS SAFETY IN SPACE, THEIR TRAINING TELLS THEM.
BUT IT WAS SPACE THAT BETRAYED THEM. SPACE THAT DESTROYED THEM.
DOOMED THEM TO THEIR PLIGHT UPON THIS BARBAROUS, UNCERTAIN WORLD.

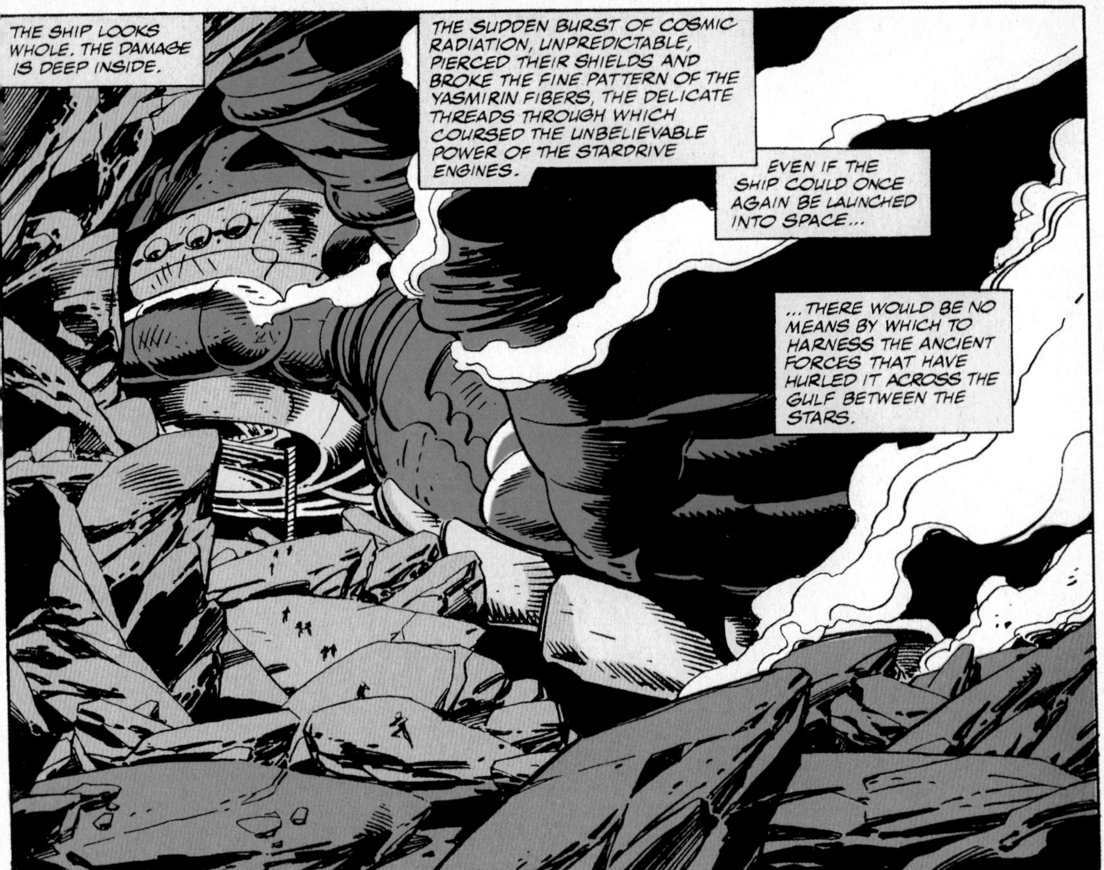
THE SHIP LOOKS WHOLE. THE DAMAGE IS DEEP INSIDE.
THE SUDDEN BURST OF COSMIC RADIATION, UNPREDICTABLE, PIERCED THEIR SHIELDS AND BROKE THE FINE PATTERN OF THE YASMIRIN FIBERS, THE DELICATE THREADS THROUGH WHICH COURSED THE UNBELIEVABLE POWER OF THE STARDRIVE ENGINES.
EVEN IF THE SHIP COULD ONCE AGAIN BE LAUNCHED INTO SPACE...
...THERE WOULD BE NO MEANS BY WHICH TO HARNESS THE ANCIENT FORCES THAT HAVE HURLED IT ACROSS THE GULF BETWEEN THE STARS.

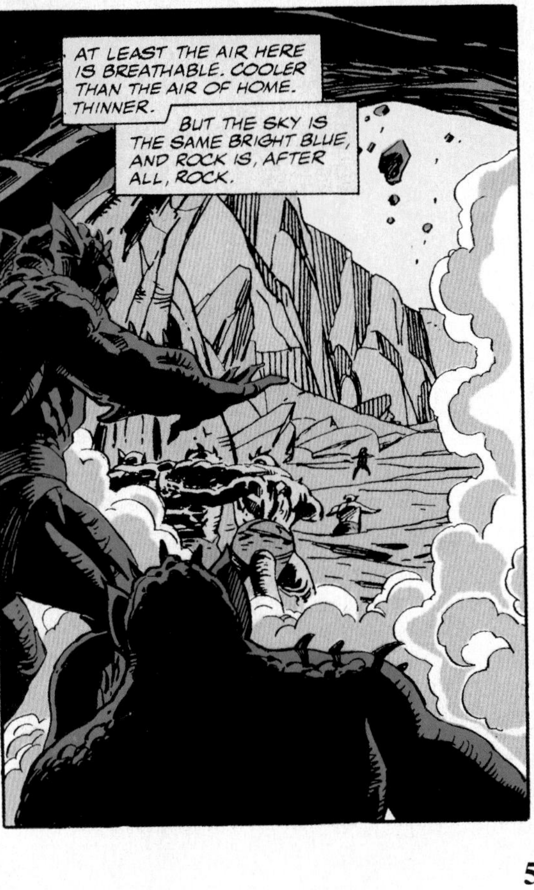
AT LEAST THE AIR HERE IS BREATHABLE. COOLER THAN THE AIR OF HOME. THINNER.
BUT THE SKY IS THE SAME BRIGHT BLUE, AND ROCK IS, AFTER ALL, ROCK.

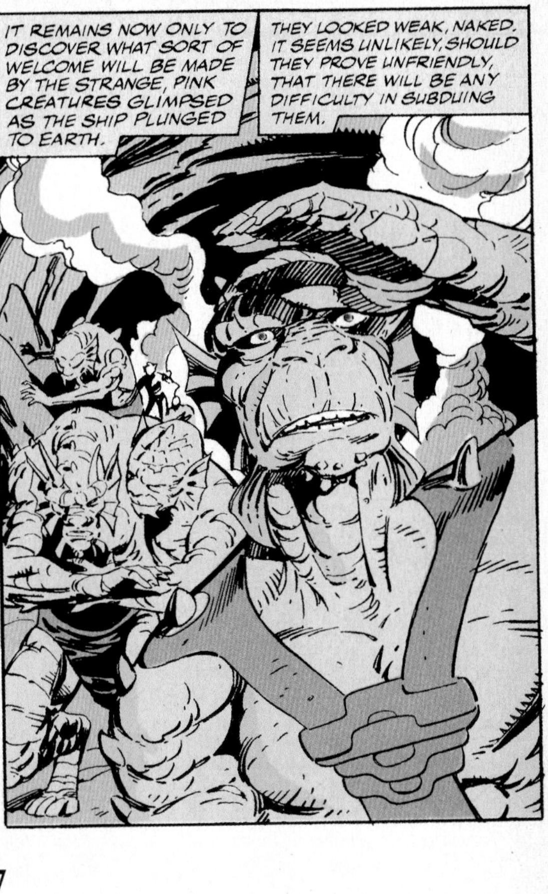
IT REMAINS NOW ONLY TO DISCOVER WHAT SORT OF WELCOME WILL BE MADE BY THE STRANGE, PINK CREATURES GLIMPSED AS THE SHIP PLUNGED TO EARTH.
THEY LOOKED WEAK, NAKED. IT SEEMS UNLIKELY, SHOULD THEY PROVE UNFRIENDLY, THAT THERE WILL BE ANY DIFFICULTY IN SUBDUING THEM.

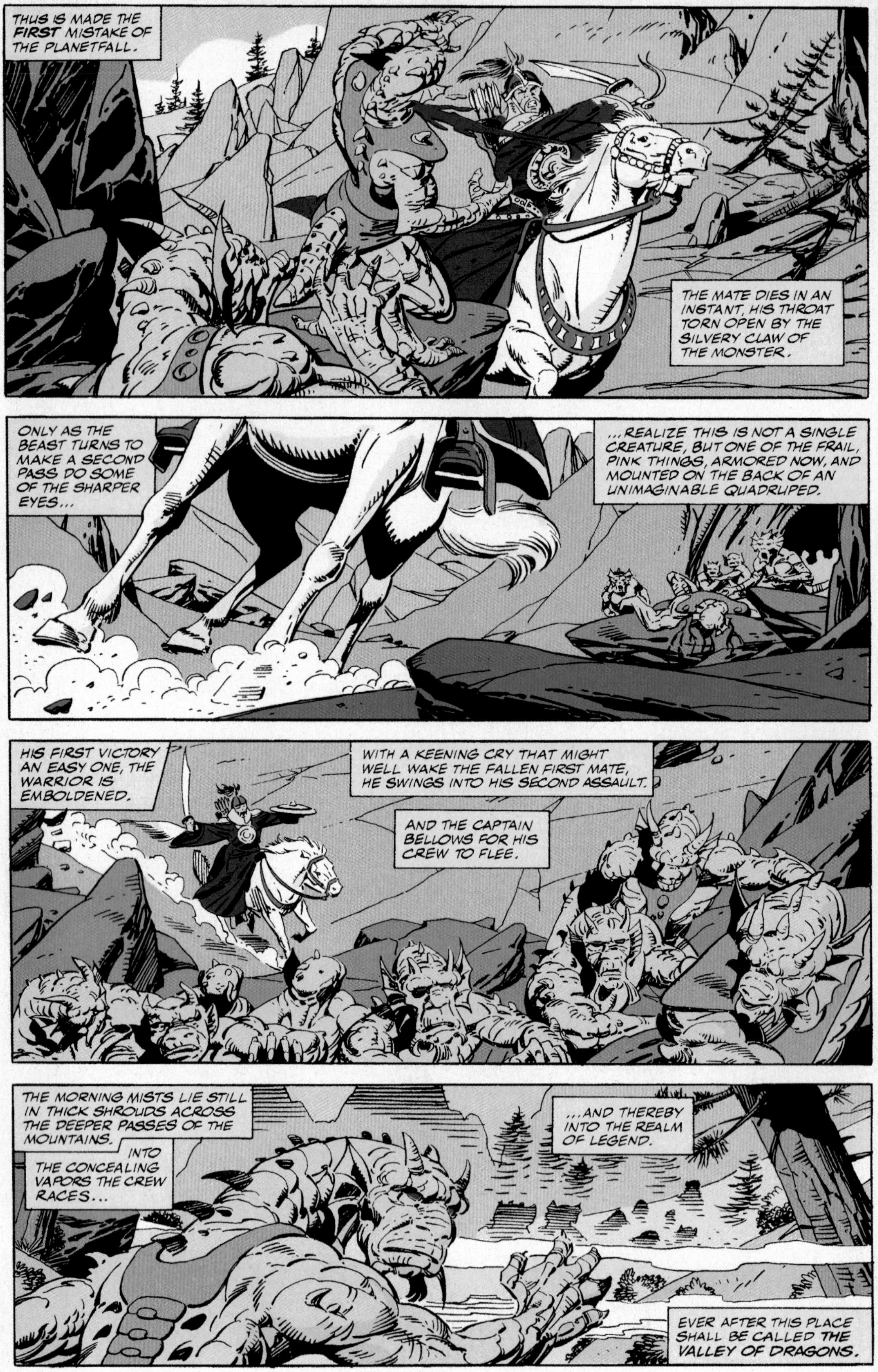
THUS IS MADE THE FIRST MISTAKE OF THE PLANETFALL.
THE MATE DIES IN AN INSTANT, HIS THROAT TORN OPEN BY THE SILVERY CLAW OF THE MONSTER.
ONLY AS THE BEAST TURNS TO MAKE A SECOND PASS DO SOME OF THE SHARPER EYES...
...REALIZE THIS IS NOT A SINGLE CREATURE, BUT ONE OF THE FRAIL, PINK THINGS, ARMORED NOW, AND MOUNTED ON THE BACK OF AN UNIMAGINABLE QUADRUPED.
HIS FIRST VICTORY AN EASY ONE, THE WARRIOR IS EMBOLDENED.
WITH A KEENING CRY THAT MIGHT WELL WAKE THE FALLEN FIRST MATE, HE SWINGS INTO HIS SECOND ASSAULT.
AND THE CAPTAIN BELLOWS FOR HIS CREW TO FLEE.
THE MORNING MISTS LIE STILL IN THICK SHROUDS ACROSS THE DEEPER PASSES OF THE MOUNTAINS.
INTO THE CONCEALING VAPORS THE CREW RACES...
...AND THEREBY INTO THE REALM OF LEGEND.
EVER AFTER THIS PLACE SHALL BE CALLED THE VALLEY OF DRAGONS.

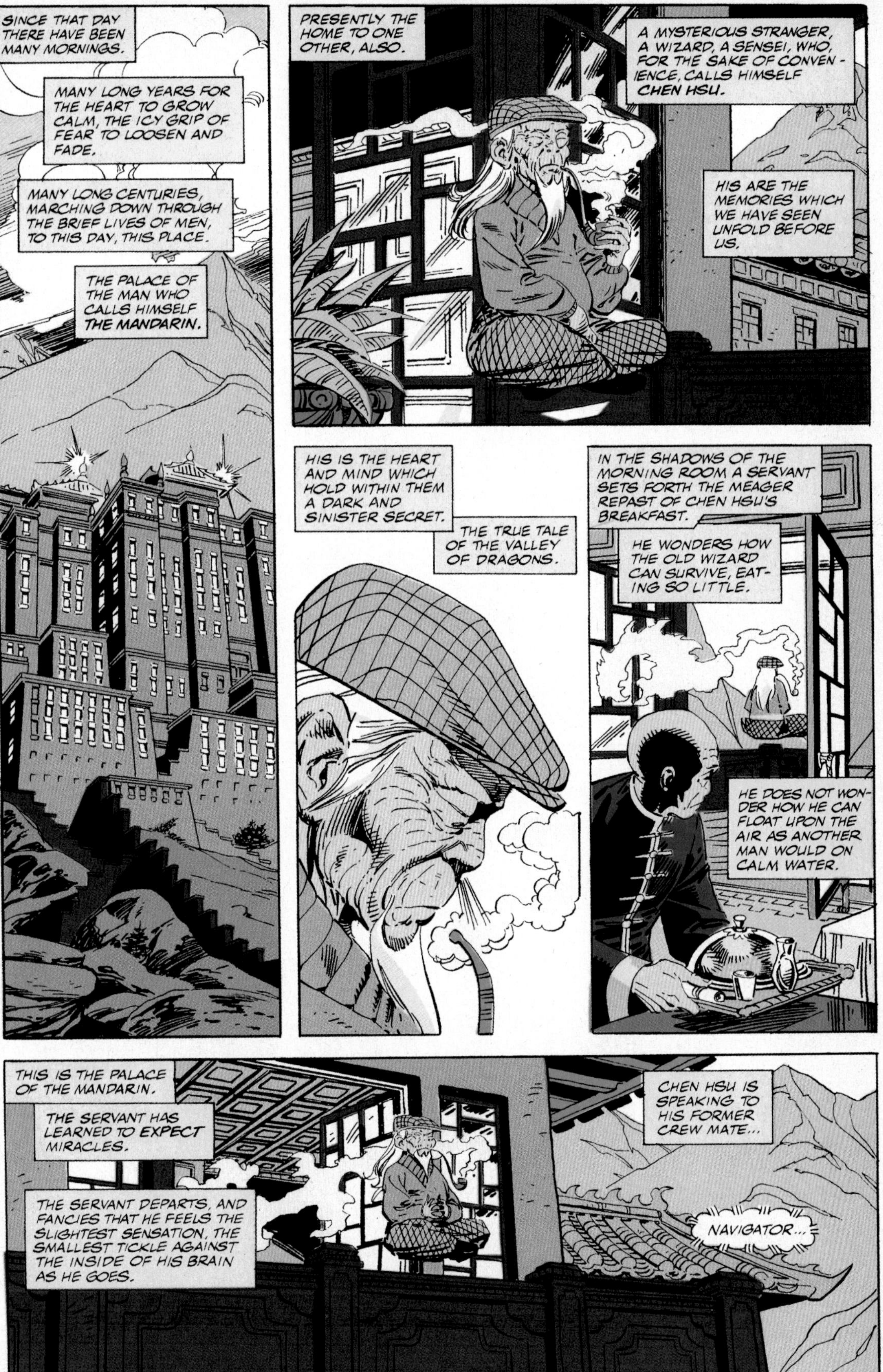
SINCE THAT DAY THERE HAVE BEEN MANY MORNINGS.
MANY LONG YEARS FOR THE HEART TO GROW CALM, THE ICY GRIP OF FEAR TO LOOSEN AND FADE.
MANY LONG CENTURIES, MARCHING DOWN THROUGH THE BRIEF LIVES OF MEN, TO THIS DAY, THIS PLACE.
THE PALACE OF THE MAN WHO CALLS HIMSELF THE MANDARIN.
PRESENTLY THE HOME TO ONE OTHER, ALSO.
A MYSTERIOUS STRANGER, A WIZARD, A SENSEI, WHO, FOR THE SAKE OF CONVENIENCE, CALLS HIMSELF CHEN HSU.
HIS ARE THE MEMORIES WHICH WE HAVE SEEN UNFOLD BEFORE US.
HIS IS THE HEART AND MIND WHICH HOLD WITHIN THEM A DARK AND SINISTER SECRET.
THE TRUE TALE OF THE VALLEY OF DRAGONS.
IN THE SHADOWS OF THE MORNING ROOM A SERVANT SETS FORTH THE MEAGER REPAST OF CHEN HSU'S BREAKFAST.
HE WONDERS HOW THE OLD WIZARD CAN SURVIVE, EATING SO LITTLE.
HE DOES NOT WONDER HOW HE CAN FLOAT UPON THE AIR AS ANOTHER MAN WOULD ON CALM WATER.
THIS IS THE PALACE OF THE MANDARIN.
THE SERVANT HAS LEARNED TO EXPECT MIRACLES.
THE SERVANT DEPARTS, AND FANCIES THAT HE FEELS THE SLIGHTEST SENSATION, THE SMALLEST TICKLE AGAINST THE INSIDE OF HIS BRAIN AS HE GOES.
CHEN HSU IS SPEAKING TO HIS FORMER CREW MATE...
NAVIGATOR...

THE GIANT TURNS, A TINY PART OF HIM REACTING WITH PLEASURE AT THE SOUND OF HIS ANCIENT, ALMOST FORGOTTEN TITLE.

MY CAPTAIN...?

DRAGON SEED

PAUL RYAN	BOB WIACEK	JOHN BYRNE	MICHAEL HEISLER
PENCILER	INKER	WRITER	LETTERER

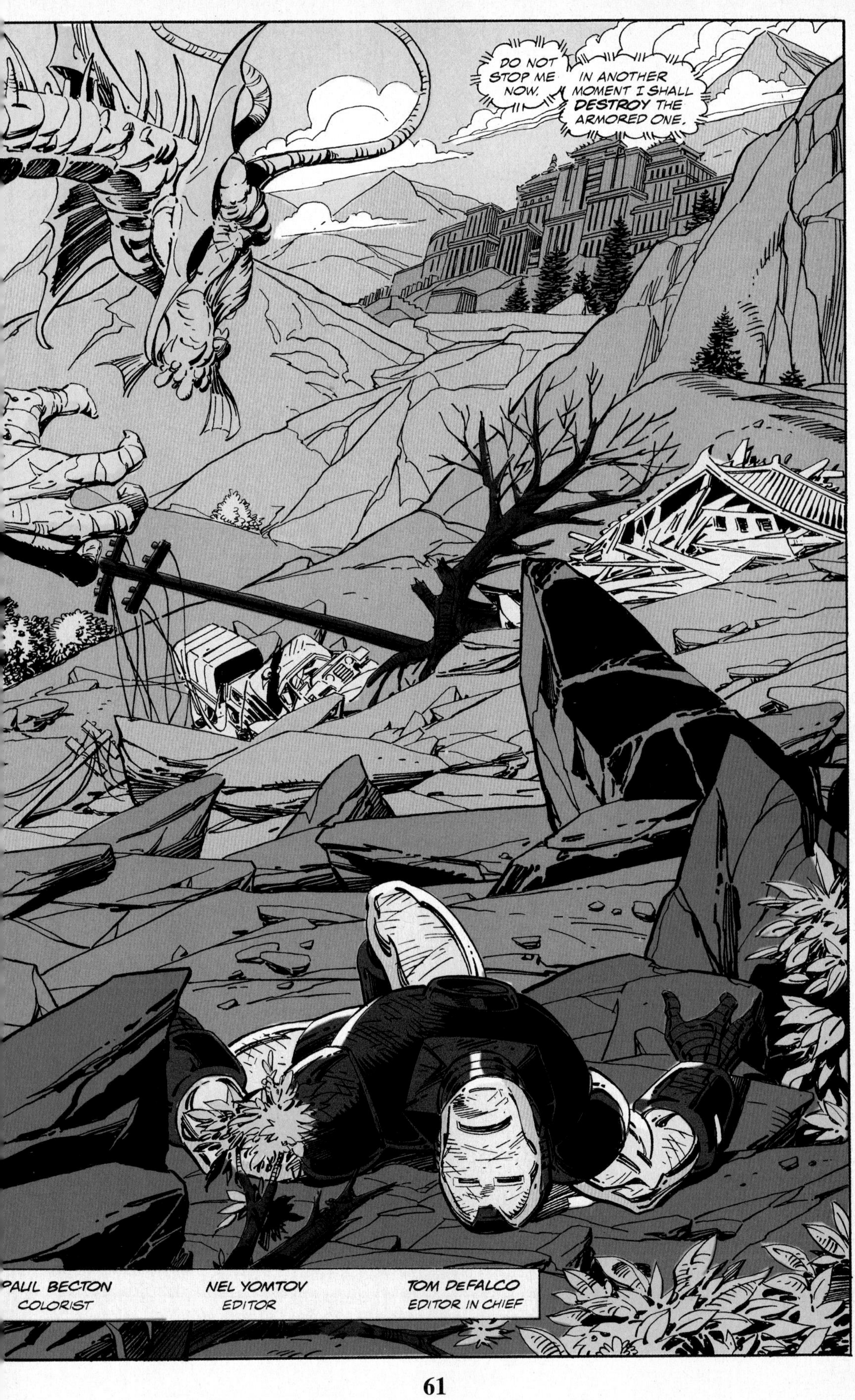
DO NOT STOP ME NOW.
IN ANOTHER MOMENT I SHALL DESTROY THE ARMORED ONE.
PAUL BECTON COLORIST
NEL YOMTOV EDITOR
TOM DEFALCO EDITOR IN CHIEF

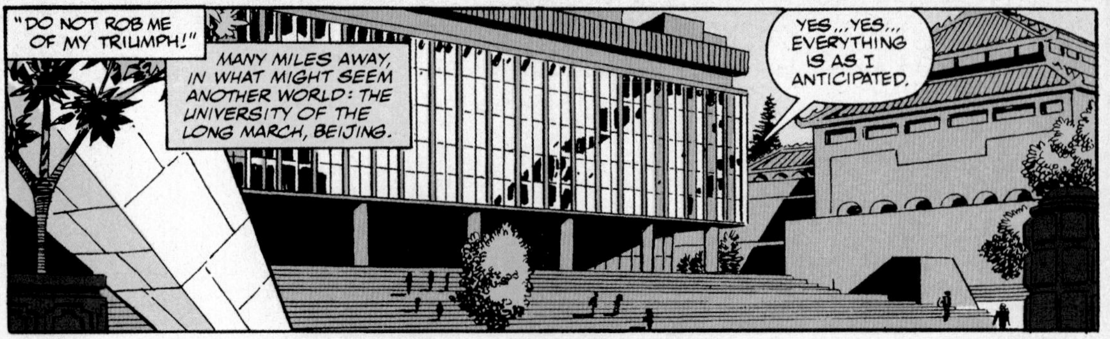
"DO NOT ROB ME OF MY TRIUMPH!"
MANY MILES AWAY, IN WHAT MIGHT SEEM ANOTHER WORLD: THE UNIVERSITY OF THE LONG MARCH, BEIJING.
YES,...YES... EVERYTHING IS AS I ANTICIPATED.

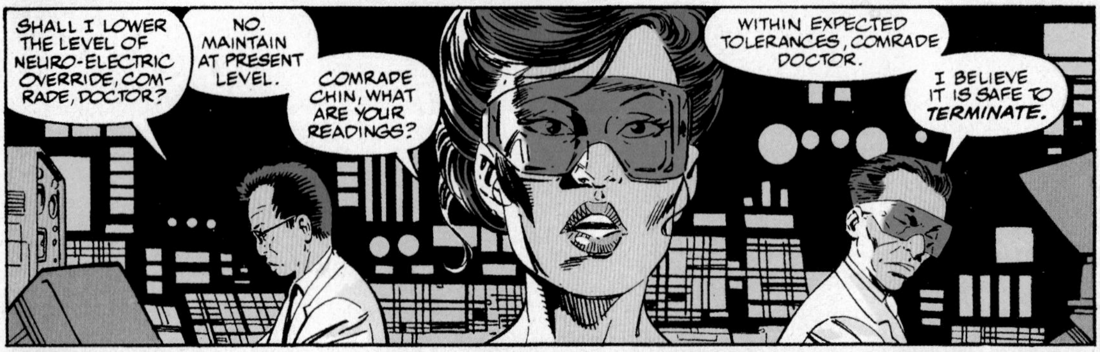
SHALL I LOWER THE LEVEL OF NEURO-ELECTRIC OVERRIDE, COMRADE, DOCTOR?
NO. MAINTAIN AT PRESENT LEVEL.
COMRADE CHIN, WHAT ARE YOUR READINGS?
WITHIN EXPECTED TOLERANCES, COMRADE DOCTOR.
I BELIEVE IT IS SAFE TO TERMINATE.

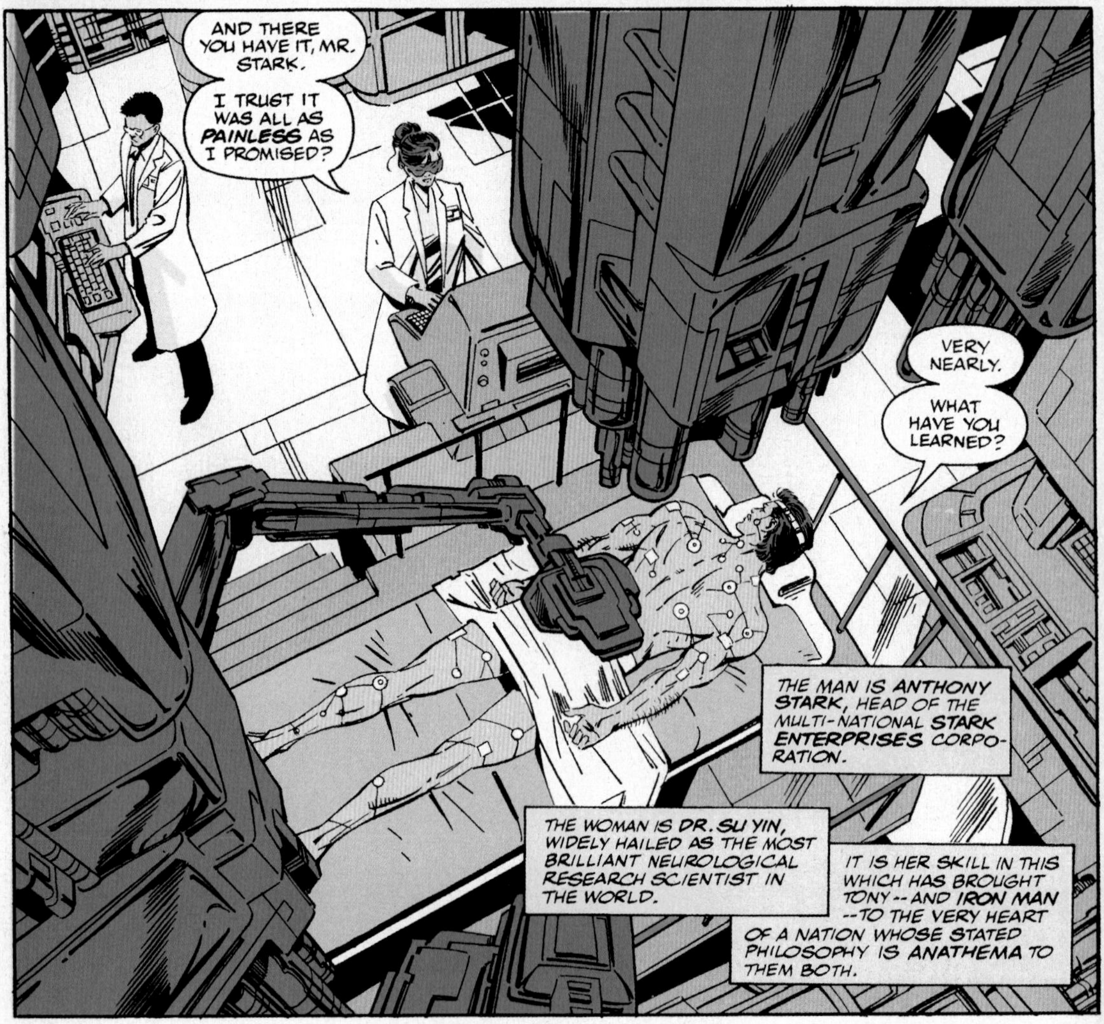
AND THERE YOU HAVE IT, MR. STARK.
I TRUST IT WAS ALL AS PAINLESS AS I PROMISED?
VERY NEARLY.
WHAT HAVE YOU LEARNED?
THE MAN IS ANTHONY STARK, HEAD OF THE MULTI-NATIONAL STARK ENTERPRISES CORPORATION.
THE WOMAN IS DR. SU YIN, WIDELY HAILED AS THE MOST BRILLIANT NEUROLOGICAL RESEARCH SCIENTIST IN THE WORLD.
IT IS HER SKILL IN THIS WHICH HAS BROUGHT TONY--AND IRON MAN--TO THE VERY HEART OF A NATION WHOSE STATED PHILOSOPHY IS ANATHEMA TO THEM BOTH.

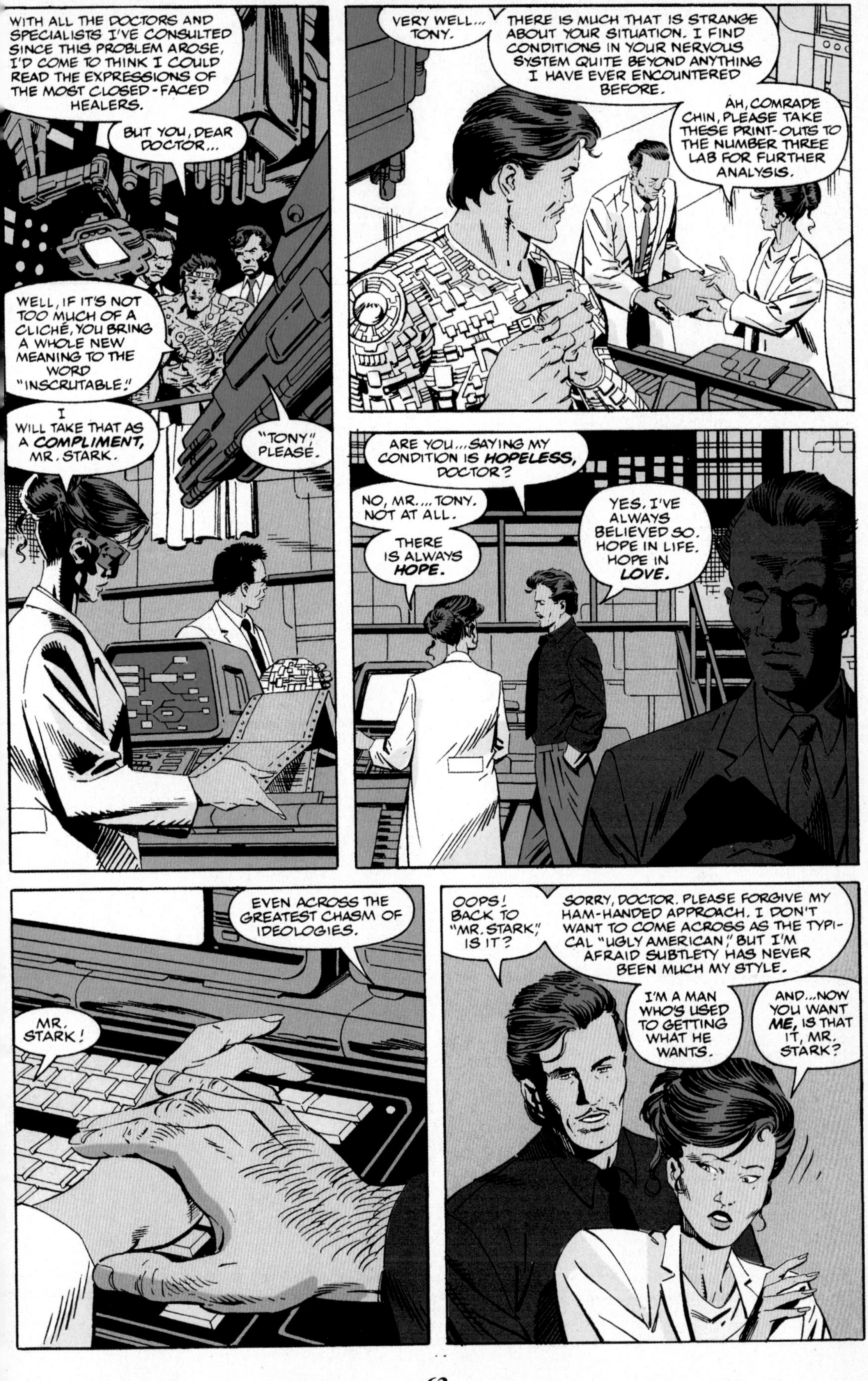
WITH ALL THE DOCTORS AND SPECIALISTS I'VE CONSULTED SINCE THIS PROBLEM AROSE, I'D COME TO THINK I COULD READ THE EXPRESSIONS OF THE MOST CLOSED-FACED HEALERS.
BUT YOU, DEAR DOCTOR...
WELL, IF IT'S NOT TOO MUCH OF A CLICHÉ, YOU BRING A WHOLE NEW MEANING TO THE WORD "INSCRUTABLE."
I WILL TAKE THAT AS A COMPLIMENT, MR. STARK.
"TONY," PLEASE.
VERY WELL... TONY.
THERE IS MUCH THAT IS STRANGE ABOUT YOUR SITUATION. I FIND CONDITIONS IN YOUR NERVOUS SYSTEM QUITE BEYOND ANYTHING I HAVE EVER ENCOUNTERED BEFORE.
AH, COMRADE CHIN, PLEASE TAKE THESE PRINT-OUTS TO THE NUMBER THREE LAB FOR FURTHER ANALYSIS.
ARE YOU...SAYING MY CONDITION IS HOPELESS, DOCTOR?
NO, MR.... TONY. NOT AT ALL.
THERE IS ALWAYS HOPE.
YES. I'VE ALWAYS BELIEVED SO. HOPE IN LIFE. HOPE IN LOVE.
EVEN ACROSS THE GREATEST CHASM OF IDEOLOGIES.
MR. STARK!
OOPS! BACK TO "MR. STARK," IS IT?
SORRY, DOCTOR. PLEASE FORGIVE MY HAM-HANDED APPROACH. I DON'T WANT TO COME ACROSS AS THE TYPICAL "UGLY AMERICAN," BUT I'M AFRAID SUBTLETY HAS NEVER BEEN MUCH MY STYLE.
I'M A MAN WHO'S USED TO GETTING WHAT HE WANTS.
AND...NOW YOU WANT ME, IS THAT IT, MR. STARK?

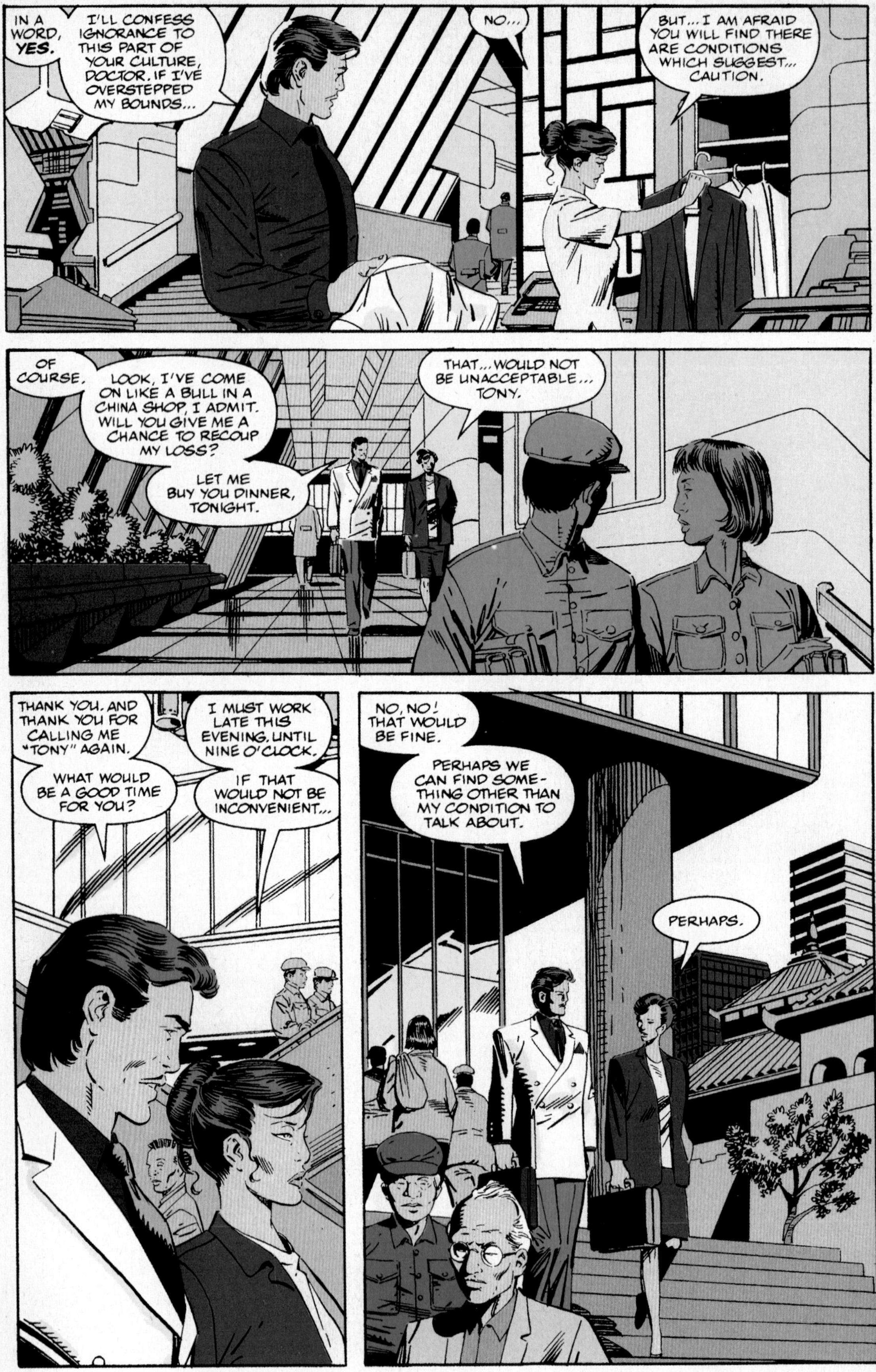
IN A WORD, YES.
I'LL CONFESS IGNORANCE TO THIS PART OF YOUR CULTURE, DOCTOR. IF I'VE OVERSTEPPED MY BOUNDS...
NO...
BUT... I AM AFRAID YOU WILL FIND THERE ARE CONDITIONS WHICH SUGGEST... CAUTION.
OF COURSE.
LOOK, I'VE COME ON LIKE A BULL IN A CHINA SHOP, I ADMIT. WILL YOU GIVE ME A CHANCE TO RECOUP MY LOSS?
LET ME BUY YOU DINNER, TONIGHT.
THAT... WOULD NOT BE UNACCEPTABLE... TONY.
THANK YOU. AND THANK YOU FOR CALLING ME "TONY" AGAIN.
WHAT WOULD BE A GOOD TIME FOR YOU?
I MUST WORK LATE THIS EVENING. UNTIL NINE O'CLOCK.
IF THAT WOULD NOT BE INCONVENIENT...
NO, NO! THAT WOULD BE FINE.
PERHAPS WE CAN FIND SOMETHING OTHER THAN MY CONDITION TO TALK ABOUT.
PERHAPS.

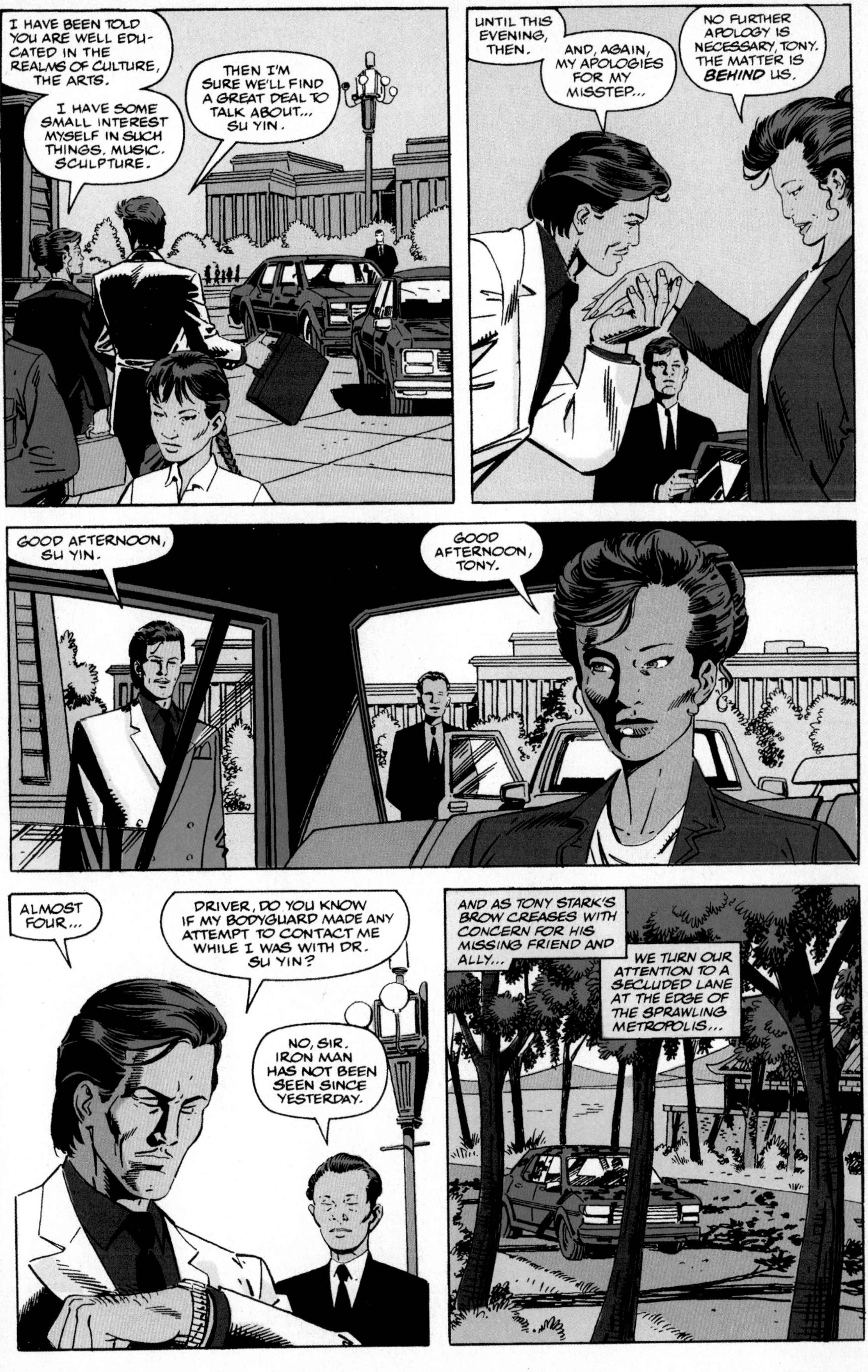
I HAVE BEEN TOLD YOU ARE WELL EDUCATED IN THE REALMS OF CULTURE, THE ARTS.
I HAVE SOME SMALL INTEREST MYSELF IN SUCH THINGS. MUSIC. SCULPTURE.
THEN I'M SURE WE'LL FIND A GREAT DEAL TO TALK ABOUT... SU YIN.
UNTIL THIS EVENING, THEN.
AND, AGAIN, MY APOLOGIES FOR MY MISSTEP...
NO FURTHER APOLOGY IS NECESSARY, TONY. THE MATTER IS BEHIND US.
GOOD AFTERNOON, SU YIN.
GOOD AFTERNOON, TONY.
ALMOST FOUR...
DRIVER, DO YOU KNOW IF MY BODYGUARD MADE ANY ATTEMPT TO CONTACT ME WHILE I WAS WITH DR. SU YIN?
NO, SIR. IRON MAN HAS NOT BEEN SEEN SINCE YESTERDAY.
AND AS TONY STARK'S BROW CREASES WITH CONCERN FOR HIS MISSING FRIEND AND ALLY...
WE TURN OUR ATTENTION TO A SECLUDED LANE AT THE EDGE OF THE SPRAWLING METROPOLIS...

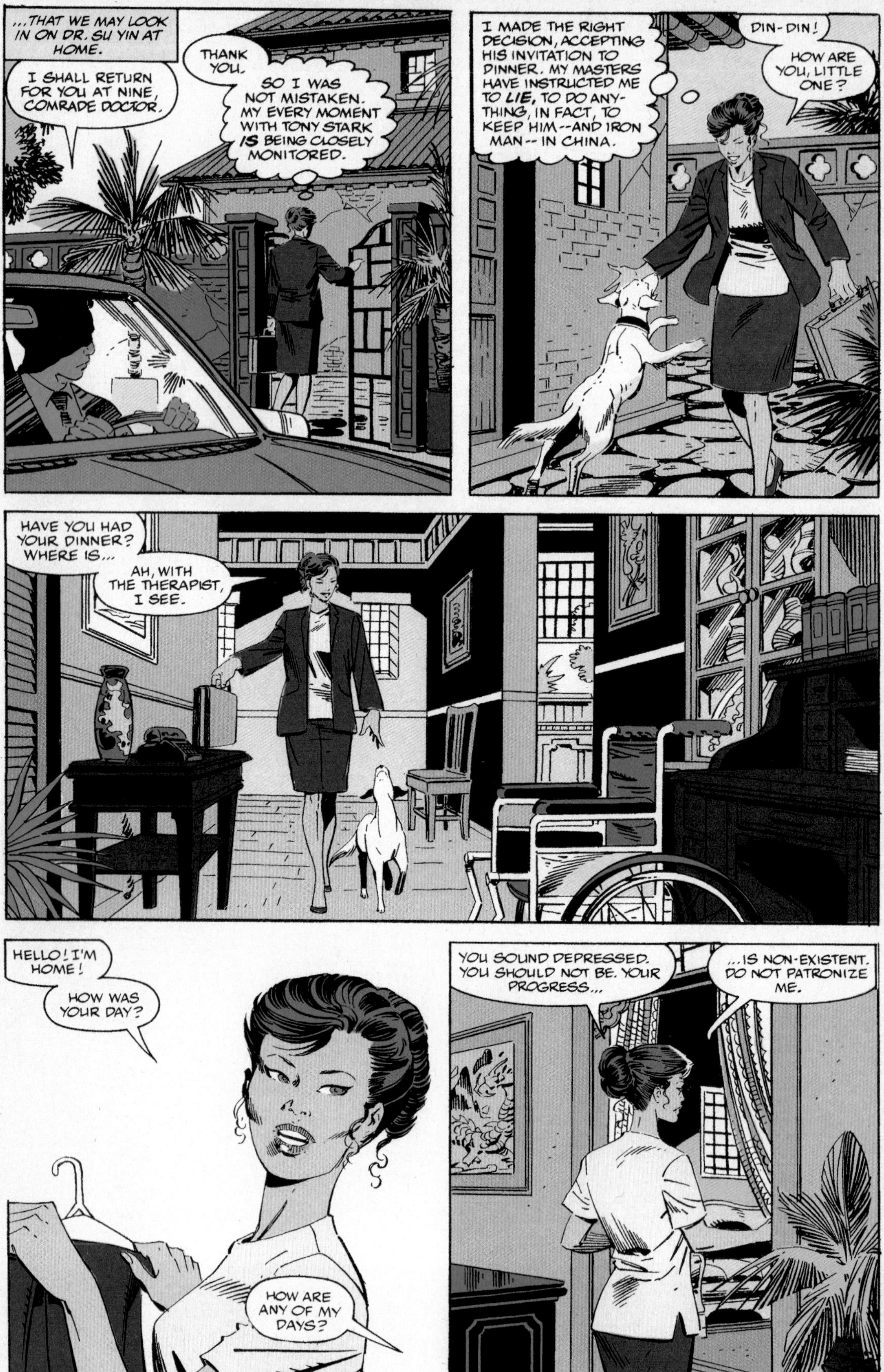
...THAT WE MAY LOOK IN ON DR. SU YIN AT HOME.
I SHALL RETURN FOR YOU AT NINE, COMRADE DOCTOR.
THANK YOU.
SO I WAS NOT MISTAKEN. MY EVERY MOMENT WITH TONY STARK IS BEING CLOSELY MONITORED.
I MADE THE RIGHT DECISION, ACCEPTING HIS INVITATION TO DINNER. MY MASTERS HAVE INSTRUCTED ME TO LIE, TO DO ANYTHING, IN FACT, TO KEEP HIM--AND IRON MAN--IN CHINA.
DIN-DIN!
HOW ARE YOU, LITTLE ONE?
HAVE YOU HAD YOUR DINNER? WHERE IS...
AH, WITH THE THERAPIST, I SEE.
HELLO! I'M HOME!
HOW WAS YOUR DAY?
HOW ARE ANY OF MY DAYS?
YOU SOUND DEPRESSED. YOU SHOULD NOT BE. YOUR PROGRESS...
...IS NON-EXISTENT. DO NOT PATRONIZE ME.

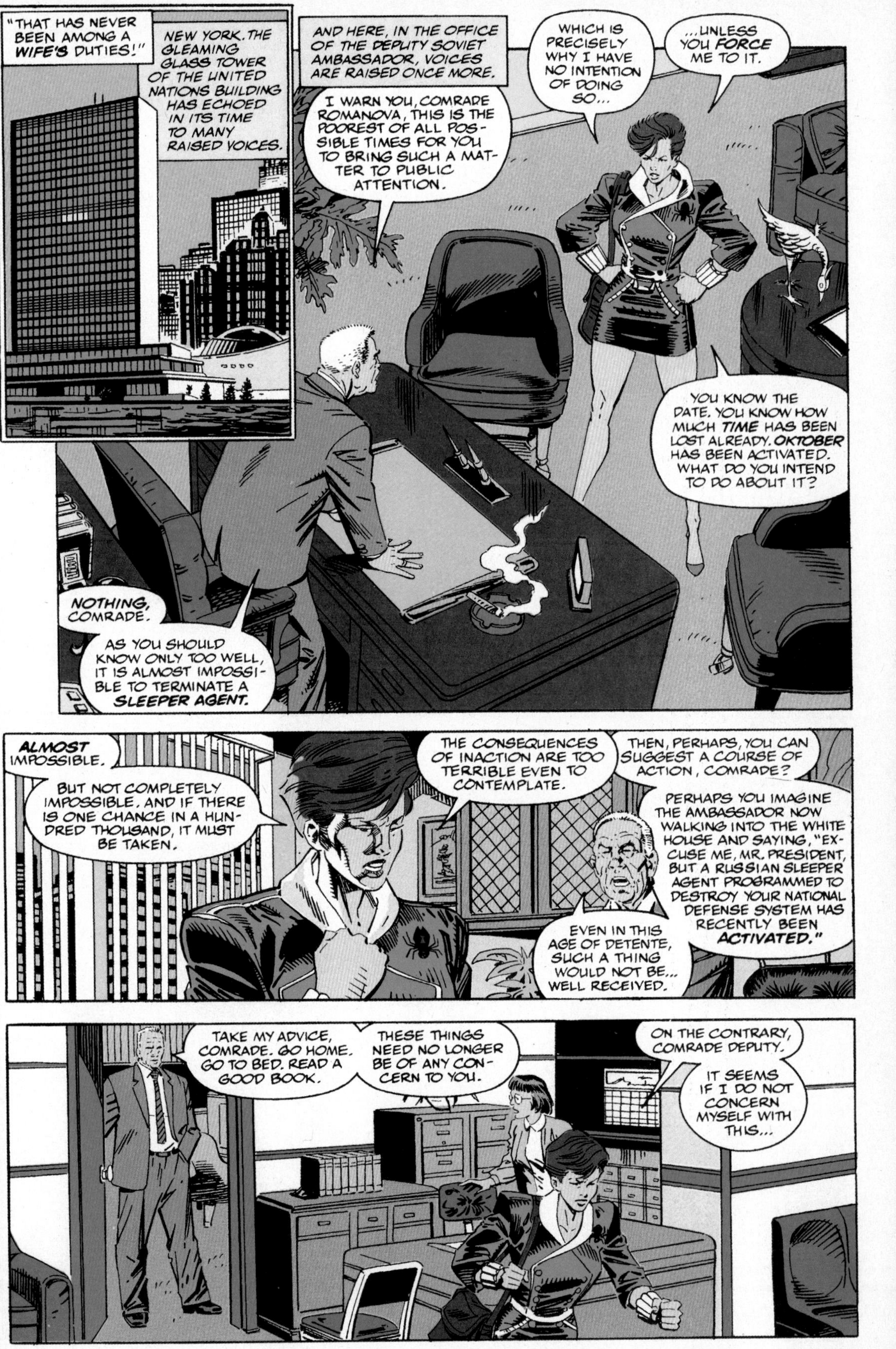
"THAT HAS NEVER BEEN AMONG A WIFE'S DUTIES!"
NEW YORK. THE GLEAMING GLASS TOWER OF THE UNITED NATIONS BUILDING HAS ECHOED IN ITS TIME TO MANY RAISED VOICES.
AND HERE, IN THE OFFICE OF THE DEPUTY SOVIET AMBASSADOR, VOICES ARE RAISED ONCE MORE.
I WARN YOU, COMRADE ROMANOVA, THIS IS THE POOREST OF ALL POSSIBLE TIMES FOR YOU TO BRING SUCH A MATTER TO PUBLIC ATTENTION.
WHICH IS PRECISELY WHY I HAVE NO INTENTION OF DOING SO...
...UNLESS YOU FORCE ME TO IT.
YOU KNOW THE DATE. YOU KNOW HOW MUCH TIME HAS BEEN LOST ALREADY. OKTOBER HAS BEEN ACTIVATED. WHAT DO YOU INTEND TO DO ABOUT IT?
NOTHING, COMRADE.
AS YOU SHOULD KNOW ONLY TOO WELL, IT IS ALMOST IMPOSSIBLE TO TERMINATE A SLEEPER AGENT.
ALMOST IMPOSSIBLE.
BUT NOT COMPLETELY IMPOSSIBLE. AND IF THERE IS ONE CHANCE IN A HUNDRED THOUSAND, IT MUST BE TAKEN.
THE CONSEQUENCES OF INACTION ARE TOO TERRIBLE EVEN TO CONTEMPLATE.
THEN, PERHAPS, YOU CAN SUGGEST A COURSE OF ACTION, COMRADE?
PERHAPS YOU IMAGINE THE AMBASSADOR NOW WALKING INTO THE WHITE HOUSE AND SAYING, "EXCUSE ME, MR. PRESIDENT, BUT A RUSSIAN SLEEPER AGENT PROGRAMMED TO DESTROY YOUR NATIONAL DEFENSE SYSTEM HAS RECENTLY BEEN ACTIVATED."
EVEN IN THIS AGE OF DETENTE, SUCH A THING WOULD NOT BE... WELL RECEIVED.
TAKE MY ADVICE, COMRADE. GO HOME. GO TO BED. READ A GOOD BOOK.
THESE THINGS NEED NO LONGER BE OF ANY CONCERN TO YOU.
ON THE CONTRARY, COMRADE DEPUTY.
IT SEEMS IF I DO NOT CONCERN MYSELF WITH THIS...

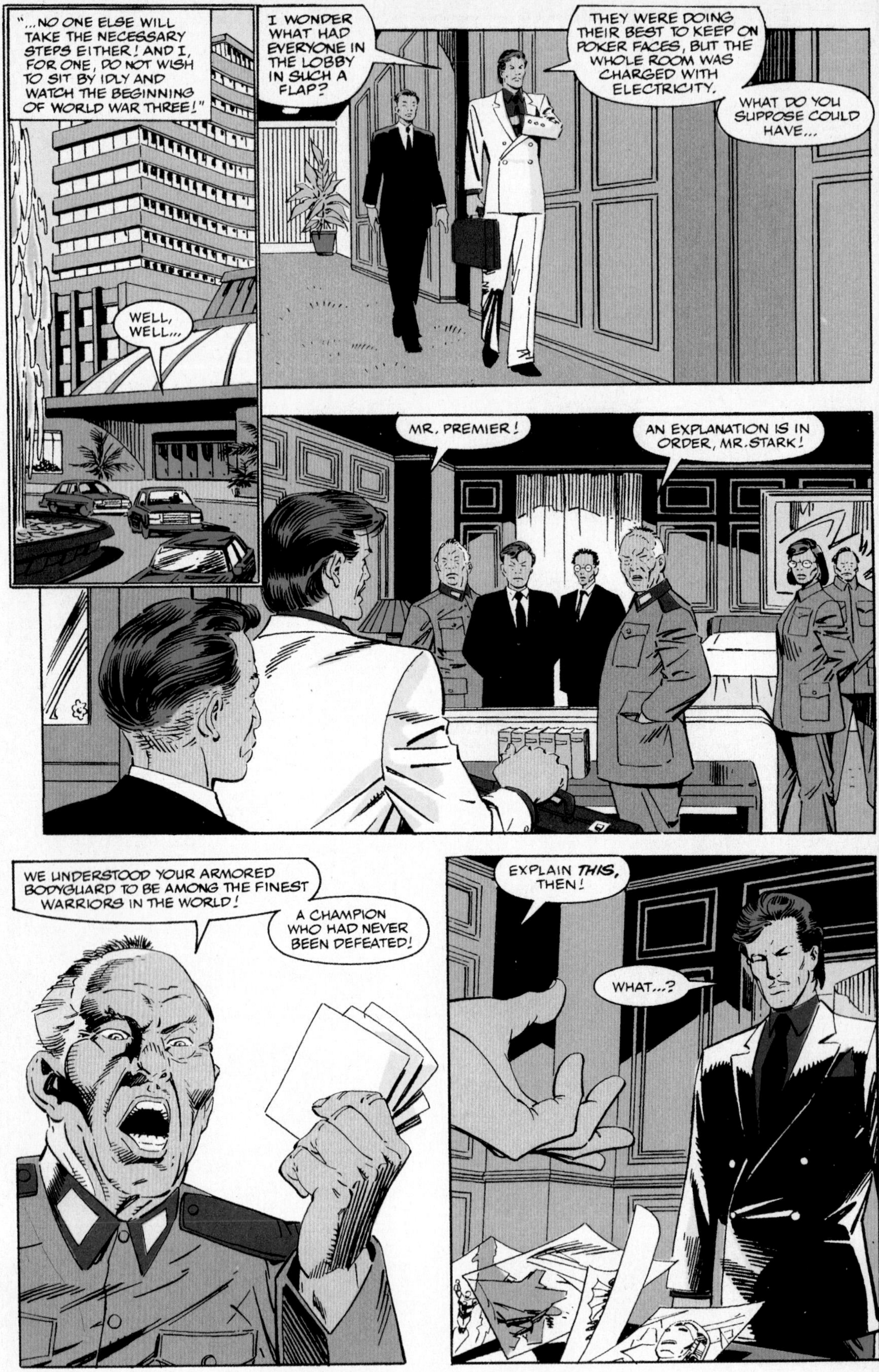
"...NO ONE ELSE WILL TAKE THE NECESSARY STEPS EITHER! AND I, FOR ONE, DO NOT WISH TO SIT BY IDLY AND WATCH THE BEGINNING OF WORLD WAR THREE!"
WELL, WELL...
I WONDER WHAT HAD EVERYONE IN THE LOBBY IN SUCH A FLAP?
THEY WERE DOING THEIR BEST TO KEEP ON POKER FACES, BUT THE WHOLE ROOM WAS CHARGED WITH ELECTRICITY.
WHAT DO YOU SUPPOSE COULD HAVE...
MR. PREMIER!
AN EXPLANATION IS IN ORDER, MR. STARK!
WE UNDERSTOOD YOUR ARMORED BODYGUARD TO BE AMONG THE FINEST WARRIORS IN THE WORLD!
A CHAMPION WHO HAD NEVER BEEN DEFEATED!
EXPLAIN *THIS*, THEN!
WHAT...?

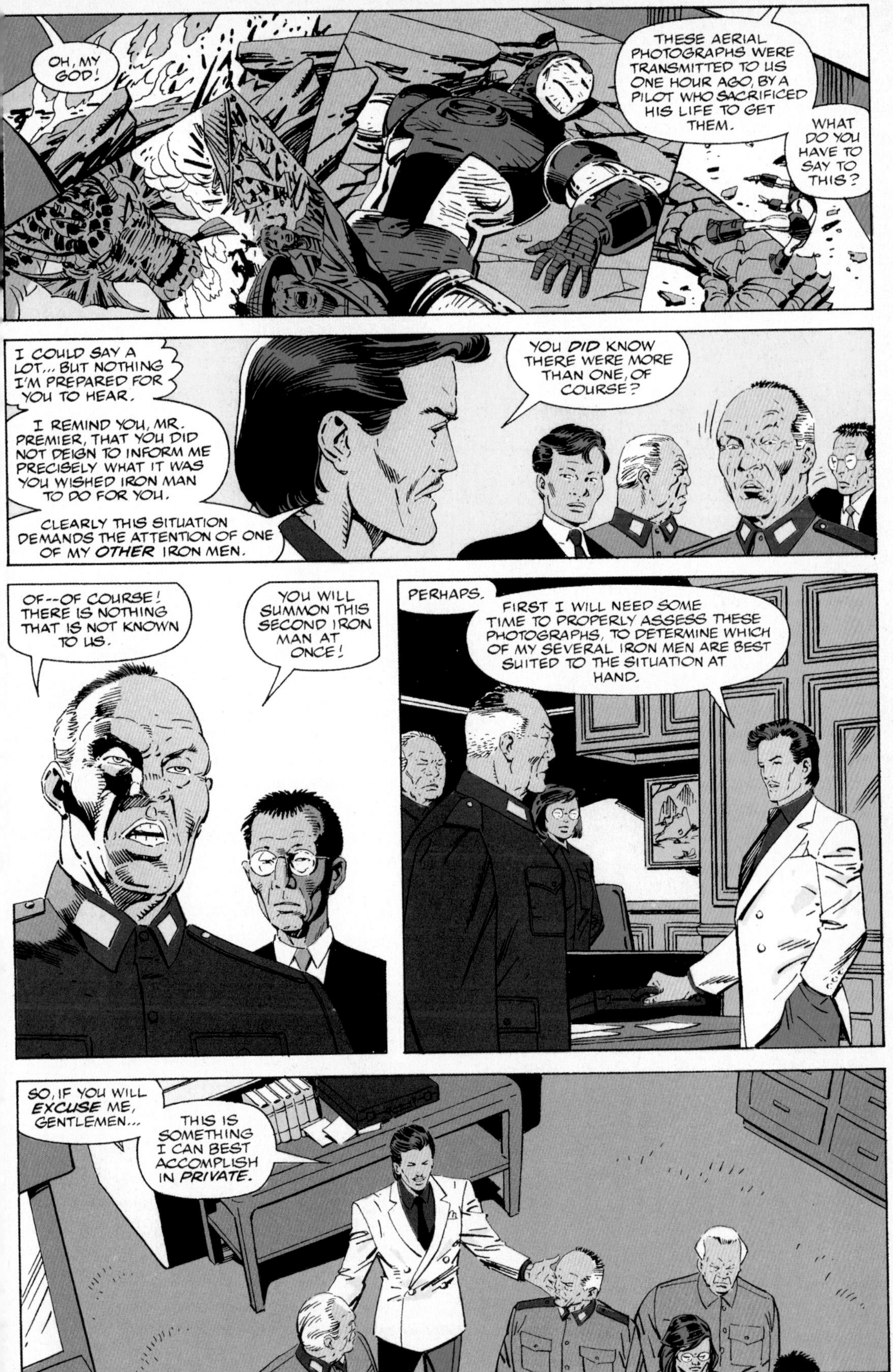
OH, MY GOD!
THESE AERIAL PHOTOGRAPHS WERE TRANSMITTED TO US ONE HOUR AGO, BY A PILOT WHO SACRIFICED HIS LIFE TO GET THEM.
WHAT DO YOU HAVE TO SAY TO THIS?
I COULD SAY A LOT... BUT NOTHING I'M PREPARED FOR YOU TO HEAR.
I REMIND YOU, MR. PREMIER, THAT YOU DID NOT DEIGN TO INFORM ME PRECISELY WHAT IT WAS YOU WISHED IRON MAN TO DO FOR YOU.
CLEARLY THIS SITUATION DEMANDS THE ATTENTION OF ONE OF MY *OTHER* IRON MEN.
YOU *DID* KNOW THERE WERE MORE THAN ONE, OF COURSE?
OF--OF COURSE! THERE IS NOTHING THAT IS NOT KNOWN TO US.
YOU WILL SUMMON THIS SECOND IRON MAN AT ONCE!
PERHAPS.
FIRST I WILL NEED SOME TIME TO PROPERLY ASSESS THESE PHOTOGRAPHS, TO DETERMINE WHICH OF MY SEVERAL IRON MEN ARE BEST SUITED TO THE SITUATION AT HAND.
SO, IF YOU WILL *EXCUSE* ME, GENTLEMEN...
THIS IS SOMETHING I CAN BEST ACCOMPLISH IN *PRIVATE*.

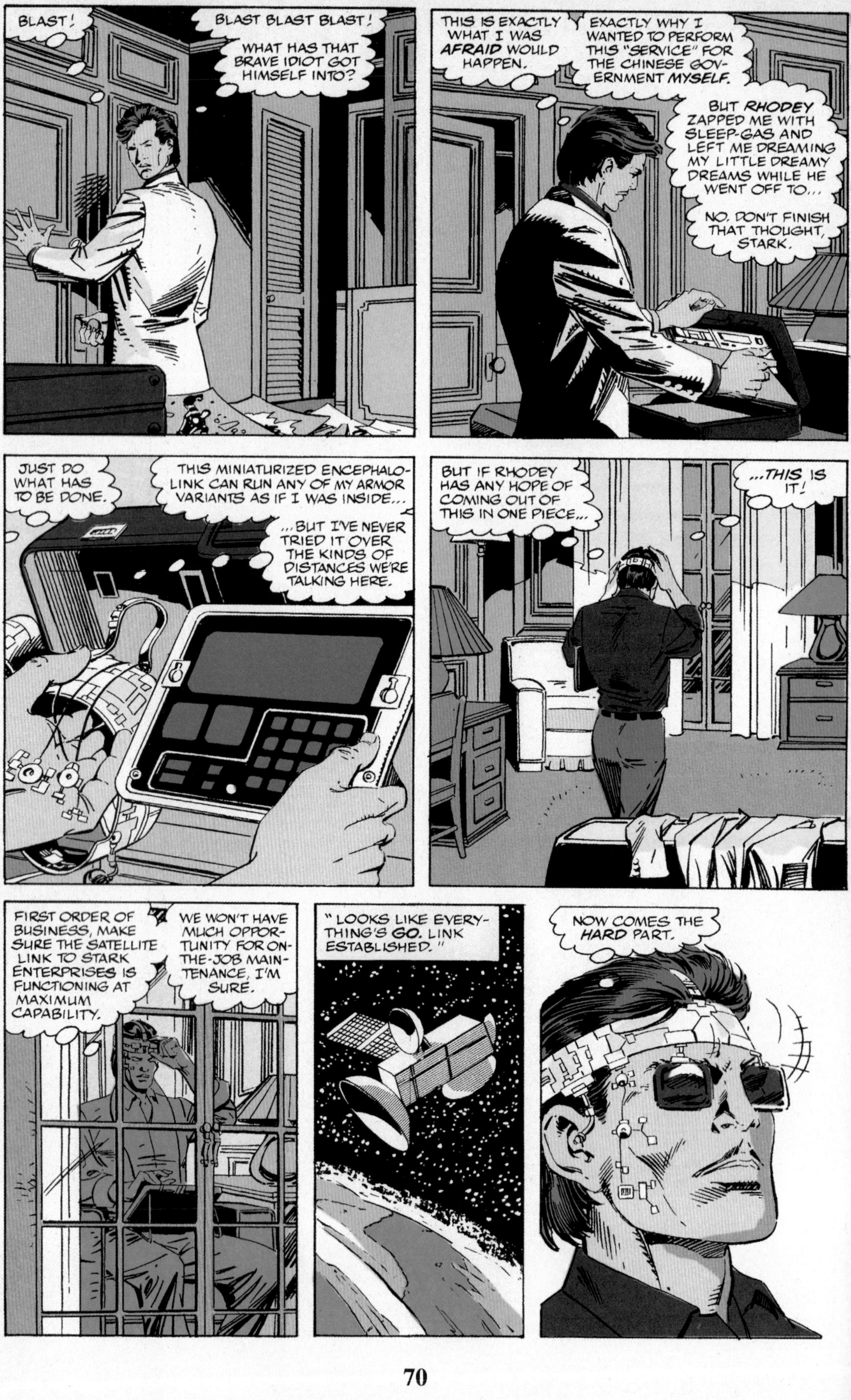

BLAST!
BLAST BLAST BLAST!
WHAT HAS THAT BRAVE IDIOT GOT HIMSELF INTO?
THIS IS EXACTLY WHAT I WAS AFRAID WOULD HAPPEN.
EXACTLY WHY I WANTED TO PERFORM THIS "SERVICE" FOR THE CHINESE GOVERNMENT MYSELF.
BUT RHODEY ZAPPED ME WITH SLEEP-GAS AND LEFT ME DREAMING MY LITTLE DREAMY DREAMS WHILE HE WENT OFF TO...
NO. DON'T FINISH THAT THOUGHT, STARK.
JUST DO WHAT HAS TO BE DONE.
THIS MINIATURIZED ENCEPHALO-LINK CAN RUN ANY OF MY ARMOR VARIANTS AS IF I WAS INSIDE...
...BUT I'VE NEVER TRIED IT OVER THE KINDS OF DISTANCES WE'RE TALKING HERE.
BUT IF RHODEY HAS ANY HOPE OF COMING OUT OF THIS IN ONE PIECE...
...THIS IS IT!
FIRST ORDER OF BUSINESS, MAKE SURE THE SATELLITE LINK TO STARK ENTERPRISES IS FUNCTIONING AT MAXIMUM CAPABILITY.
WE WON'T HAVE MUCH OPPORTUNITY FOR ON-THE-JOB MAINTENANCE, I'M SURE.
"LOOKS LIKE EVERYTHING'S GO. LINK ESTABLISHED."
NOW COMES THE HARD PART.

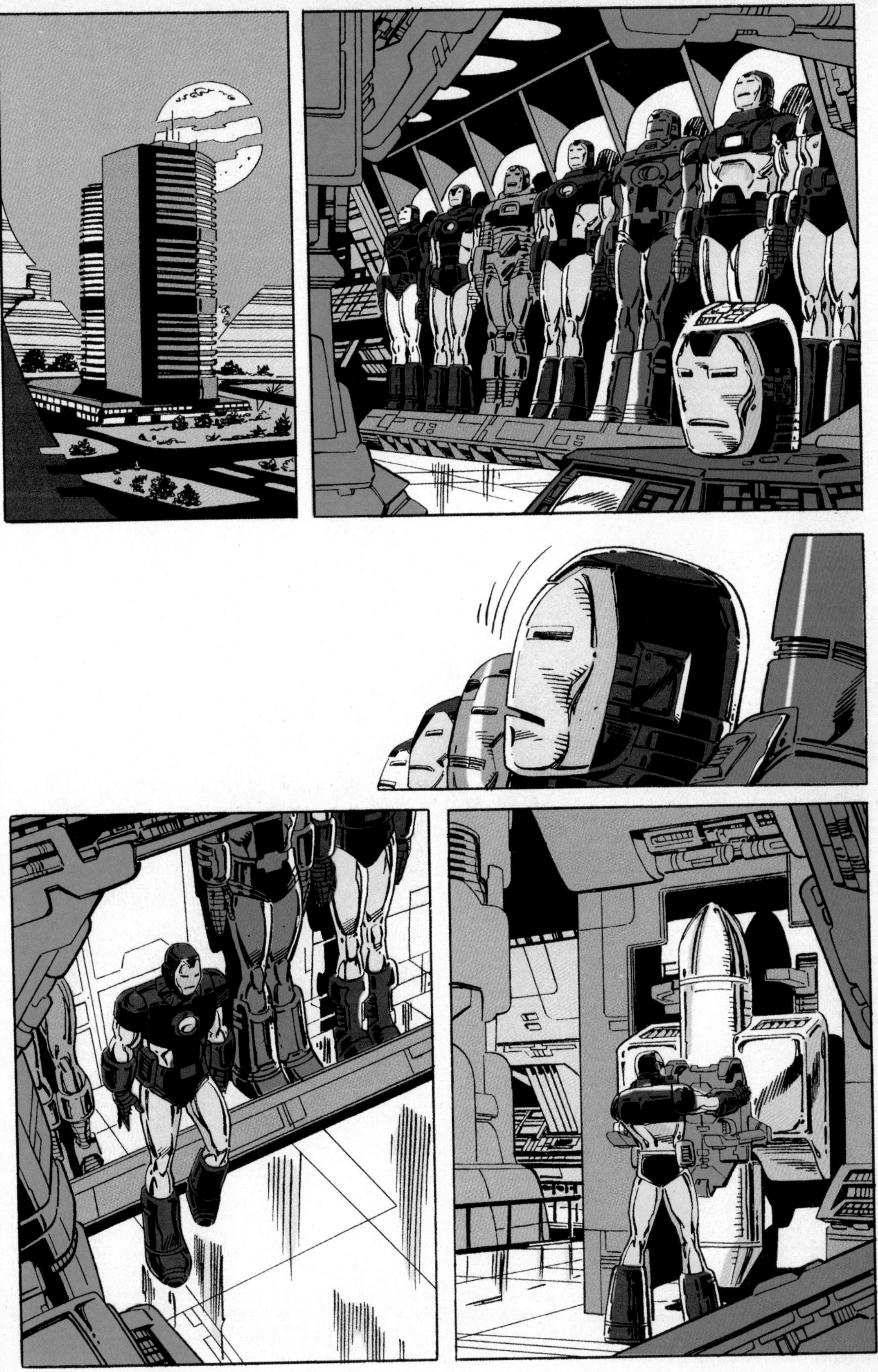

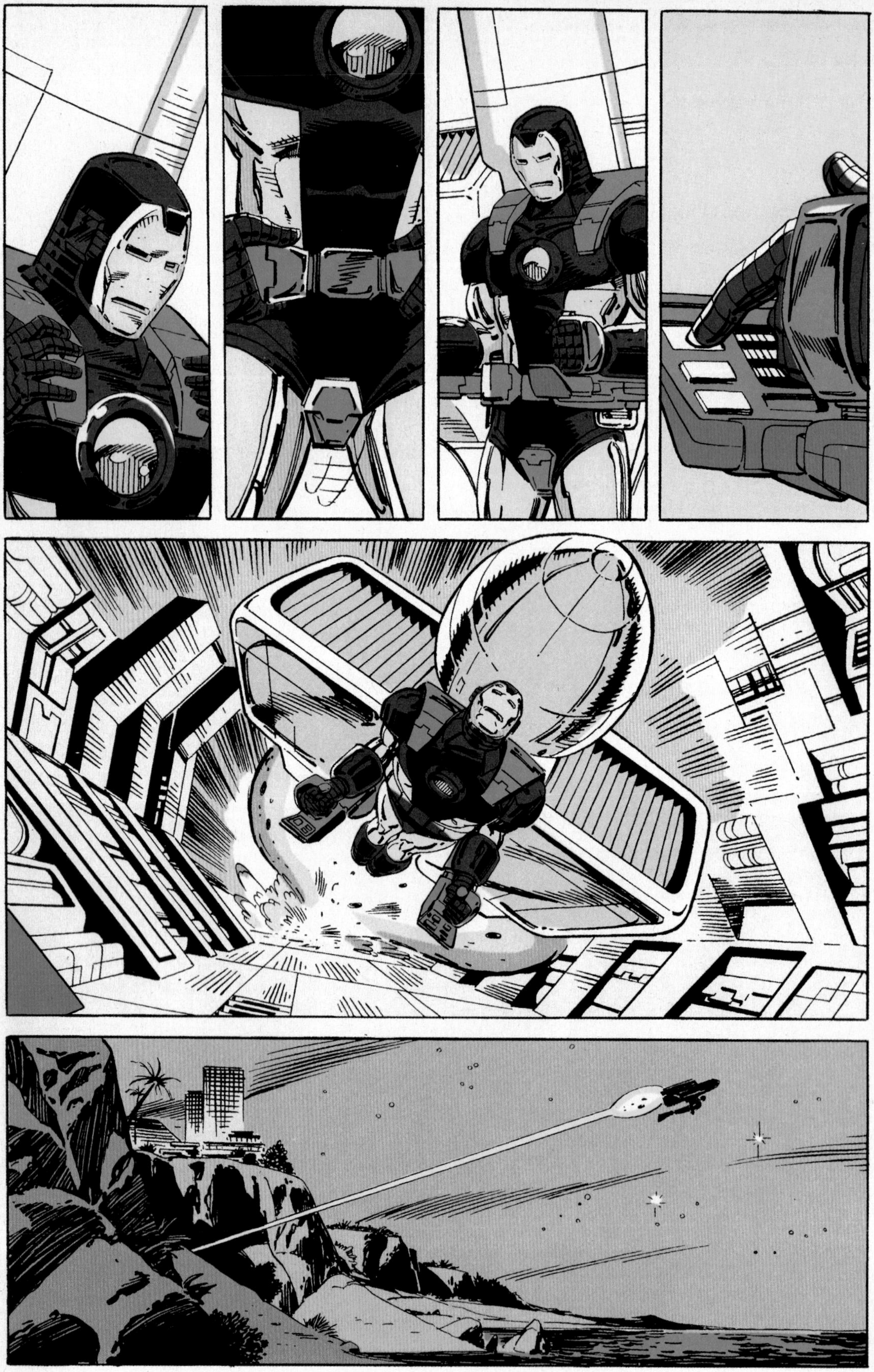

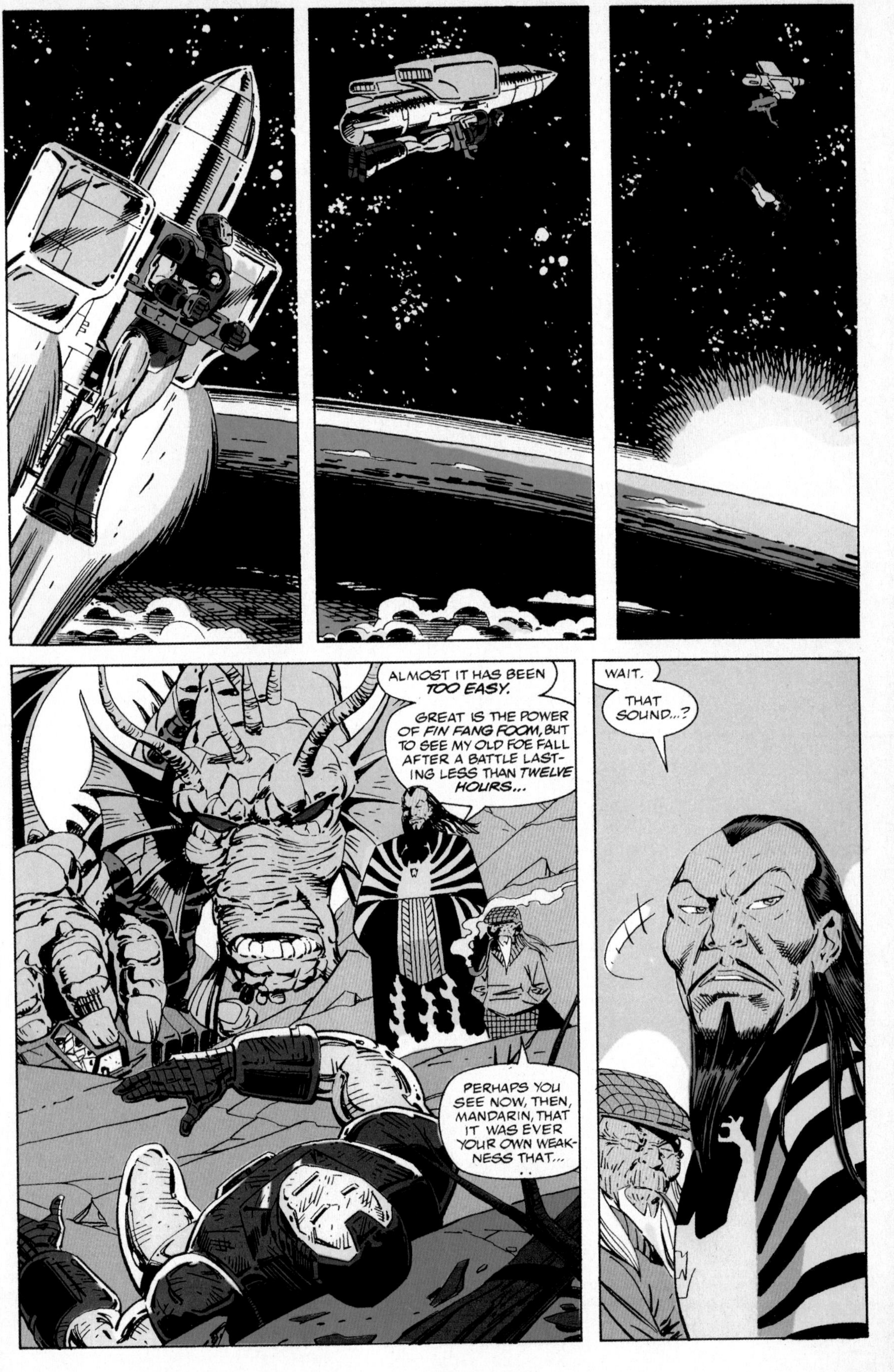
ALMOST IT HAS BEEN *TOO EASY.*
GREAT IS THE POWER OF *FIN FANG FOOM,* BUT TO SEE MY OLD FOE FALL AFTER A BATTLE LASTING LESS THAN *TWELVE HOURS...*
PERHAPS YOU SEE NOW, THEN, MANDARIN, THAT IT WAS EVER YOUR OWN WEAKNESS THAT...
WAIT.
THAT SOUND...?

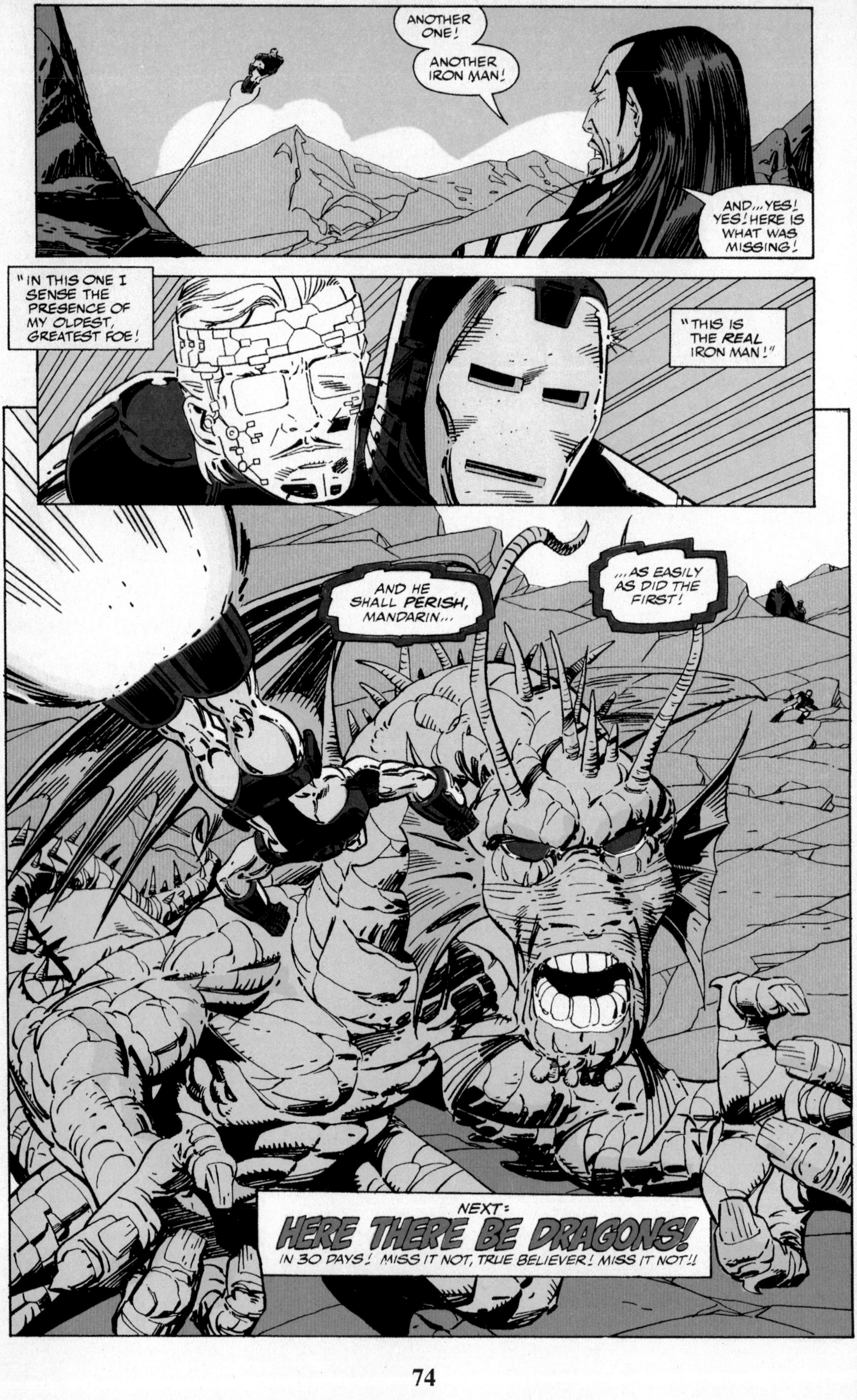

ANOTHER ONE!
ANOTHER IRON MAN!
AND... YES! YES! HERE IS WHAT WAS MISSING!
"IN THIS ONE I SENSE THE PRESENCE OF MY OLDEST, GREATEST FOE!
"THIS IS THE REAL IRON MAN!"
AND HE SHALL PERISH, MANDARIN...
...AS EASILY AS DID THE FIRST!
NEXT:
HERE THERE BE DRAGONS!
IN 30 DAYS! MISS IT NOT, TRUE BELIEVER! MISS IT NOT!!

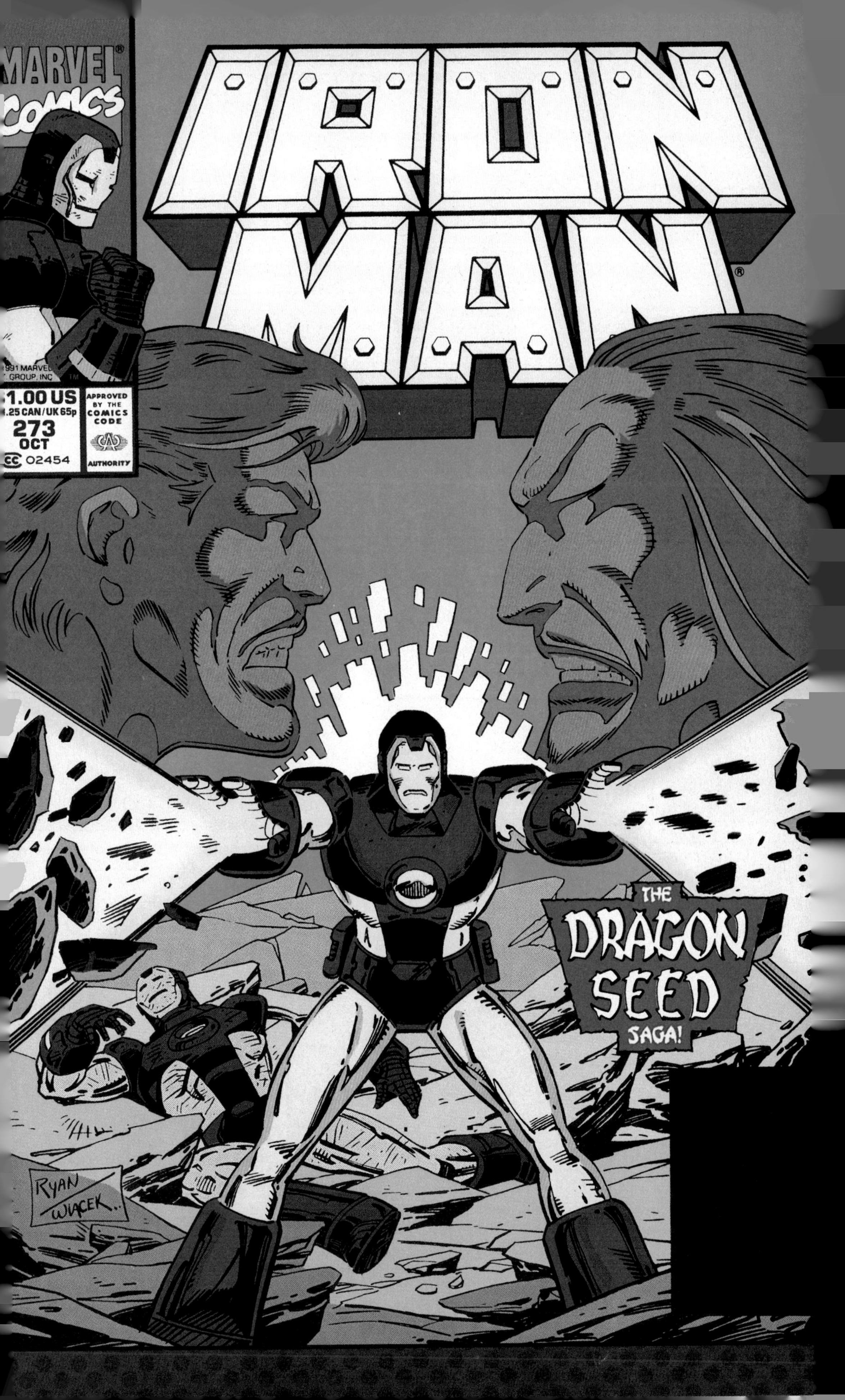

MARVEL COMICS
IRON MAN
1.00 US
.25 CAN/UK 65p
273
OCT
CC 02454
APPROVED BY THE COMICS CODE AUTHORITY
THE DRAGON SEED SAGA!
RYAN
WIACEK

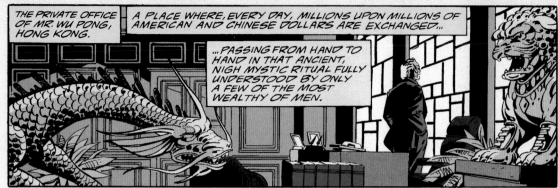

THE PRIVATE OFFICE OF MR. WU PONG, HONG KONG.

A PLACE WHERE, EVERY DAY, MILLIONS UPON MILLIONS OF AMERICAN AND CHINESE DOLLARS ARE EXCHANGED...

...PASSING FROM HAND TO HAND IN THAT ANCIENT, NIGH MYSTIC RITUAL FULLY UNDERSTOOD BY ONLY A FEW OF THE MOST WEALTHY OF MEN.

AND WU PONG, IF HE IS NOTHING ELSE, IS A WEALTHY MAN.

HE HAS, AFTER ALL, HAD THREE THOUSAND YEARS TO AMASS HIS FORTUNE.

MR. WU...

I HAVE THE PAPERS YOU REQUESTED ON THE FALSWORTH PROPERTIES.

I THINK YOU WILL FIND EVERYTHING IS IN ORDER.

I'M CERTAIN IT IS, MISS LING.

YOU HAVE SERVED ME MOST EFFICIENTLY, IN ALL THE SEVEN YEARS YOU HAVE BEEN WITH WU PONG EXPORTS.

HOWEVER, AS IT TURNS OUT, I HAVE NO NEED FOR THESE PAPERS AFTER ALL.

YOU DON'T?

BUT, SIR, I THOUGHT...

I...

M-MR. WU...?

N-NOOOO-OOHH!!!

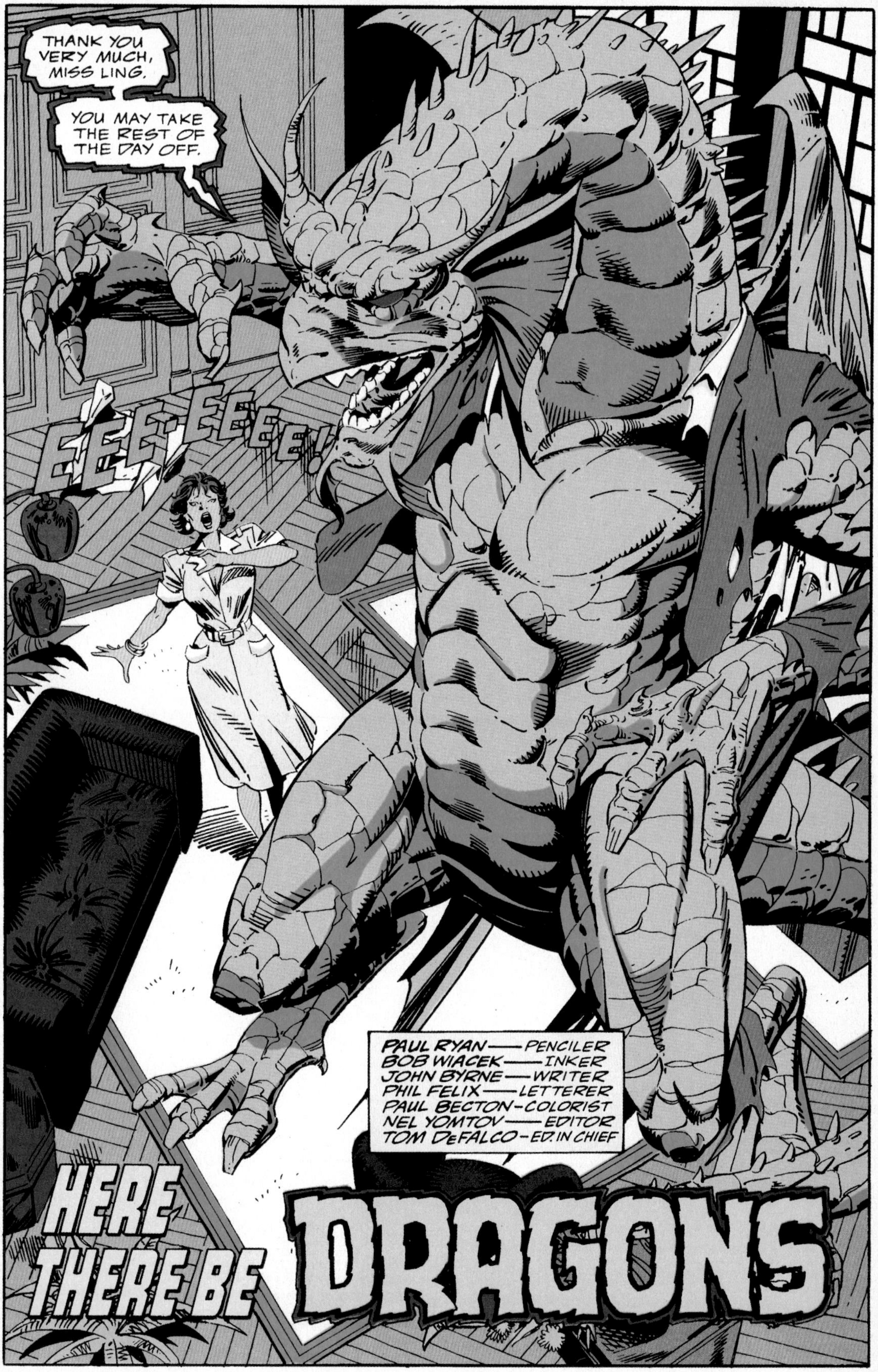

THANK YOU VERY MUCH, MISS LING.
YOU MAY TAKE THE REST OF THE DAY OFF.
EEE-EEEEE!
PAUL RYAN—PENCILER
BOB WIACEK—INKER
JOHN BYRNE—WRITER
PHIL FELIX—LETTERER
PAUL BECTON-COLORIST
NEL YOMTOV—EDITOR
TOM DEFALCO-ED. IN CHIEF
HERE THERE BE DRAGONS

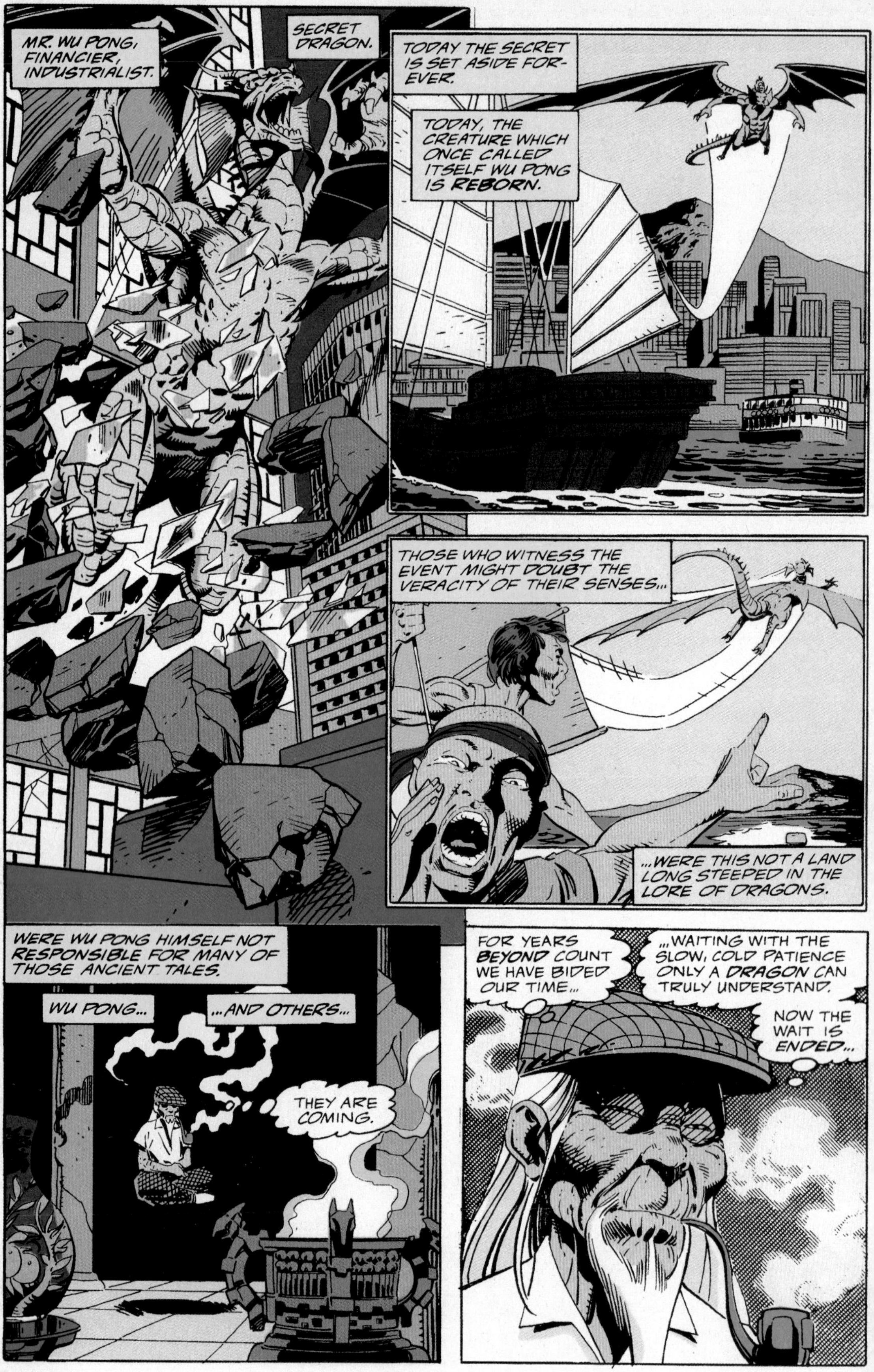
MR. WU PONG, FINANCIER, INDUSTRIALIST.
SECRET DRAGON.
TODAY THE SECRET IS SET ASIDE FOREVER.
TODAY, THE CREATURE WHICH ONCE CALLED ITSELF WU PONG IS REBORN.
THOSE WHO WITNESS THE EVENT MIGHT DOUBT THE VERACITY OF THEIR SENSES...
...WERE THIS NOT A LAND LONG STEEPED IN THE LORE OF DRAGONS.
WERE WU PONG HIMSELF NOT RESPONSIBLE FOR MANY OF THOSE ANCIENT TALES.
WU PONG...
...AND OTHERS...
THEY ARE COMING.
FOR YEARS BEYOND COUNT WE HAVE BIDED OUR TIME...
...WAITING WITH THE SLOW, COLD PATIENCE ONLY A DRAGON CAN TRULY UNDERSTAND.
NOW THE WAIT IS ENDED...

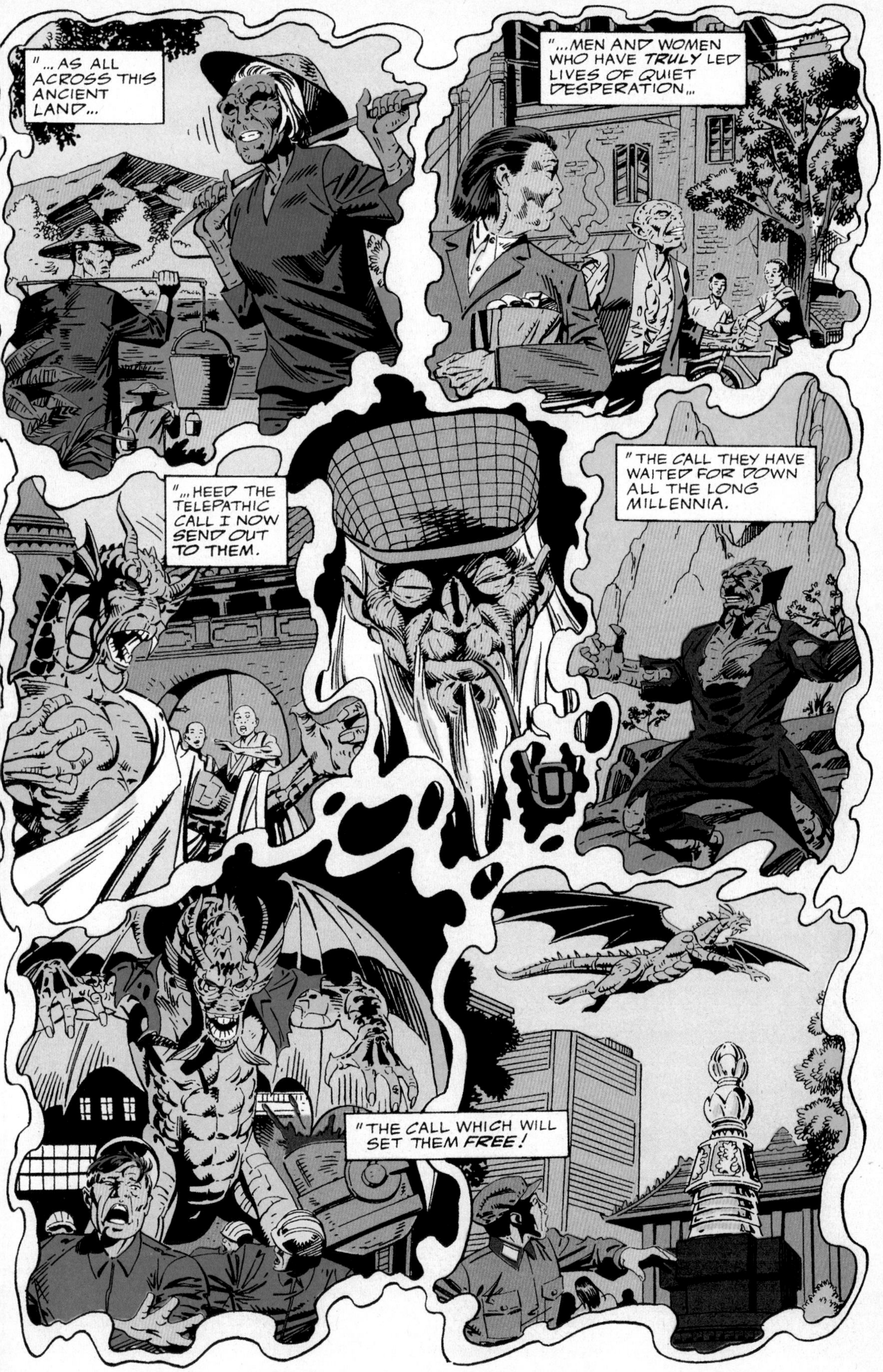
"...AS ALL ACROSS THIS ANCIENT LAND...
"...MEN AND WOMEN WHO HAVE TRULY LED LIVES OF QUIET DESPERATION...
"...HEED THE TELEPATHIC CALL I NOW SEND OUT TO THEM.
"THE CALL THEY HAVE WAITED FOR DOWN ALL THE LONG MILLENNIA.
"THE CALL WHICH WILL SET THEM FREE!

"AND I HEAR THE JOYOUS SHOUTS THAT FILL THEIR MINDS...

"...REACHING OUT TO THOSE OF THEIR KIND, OTHERS THEY HAVE NOT SEEN IN *CENTURIES!*

"GREAT IS THEIR JUBILATION.

"CAN THEY NOT, THEREFORE, BE *FORGIVEN* IF THEIR JOCUNDITY ENCOURAGES IN SOME A SMALL *EXCESS* OF BEHAVIOR?

"...AND I CAN FIND IN MY HEART NO *ANGER*, NO HARSH WORDS.

"MY BROTHER'S ROAR FILLS THE SLEEPY VALLEY...

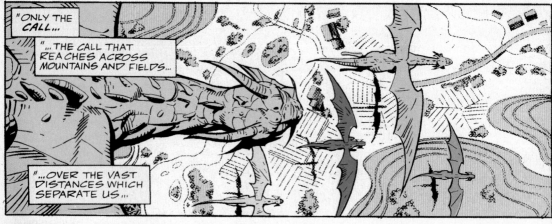

"ONLY THE *CALL*...

"...THE CALL THAT REACHES ACROSS MOUNTAINS AND FIELDS...

"...OVER THE VAST DISTANCES WHICH SEPARATE US...

"...CALLING MY BRETHREN *HOME.*

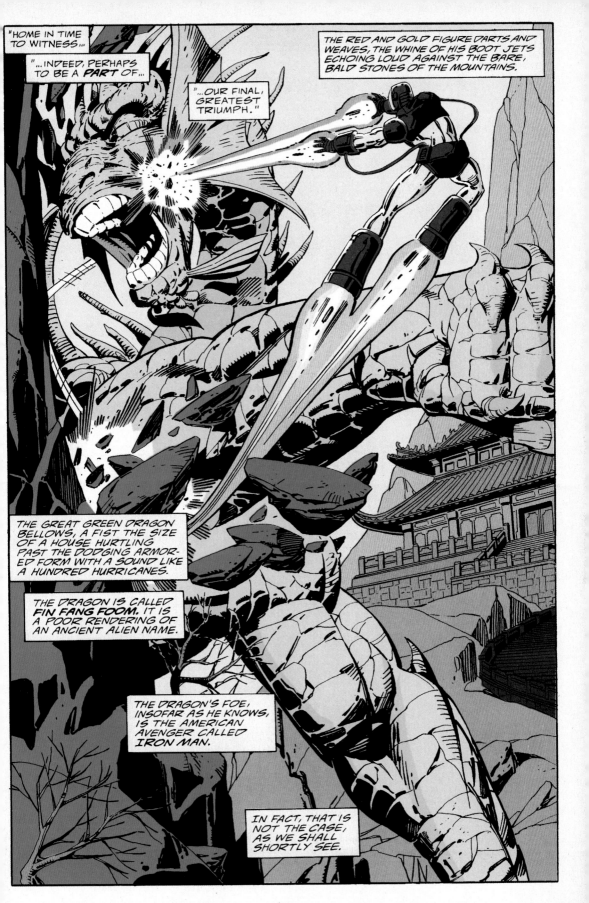

"HOME IN TIME TO WITNESS..."

"...INDEED, PERHAPS TO BE A *PART* OF..."

"...OUR FINAL, GREATEST TRIUMPH."

THE RED AND GOLD FIGURE DARTS AND WEAVES, THE WHINE OF HIS BOOT JETS ECHOING LOUD AGAINST THE BARE, BALD STONES OF THE MOUNTAINS.

THE GREAT GREEN DRAGON BELLOWS, A FIST THE SIZE OF A HOUSE HURTLING PAST THE DODGING ARMORED FORM WITH A SOUND LIKE A HUNDRED HURRICANES.

THE DRAGON IS CALLED *FIN FANG FOOM.* IT IS A POOR RENDERING OF AN ANCIENT ALIEN NAME.

THE DRAGON'S FOE, INSOFAR AS HE KNOWS, IS THE AMERICAN AVENGER CALLED *IRON MAN.*

IN FACT, THAT IS NOT THE CASE, AS WE SHALL SHORTLY SEE.

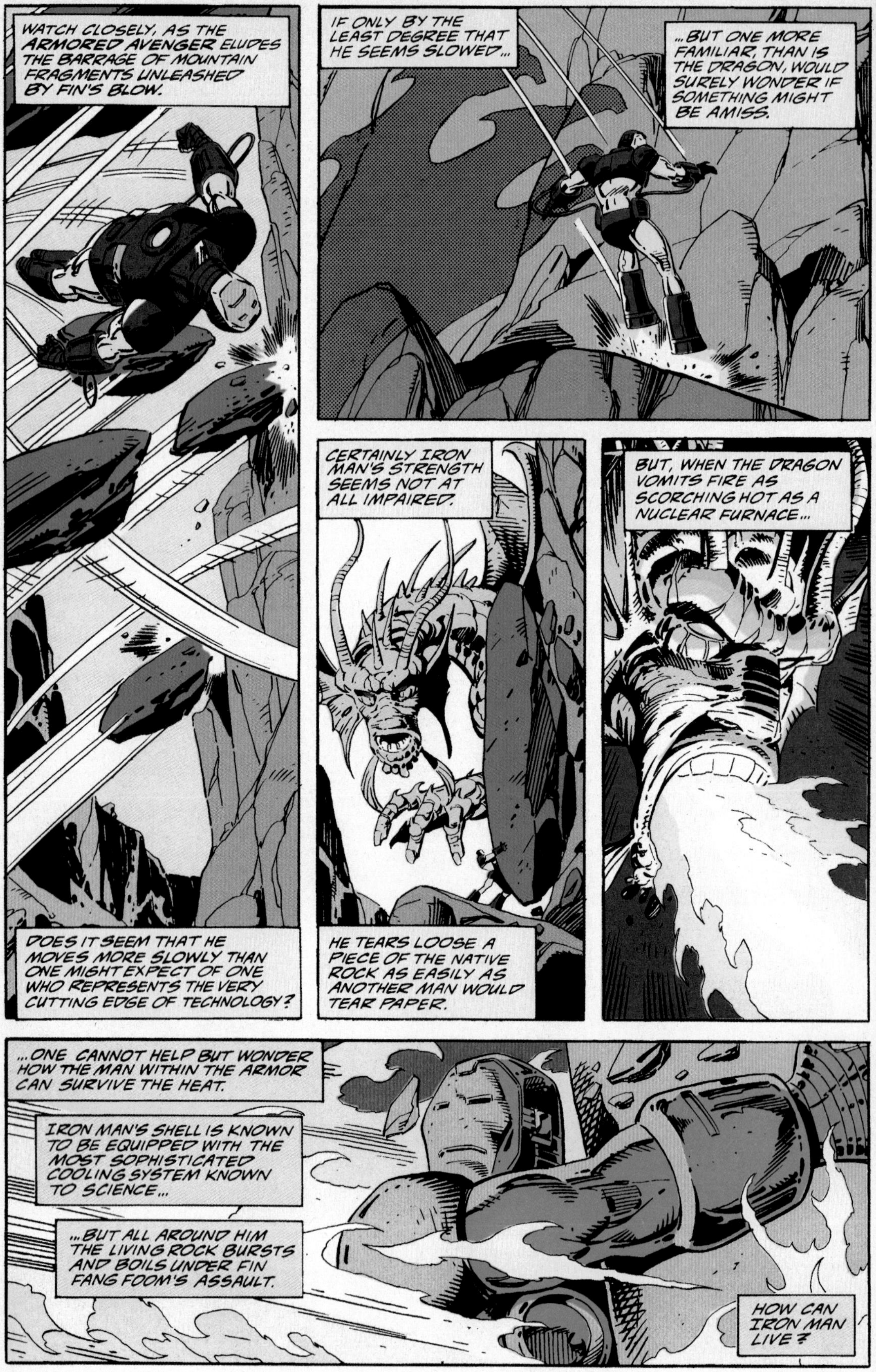
WATCH CLOSELY, AS THE ARMORED AVENGER ELUDES THE BARRAGE OF MOUNTAIN FRAGMENTS UNLEASHED BY FIN'S BLOW.
DOES IT SEEM THAT HE MOVES MORE SLOWLY THAN ONE MIGHT EXPECT OF ONE WHO REPRESENTS THE VERY CUTTING EDGE OF TECHNOLOGY?
IF ONLY BY THE LEAST DEGREE THAT HE SEEMS SLOWED...
...BUT ONE MORE FAMILIAR, THAN IS THE DRAGON, WOULD SURELY WONDER IF SOMETHING MIGHT BE AMISS.
CERTAINLY IRON MAN'S STRENGTH SEEMS NOT AT ALL IMPAIRED.
HE TEARS LOOSE A PIECE OF THE NATIVE ROCK AS EASILY AS ANOTHER MAN WOULD TEAR PAPER.
BUT, WHEN THE DRAGON VOMITS FIRE AS SCORCHING HOT AS A NUCLEAR FURNACE...
...ONE CANNOT HELP BUT WONDER HOW THE MAN WITHIN THE ARMOR CAN SURVIVE THE HEAT.
IRON MAN'S SHELL IS KNOWN TO BE EQUIPPED WITH THE MOST SOPHISTICATED COOLING SYSTEM KNOWN TO SCIENCE...
...BUT ALL AROUND HIM THE LIVING ROCK BURSTS AND BOILS UNDER FIN FANG FOOM'S ASSAULT.
HOW CAN IRON MAN LIVE?

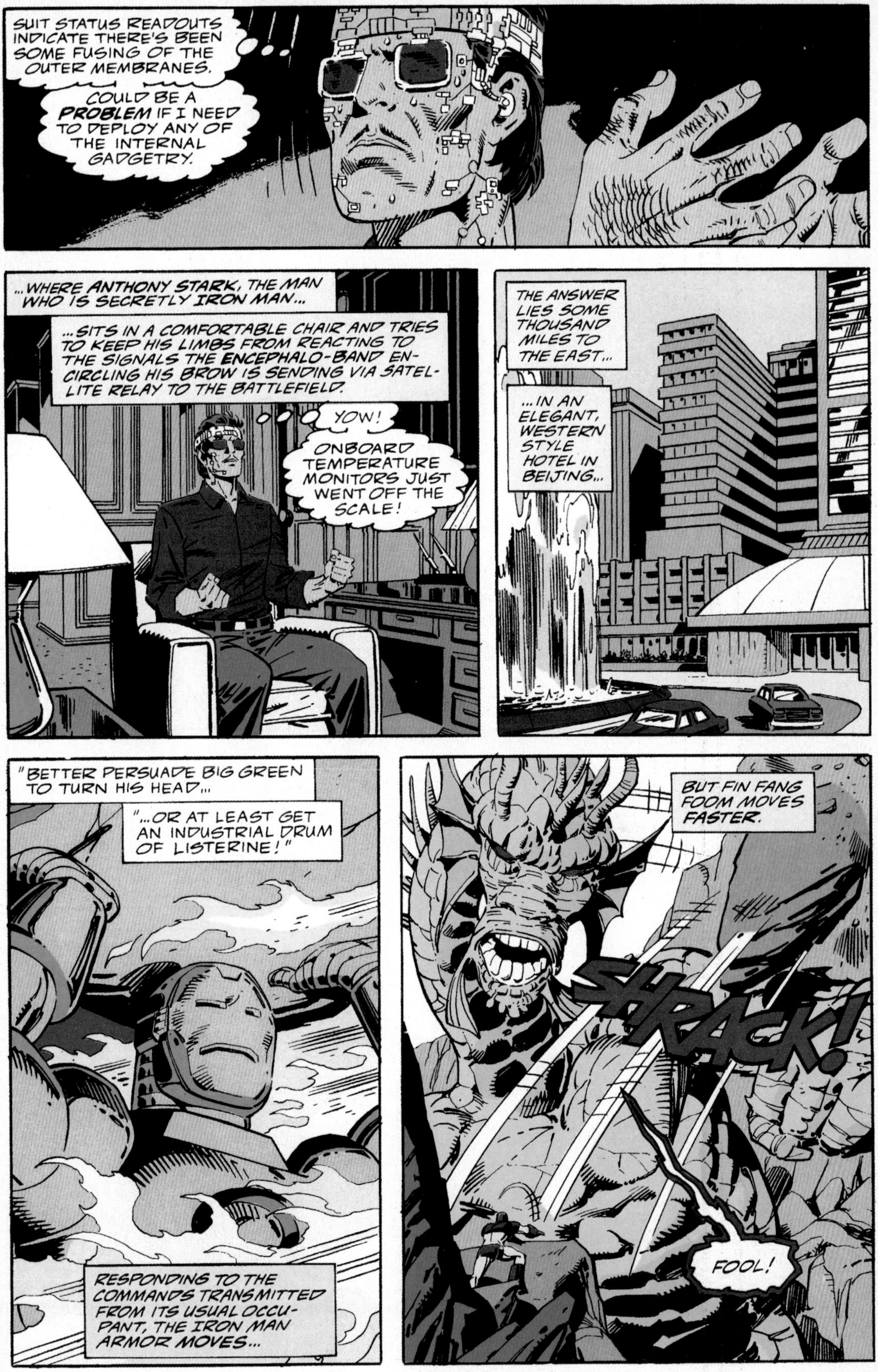
SUIT STATUS READOUTS INDICATE THERE'S BEEN SOME FUSING OF THE OUTER MEMBRANES.
COULD BE A **PROBLEM** IF I NEED TO DEPLOY ANY OF THE INTERNAL GADGETRY.
...WHERE **ANTHONY STARK**, THE MAN WHO IS SECRETLY **IRON MAN**...
...SITS IN A COMFORTABLE CHAIR AND TRIES TO KEEP HIS LIMBS FROM REACTING TO THE SIGNALS THE **ENCEPHALO-BAND** ENCIRCLING HIS BROW IS SENDING VIA SATELLITE RELAY TO THE BATTLEFIELD.
YOW!
ONBOARD TEMPERATURE MONITORS JUST WENT OFF THE SCALE!
THE ANSWER LIES SOME THOUSAND MILES TO THE EAST...
...IN AN ELEGANT, WESTERN STYLE HOTEL IN BEIJING...
"BETTER PERSUADE BIG GREEN TO TURN HIS HEAD...
"...OR AT LEAST GET AN INDUSTRIAL DRUM OF LISTERINE!"
RESPONDING TO THE COMMANDS TRANSMITTED FROM ITS USUAL OCCUPANT, THE IRON MAN ARMOR MOVES...
BUT FIN FANG FOOM MOVES **FASTER**.
SHRACK!
FOOL!

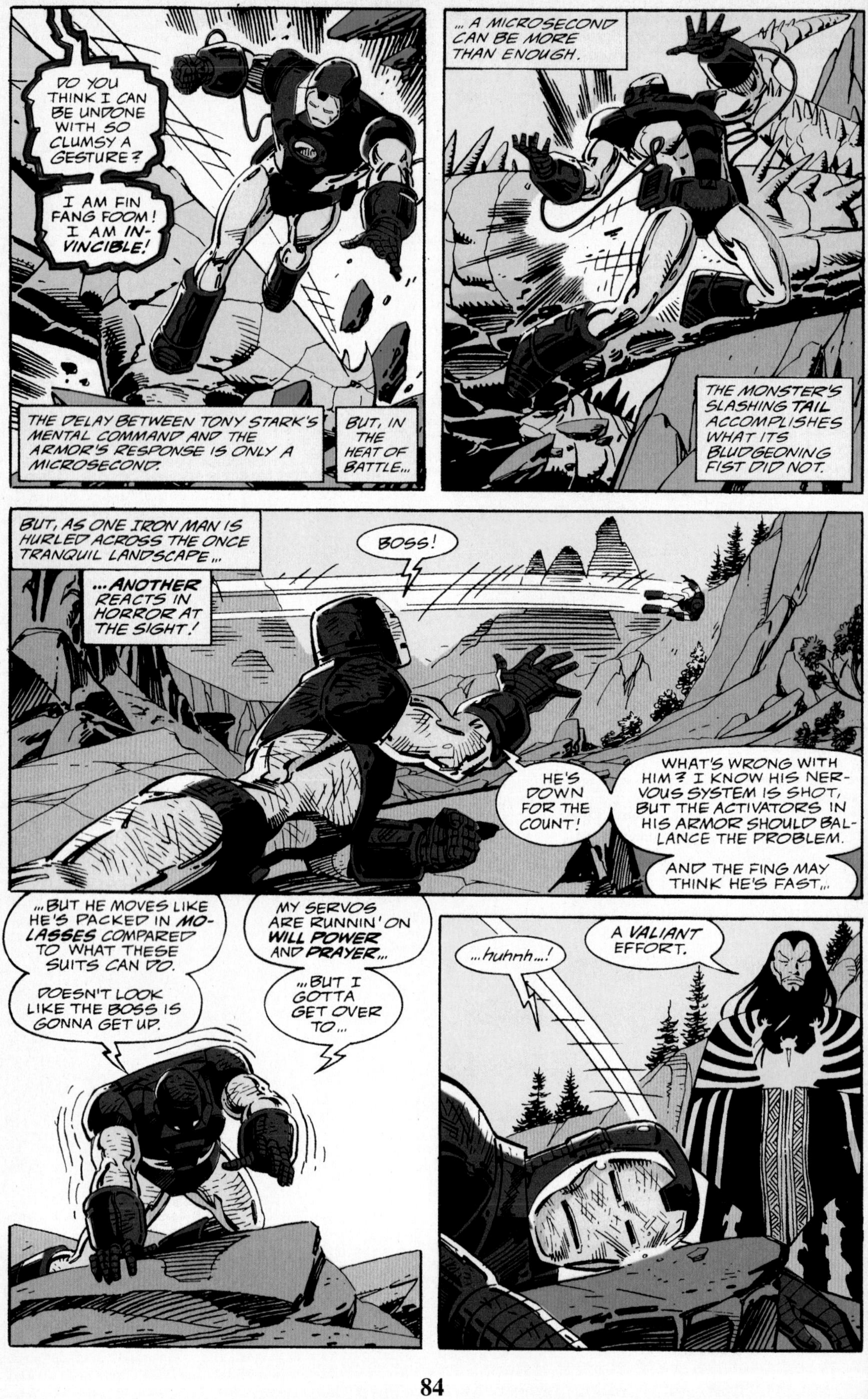
DO YOU THINK I CAN BE UNDONE WITH SO CLUMSY A GESTURE?
I AM FIN FANG FOOM! I AM IN-VINCIBLE!
THE DELAY BETWEEN TONY STARK'S MENTAL COMMAND AND THE ARMOR'S RESPONSE IS ONLY A MICROSECOND.
BUT, IN THE HEAT OF BATTLE...
...A MICROSECOND CAN BE MORE THAN ENOUGH.
THE MONSTER'S SLASHING TAIL ACCOMPLISHES WHAT ITS BLUDGEONING FIST DID NOT.
BUT, AS ONE IRON MAN IS HURLED ACROSS THE ONCE TRANQUIL LANDSCAPE...
BOSS!
...ANOTHER REACTS IN HORROR AT THE SIGHT!
HE'S DOWN FOR THE COUNT!
WHAT'S WRONG WITH HIM? I KNOW HIS NER-VOUS SYSTEM IS SHOT, BUT THE ACTIVATORS IN HIS ARMOR SHOULD BAL-LANCE THE PROBLEM.
AND THE FING MAY THINK HE'S FAST...
...BUT HE MOVES LIKE HE'S PACKED IN MO-LASSES COMPARED TO WHAT THESE SUITS CAN DO.
DOESN'T LOOK LIKE THE BOSS IS GONNA GET UP.
MY SERVOS ARE RUNNIN' ON WILL POWER AND PRAYER...
...BUT I GOTTA GET OVER TO...
...huhhh...!
A VALIANT EFFORT.

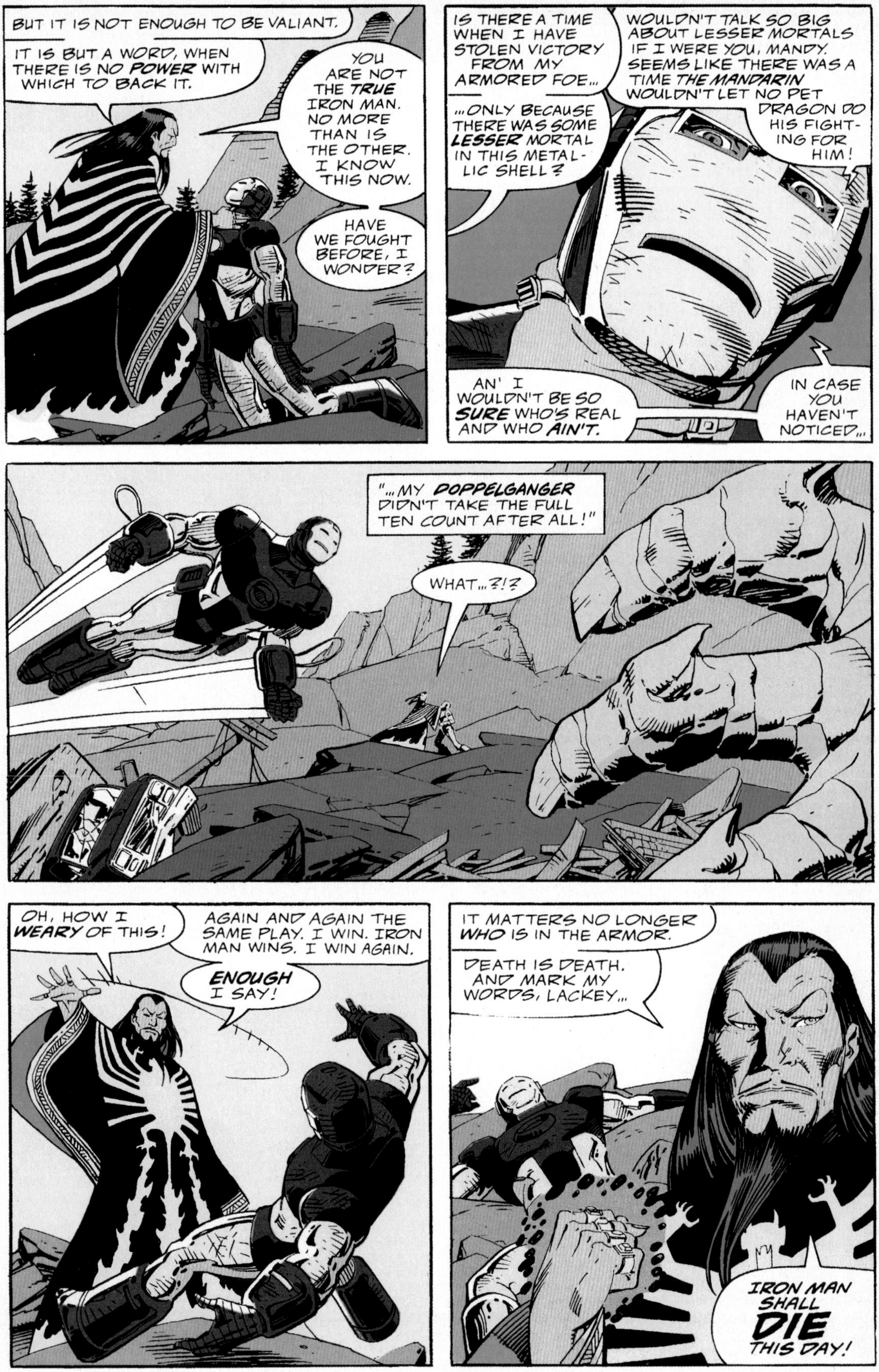
BUT IT IS NOT ENOUGH TO BE VALIANT.
IT IS BUT A WORD, WHEN THERE IS NO POWER WITH WHICH TO BACK IT.
YOU ARE NOT THE TRUE IRON MAN. NO MORE THAN IS THE OTHER. I KNOW THIS NOW.
HAVE WE FOUGHT BEFORE, I WONDER?
IS THERE A TIME WHEN I HAVE STOLEN VICTORY FROM MY ARMORED FOE...
...ONLY BECAUSE THERE WAS SOME LESSER MORTAL IN THIS METALLIC SHELL?
WOULDN'T TALK SO BIG ABOUT LESSER MORTALS IF I WERE YOU, MANDY. SEEMS LIKE THERE WAS A TIME THE MANDARIN WOULDN'T LET NO PET DRAGON DO HIS FIGHTING FOR HIM!
AN' I WOULDN'T BE SO SURE WHO'S REAL AND WHO AIN'T.
IN CASE YOU HAVEN'T NOTICED...
"...MY DOPPELGANGER DIDN'T TAKE THE FULL TEN COUNT AFTER ALL!"
WHAT...?!?
OH, HOW I WEARY OF THIS!
AGAIN AND AGAIN THE SAME PLAY. I WIN. IRON MAN WINS. I WIN AGAIN.
ENOUGH I SAY!
IT MATTERS NO LONGER WHO IS IN THE ARMOR.
DEATH IS DEATH. AND MARK MY WORDS, LACKEY...
IRON MAN SHALL DIE THIS DAY!

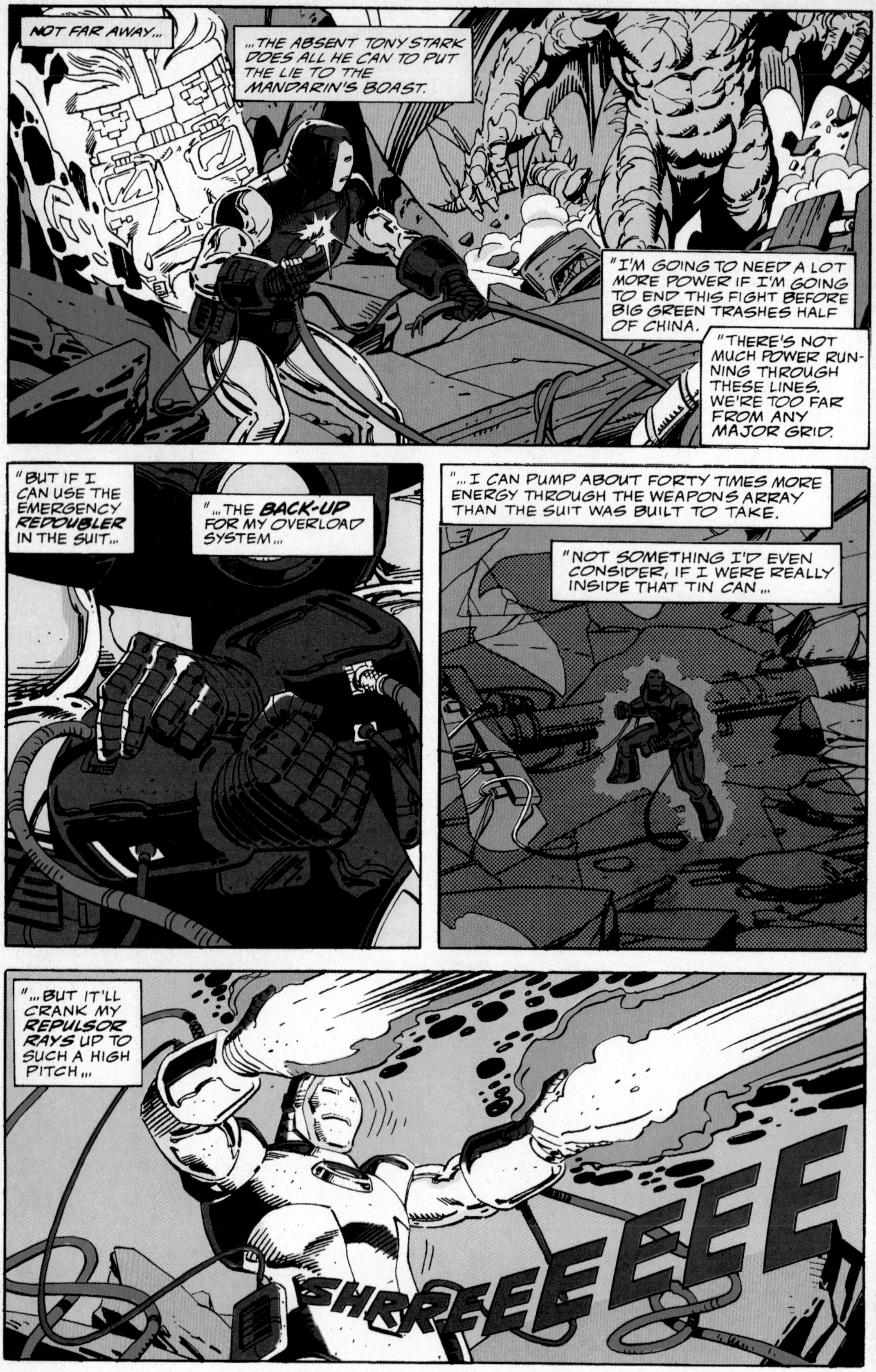
NOT FAR AWAY...
...THE ABSENT TONY STARK DOES ALL HE CAN TO PUT THE LIE TO THE MANDARIN'S BOAST.
"I'M GOING TO NEED A LOT MORE POWER IF I'M GOING TO END THIS FIGHT BEFORE BIG GREEN TRASHES HALF OF CHINA.
"THERE'S NOT MUCH POWER RUNNING THROUGH THESE LINES. WE'RE TOO FAR FROM ANY MAJOR GRID.
"BUT IF I CAN USE THE EMERGENCY REDOUBLER IN THE SUIT...
"...THE BACK-UP FOR MY OVERLOAD SYSTEM...
"...I CAN PUMP ABOUT FORTY TIMES MORE ENERGY THROUGH THE WEAPONS ARRAY THAN THE SUIT WAS BUILT TO TAKE.
"NOT SOMETHING I'D EVEN CONSIDER, IF I WERE REALLY INSIDE THAT TIN CAN...
"...BUT IT'LL CRANK MY REPULSOR RAYS UP TO SUCH A HIGH PITCH...
SHRREEEEEEE

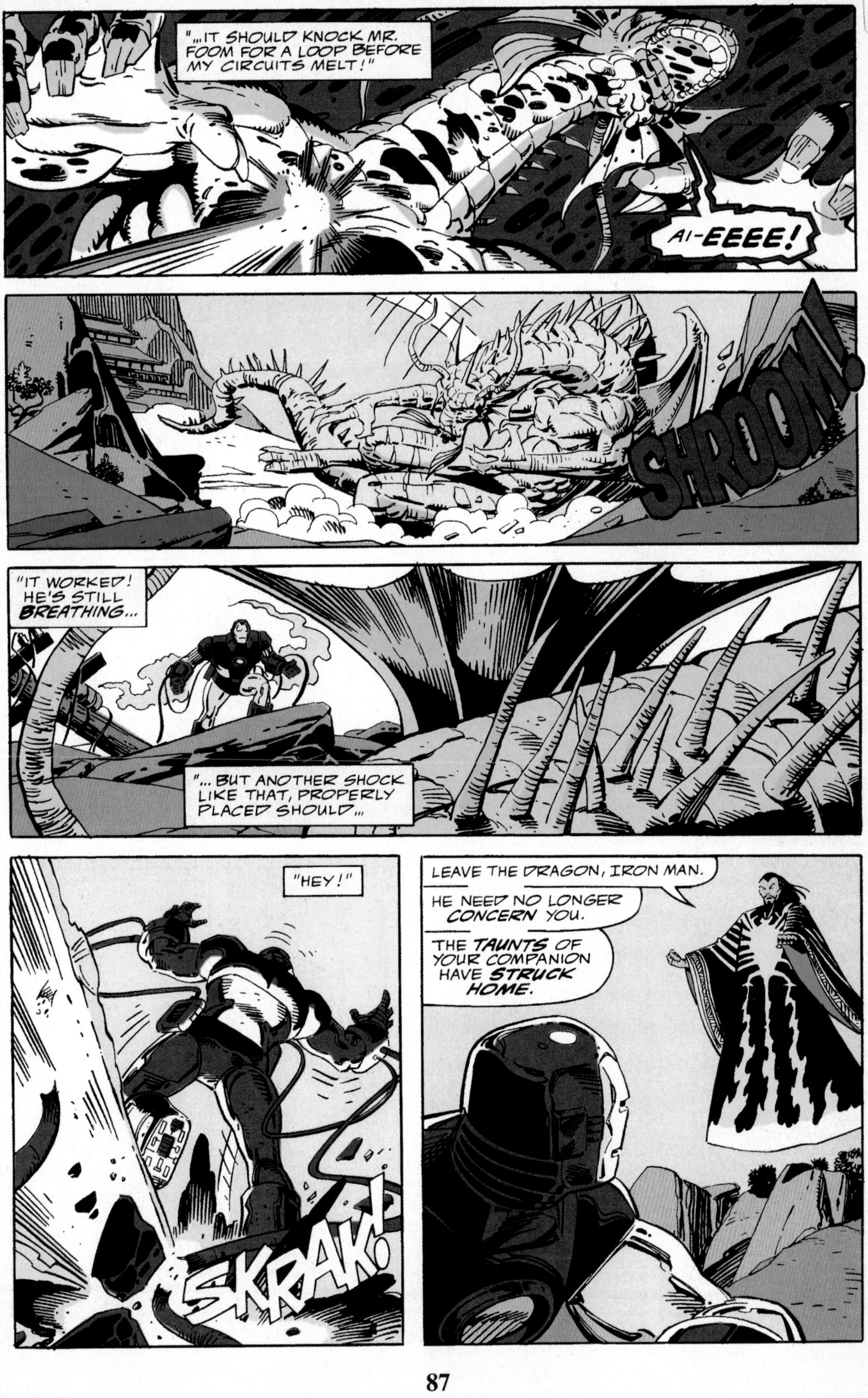
"...IT SHOULD KNOCK MR. FOOM FOR A LOOP BEFORE MY CIRCUITS MELT!"
AI-EEEE!
SHROOM!
"IT WORKED! HE'S STILL BREATHING...
"... BUT ANOTHER SHOCK LIKE THAT, PROPERLY PLACED SHOULD...
"HEY!"
SKRAK!
LEAVE THE DRAGON, IRON MAN.
HE NEED NO LONGER CONCERN YOU.
THE TAUNTS OF YOUR COMPANION HAVE STRUCK HOME.

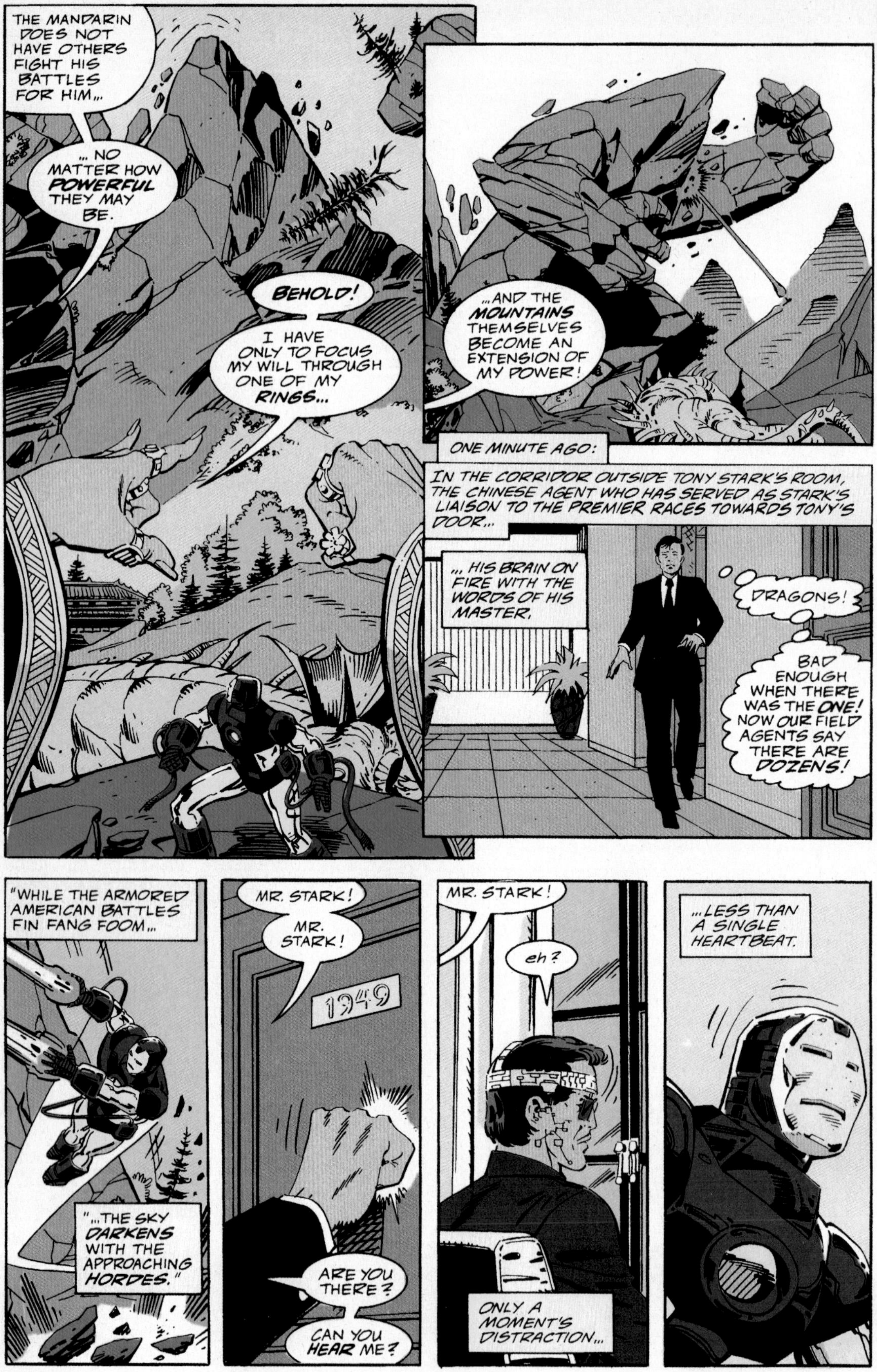
THE MANDARIN DOES NOT HAVE OTHERS FIGHT HIS BATTLES FOR HIM...
... NO MATTER HOW POWERFUL THEY MAY BE.
BEHOLD!
I HAVE ONLY TO FOCUS MY WILL THROUGH ONE OF MY RINGS...
...AND THE MOUNTAINS THEMSELVES BECOME AN EXTENSION OF MY POWER!
ONE MINUTE AGO:
IN THE CORRIDOR OUTSIDE TONY STARK'S ROOM, THE CHINESE AGENT WHO HAS SERVED AS STARK'S LIAISON TO THE PREMIER RACES TOWARDS TONY'S DOOR...
... HIS BRAIN ON FIRE WITH THE WORDS OF HIS MASTER.
DRAGONS!
BAD ENOUGH WHEN THERE WAS THE ONE! NOW OUR FIELD AGENTS SAY THERE ARE DOZENS!
"WHILE THE ARMORED AMERICAN BATTLES FIN FANG FOOM...
"...THE SKY DARKENS WITH THE APPROACHING HORDES."
MR. STARK!
MR. STARK!
1949
ARE YOU THERE?
CAN YOU HEAR ME?
MR. STARK!
eh?
ONLY A MOMENT'S DISTRACTION...
...LESS THAN A SINGLE HEARTBEAT.

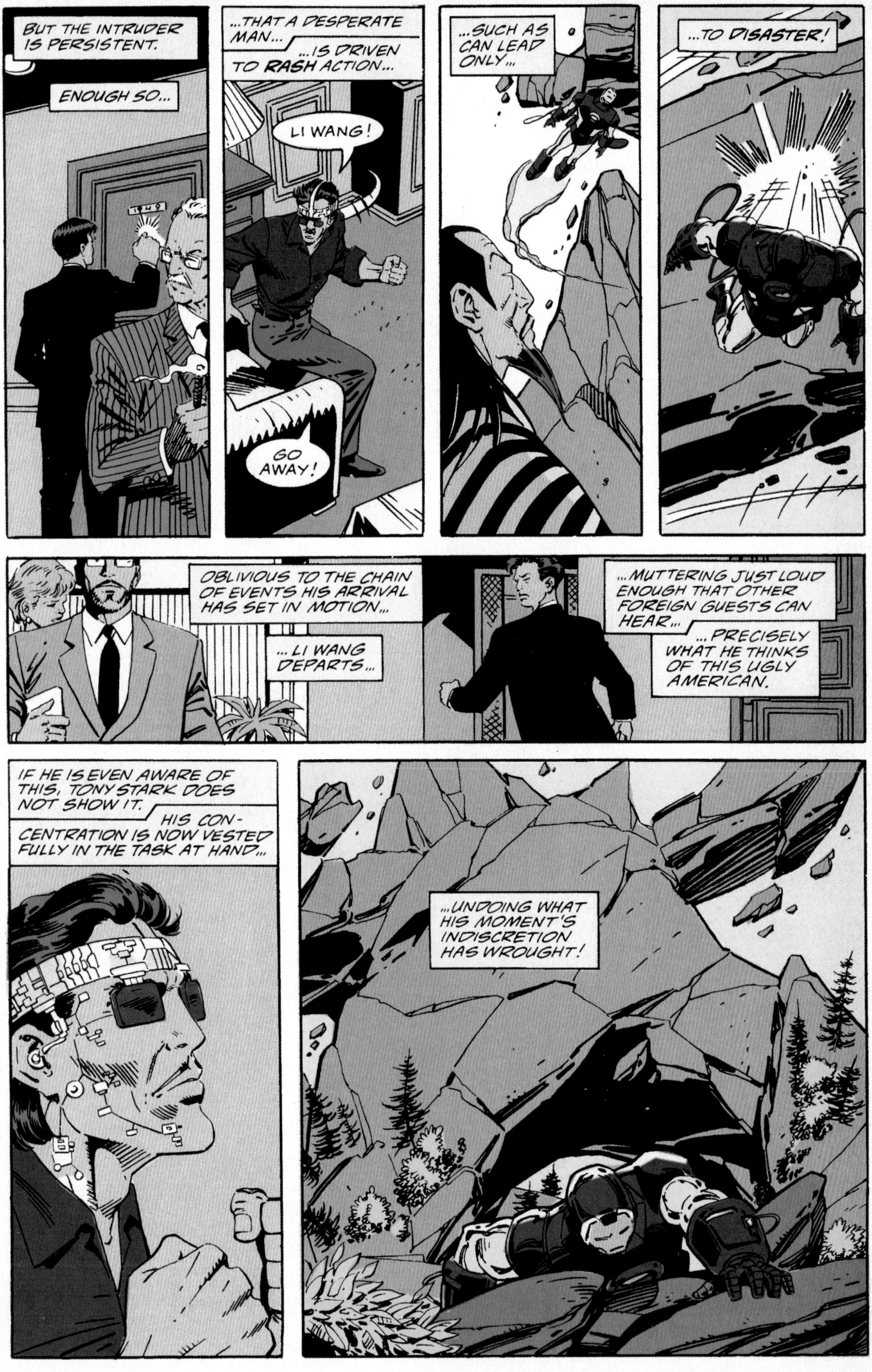
BUT THE INTRUDER IS PERSISTENT.
ENOUGH SO...
...THAT A DESPERATE MAN...
...IS DRIVEN TO RASH ACTION...
LI WANG!
GO AWAY!
...SUCH AS CAN LEAD ONLY...
...TO DISASTER!
OBLIVIOUS TO THE CHAIN OF EVENTS HIS ARRIVAL HAS SET IN MOTION...
...LI WANG DEPARTS...
...MUTTERING JUST LOUD ENOUGH THAT OTHER FOREIGN GUESTS CAN HEAR...
...PRECISELY WHAT HE THINKS OF THIS UGLY AMERICAN.
IF HE IS EVEN AWARE OF THIS, TONY STARK DOES NOT SHOW IT.
HIS CONCENTRATION IS NOW VESTED FULLY IN THE TASK AT HAND...
...UNDOING WHAT HIS MOMENT'S INDISCRETION HAS WROUGHT!

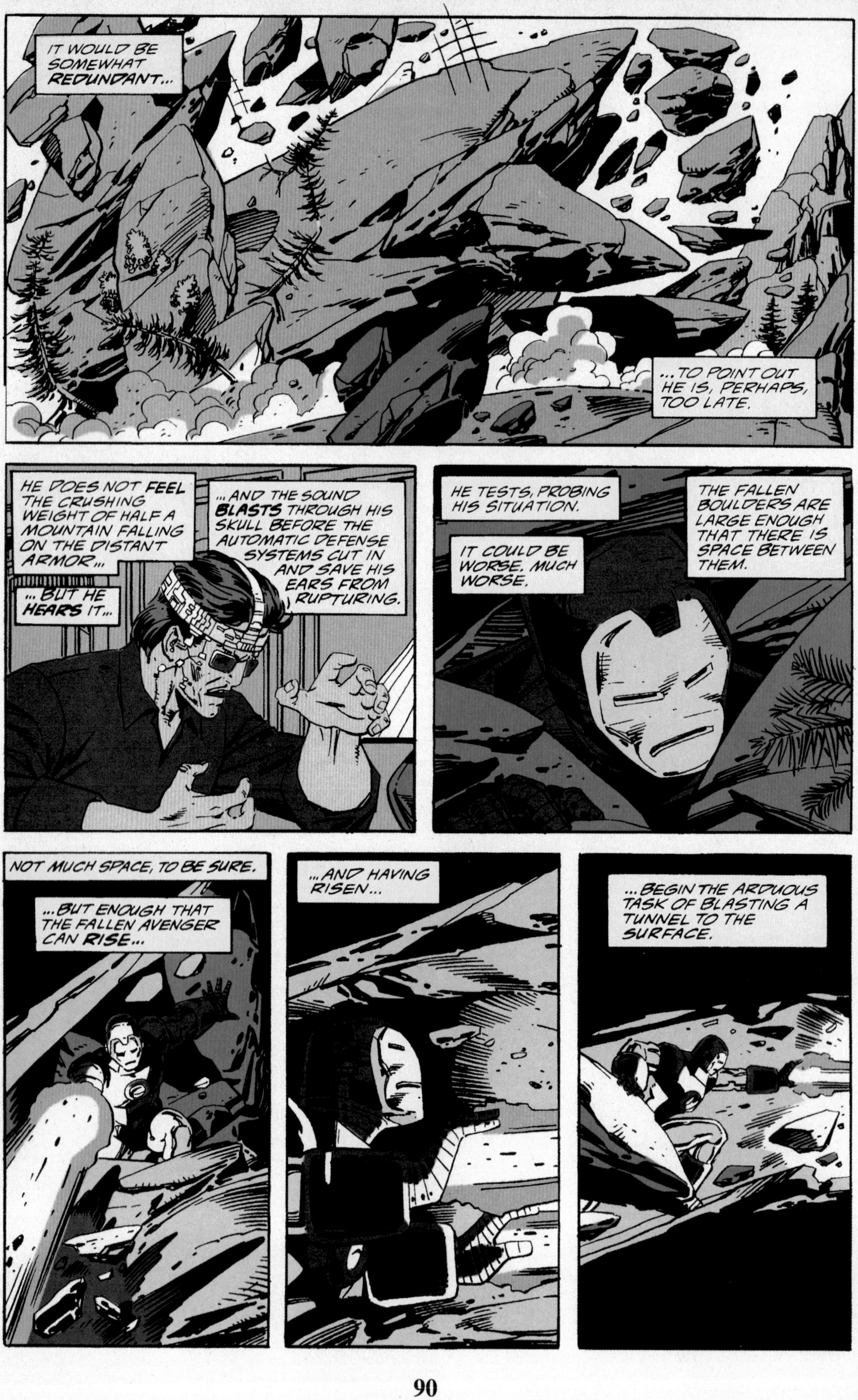
IT WOULD BE SOMEWHAT REDUNDANT...
...TO POINT OUT HE IS, PERHAPS, TOO LATE.
HE DOES NOT FEEL THE CRUSHING WEIGHT OF HALF A MOUNTAIN FALLING ON THE DISTANT ARMOR...
...BUT HE HEARS IT...
...AND THE SOUND BLASTS THROUGH HIS SKULL BEFORE THE AUTOMATIC DEFENSE SYSTEMS CUT IN AND SAVE HIS EARS FROM RUPTURING.
HE TESTS, PROBING HIS SITUATION.
IT COULD BE WORSE. MUCH WORSE.
THE FALLEN BOULDERS ARE LARGE ENOUGH THAT THERE IS SPACE BETWEEN THEM.
NOT MUCH SPACE, TO BE SURE.
...BUT ENOUGH THAT THE FALLEN AVENGER CAN RISE...
...AND HAVING RISEN...
...BEGIN THE ARDUOUS TASK OF BLASTING A TUNNEL TO THE SURFACE.

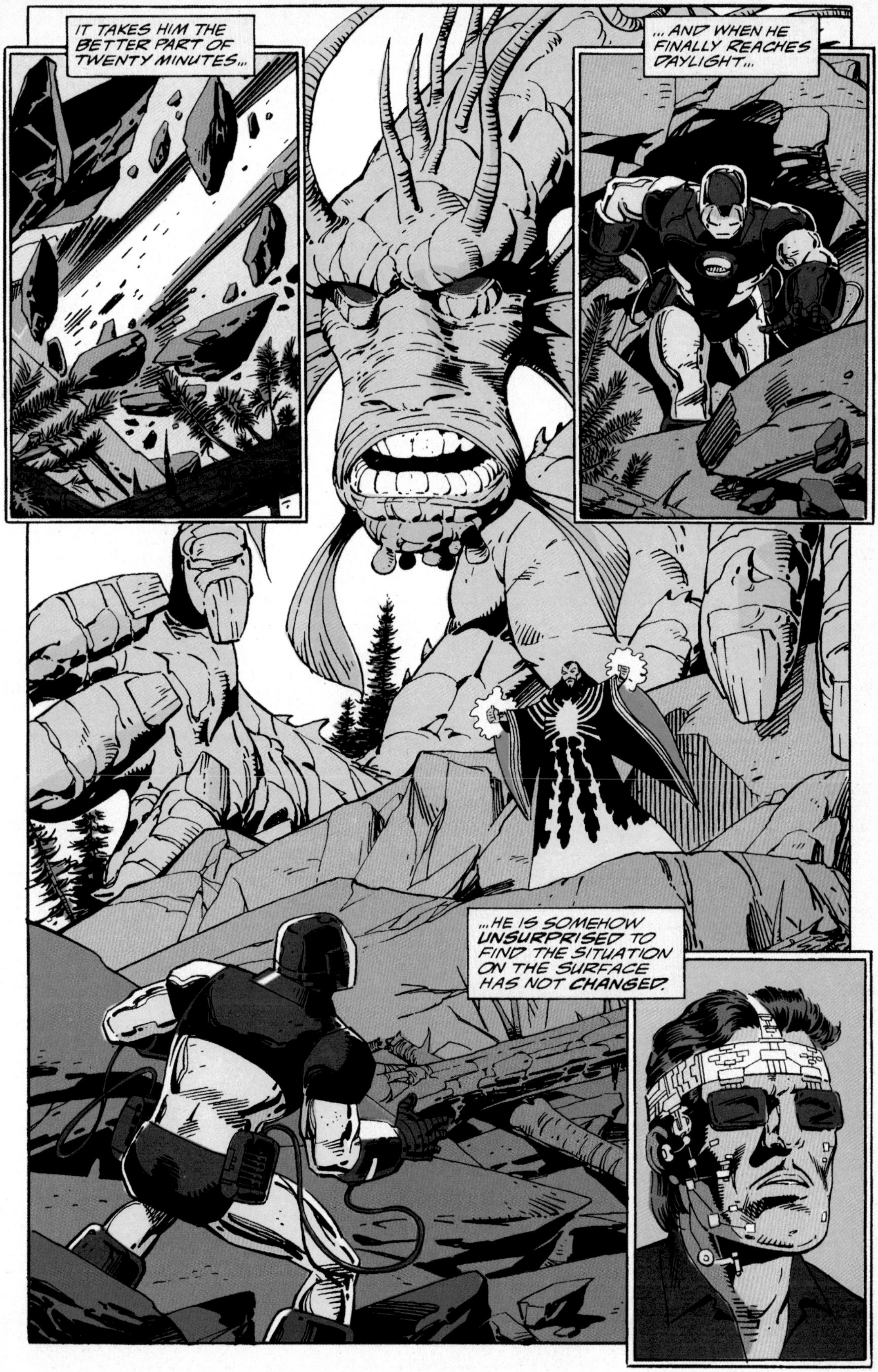
IT TAKES HIM THE BETTER PART OF TWENTY MINUTES...
...AND WHEN HE FINALLY REACHES DAYLIGHT...
...HE IS SOMEHOW UNSURPRISED TO FIND THE SITUATION ON THE SURFACE HAS NOT CHANGED.

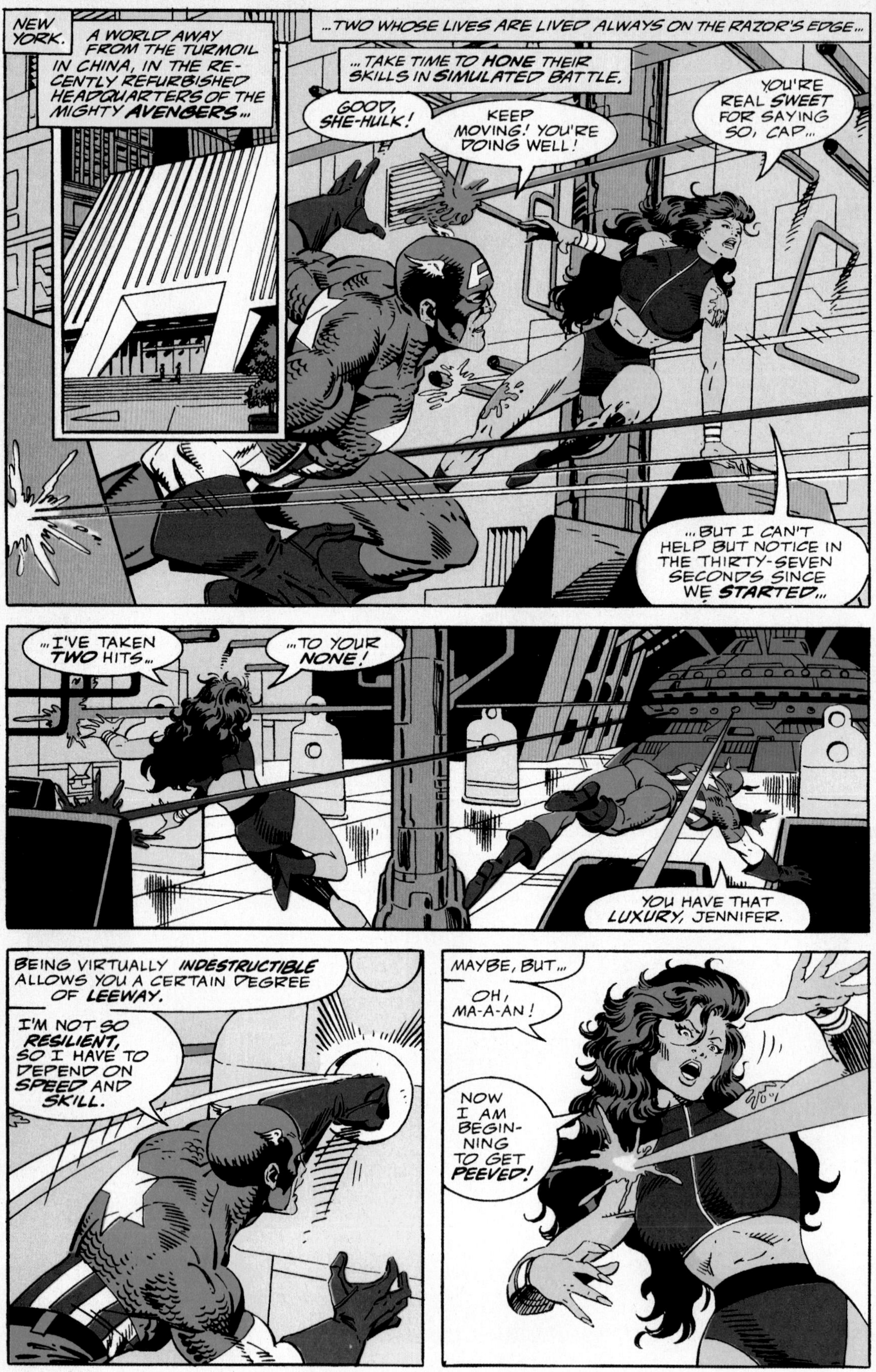
NEW YORK.
A WORLD AWAY FROM THE TURMOIL IN CHINA, IN THE RECENTLY REFURBISHED HEADQUARTERS OF THE MIGHTY AVENGERS...
...TWO WHOSE LIVES ARE LIVED ALWAYS ON THE RAZOR'S EDGE...
...TAKE TIME TO HONE THEIR SKILLS IN SIMULATED BATTLE.
GOOD, SHE-HULK!
KEEP MOVING! YOU'RE DOING WELL!
YOU'RE REAL SWEET FOR SAYING SO, CAP...
...BUT I CAN'T HELP BUT NOTICE IN THE THIRTY-SEVEN SECONDS SINCE WE STARTED...
...I'VE TAKEN TWO HITS...
...TO YOUR NONE!
YOU HAVE THAT LUXURY, JENNIFER.
BEING VIRTUALLY INDESTRUCTIBLE ALLOWS YOU A CERTAIN DEGREE OF LEEWAY.
I'M NOT SO RESILIENT, SO I HAVE TO DEPEND ON SPEED AND SKILL.
MAYBE, BUT...
OH, MA-A-AN!
NOW I AM BEGINNING TO GET PEEVED!

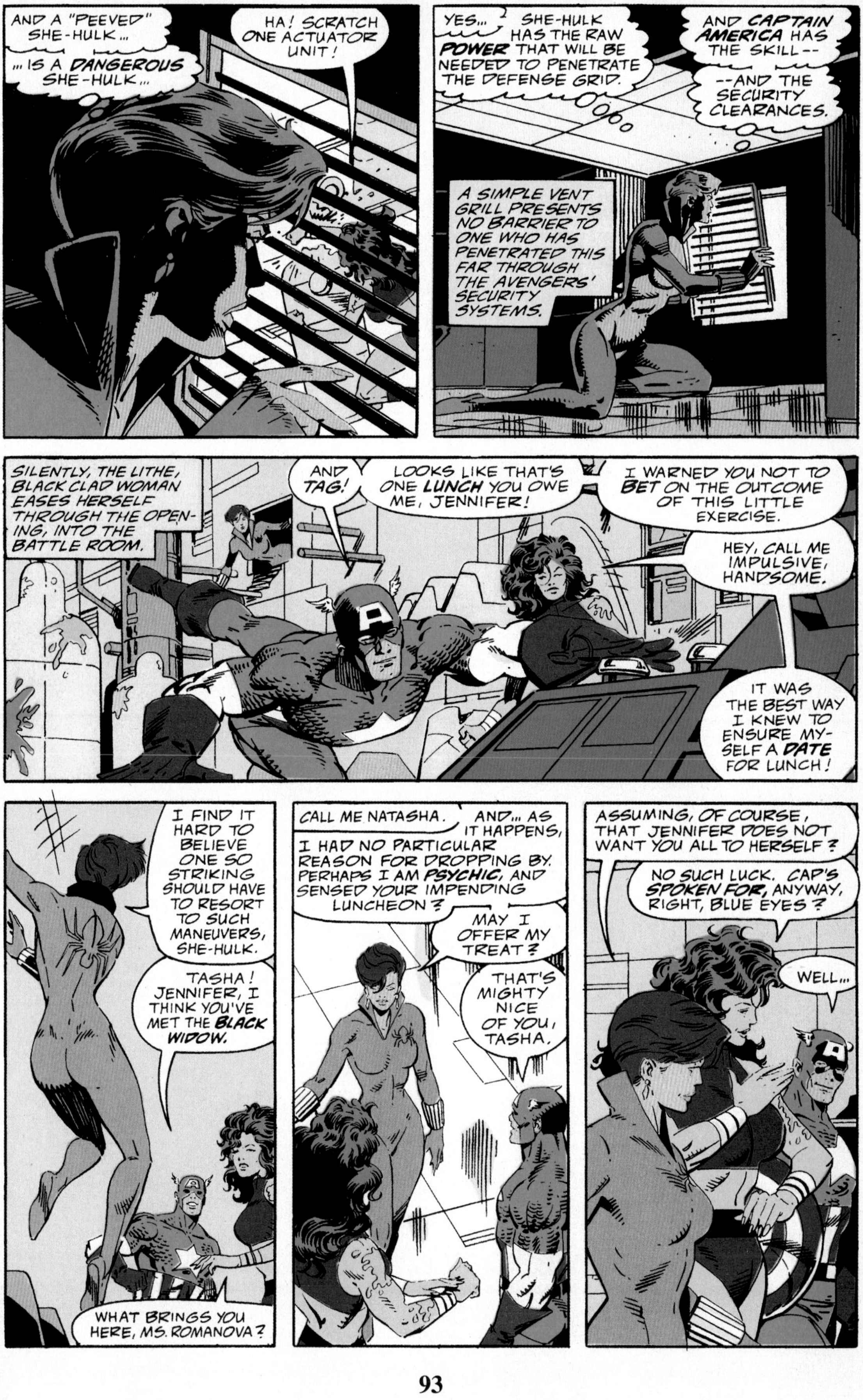
AND A "PEEVED" SHE-HULK...
...IS A DANGEROUS SHE-HULK...
HA! SCRATCH ONE ACTUATOR UNIT!
YES... SHE-HULK HAS THE RAW POWER THAT WILL BE NEEDED TO PENETRATE THE DEFENSE GRID.
AND CAPTAIN AMERICA HAS THE SKILL--
--AND THE SECURITY CLEARANCES.
A SIMPLE VENT GRILL PRESENTS NO BARRIER TO ONE WHO HAS PENETRATED THIS FAR THROUGH THE AVENGERS' SECURITY SYSTEMS.
SILENTLY, THE LITHE, BLACK CLAD WOMAN EASES HERSELF THROUGH THE OPENING, INTO THE BATTLE ROOM.
AND TAG!
LOOKS LIKE THAT'S ONE LUNCH YOU OWE ME, JENNIFER!
I WARNED YOU NOT TO BET ON THE OUTCOME OF THIS LITTLE EXERCISE.
HEY, CALL ME IMPULSIVE, HANDSOME.
IT WAS THE BEST WAY I KNEW TO ENSURE MYSELF A DATE FOR LUNCH!
I FIND IT HARD TO BELIEVE ONE SO STRIKING SHOULD HAVE TO RESORT TO SUCH MANEUVERS, SHE-HULK.
TASHA! JENNIFER, I THINK YOU'VE MET THE BLACK WIDOW.
WHAT BRINGS YOU HERE, MS. ROMANOVA?
CALL ME NATASHA.
AND... AS IT HAPPENS, I HAD NO PARTICULAR REASON FOR DROPPING BY. PERHAPS I AM PSYCHIC, AND SENSED YOUR IMPENDING LUNCHEON?
MAY I OFFER MY TREAT?
THAT'S MIGHTY NICE OF YOU, TASHA.
ASSUMING, OF COURSE, THAT JENNIFER DOES NOT WANT YOU ALL TO HERSELF?
NO SUCH LUCK. CAP'S SPOKEN FOR, ANYWAY, RIGHT, BLUE EYES?
WELL...

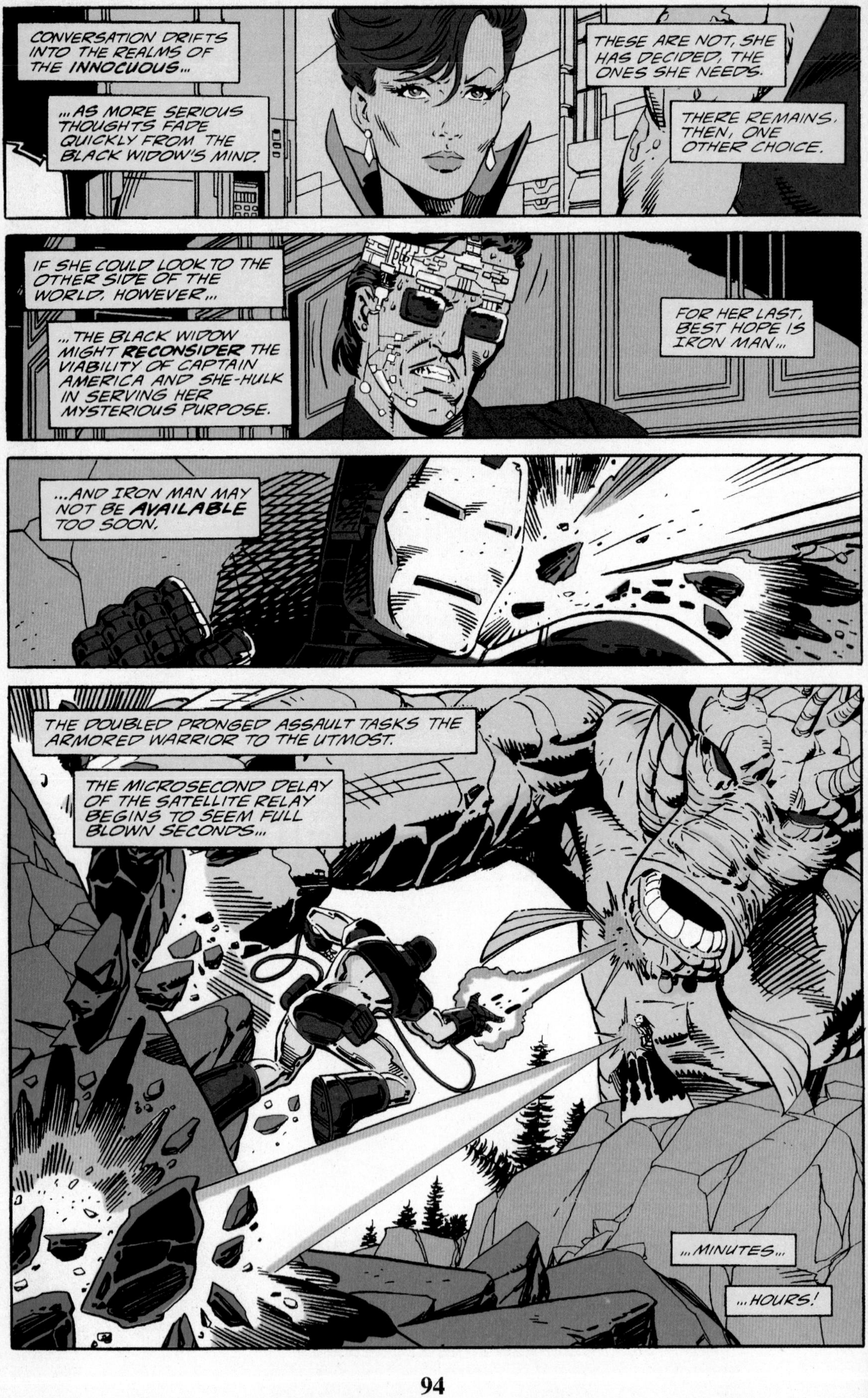
CONVERSATION DRIFTS INTO THE REALMS OF THE INNOCUOUS...
...AS MORE SERIOUS THOUGHTS FADE QUICKLY FROM THE BLACK WIDOW'S MIND.
THESE ARE NOT, SHE HAS DECIDED, THE ONES SHE NEEDS.
THERE REMAINS, THEN, ONE OTHER CHOICE.
IF SHE COULD LOOK TO THE OTHER SIDE OF THE WORLD, HOWEVER...
...THE BLACK WIDOW MIGHT RECONSIDER THE VIABILITY OF CAPTAIN AMERICA AND SHE-HULK IN SERVING HER MYSTERIOUS PURPOSE.
FOR HER LAST, BEST HOPE IS IRON MAN...
...AND IRON MAN MAY NOT BE AVAILABLE TOO SOON.
THE DOUBLED PRONGED ASSAULT TASKS THE ARMORED WARRIOR TO THE UTMOST.
THE MICROSECOND DELAY OF THE SATELLITE RELAY BEGINS TO SEEM FULL BLOWN SECONDS...
...MINUTES...
...HOURS!

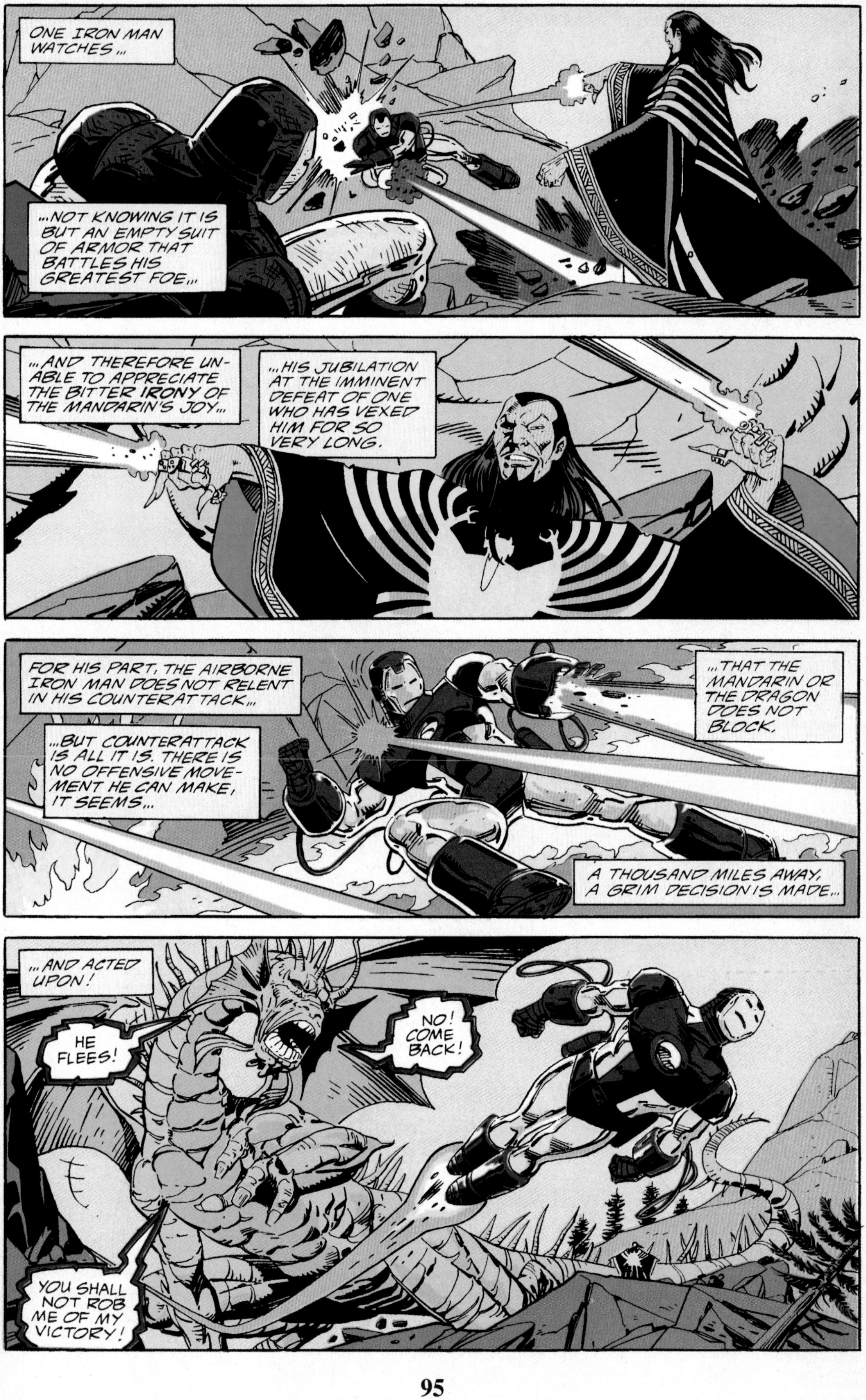
ONE IRON MAN WATCHES...
...NOT KNOWING IT IS BUT AN EMPTY SUIT OF ARMOR THAT BATTLES HIS GREATEST FOE...
...AND THEREFORE UNABLE TO APPRECIATE THE BITTER IRONY OF THE MANDARIN'S JOY...
...HIS JUBILATION AT THE IMMINENT DEFEAT OF ONE WHO HAS VEXED HIM FOR SO VERY LONG.
FOR HIS PART, THE AIRBORNE IRON MAN DOES NOT RELENT IN HIS COUNTERATTACK...
...BUT COUNTERATTACK IS ALL IT IS. THERE IS NO OFFENSIVE MOVEMENT HE CAN MAKE, IT SEEMS...
...THAT THE MANDARIN OR THE DRAGON DOES NOT BLOCK.
A THOUSAND MILES AWAY, A GRIM DECISION IS MADE...
...AND ACTED UPON!
HE FLEES!
NO! COME BACK!
YOU SHALL NOT ROB ME OF MY VICTORY!

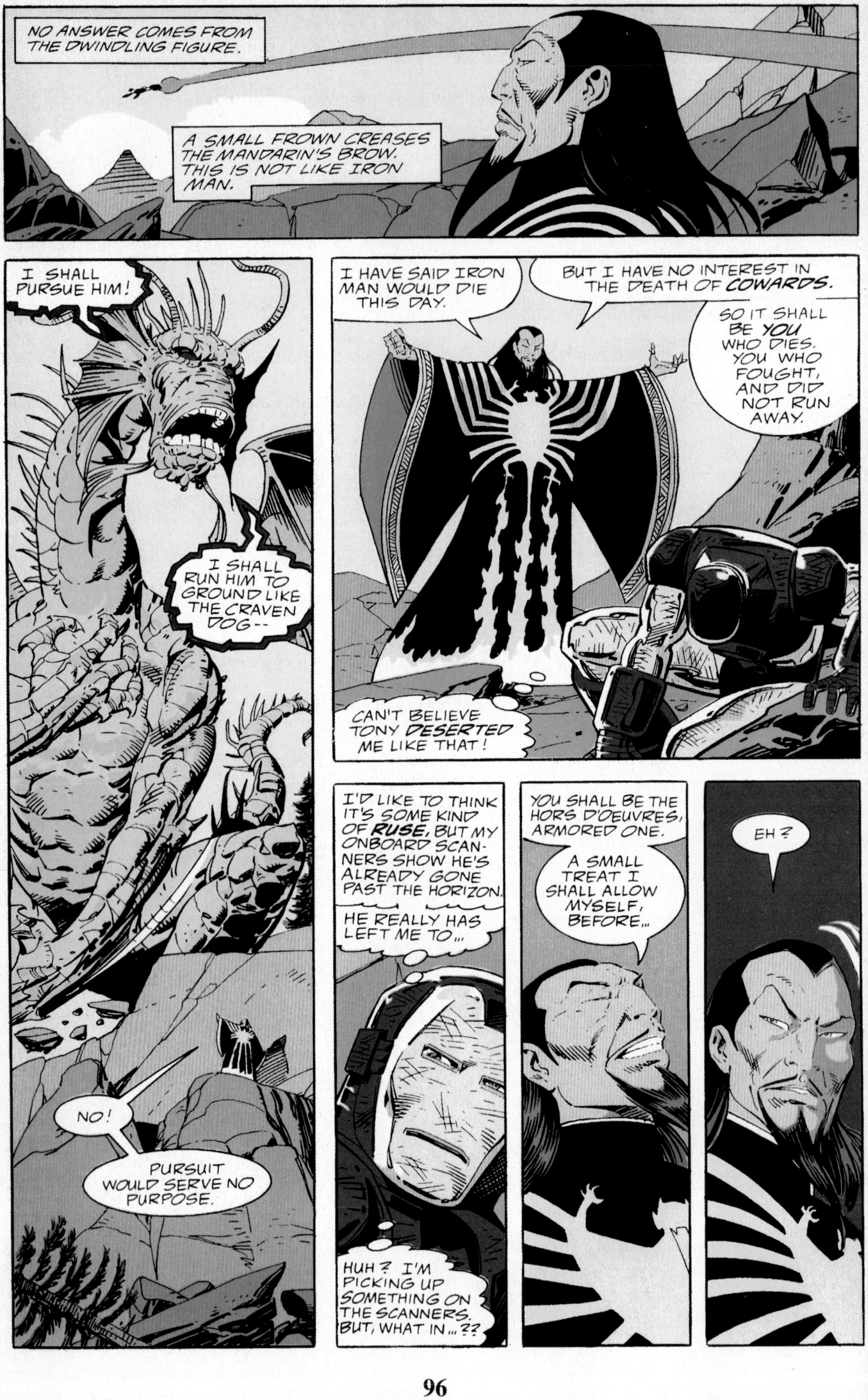
NO ANSWER COMES FROM THE DWINDLING FIGURE.
A SMALL FROWN CREASES THE MANDARIN'S BROW. THIS IS NOT LIKE IRON MAN.
I SHALL PURSUE HIM!
I SHALL RUN HIM TO GROUND LIKE THE CRAVEN DOG--
NO!
PURSUIT WOULD SERVE NO PURPOSE.
I HAVE SAID IRON MAN WOULD DIE THIS DAY.
BUT I HAVE NO INTEREST IN THE DEATH OF COWARDS.
SO IT SHALL BE YOU WHO DIES. YOU WHO FOUGHT, AND DID NOT RUN AWAY.
CAN'T BELIEVE TONY DESERTED ME LIKE THAT!
I'D LIKE TO THINK IT'S SOME KIND OF RUSE, BUT MY ONBOARD SCANNERS SHOW HE'S ALREADY GONE PAST THE HORIZON.
HE REALLY HAS LEFT ME TO...
HUH? I'M PICKING UP SOMETHING ON THE SCANNERS. BUT, WHAT IN...??
YOU SHALL BE THE HORS D'OEUVRES, ARMORED ONE.
A SMALL TREAT I SHALL ALLOW MYSELF, BEFORE...
EH?

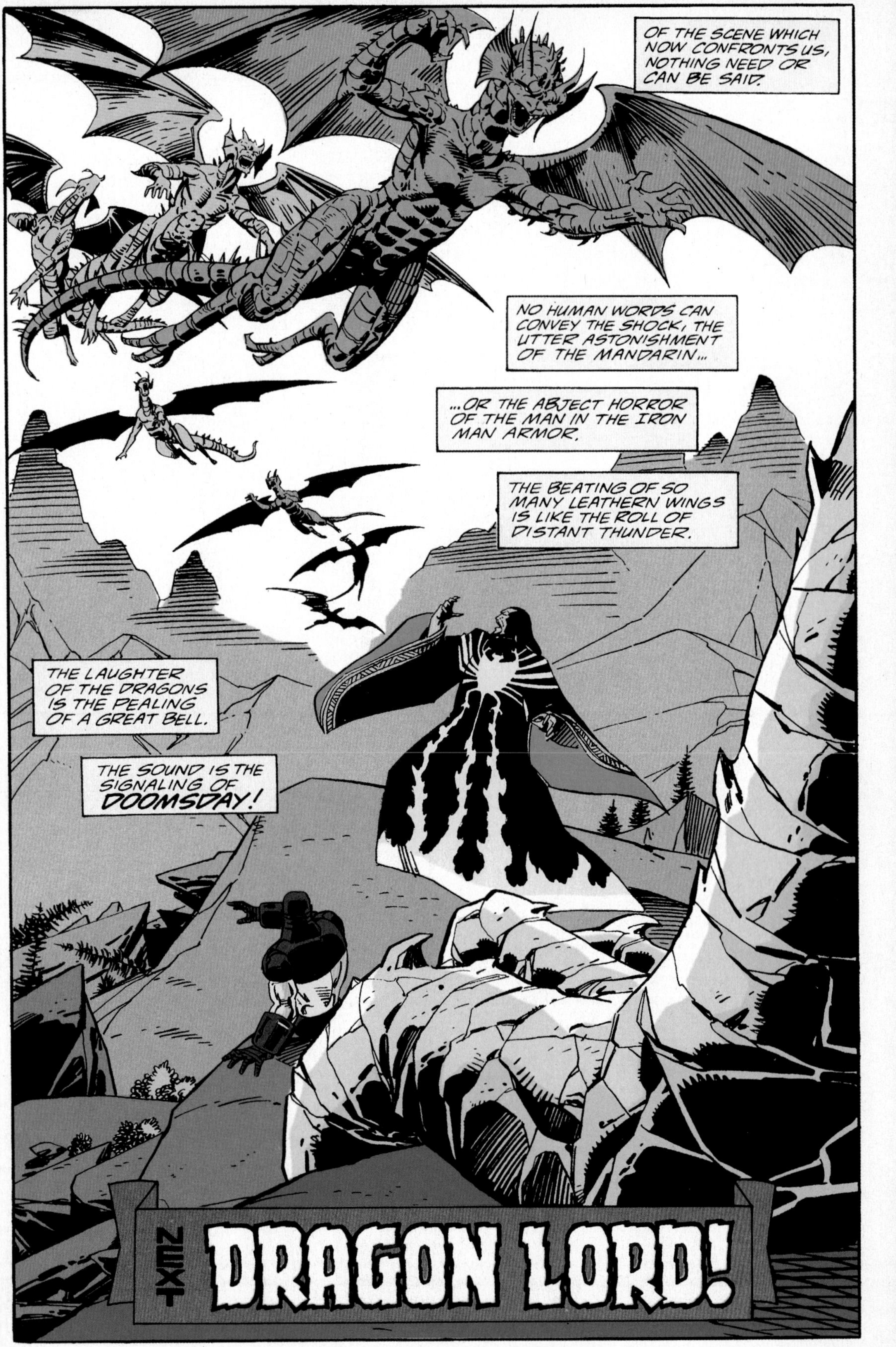

OF THE SCENE WHICH NOW CONFRONTS US, NOTHING NEED OR CAN BE SAID.
NO HUMAN WORDS CAN CONVEY THE SHOCK, THE UTTER ASTONISHMENT OF THE MANDARIN...
...OR THE ABJECT HORROR OF THE MAN IN THE IRON MAN ARMOR.
THE BEATING OF SO MANY LEATHERN WINGS IS LIKE THE ROLL OF DISTANT THUNDER.
THE LAUGHTER OF THE DRAGONS IS THE PEALING OF A GREAT BELL.
THE SOUND IS THE SIGNALING OF DOOMSDAY!
NEXT DRAGON LORD!

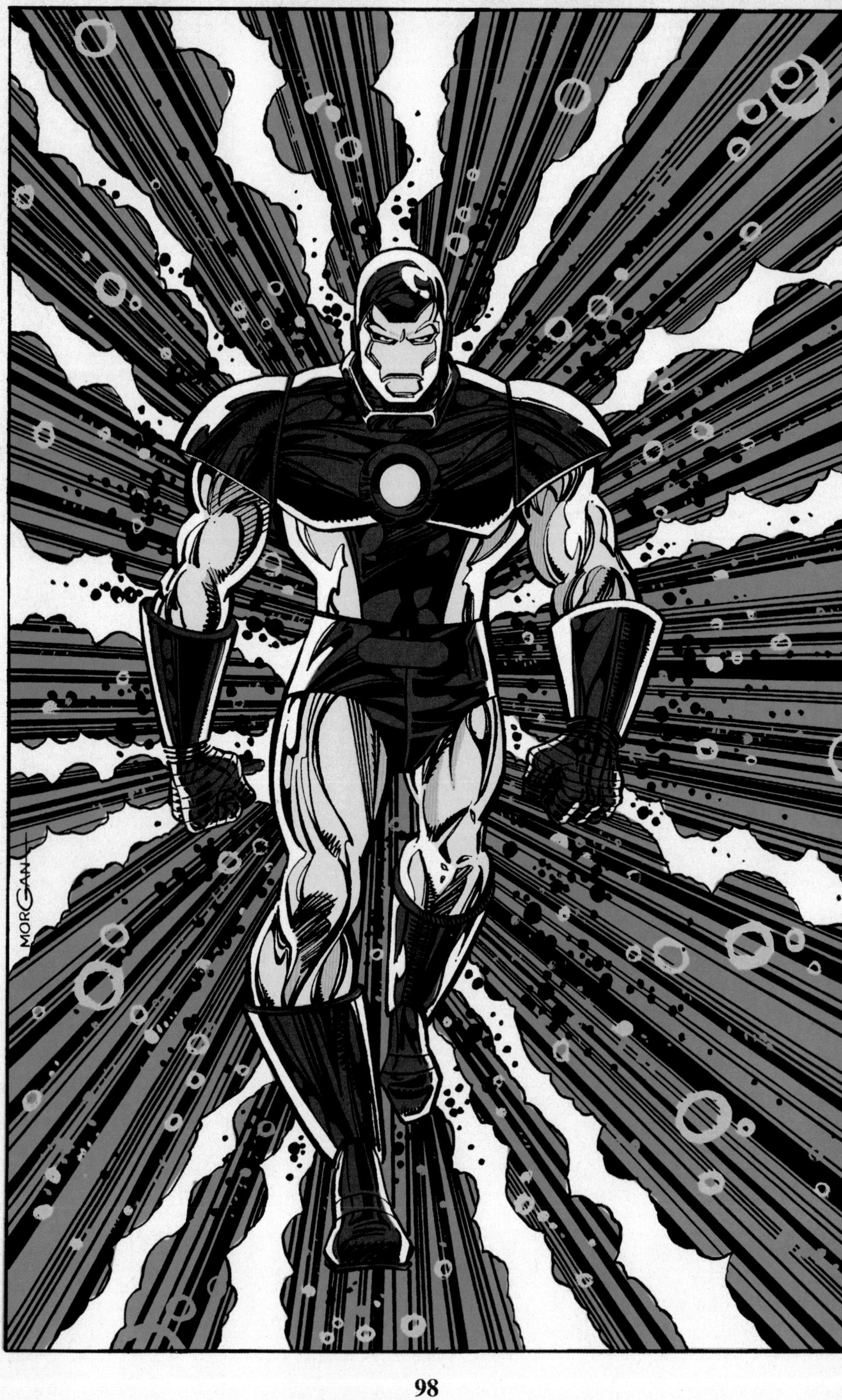
MORGAN

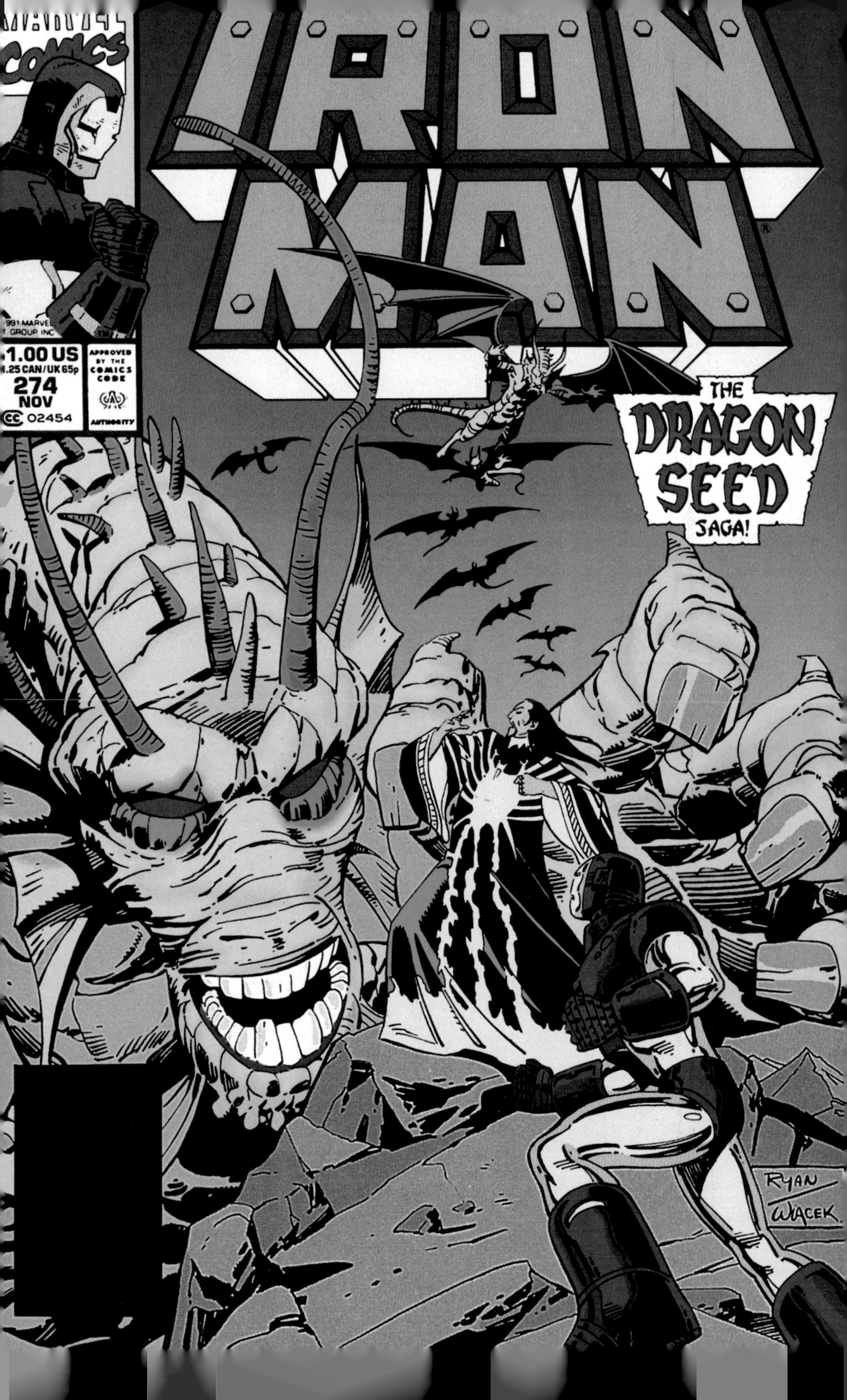
IRON MAN
274
NOV
APPROVED BY THE COMICS CODE AUTHORITY
THE DRAGON SEED SAGA!
RYAN
WIACEK

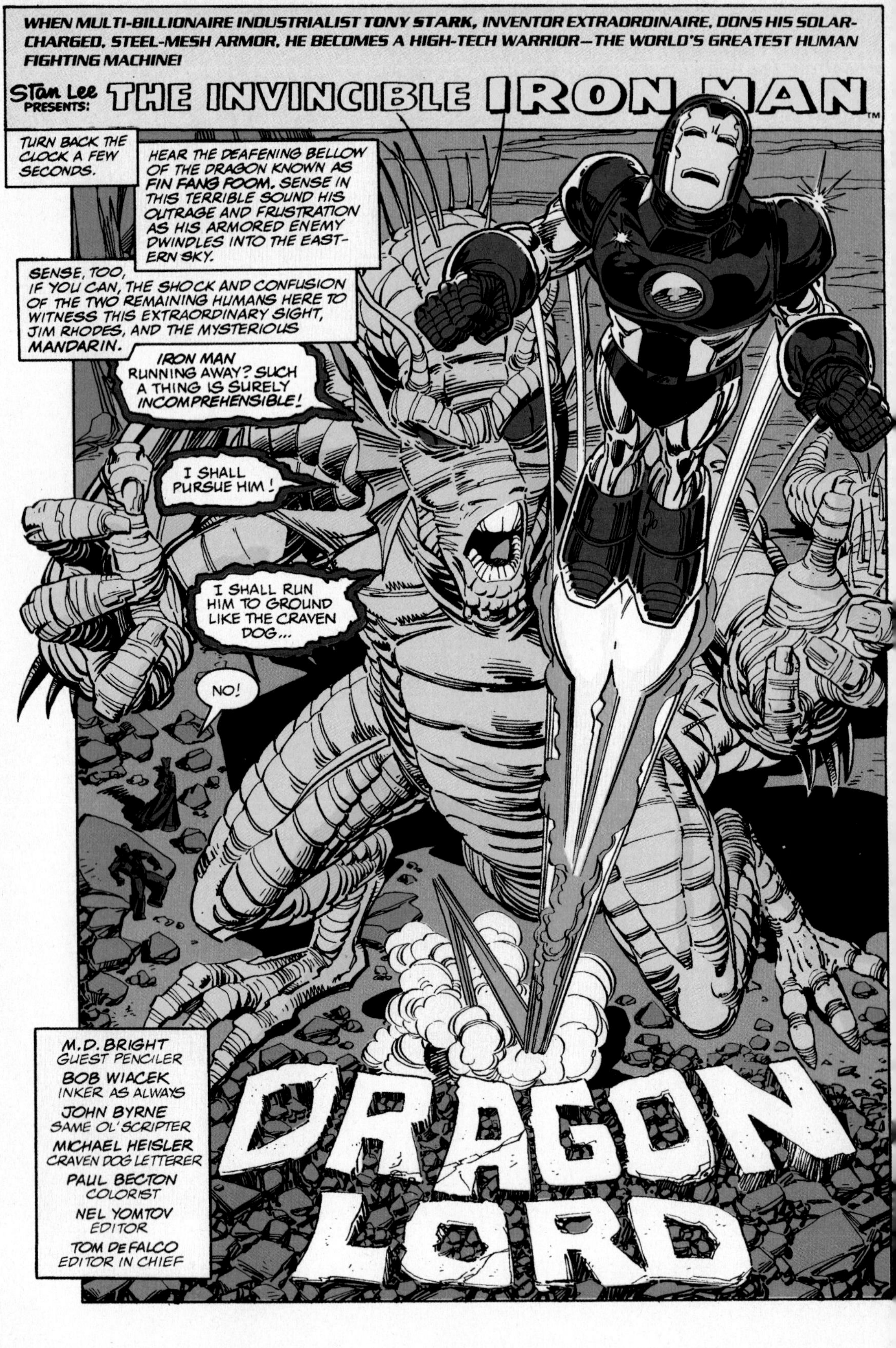
WHEN MULTI-BILLIONAIRE INDUSTRIALIST TONY STARK, INVENTOR EXTRAORDINAIRE, DONS HIS SOLAR-CHARGED, STEEL-MESH ARMOR, HE BECOMES A HIGH-TECH WARRIOR—THE WORLD'S GREATEST HUMAN FIGHTING MACHINE!
Stan Lee PRESENTS: THE INVINCIBLE IRON MAN™
TURN BACK THE CLOCK A FEW SECONDS.
HEAR THE DEAFENING BELLOW OF THE DRAGON KNOWN AS FIN FANG FOOM. SENSE IN THIS TERRIBLE SOUND HIS OUTRAGE AND FRUSTRATION AS HIS ARMORED ENEMY DWINDLES INTO THE EASTERN SKY.
SENSE, TOO, IF YOU CAN, THE SHOCK AND CONFUSION OF THE TWO REMAINING HUMANS HERE TO WITNESS THIS EXTRAORDINARY SIGHT, JIM RHODES, AND THE MYSTERIOUS MANDARIN.
IRON MAN RUNNING AWAY? SUCH A THING IS SURELY INCOMPREHENSIBLE!
I SHALL PURSUE HIM!
I SHALL RUN HIM TO GROUND LIKE THE CRAVEN DOG...
NO!
M.D. BRIGHT GUEST PENCILER
BOB WIACEK INKER AS ALWAYS
JOHN BYRNE SAME OL' SCRIPTER
MICHAEL HEISLER CRAVEN DOG LETTERER
PAUL BECTON COLORIST
NEL YOMTOV EDITOR
TOM DEFALCO EDITOR IN CHIEF
DRAGON LORD

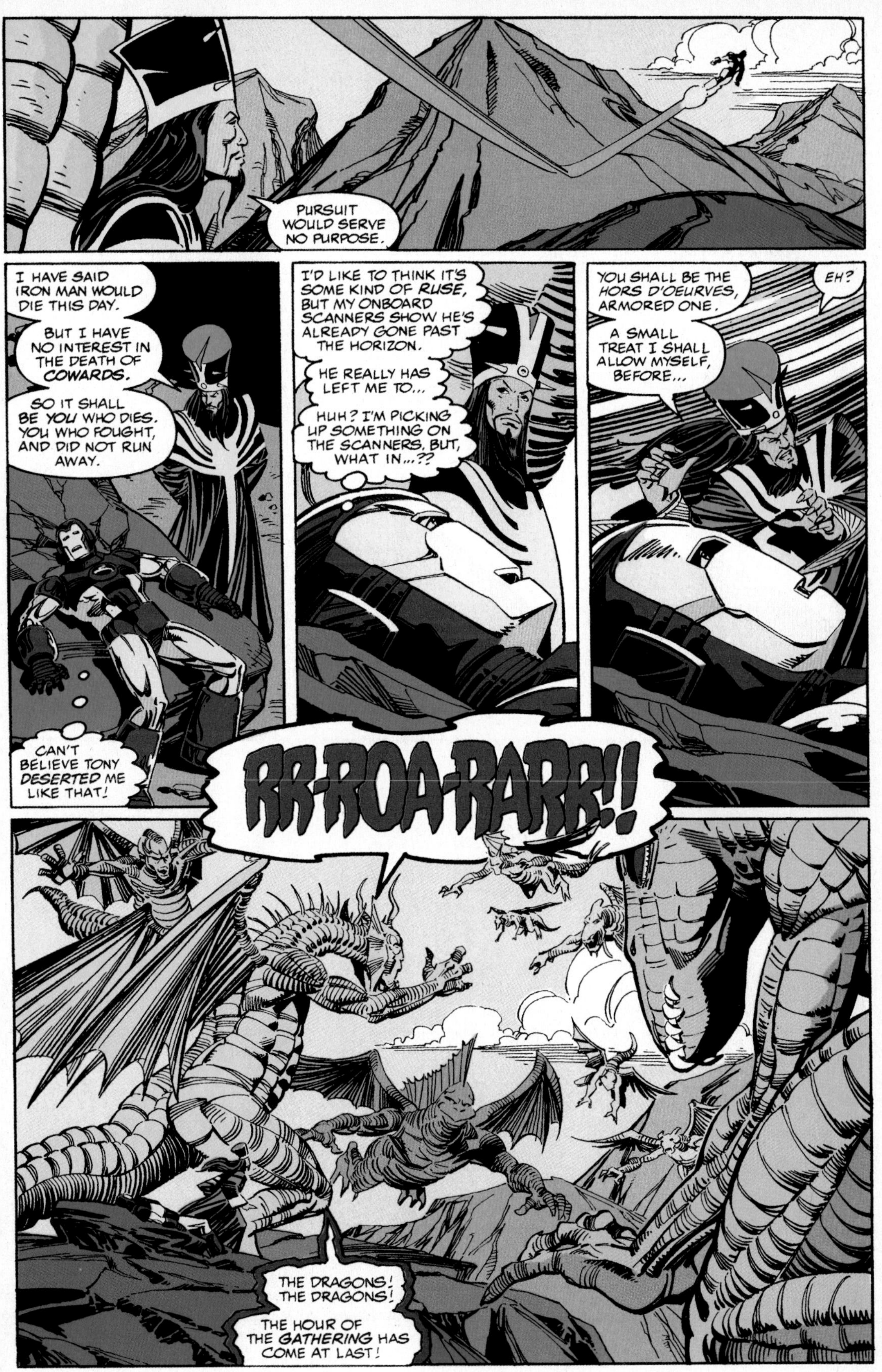
PURSUIT WOULD SERVE NO PURPOSE.
I HAVE SAID IRON MAN WOULD DIE THIS DAY.
BUT I HAVE NO INTEREST IN THE DEATH OF COWARDS.
SO IT SHALL BE YOU WHO DIES. YOU WHO FOUGHT, AND DID NOT RUN AWAY.
CAN'T BELIEVE TONY DESERTED ME LIKE THAT!
I'D LIKE TO THINK IT'S SOME KIND OF RUSE, BUT MY ONBOARD SCANNERS SHOW HE'S ALREADY GONE PAST THE HORIZON.
HE REALLY HAS LEFT ME TO...
HUH? I'M PICKING UP SOMETHING ON THE SCANNERS, BUT, WHAT IN...??
YOU SHALL BE THE HORS D'OEURVES, ARMORED ONE.
EH?
A SMALL TREAT I SHALL ALLOW MYSELF, BEFORE...
RR-ROA-RARR!!
THE DRAGONS! THE DRAGONS!
THE HOUR OF THE GATHERING HAS COME AT LAST!

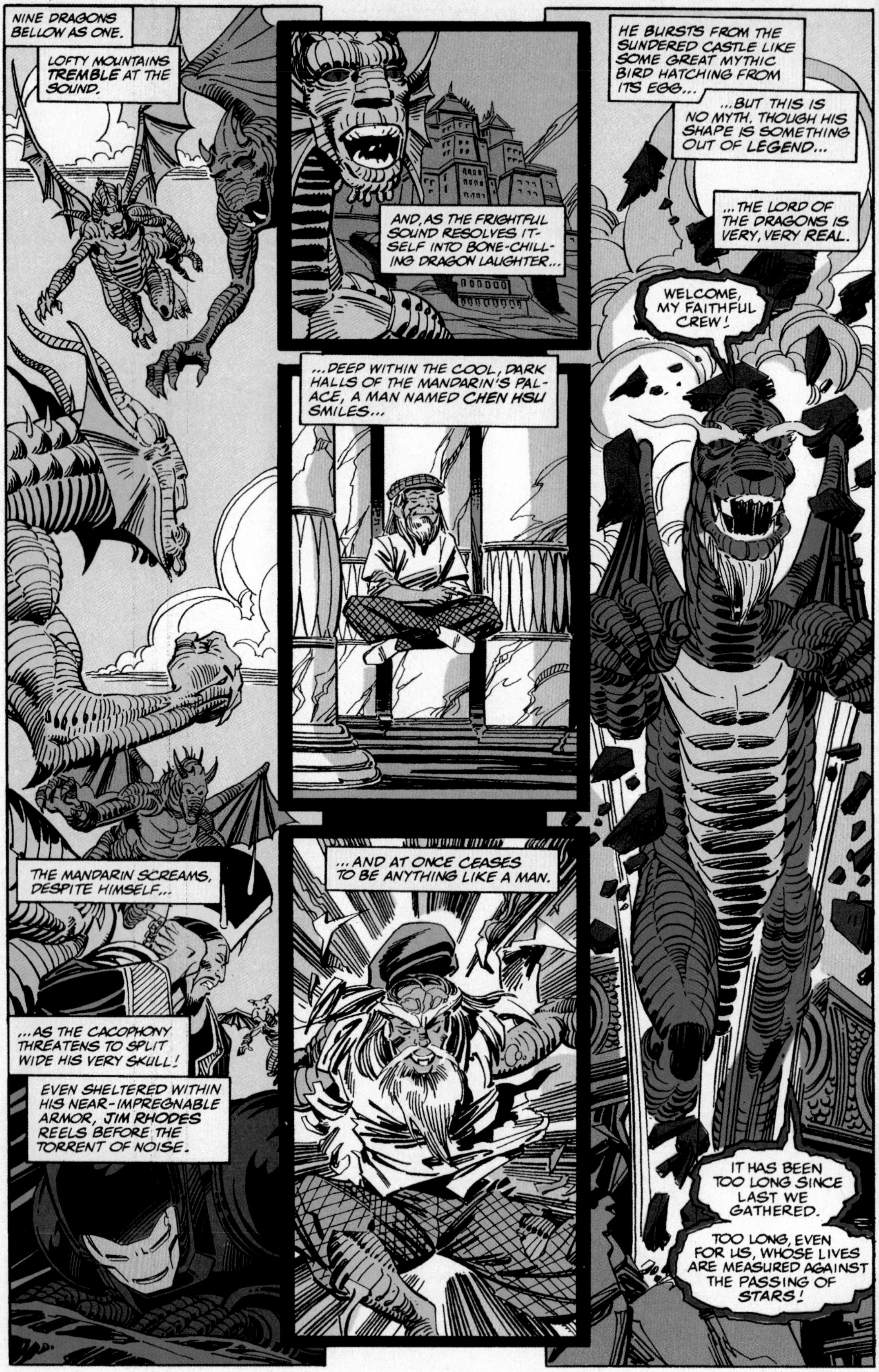
NINE DRAGONS BELLOW AS ONE.
LOFTY MOUNTAINS TREMBLE AT THE SOUND.
THE MANDARIN SCREAMS, DESPITE HIMSELF...
...AS THE CACOPHONY THREATENS TO SPLIT WIDE HIS VERY SKULL!
EVEN SHELTERED WITHIN HIS NEAR-IMPREGNABLE ARMOR, JIM RHODES REELS BEFORE THE TORRENT OF NOISE.
AND, AS THE FRIGHTFUL SOUND RESOLVES ITSELF INTO BONE-CHILLING DRAGON LAUGHTER...
...DEEP WITHIN THE COOL, DARK HALLS OF THE MANDARIN'S PALACE, A MAN NAMED CHEN HSU SMILES...
...AND AT ONCE CEASES TO BE ANYTHING LIKE A MAN.
HE BURSTS FROM THE SUNDERED CASTLE LIKE SOME GREAT MYTHIC BIRD HATCHING FROM ITS EGG...
...BUT THIS IS NO MYTH. THOUGH HIS SHAPE IS SOMETHING OUT OF LEGEND...
...THE LORD OF THE DRAGONS IS VERY, VERY REAL.
WELCOME, MY FAITHFUL CREW!
IT HAS BEEN TOO LONG SINCE LAST WE GATHERED.
TOO LONG, EVEN FOR US, WHOSE LIVES ARE MEASURED AGAINST THE PASSING OF STARS!

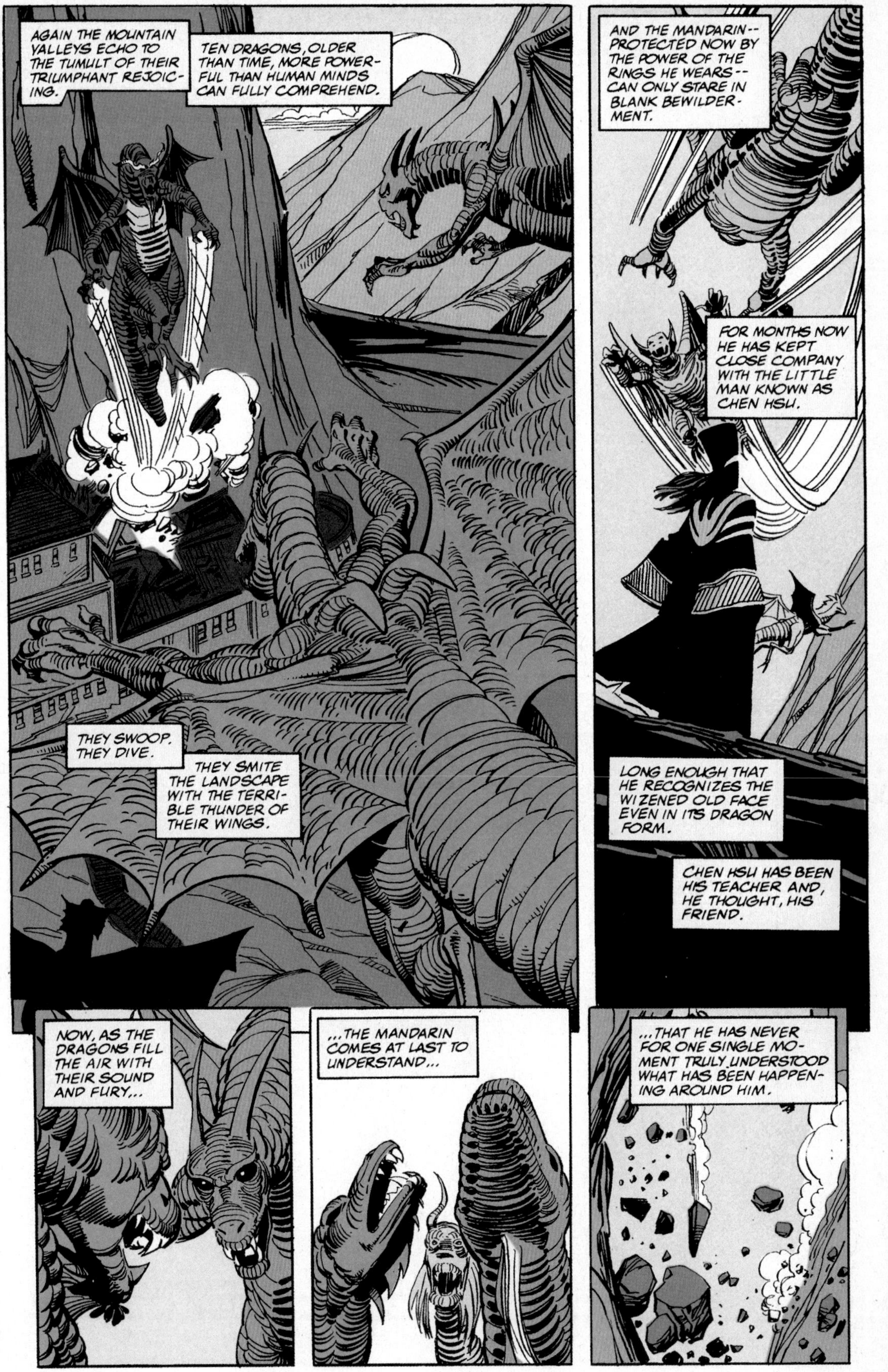
AGAIN THE MOUNTAIN VALLEYS ECHO TO THE TUMULT OF THEIR TRIUMPHANT REJOICING.
TEN DRAGONS, OLDER THAN TIME, MORE POWERFUL THAN HUMAN MINDS CAN FULLY COMPREHEND.
THEY SWOOP. THEY DIVE.
THEY SMITE THE LANDSCAPE WITH THE TERRIBLE THUNDER OF THEIR WINGS.
AND THE MANDARIN-- PROTECTED NOW BY THE POWER OF THE RINGS HE WEARS-- CAN ONLY STARE IN BLANK BEWILDERMENT.
FOR MONTHS NOW HE HAS KEPT CLOSE COMPANY WITH THE LITTLE MAN KNOWN AS CHEN HSU.
LONG ENOUGH THAT HE RECOGNIZES THE WIZENED OLD FACE EVEN IN ITS DRAGON FORM.
CHEN HSU HAS BEEN HIS TEACHER AND, HE THOUGHT, HIS FRIEND.
NOW, AS THE DRAGONS FILL THE AIR WITH THEIR SOUND AND FURY,..
...THE MANDARIN COMES AT LAST TO UNDERSTAND...
...THAT HE HAS NEVER FOR ONE SINGLE MOMENT TRULY UNDERSTOOD WHAT HAS BEEN HAPPENING AROUND HIM.

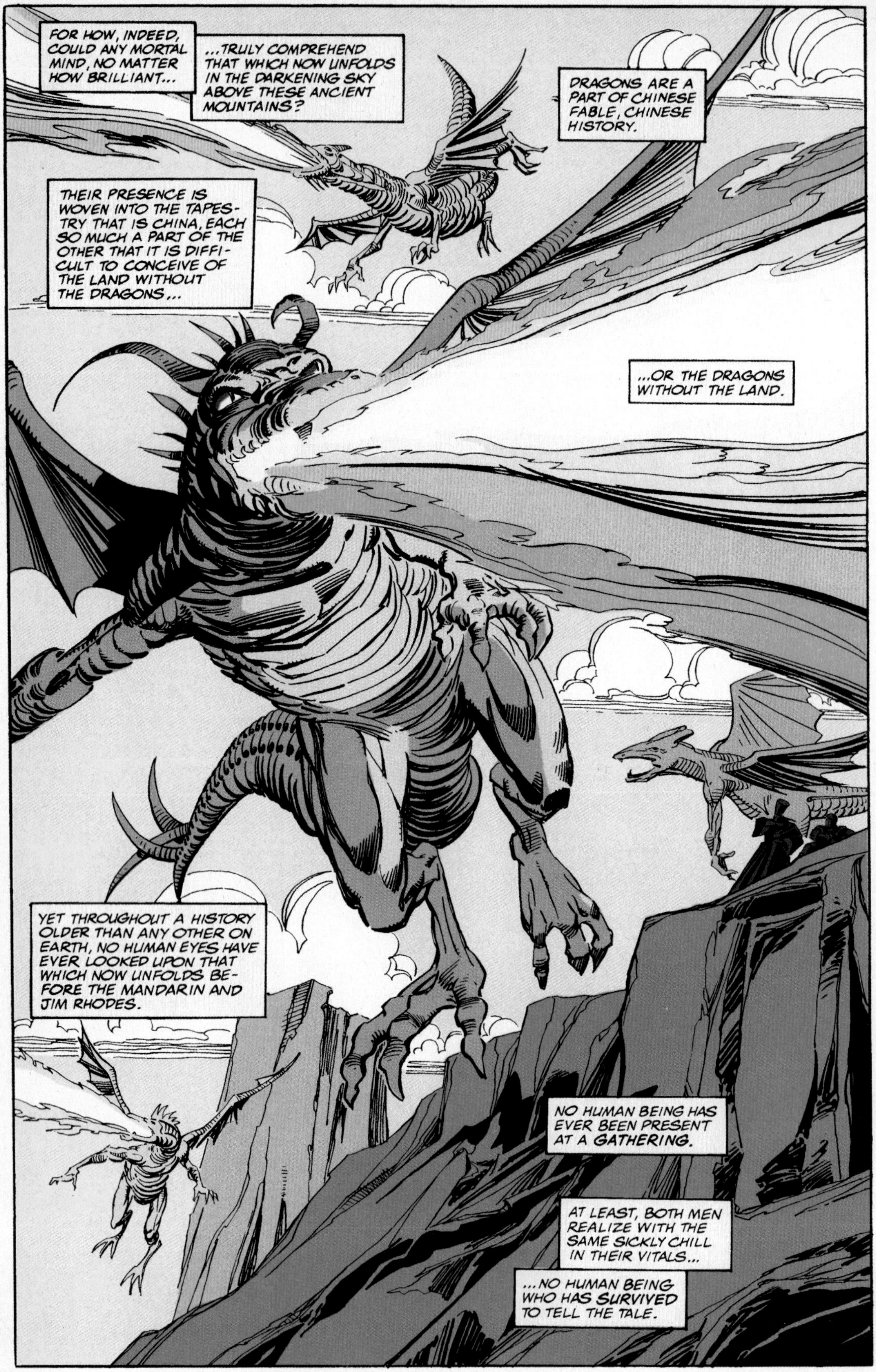
FOR HOW, INDEED, COULD ANY MORTAL MIND, NO MATTER HOW BRILLIANT...
...TRULY COMPREHEND THAT WHICH NOW UNFOLDS IN THE DARKENING SKY ABOVE THESE ANCIENT MOUNTAINS?
DRAGONS ARE A PART OF CHINESE FABLE, CHINESE HISTORY.
THEIR PRESENCE IS WOVEN INTO THE TAPESTRY THAT IS CHINA, EACH SO MUCH A PART OF THE OTHER THAT IT IS DIFFICULT TO CONCEIVE OF THE LAND WITHOUT THE DRAGONS...
...OR THE DRAGONS WITHOUT THE LAND.
YET THROUGHOUT A HISTORY OLDER THAN ANY OTHER ON EARTH, NO HUMAN EYES HAVE EVER LOOKED UPON THAT WHICH NOW UNFOLDS BEFORE THE MANDARIN AND JIM RHODES.
NO HUMAN BEING HAS EVER BEEN PRESENT AT A GATHERING.
AT LEAST, BOTH MEN REALIZE WITH THE SAME SICKLY CHILL IN THEIR VITALS...
...NO HUMAN BEING WHO HAS SURVIVED TO TELL THE TALE.

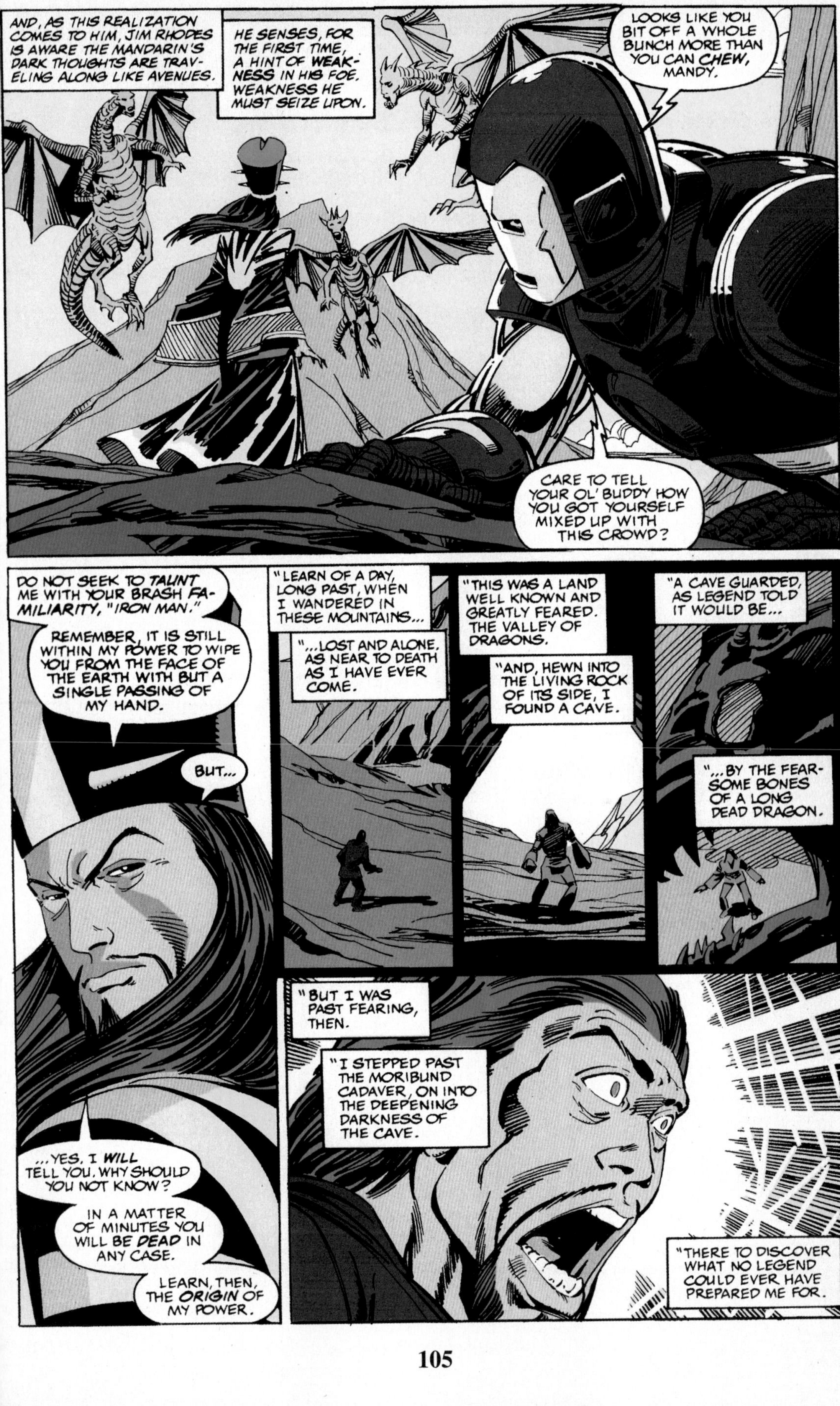
AND, AS THIS REALIZATION COMES TO HIM, JIM RHODES IS AWARE THE MANDARIN'S DARK THOUGHTS ARE TRAVELING ALONG LIKE AVENUES.
HE SENSES, FOR THE FIRST TIME, A HINT OF WEAKNESS IN HIS FOE. WEAKNESS HE MUST SEIZE UPON.
LOOKS LIKE YOU BIT OFF A WHOLE BUNCH MORE THAN YOU CAN CHEW, MANDY.
CARE TO TELL YOUR OL' BUDDY HOW YOU GOT YOURSELF MIXED UP WITH THIS CROWD?
DO NOT SEEK TO TAUNT ME WITH YOUR BRASH FAMILIARITY, "IRON MAN."
REMEMBER, IT IS STILL WITHIN MY POWER TO WIPE YOU FROM THE FACE OF THE EARTH WITH BUT A SINGLE PASSING OF MY HAND.
BUT...
...YES, I WILL TELL YOU. WHY SHOULD YOU NOT KNOW?
IN A MATTER OF MINUTES YOU WILL BE DEAD IN ANY CASE.
LEARN, THEN, THE ORIGIN OF MY POWER.
"LEARN OF A DAY, LONG PAST, WHEN I WANDERED IN THESE MOUNTAINS...
"...LOST AND ALONE, AS NEAR TO DEATH AS I HAVE EVER COME.
"THIS WAS A LAND WELL KNOWN AND GREATLY FEARED. THE VALLEY OF DRAGONS.
"AND, HEWN INTO THE LIVING ROCK OF ITS SIDE, I FOUND A CAVE.
"A CAVE GUARDED, AS LEGEND TOLD IT WOULD BE...
"...BY THE FEARSOME BONES OF A LONG DEAD DRAGON.
"BUT I WAS PAST FEARING, THEN.
"I STEPPED PAST THE MORIBUND CADAVER, ON INTO THE DEEPENING DARKNESS OF THE CAVE.
"THERE TO DISCOVER WHAT NO LEGEND COULD EVER HAVE PREPARED ME FOR.

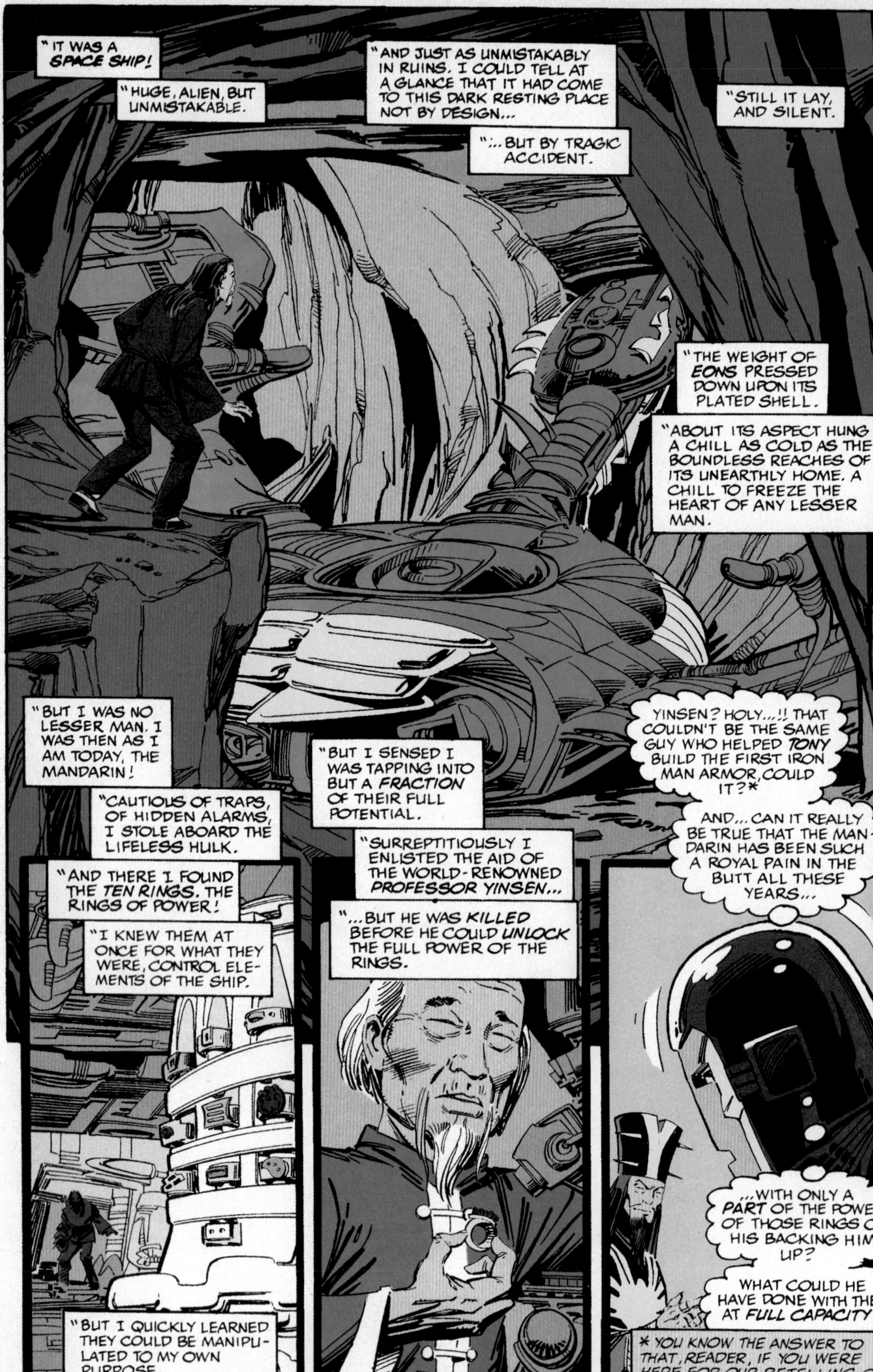
"IT WAS A SPACE SHIP!
"HUGE, ALIEN, BUT UNMISTAKABLE.
"AND JUST AS UNMISTAKABLY IN RUINS. I COULD TELL AT A GLANCE THAT IT HAD COME TO THIS DARK RESTING PLACE NOT BY DESIGN...
"...BUT BY TRAGIC ACCIDENT.
"STILL IT LAY, AND SILENT.
"THE WEIGHT OF EONS PRESSED DOWN UPON ITS PLATED SHELL.
"ABOUT ITS ASPECT HUNG A CHILL AS COLD AS THE BOUNDLESS REACHES OF ITS UNEARTHLY HOME. A CHILL TO FREEZE THE HEART OF ANY LESSER MAN.
"BUT I WAS NO LESSER MAN. I WAS THEN AS I AM TODAY, THE MANDARIN!
"CAUTIOUS OF TRAPS, OF HIDDEN ALARMS, I STOLE ABOARD THE LIFELESS HULK.
"AND THERE I FOUND THE TEN RINGS. THE RINGS OF POWER!
"I KNEW THEM AT ONCE FOR WHAT THEY WERE, CONTROL ELEMENTS OF THE SHIP.
"BUT I QUICKLY LEARNED THEY COULD BE MANIPULATED TO MY OWN PURPOSE.
"BUT I SENSED I WAS TAPPING INTO BUT A FRACTION OF THEIR FULL POTENTIAL.
"SURREPTITIOUSLY I ENLISTED THE AID OF THE WORLD-RENOWNED PROFESSOR YINSEN...
"...BUT HE WAS KILLED BEFORE HE COULD UNLOCK THE FULL POWER OF THE RINGS.
YINSEN? HOLY...!! THAT COULDN'T BE THE SAME GUY WHO HELPED TONY BUILD THE FIRST IRON MAN ARMOR, COULD IT?*
AND... CAN IT REALLY BE TRUE THAT THE MANDARIN HAS BEEN SUCH A ROYAL PAIN IN THE BUTT ALL THESE YEARS...
...WITH ONLY A PART OF THE POWER OF THOSE RINGS OF HIS BACKING HIM UP?
WHAT COULD HE HAVE DONE WITH THEM AT FULL CAPACITY?
* YOU KNOW THE ANSWER TO THAT, READER, IF YOU WERE HERE FOR OUR RETELLING OF IRON MAN'S ORIGIN IN ISSUE #'S 267-268. --NEL

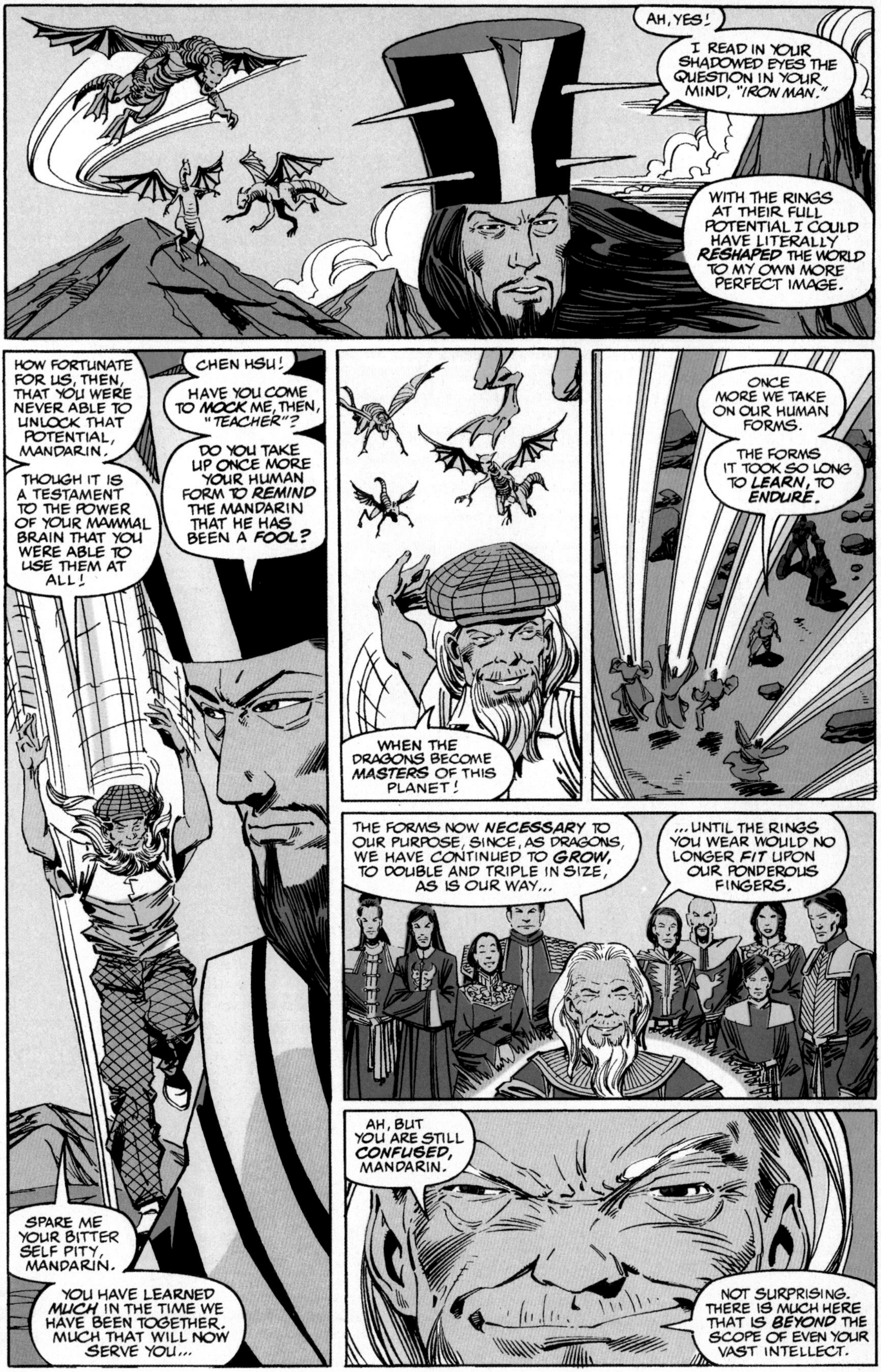
AH, YES!
I READ IN YOUR SHADOWED EYES THE QUESTION IN YOUR MIND, "IRON MAN."
WITH THE RINGS AT THEIR FULL POTENTIAL I COULD HAVE LITERALLY RESHAPED THE WORLD TO MY OWN MORE PERFECT IMAGE.
HOW FORTUNATE FOR US, THEN, THAT YOU WERE NEVER ABLE TO UNLOCK THAT POTENTIAL, MANDARIN.
THOUGH IT IS A TESTAMENT TO THE POWER OF YOUR MAMMAL BRAIN THAT YOU WERE ABLE TO USE THEM AT ALL!
CHEN HSU!
HAVE YOU COME TO MOCK ME, THEN, "TEACHER"?
DO YOU TAKE UP ONCE MORE YOUR HUMAN FORM TO REMIND THE MANDARIN THAT HE HAS BEEN A FOOL?
SPARE ME YOUR BITTER SELF PITY, MANDARIN.
YOU HAVE LEARNED MUCH IN THE TIME WE HAVE BEEN TOGETHER. MUCH THAT WILL NOW SERVE YOU...
WHEN THE DRAGONS BECOME MASTERS OF THIS PLANET!
ONCE MORE WE TAKE ON OUR HUMAN FORMS.
THE FORMS IT TOOK SO LONG TO LEARN, TO ENDURE.
THE FORMS NOW NECESSARY TO OUR PURPOSE, SINCE, AS DRAGONS, WE HAVE CONTINUED TO GROW, TO DOUBLE AND TRIPLE IN SIZE, AS IS OUR WAY...
...UNTIL THE RINGS YOU WEAR WOULD NO LONGER FIT UPON OUR PONDEROUS FINGERS.
AH, BUT YOU ARE STILL CONFUSED, MANDARIN.
NOT SURPRISING. THERE IS MUCH HERE THAT IS BEYOND THE SCOPE OF EVEN YOUR VAST INTELLECT.

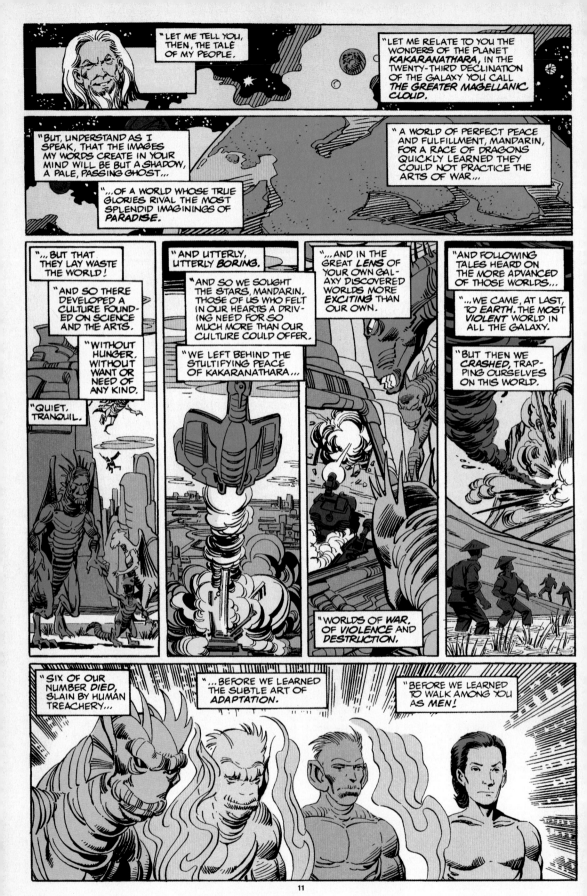

"LET ME TELL YOU, THEN, THE TALE OF MY PEOPLE.

"LET ME RELATE TO YOU THE WONDERS OF THE PLANET *KAKARANATHARA*, IN THE TWENTY-THIRD DECLINATION OF THE GALAXY YOU CALL *THE GREATER MAGELLANIC CLOUD.*

"BUT, UNDERSTAND AS I SPEAK, THAT THE IMAGES MY WORDS CREATE IN YOUR MIND WILL BE BUT A SHADOW, A PALE, PASSING GHOST...

"...OF A WORLD WHOSE TRUE GLORIES RIVAL THE MOST SPLENDID IMAGININGS OF *PARADISE.*

"A WORLD OF PERFECT PEACE AND FULFILLMENT, MANDARIN, FOR A RACE OF DRAGONS QUICKLY LEARNED THEY COULD NOT PRACTICE THE ARTS OF WAR...

"...BUT THAT THEY LAY WASTE THE WORLD!

"AND SO THERE DEVELOPED A CULTURE FOUNDED ON SCIENCE AND THE ARTS.

"WITHOUT HUNGER, WITHOUT WANT OR NEED OF ANY KIND.

"QUIET, TRANQUIL.

"AND UTTERLY, UTTERLY *BORING.*

"AND SO WE SOUGHT THE STARS, MANDARIN, THOSE OF US WHO FELT IN OUR HEARTS A DRIVING NEED FOR SO MUCH MORE THAN OUR CULTURE COULD OFFER.

"WE LEFT BEHIND THE STULTIFYING PEACE OF KAKARANATHARA...

"...AND IN THE GREAT *LENS* OF YOUR OWN GALAXY DISCOVERED WORLDS MORE *EXCITING* THAN OUR OWN.

"WORLDS OF WAR, OF *VIOLENCE* AND *DESTRUCTION.*

"AND FOLLOWING TALES HEARD ON THE MORE ADVANCED OF THOSE WORLDS...

"...WE CAME, AT LAST, TO *EARTH.* THE MOST *VIOLENT* WORLD IN ALL THE GALAXY.

"BUT THEN WE *CRASHED,* TRAPPING OURSELVES ON THIS WORLD.

"SIX OF OUR NUMBER *DIED,* SLAIN BY HUMAN TREACHERY...

"...BEFORE WE LEARNED THE SUBTLE ART OF ADAPTATION.

"BEFORE WE LEARNED TO WALK AMONG YOU AS MEN!

11

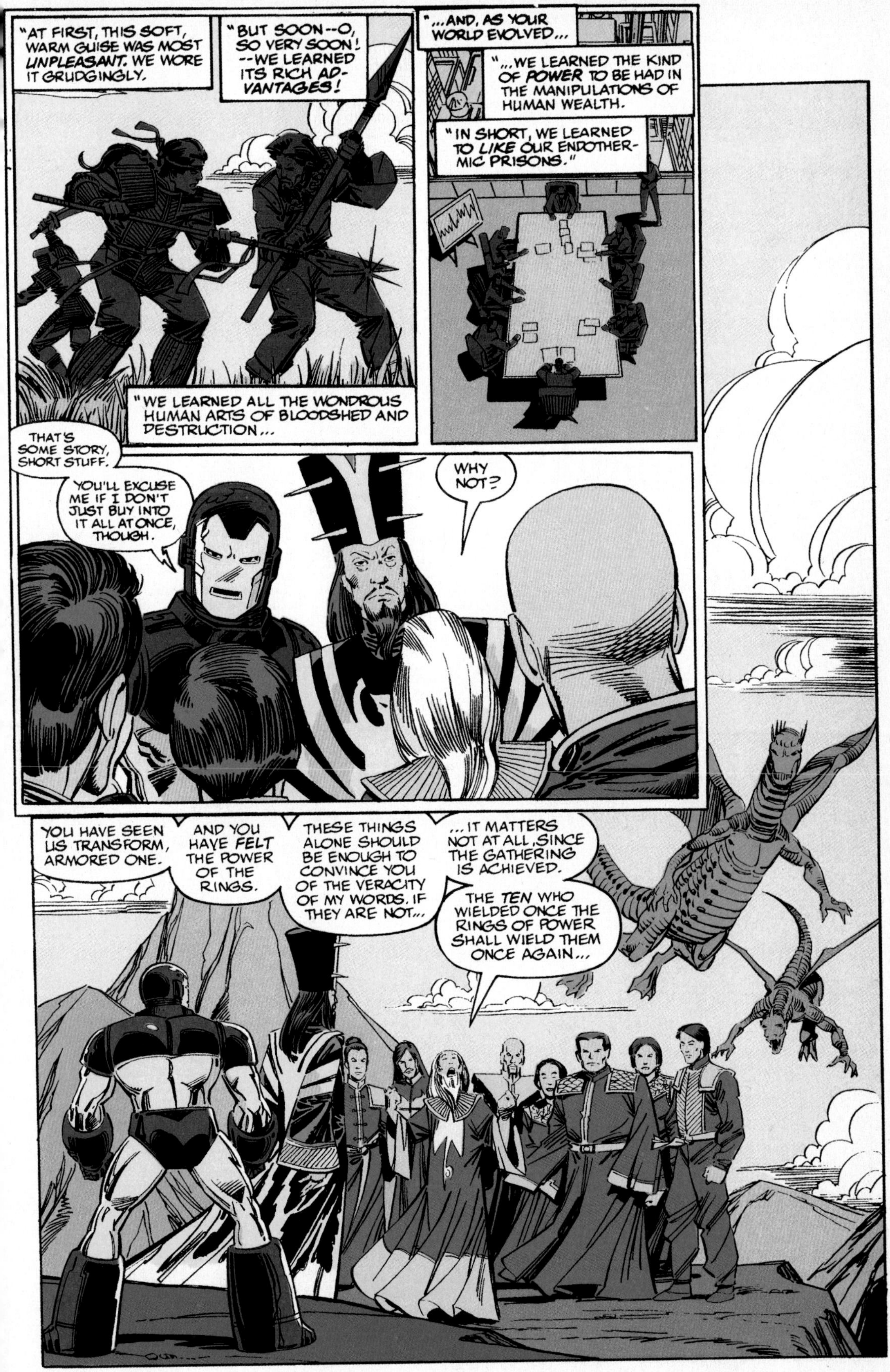
"AT FIRST, THIS SOFT, WARM GUISE WAS MOST UNPLEASANT. WE WORE IT GRUDGINGLY.
"BUT SOON--O, SO VERY SOON! --WE LEARNED ITS RICH ADVANTAGES!
"WE LEARNED ALL THE WONDROUS HUMAN ARTS OF BLOODSHED AND DESTRUCTION...
"...AND, AS YOUR WORLD EVOLVED...
"...WE LEARNED THE KIND OF POWER TO BE HAD IN THE MANIPULATIONS OF HUMAN WEALTH.
"IN SHORT, WE LEARNED TO LIKE OUR ENDOTHERMIC PRISONS."
THAT'S SOME STORY, SHORT STUFF.
YOU'LL EXCUSE ME IF I DON'T JUST BUY INTO IT ALL AT ONCE, THOUGH.
WHY NOT?
YOU HAVE SEEN US TRANSFORM, ARMORED ONE.
AND YOU HAVE FELT THE POWER OF THE RINGS.
THESE THINGS ALONE SHOULD BE ENOUGH TO CONVINCE YOU OF THE VERACITY OF MY WORDS. IF THEY ARE NOT...
...IT MATTERS NOT AT ALL, SINCE THE GATHERING IS ACHIEVED.
THE TEN WHO WIELDED ONCE THE RINGS OF POWER SHALL WIELD THEM ONCE AGAIN...

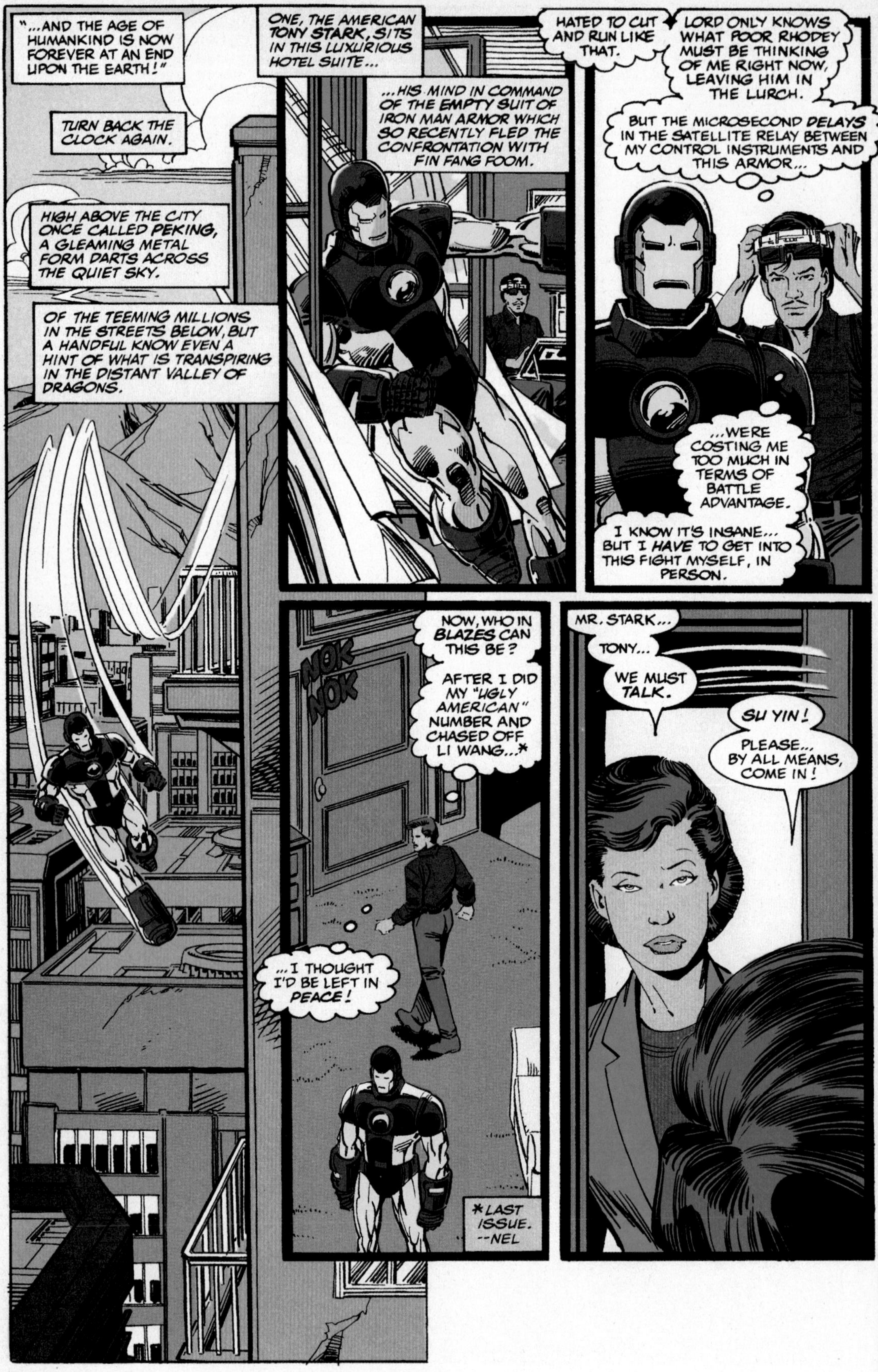
"...AND THE AGE OF HUMANKIND IS NOW FOREVER AT AN END UPON THE EARTH!"
TURN BACK THE CLOCK AGAIN.
HIGH ABOVE THE CITY ONCE CALLED PEKING, A GLEAMING METAL FORM DARTS ACROSS THE QUIET SKY.
OF THE TEEMING MILLIONS IN THE STREETS BELOW, BUT A HANDFUL KNOW EVEN A HINT OF WHAT IS TRANSPIRING IN THE DISTANT VALLEY OF DRAGONS.
ONE, THE AMERICAN TONY STARK, SITS IN THIS LUXURIOUS HOTEL SUITE...
...HIS MIND IN COMMAND OF THE EMPTY SUIT OF IRON MAN ARMOR WHICH SO RECENTLY FLED THE CONFRONTATION WITH FIN FANG FOOM.
HATED TO CUT AND RUN LIKE THAT.
LORD ONLY KNOWS WHAT POOR RHODEY MUST BE THINKING OF ME RIGHT NOW, LEAVING HIM IN THE LURCH.
BUT THE MICROSECOND DELAYS IN THE SATELLITE RELAY BETWEEN MY CONTROL INSTRUMENTS AND THIS ARMOR...
...WERE COSTING ME TOO MUCH IN TERMS OF BATTLE ADVANTAGE.
I KNOW IT'S INSANE... BUT I HAVE TO GET INTO THIS FIGHT MYSELF, IN PERSON.
NOK NOK
NOW, WHO IN BLAZES CAN THIS BE?
AFTER I DID MY "UGLY AMERICAN" NUMBER AND CHASED OFF LI WANG...*
...I THOUGHT I'D BE LEFT IN PEACE!
*LAST ISSUE. --NEL
MR. STARK...
TONY...
WE MUST TALK.
SU YIN!
PLEASE... BY ALL MEANS, COME IN!

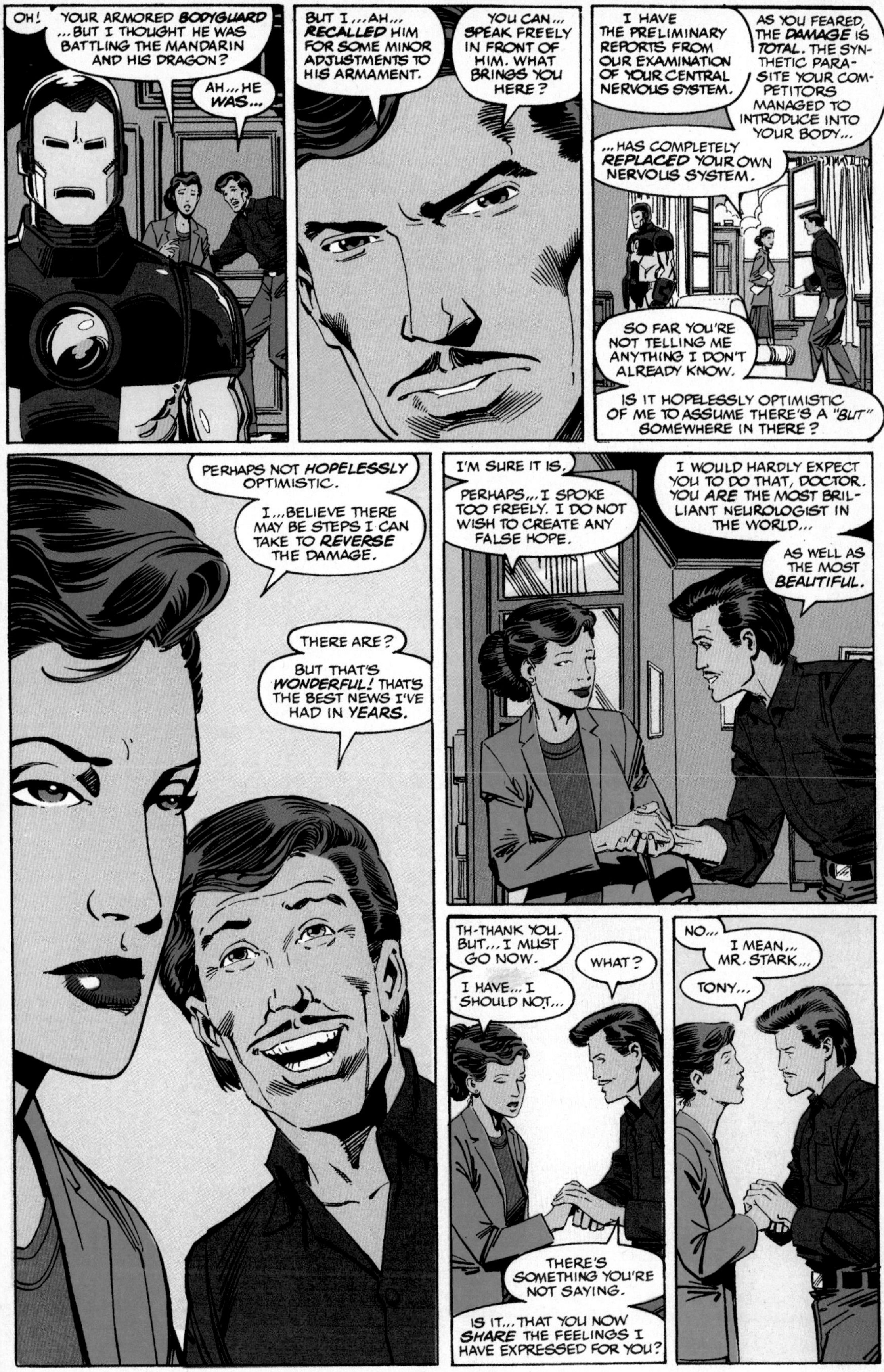
OH!
YOUR ARMORED BODYGUARD ...BUT I THOUGHT HE WAS BATTLING THE MANDARIN AND HIS DRAGON?
AH... HE WAS...
BUT I... AH... RECALLED HIM FOR SOME MINOR ADJUSTMENTS TO HIS ARMAMENT.
YOU CAN... SPEAK FREELY IN FRONT OF HIM. WHAT BRINGS YOU HERE?
I HAVE THE PRELIMINARY REPORTS FROM OUR EXAMINATION OF YOUR CENTRAL NERVOUS SYSTEM.
AS YOU FEARED, THE DAMAGE IS TOTAL. THE SYNTHETIC PARASITE YOUR COMPETITORS MANAGED TO INTRODUCE INTO YOUR BODY...
...HAS COMPLETELY REPLACED YOUR OWN NERVOUS SYSTEM.
SO FAR YOU'RE NOT TELLING ME ANYTHING I DON'T ALREADY KNOW.
IS IT HOPELESSLY OPTIMISTIC OF ME TO ASSUME THERE'S A "BUT" SOMEWHERE IN THERE?
PERHAPS NOT HOPELESSLY OPTIMISTIC.
I... BELIEVE THERE MAY BE STEPS I CAN TAKE TO REVERSE THE DAMAGE.
THERE ARE?
BUT THAT'S WONDERFUL! THAT'S THE BEST NEWS I'VE HAD IN YEARS.
I'M SURE IT IS.
PERHAPS... I SPOKE TOO FREELY. I DO NOT WISH TO CREATE ANY FALSE HOPE.
I WOULD HARDLY EXPECT YOU TO DO THAT, DOCTOR. YOU ARE THE MOST BRILLIANT NEUROLOGIST IN THE WORLD...
AS WELL AS THE MOST BEAUTIFUL.
TH-THANK YOU. BUT... I MUST GO NOW.
I HAVE... I SHOULD NOT...
WHAT?
THERE'S SOMETHING YOU'RE NOT SAYING.
IS IT... THAT YOU NOW SHARE THE FEELINGS I HAVE EXPRESSED FOR YOU?
NO...
I MEAN... MR. STARK...
TONY...

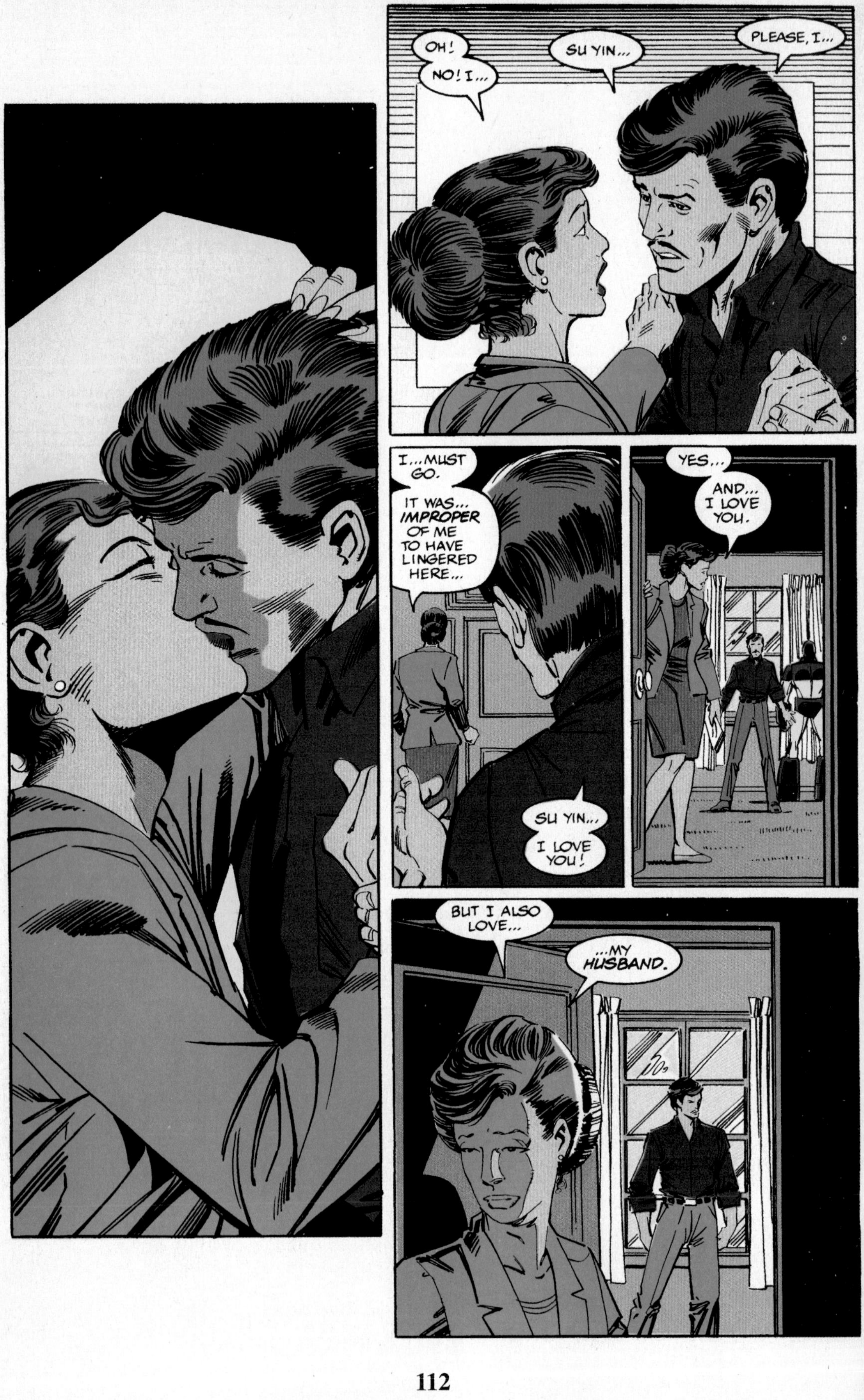
OH! NO! I...
SU YIN...
PLEASE, I...
I...MUST GO.
IT WAS... IMPROPER OF ME TO HAVE LINGERED HERE...
SU YIN... I LOVE YOU!
YES...
AND... I LOVE YOU.
BUT I ALSO LOVE...
...MY HUSBAND.

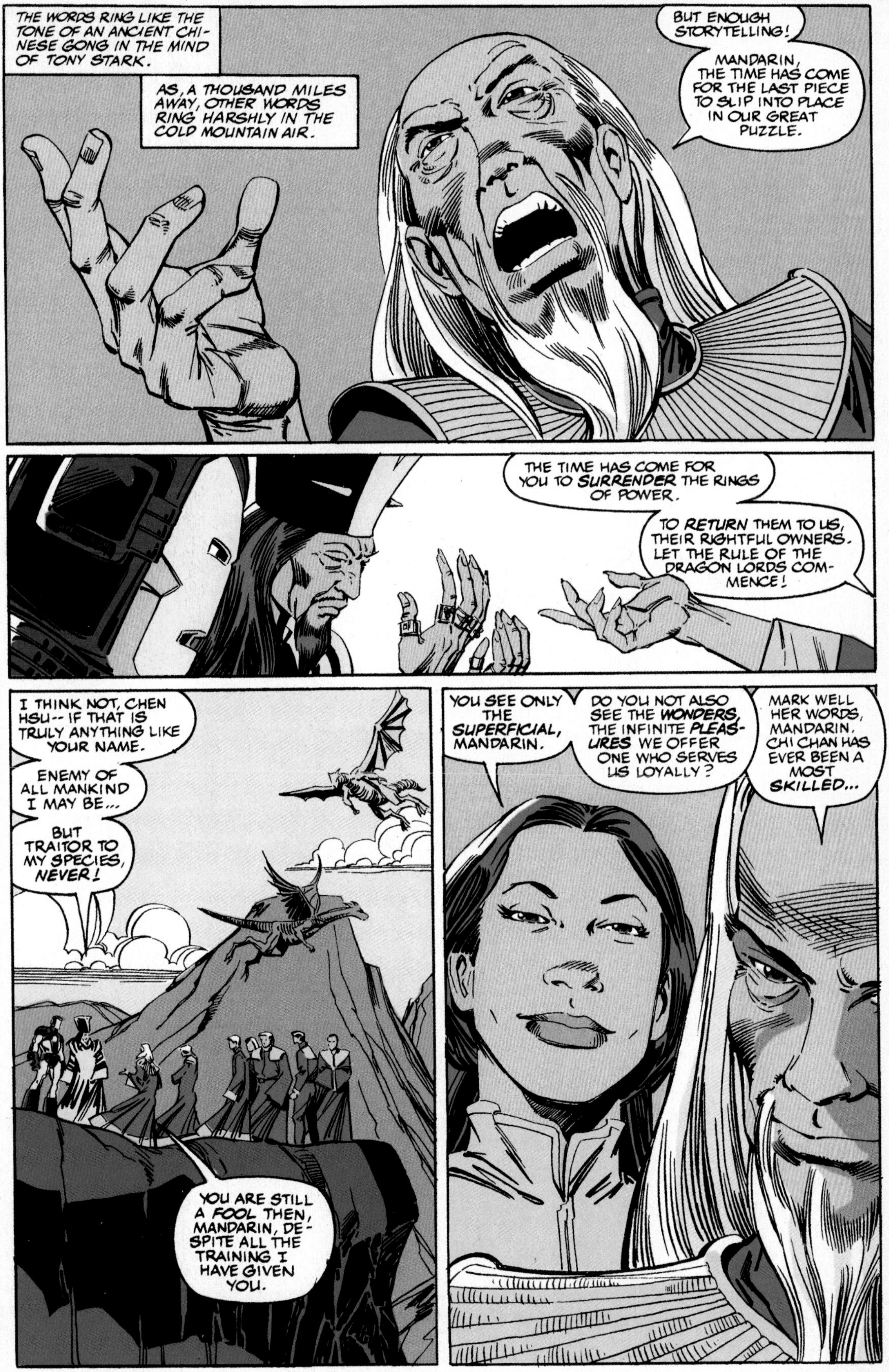
THE WORDS RING LIKE THE TONE OF AN ANCIENT CHINESE GONG IN THE MIND OF TONY STARK.
AS, A THOUSAND MILES AWAY, OTHER WORDS RING HARSHLY IN THE COLD MOUNTAIN AIR.
BUT ENOUGH STORYTELLING!
MANDARIN, THE TIME HAS COME FOR THE LAST PIECE TO SLIP INTO PLACE IN OUR GREAT PUZZLE.
THE TIME HAS COME FOR YOU TO SURRENDER THE RINGS OF POWER.
TO RETURN THEM TO US, THEIR RIGHTFUL OWNERS. LET THE RULE OF THE DRAGON LORDS COMMENCE!
I THINK NOT, CHEN HSU-- IF THAT IS TRULY ANYTHING LIKE YOUR NAME.
ENEMY OF ALL MANKIND I MAY BE...
BUT TRAITOR TO MY SPECIES, NEVER!
YOU ARE STILL A FOOL THEN, MANDARIN, DESPITE ALL THE TRAINING I HAVE GIVEN YOU.
YOU SEE ONLY THE SUPERFICIAL, MANDARIN.
DO YOU NOT ALSO SEE THE WONDERS, THE INFINITE PLEASURES WE OFFER ONE WHO SERVES US LOYALLY?
MARK WELL HER WORDS, MANDARIN. CHI CHAN HAS EVER BEEN A MOST SKILLED...

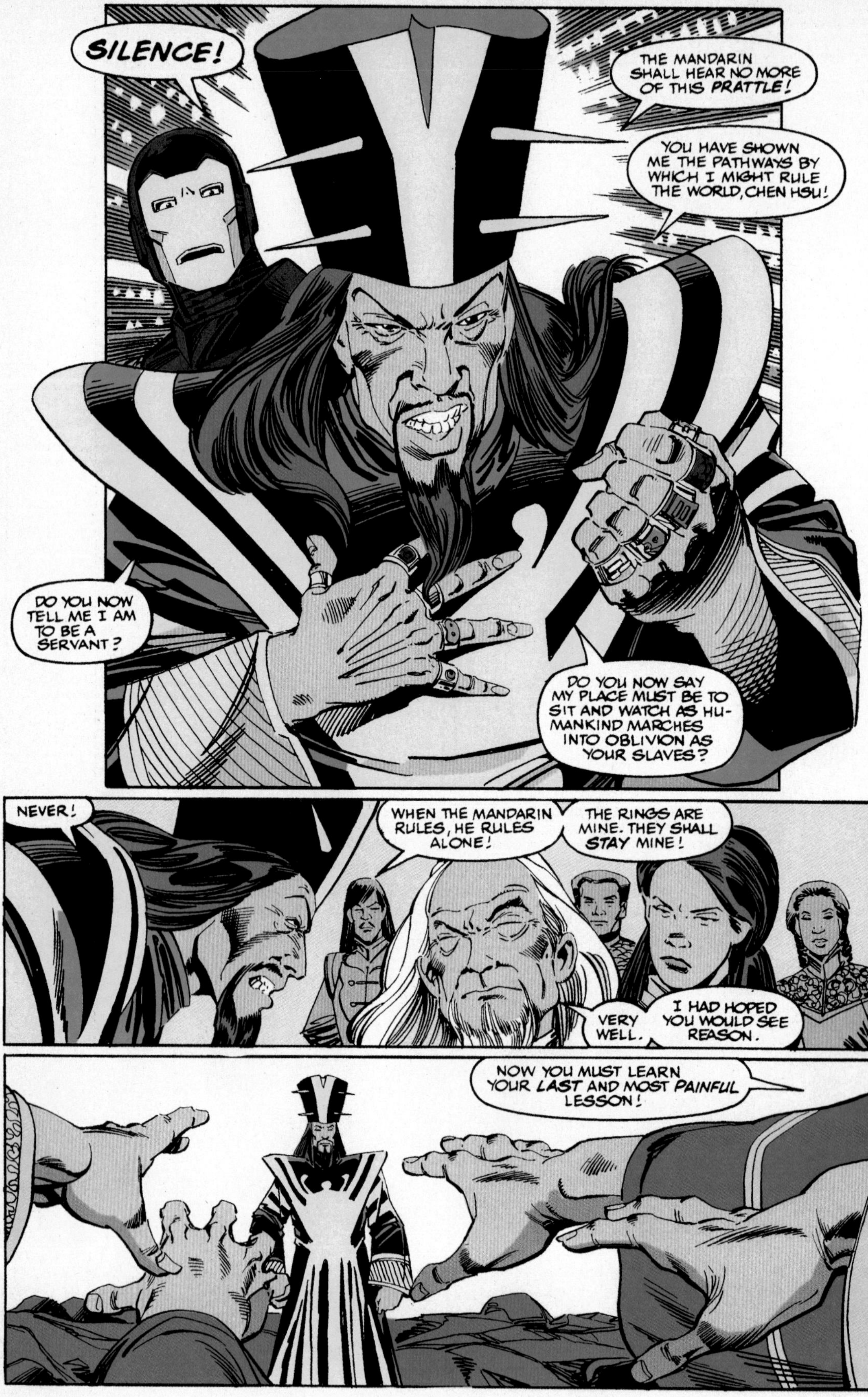
SILENCE!
THE MANDARIN SHALL HEAR NO MORE OF THIS PRATTLE!
YOU HAVE SHOWN ME THE PATHWAYS BY WHICH I MIGHT RULE THE WORLD, CHEN HSU!
DO YOU NOW TELL ME I AM TO BE A SERVANT?
DO YOU NOW SAY MY PLACE MUST BE TO SIT AND WATCH AS HU-MANKIND MARCHES INTO OBLIVION AS YOUR SLAVES?
NEVER!
WHEN THE MANDARIN RULES, HE RULES ALONE!
THE RINGS ARE MINE. THEY SHALL STAY MINE!
VERY WELL.
I HAD HOPED YOU WOULD SEE REASON.
NOW YOU MUST LEARN YOUR LAST AND MOST PAINFUL LESSON!

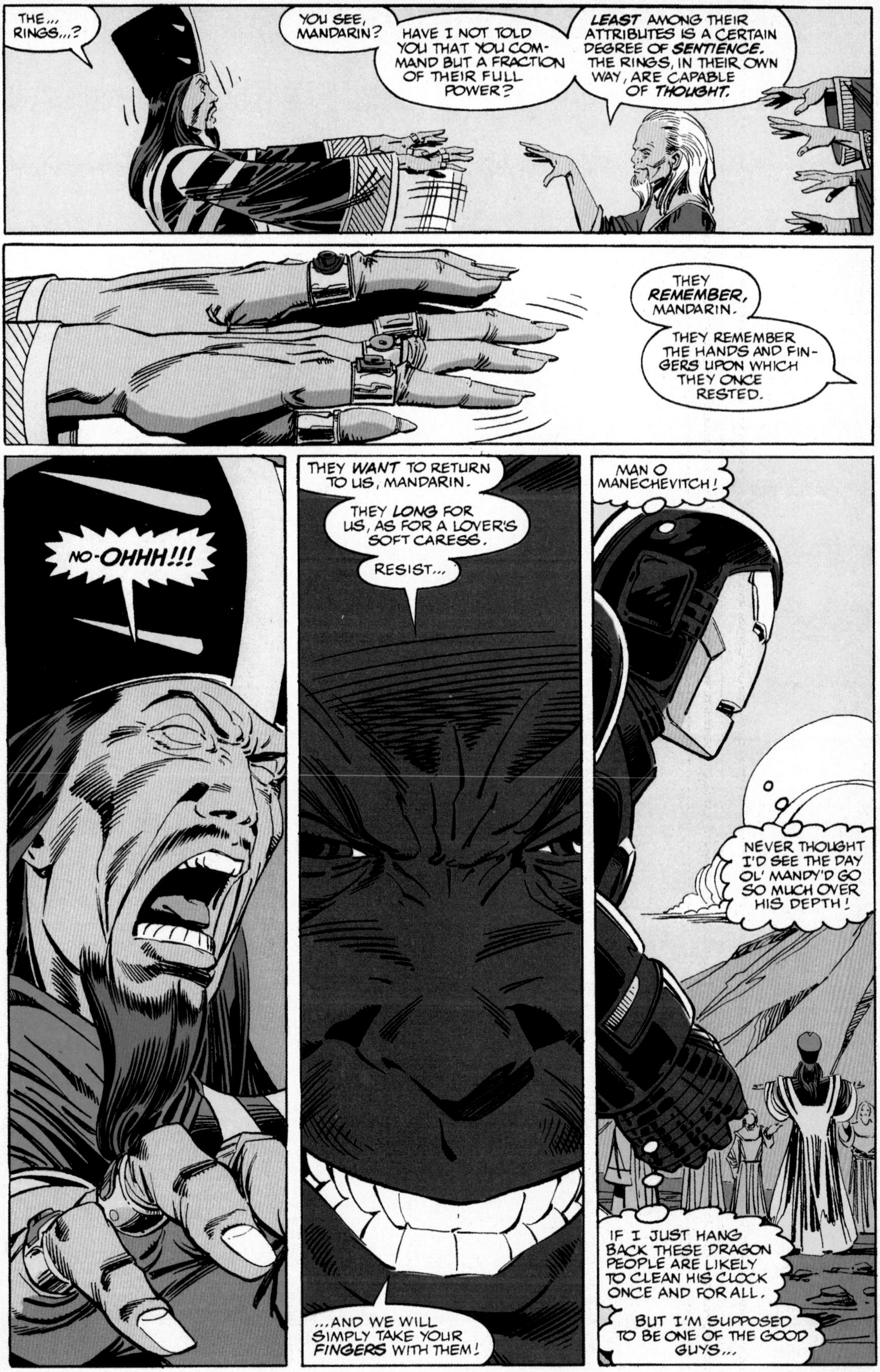
THE... RINGS...?
YOU SEE, MANDARIN?
HAVE I NOT TOLD YOU THAT YOU COMMAND BUT A FRACTION OF THEIR FULL POWER?
LEAST AMONG THEIR ATTRIBUTES IS A CERTAIN DEGREE OF SENTIENCE. THE RINGS, IN THEIR OWN WAY, ARE CAPABLE OF THOUGHT.
THEY REMEMBER, MANDARIN.
THEY REMEMBER THE HANDS AND FINGERS UPON WHICH THEY ONCE RESTED.
NO-OHHH!!!
THEY WANT TO RETURN TO US, MANDARIN.
THEY LONG FOR US, AS FOR A LOVER'S SOFT CARESS.
RESIST...
...AND WE WILL SIMPLY TAKE YOUR FINGERS WITH THEM!
MAN O MANECHEVITCH!
NEVER THOUGHT I'D SEE THE DAY OL' MANDY'D GO SO MUCH OVER HIS DEPTH!
IF I JUST HANG BACK THESE DRAGON PEOPLE ARE LIKELY TO CLEAN HIS CLOCK ONCE AND FOR ALL.
BUT I'M SUPPOSED TO BE ONE OF THE GOOD GUYS...

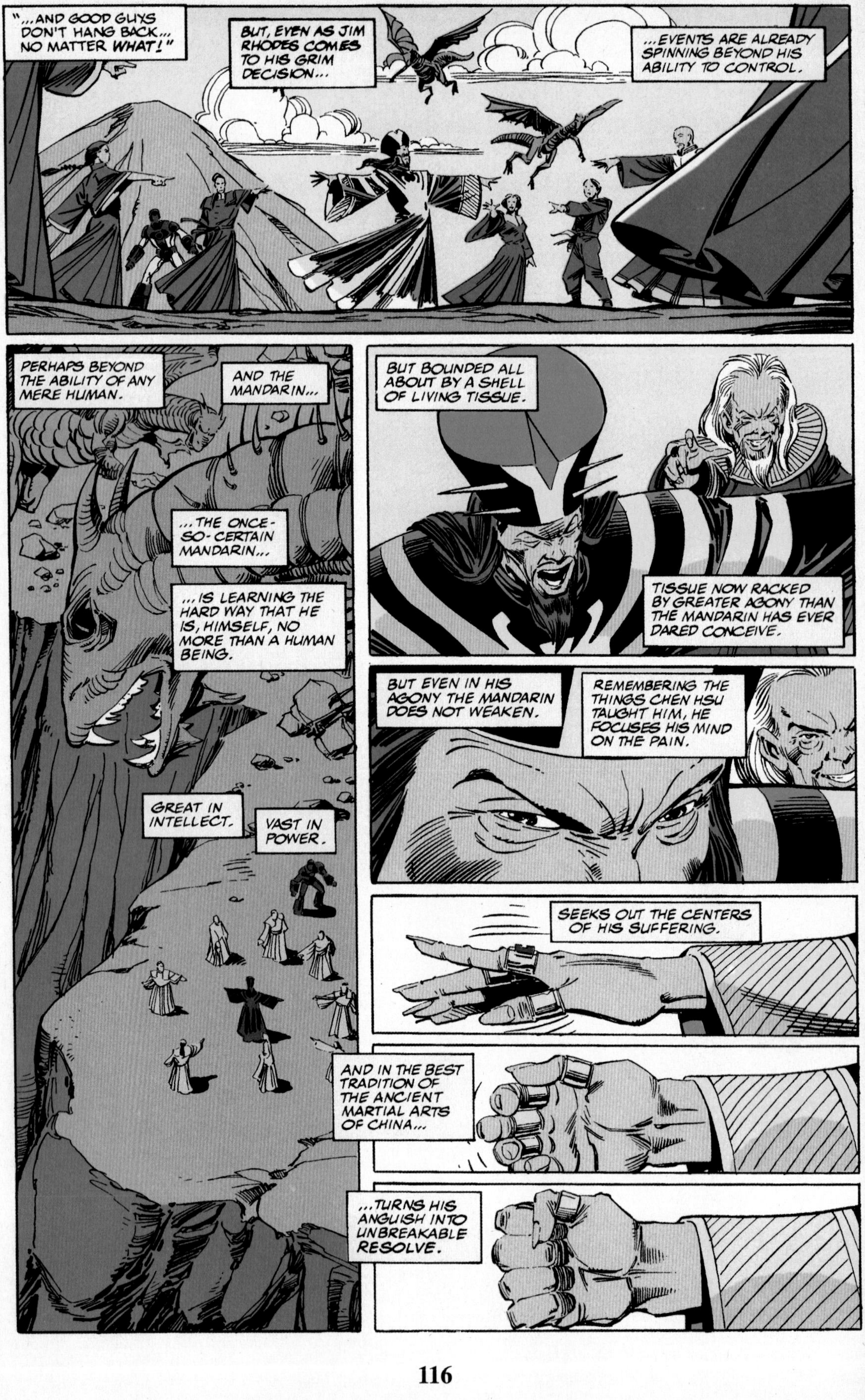
"...AND GOOD GUYS DON'T HANG BACK... NO MATTER WHAT!"
BUT, EVEN AS JIM RHODES COMES TO HIS GRIM DECISION...
...EVENTS ARE ALREADY SPINNING BEYOND HIS ABILITY TO CONTROL.
PERHAPS BEYOND THE ABILITY OF ANY MERE HUMAN.
AND THE MANDARIN...
...THE ONCE-SO-CERTAIN MANDARIN...
...IS LEARNING THE HARD WAY THAT HE IS, HIMSELF, NO MORE THAN A HUMAN BEING.
GREAT IN INTELLECT.
VAST IN POWER.
BUT BOUNDED ALL ABOUT BY A SHELL OF LIVING TISSUE.
TISSUE NOW RACKED BY GREATER AGONY THAN THE MANDARIN HAS EVER DARED CONCEIVE.
BUT EVEN IN HIS AGONY THE MANDARIN DOES NOT WEAKEN.
REMEMBERING THE THINGS CHEN HSU TAUGHT HIM, HE FOCUSES HIS MIND ON THE PAIN.
SEEKS OUT THE CENTERS OF HIS SUFFERING.
AND IN THE BEST TRADITION OF THE ANCIENT MARTIAL ARTS OF CHINA...
...TURNS HIS ANGUISH INTO UNBREAKABLE RESOLVE.

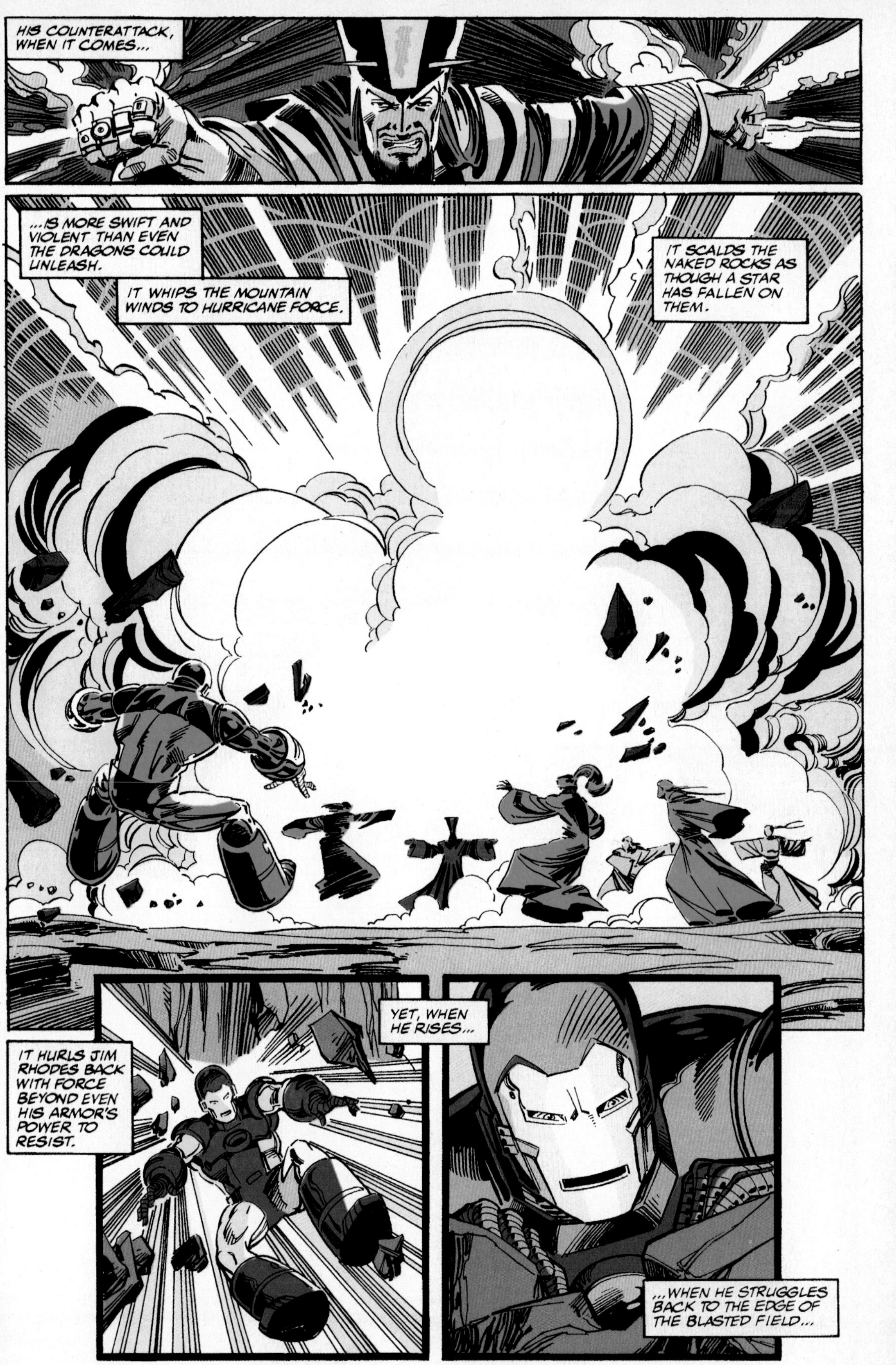
HIS COUNTERATTACK, WHEN IT COMES...
...IS MORE SWIFT AND VIOLENT THAN EVEN THE DRAGONS COULD UNLEASH.
IT WHIPS THE MOUNTAIN WINDS TO HURRICANE FORCE.
IT SCALDS THE NAKED ROCKS AS THOUGH A STAR HAS FALLEN ON THEM.
IT HURLS JIM RHODES BACK WITH FORCE BEYOND EVEN HIS ARMOR'S POWER TO RESIST.
YET, WHEN HE RISES...
...WHEN HE STRUGGLES BACK TO THE EDGE OF THE BLASTED FIELD...

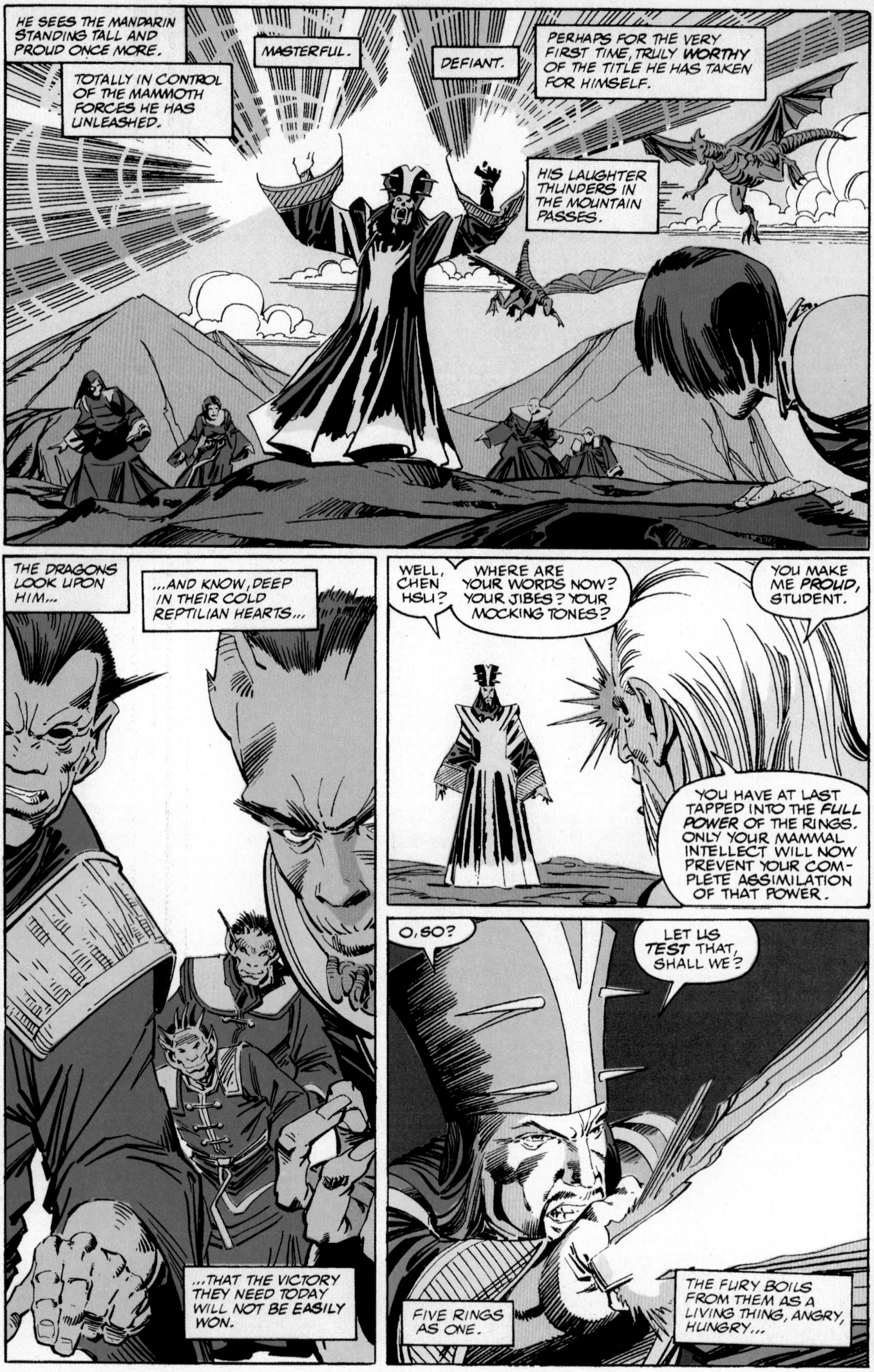
HE SEES THE MANDARIN STANDING TALL AND PROUD ONCE MORE.
TOTALLY IN CONTROL OF THE MAMMOTH FORCES HE HAS UNLEASHED.
MASTERFUL.
DEFIANT.
PERHAPS FOR THE VERY FIRST TIME, TRULY WORTHY OF THE TITLE HE HAS TAKEN FOR HIMSELF.
HIS LAUGHTER THUNDERS IN THE MOUNTAIN PASSES.
THE DRAGONS LOOK UPON HIM...
...AND KNOW, DEEP IN THEIR COLD REPTILIAN HEARTS...
...THAT THE VICTORY THEY NEED TODAY WILL NOT BE EASILY WON.
WELL, CHEN HSU?
WHERE ARE YOUR WORDS NOW? YOUR JIBES? YOUR MOCKING TONES?
YOU MAKE ME PROUD, STUDENT.
YOU HAVE AT LAST TAPPED INTO THE FULL POWER OF THE RINGS. ONLY YOUR MAMMAL INTELLECT WILL NOW PREVENT YOUR COMPLETE ASSIMILATION OF THAT POWER.
O, SO?
LET US TEST THAT, SHALL WE?
FIVE RINGS AS ONE.
THE FURY BOILS FROM THEM AS A LIVING THING, ANGRY, HUNGRY...

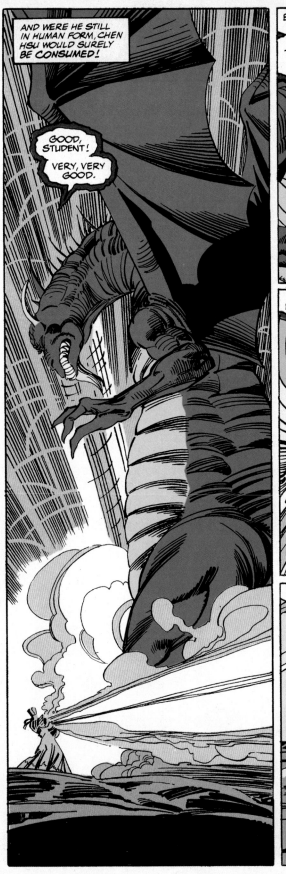

AND WERE HE STILL IN HUMAN FORM, CHEN HSU WOULD SURELY BE CONSUMED!

GOOD, STUDENT!

VERY, VERY GOOD.

BUT NOT ENOUGH, I FEAR.

NOT ENOUGH THAT YOU MIGHT CLAIM THE DAY.

DESTROY HIM, CAPTAIN! END IT NOW!

I HEAR, NAVIGATOR.

I HEAR, AND I AGREE. FAREWELL, STUDENT.

NO!

THE RINGS OBEY HIM NOW AS NEVER BEFORE.

NO CONSCIOUS THOUGHT IS NEEDED TO COMMAND THEIR POWER.

THEY ARE A PART OF HIM. THEY SENSE HIS NEED.

THEY ACT.

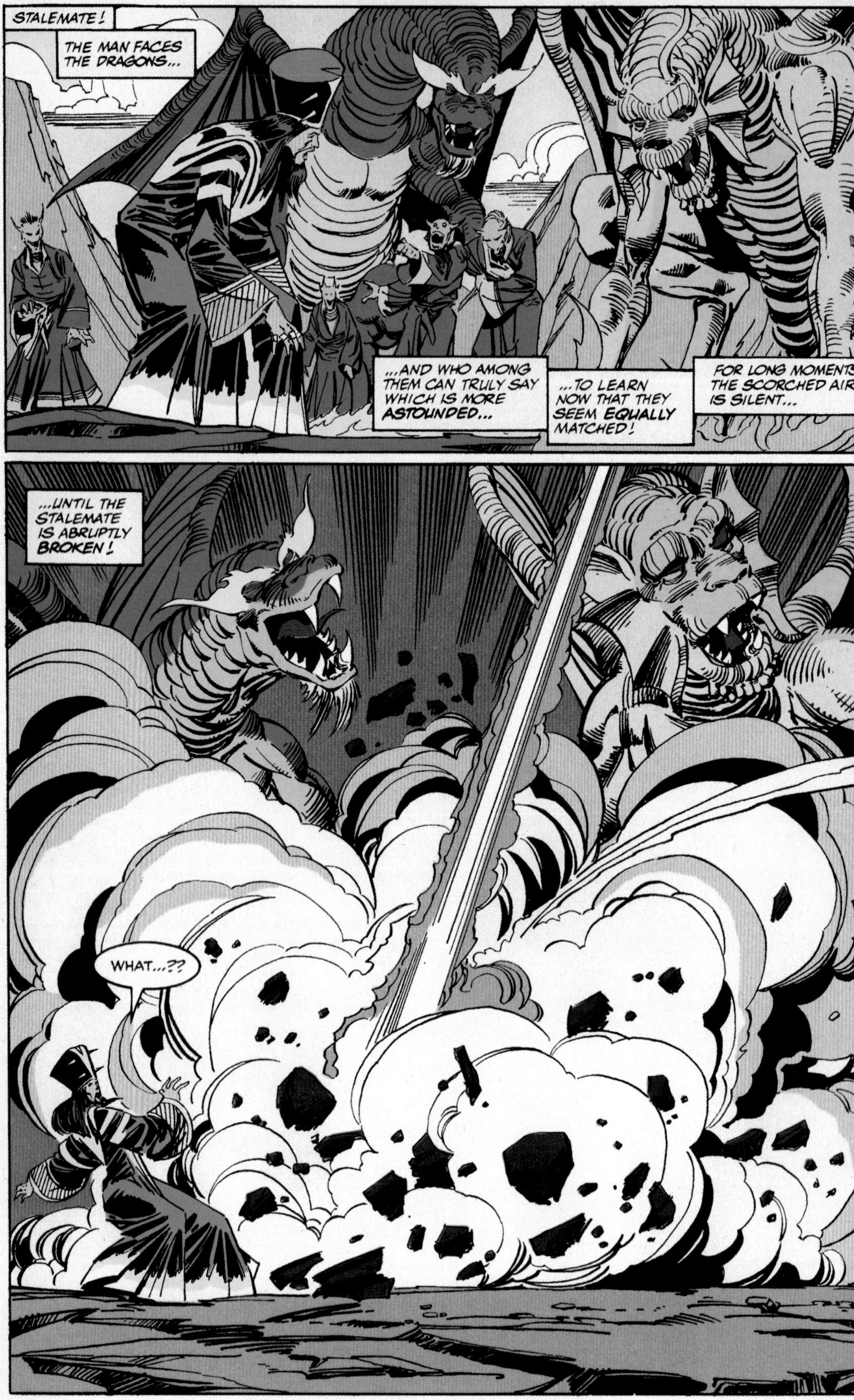
STALEMATE!
THE MAN FACES THE DRAGONS...
...AND WHO AMONG THEM CAN TRULY SAY WHICH IS MORE ASTOUNDED...
...TO LEARN NOW THAT THEY SEEM EQUALLY MATCHED!
FOR LONG MOMENTS, THE SCORCHED AIR IS SILENT...
...UNTIL THE STALEMATE IS ABRUPTLY BROKEN!
WHAT...??

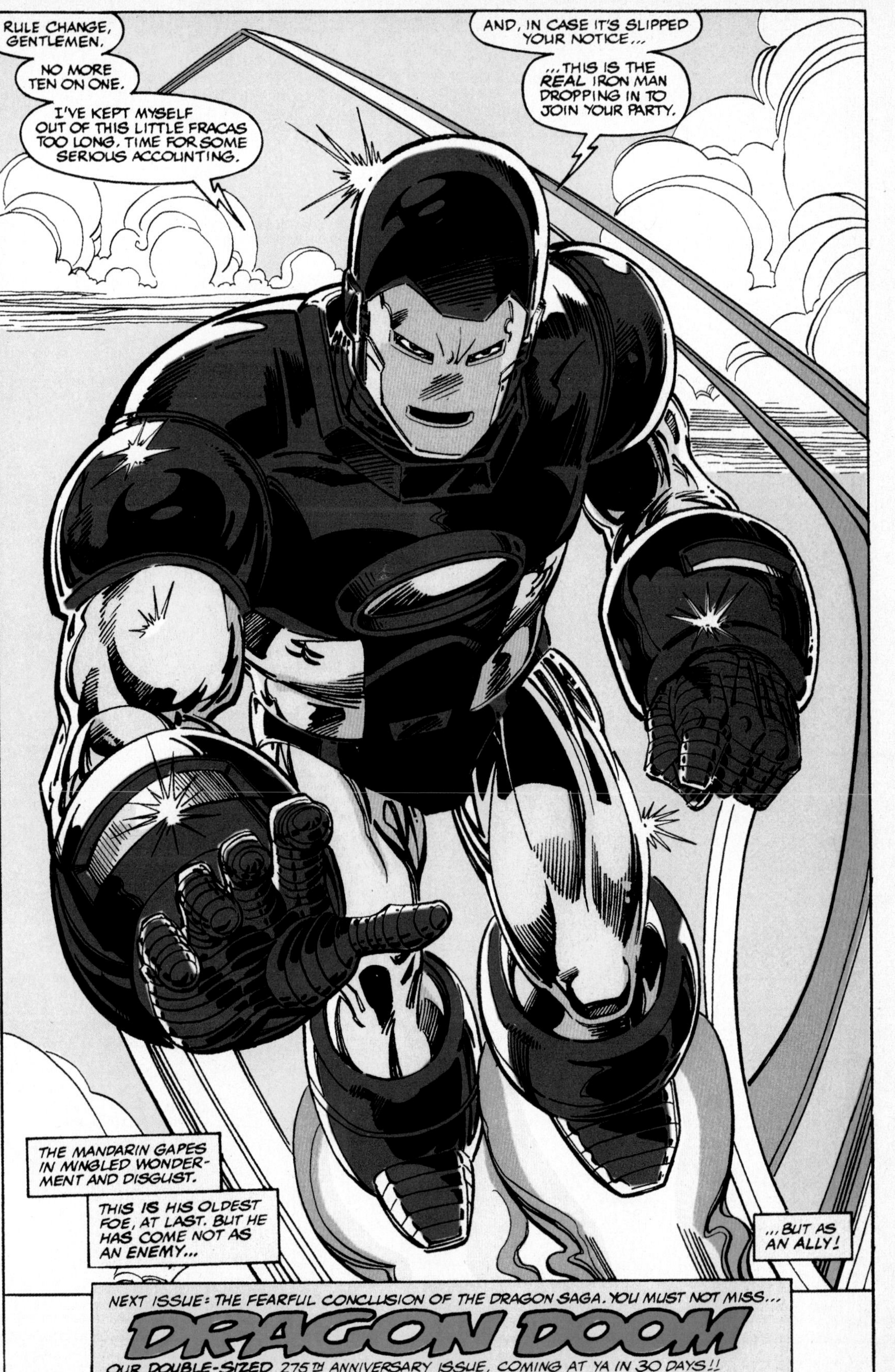
RULE CHANGE, GENTLEMEN.
NO MORE TEN ON ONE.
I'VE KEPT MYSELF OUT OF THIS LITTLE FRACAS TOO LONG. TIME FOR SOME SERIOUS ACCOUNTING.
AND, IN CASE IT'S SLIPPED YOUR NOTICE...
...THIS IS THE REAL IRON MAN DROPPING IN TO JOIN YOUR PARTY.
THE MANDARIN GAPES IN MINGLED WONDER-MENT AND DISGUST.
THIS IS HIS OLDEST FOE, AT LAST. BUT HE HAS COME NOT AS AN ENEMY...
...BUT AS AN ALLY!
NEXT ISSUE: THE FEARFUL CONCLUSION OF THE DRAGON SAGA. YOU MUST NOT MISS...
DRAGON DOOM
OUR DOUBLE-SIZED 275TH ANNIVERSARY ISSUE, COMING AT YA IN 30 DAYS!!

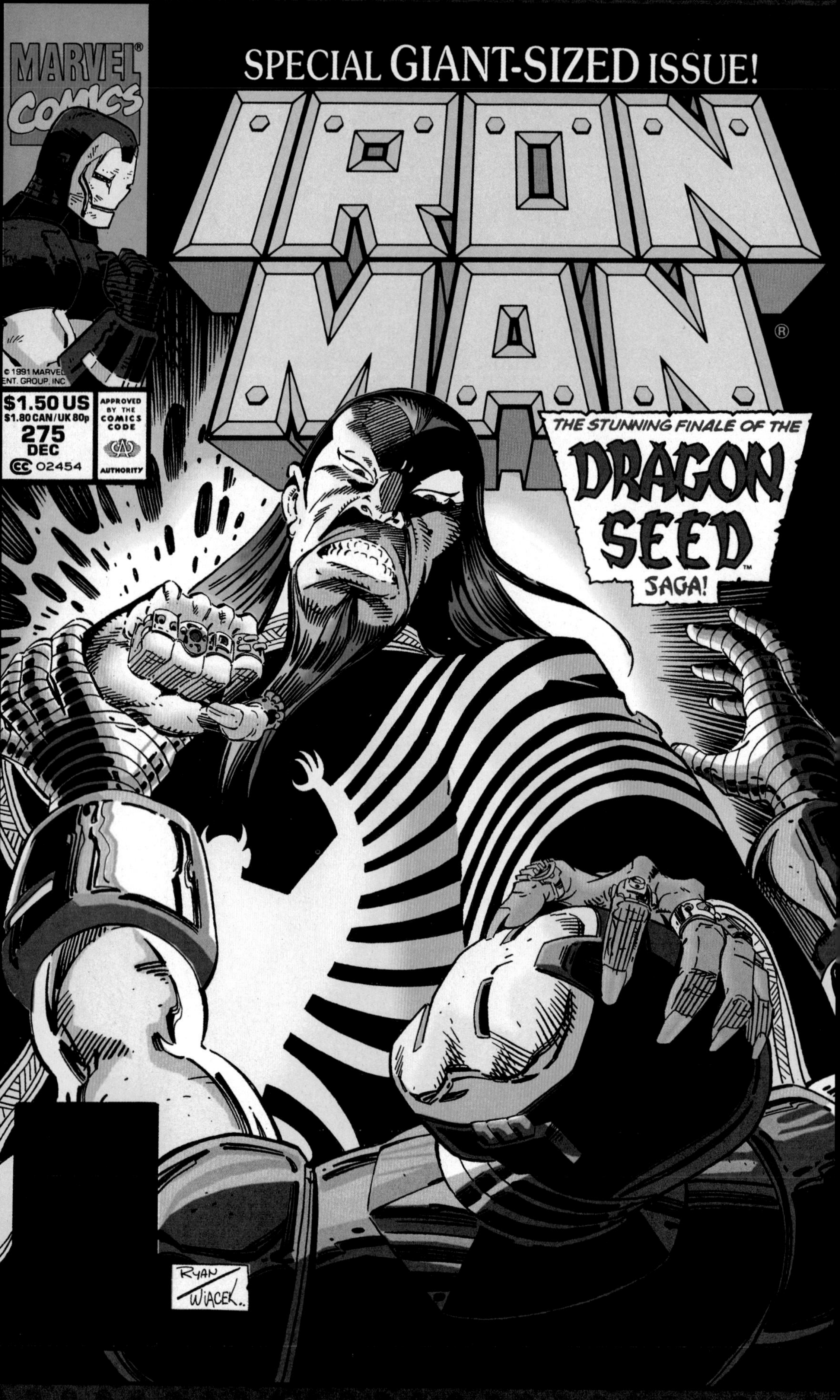
MARVEL® COMICS
SPECIAL GIANT-SIZED ISSUE!
IRON MAN®
© 1991 MARVEL ENT. GROUP, INC
$1.50 US
$1.80 CAN/UK 80p
275
DEC
02454
APPROVED BY THE COMICS CODE AUTHORITY
THE STUNNING FINALE OF THE
DRAGON SEED™
SAGA!
RYAN
WIACEK

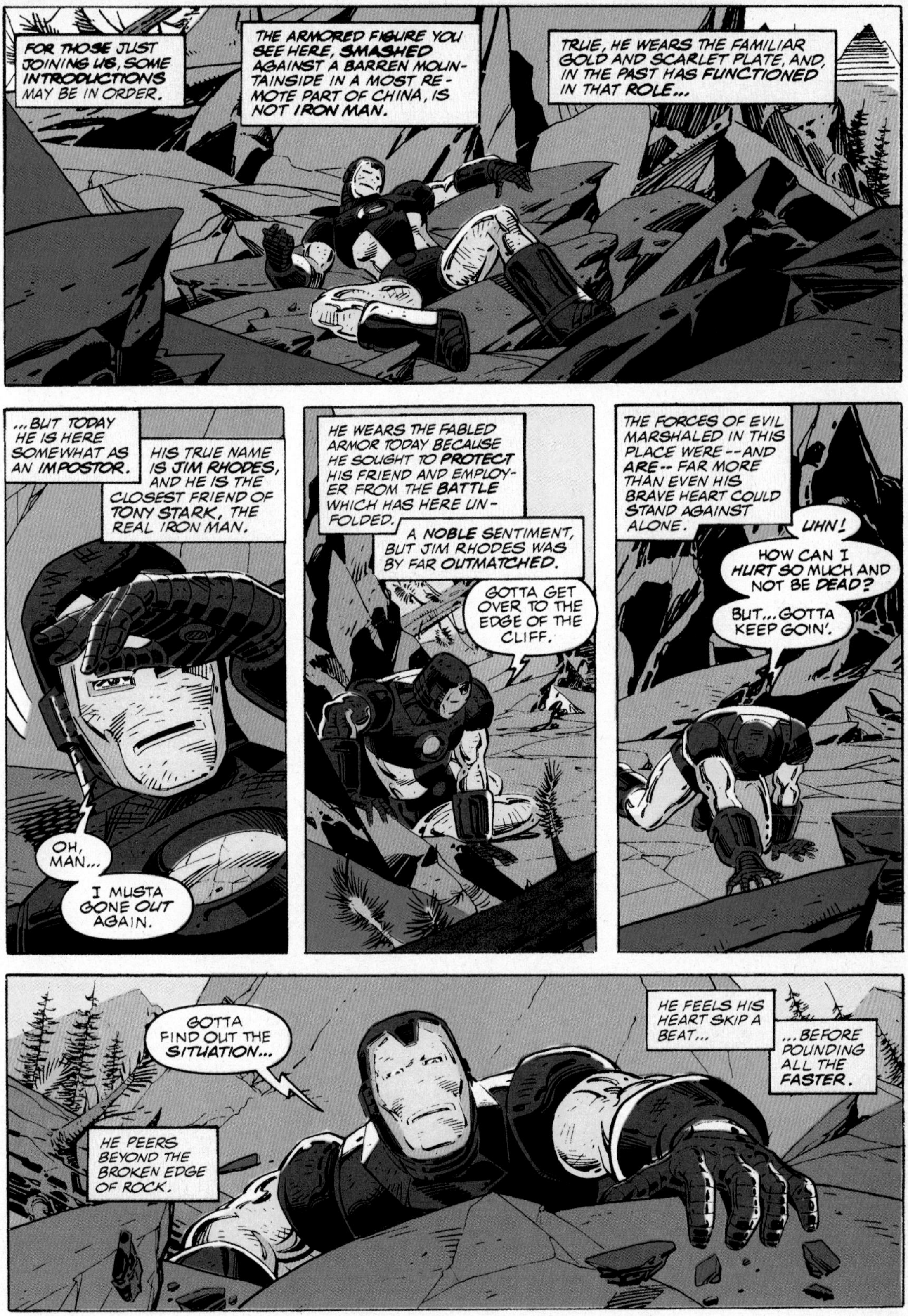
FOR THOSE JUST JOINING US, SOME INTRODUCTIONS MAY BE IN ORDER.
THE ARMORED FIGURE YOU SEE HERE, SMASHED AGAINST A BARREN MOUNTAINSIDE IN A MOST REMOTE PART OF CHINA, IS NOT IRON MAN.
TRUE, HE WEARS THE FAMILIAR GOLD AND SCARLET PLATE, AND, IN THE PAST HAS FUNCTIONED IN THAT ROLE...
...BUT TODAY HE IS HERE SOMEWHAT AS AN IMPOSTOR.
HIS TRUE NAME IS JIM RHODES, AND HE IS THE CLOSEST FRIEND OF TONY STARK, THE REAL IRON MAN.
OH, MAN...
I MUSTA GONE OUT AGAIN.
HE WEARS THE FABLED ARMOR TODAY BECAUSE HE SOUGHT TO PROTECT HIS FRIEND AND EMPLOYER FROM THE BATTLE WHICH HAS HERE UNFOLDED.
A NOBLE SENTIMENT, BUT JIM RHODES WAS BY FAR OUTMATCHED.
GOTTA GET OVER TO THE EDGE OF THE CLIFF.
THE FORCES OF EVIL MARSHALED IN THIS PLACE WERE--AND ARE-- FAR MORE THAN EVEN HIS BRAVE HEART COULD STAND AGAINST ALONE.
UHN!
HOW CAN I HURT SO MUCH AND NOT BE DEAD?
BUT... GOTTA KEEP GOIN'.
GOTTA FIND OUT THE SITUATION...
HE PEERS BEYOND THE BROKEN EDGE OF ROCK.
HE FEELS HIS HEART SKIP A BEAT...
...BEFORE POUNDING ALL THE FASTER.

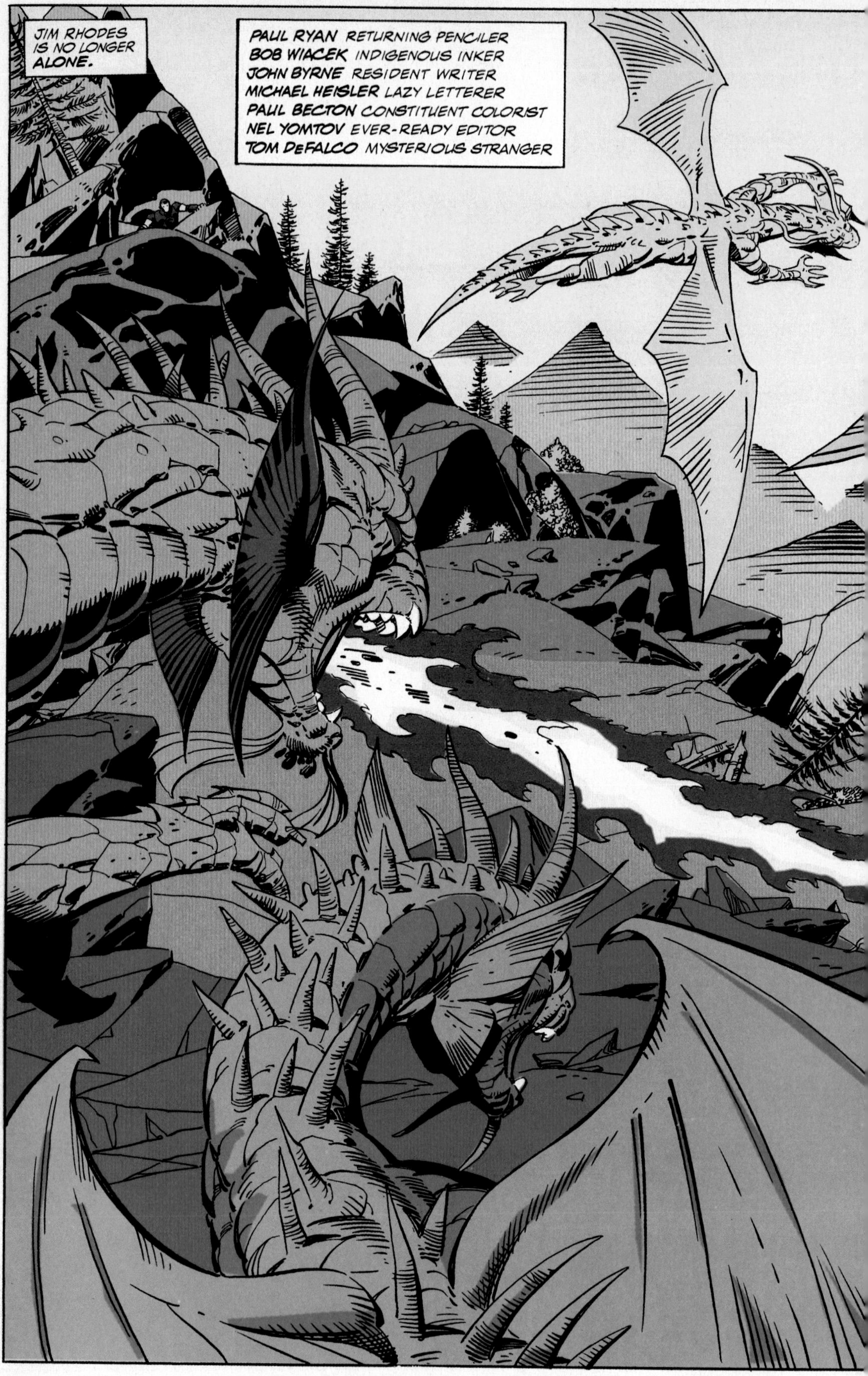
JIM RHODES IS NO LONGER ALONE.
PAUL RYAN RETURNING PENCILER
BOB WIACEK INDIGENOUS INKER
JOHN BYRNE RESIDENT WRITER
MICHAEL HEISLER LAZY LETTERER
PAUL BECTON CONSTITUENT COLORIST
NEL YOMTOV EVER-READY EDITOR
TOM DeFALCO MYSTERIOUS STRANGER

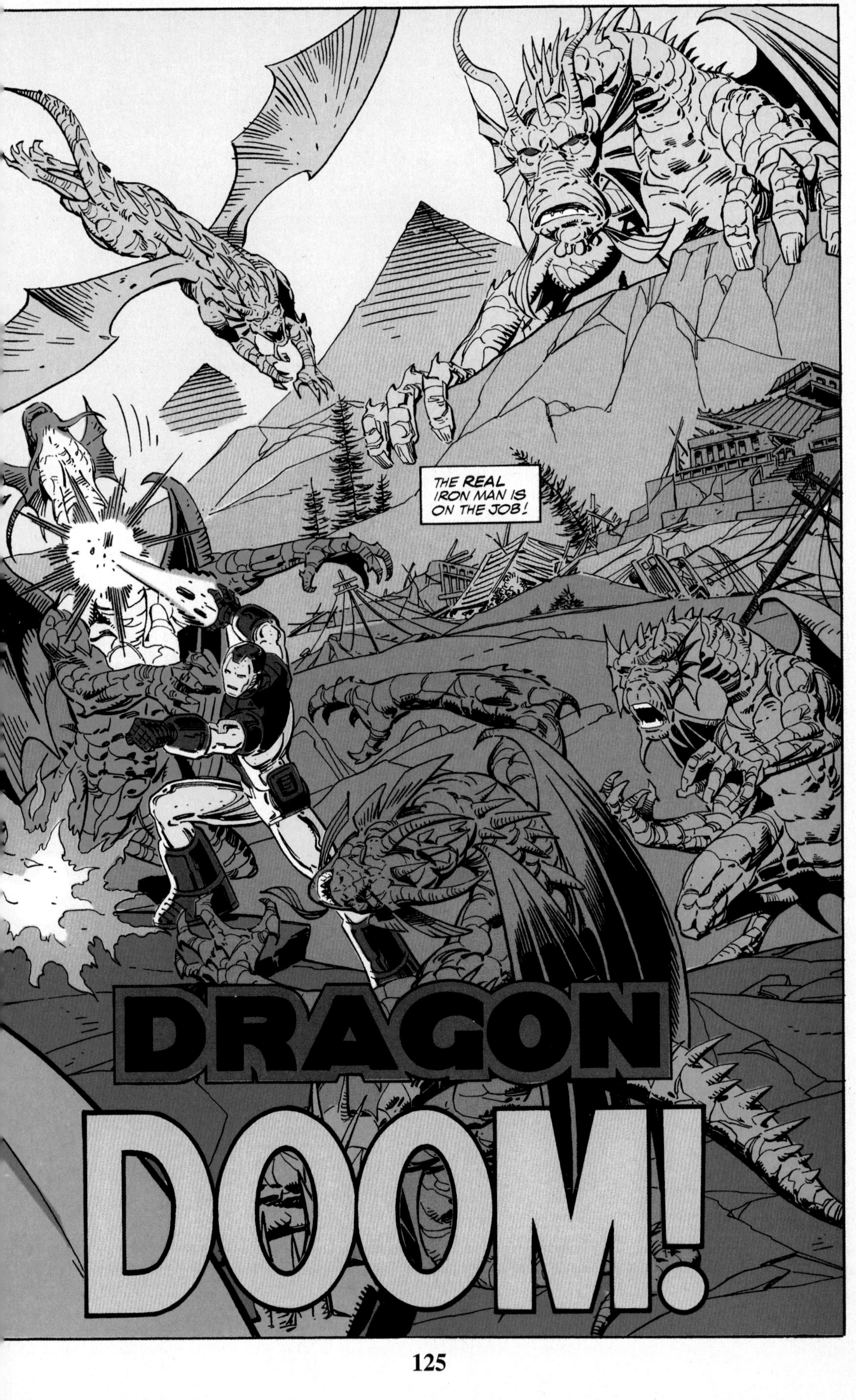
THE REAL IRON MAN IS ON THE JOB!
DRAGON
DOOM!

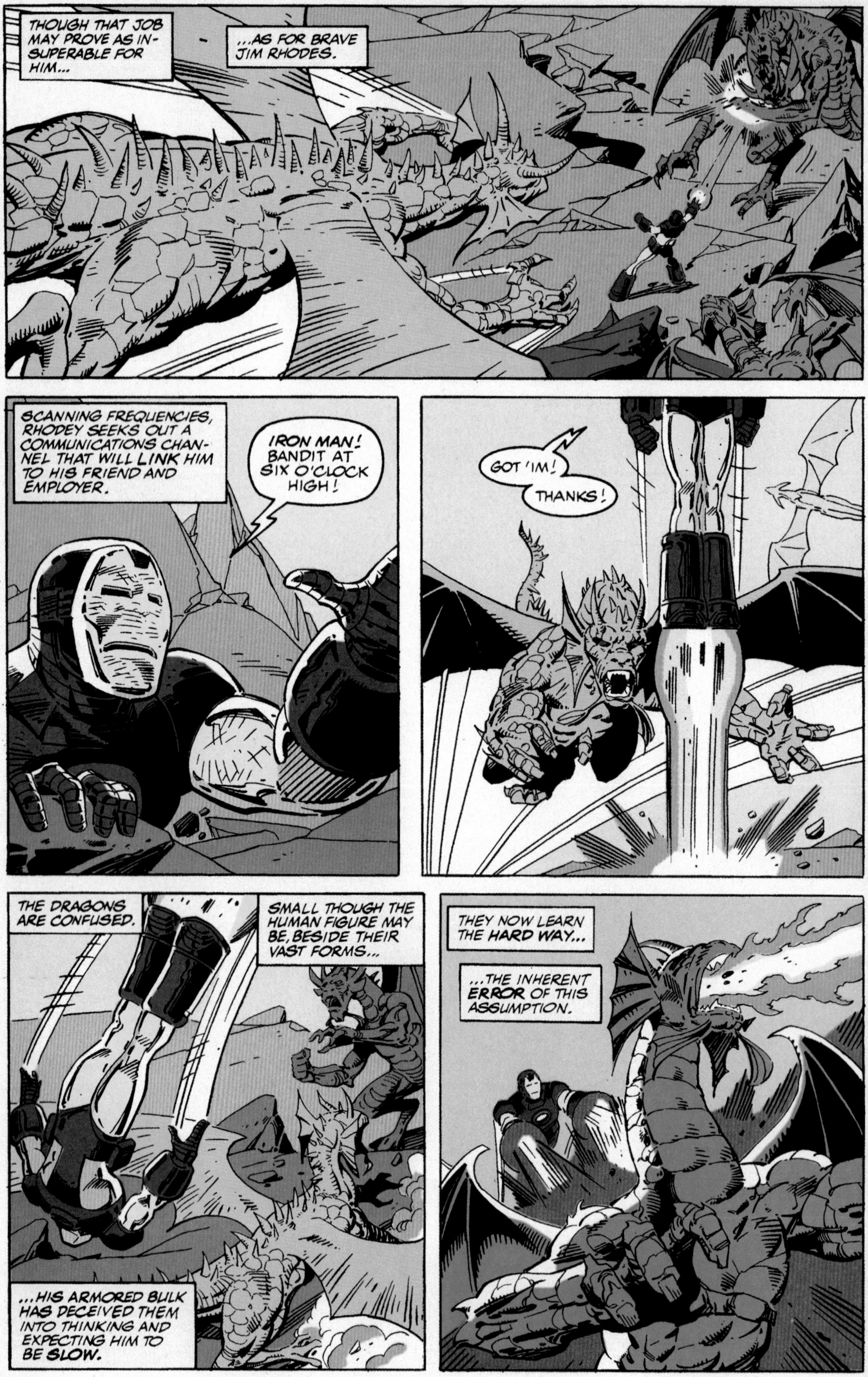
THOUGH THAT JOB MAY PROVE AS IN-SUPERABLE FOR HIM...
...AS FOR BRAVE JIM RHODES.
SCANNING FREQUENCIES, RHODEY SEEKS OUT A COMMUNICATIONS CHAN-NEL THAT WILL LINK HIM TO HIS FRIEND AND EMPLOYER.
IRON MAN! BANDIT AT SIX O'CLOCK HIGH!
GOT 'IM!
THANKS!
THE DRAGONS ARE CONFUSED.
SMALL THOUGH THE HUMAN FIGURE MAY BE, BESIDE THEIR VAST FORMS...
...HIS ARMORED BULK HAS DECEIVED THEM INTO THINKING AND EXPECTING HIM TO BE SLOW.
THEY NOW LEARN THE HARD WAY...
...THE INHERENT ERROR OF THIS ASSUMPTION.

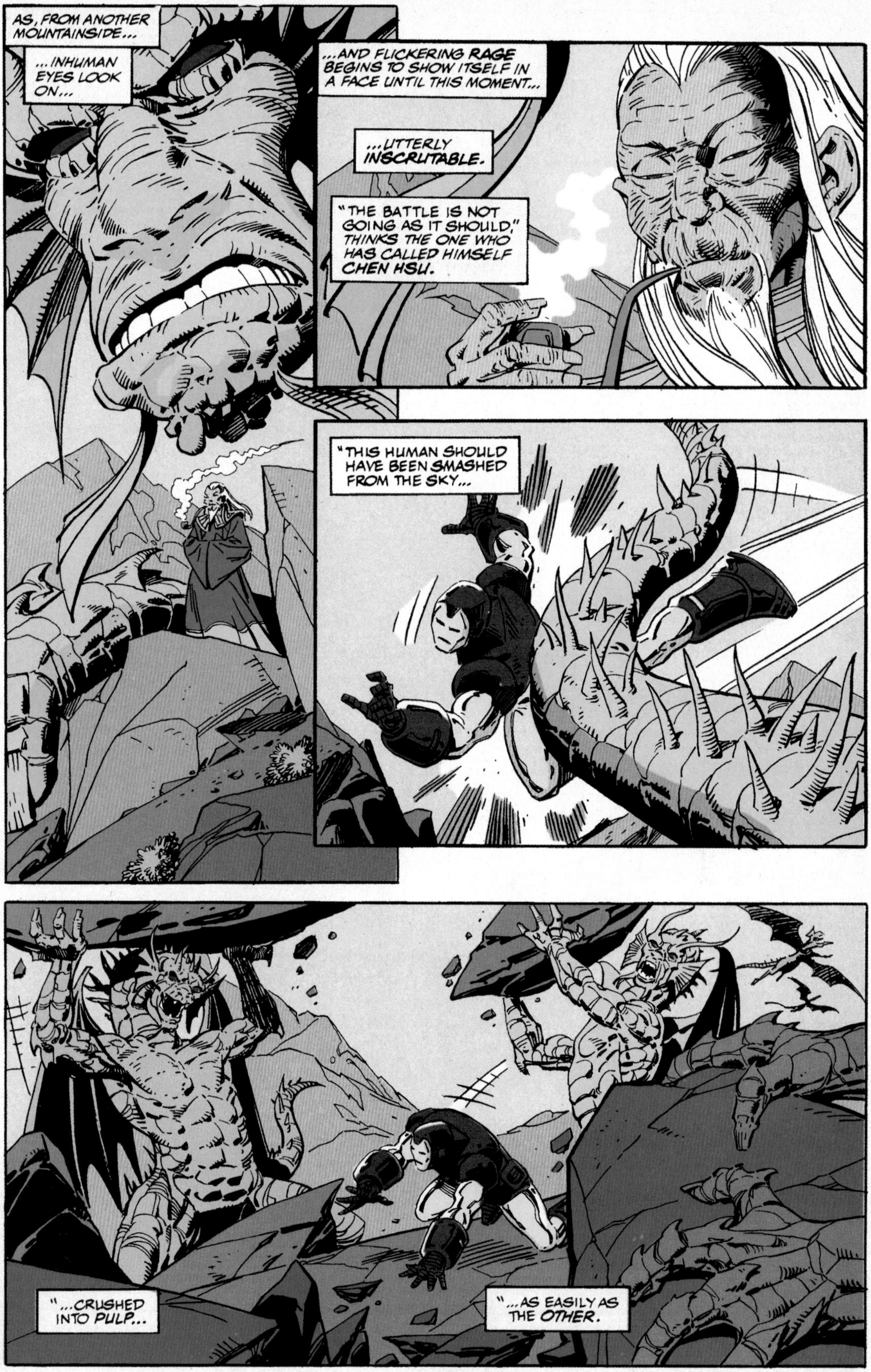
AS, FROM ANOTHER MOUNTAINSIDE...
...INHUMAN EYES LOOK ON...
...AND FLICKERING RAGE BEGINS TO SHOW ITSELF IN A FACE UNTIL THIS MOMENT...
...UTTERLY INSCRUTABLE.
"THE BATTLE IS NOT GOING AS IT SHOULD," THINKS THE ONE WHO HAS CALLED HIMSELF CHEN HSU.
"THIS HUMAN SHOULD HAVE BEEN SMASHED FROM THE SKY...
"...CRUSHED INTO PULP...
"...AS EASILY AS THE OTHER.

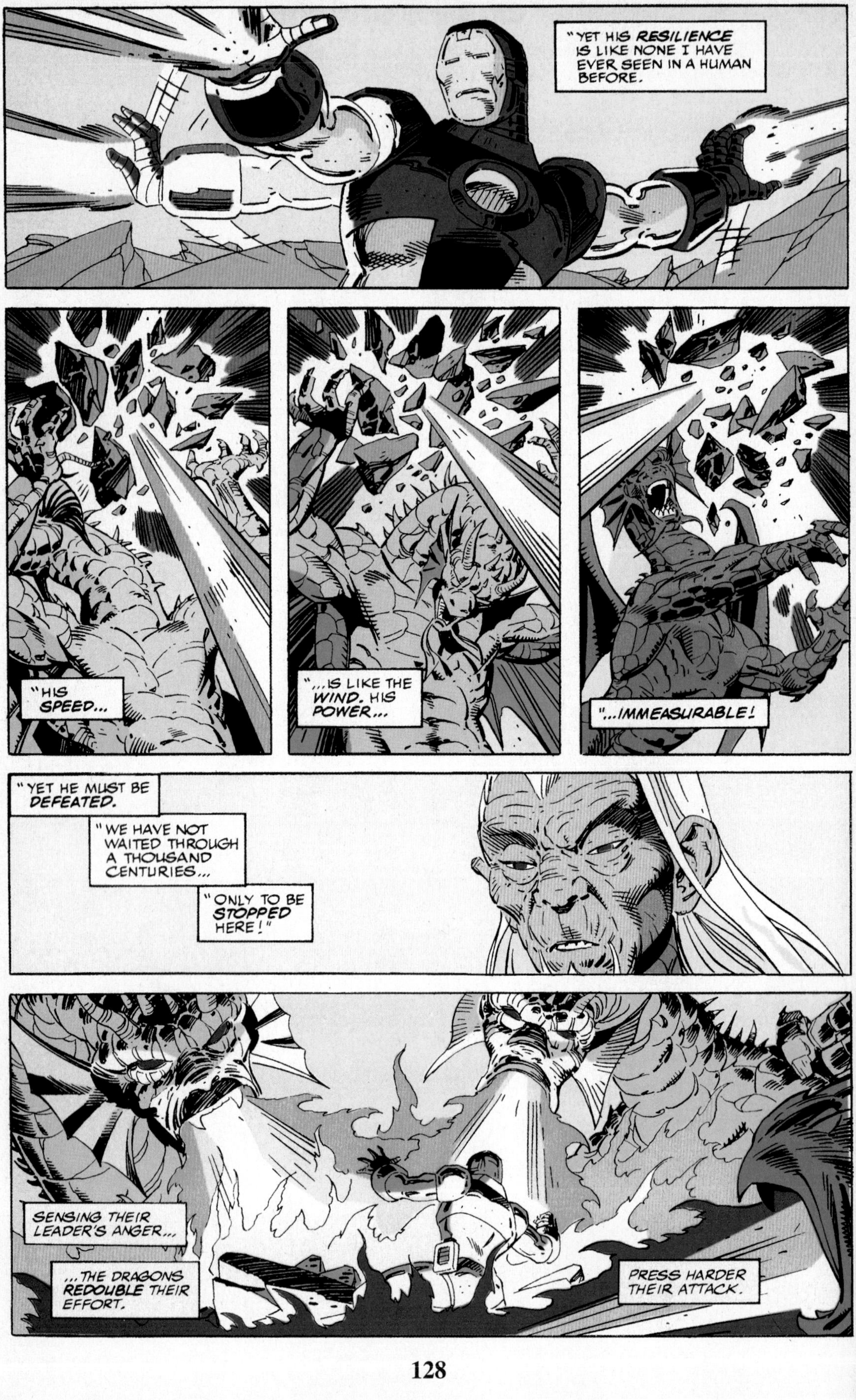
"YET HIS RESILIENCE IS LIKE NONE I HAVE EVER SEEN IN A HUMAN BEFORE.
"HIS SPEED...
"...IS LIKE THE WIND. HIS POWER...
"...IMMEASURABLE!
"YET HE MUST BE DEFEATED.
"WE HAVE NOT WAITED THROUGH A THOUSAND CENTURIES...
"ONLY TO BE STOPPED HERE!"
SENSING THEIR LEADER'S ANGER...
...THE DRAGONS REDOUBLE THEIR EFFORT.
PRESS HARDER THEIR ATTACK.

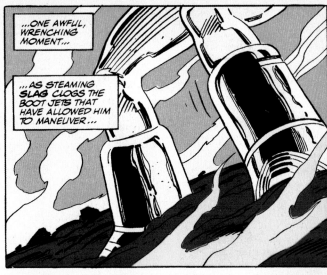

AND FOR A MOMENT...

...ONE AWFUL, WRENCHING MOMENT...

...AS STEAMING SLAG CLOGS THE BOOT JETS THAT HAVE ALLOWED HIM TO MANEUVER...

...AS ONBOARD COMPUTERS INFORM THE ARMOR'S OCCUPANT OF HIS PREDICAMENT...

...IT SEEMS FOR ALL THE WORLD...

...AS IF THIS DAY BELONGS TO THE DRAGONS!

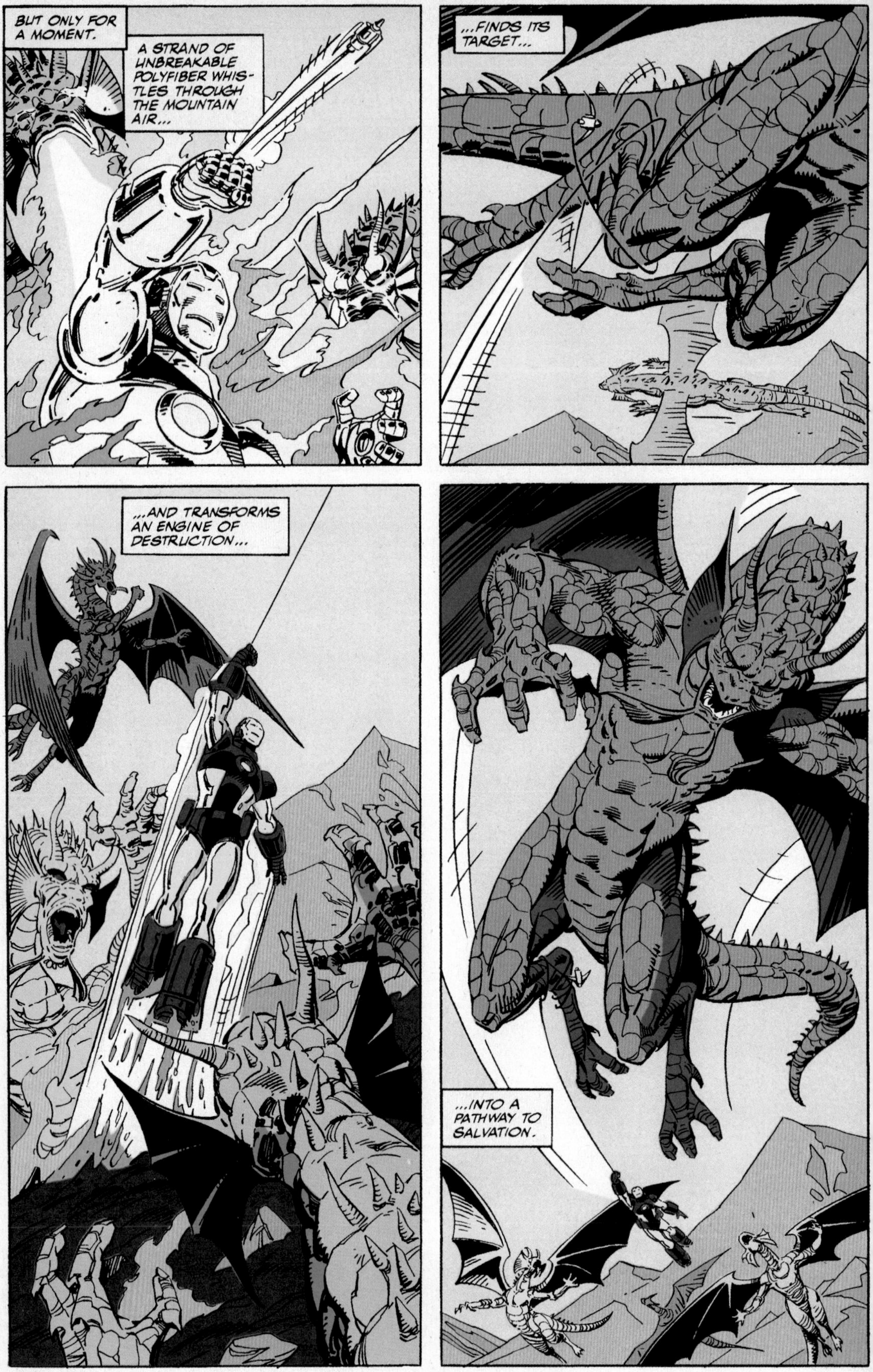
BUT ONLY FOR A MOMENT.
A STRAND OF UNBREAKABLE POLYFIBER WHISTLES THROUGH THE MOUNTAIN AIR...
...FINDS ITS TARGET...
...AND TRANSFORMS AN ENGINE OF DESTRUCTION...
...INTO A PATHWAY TO SALVATION.

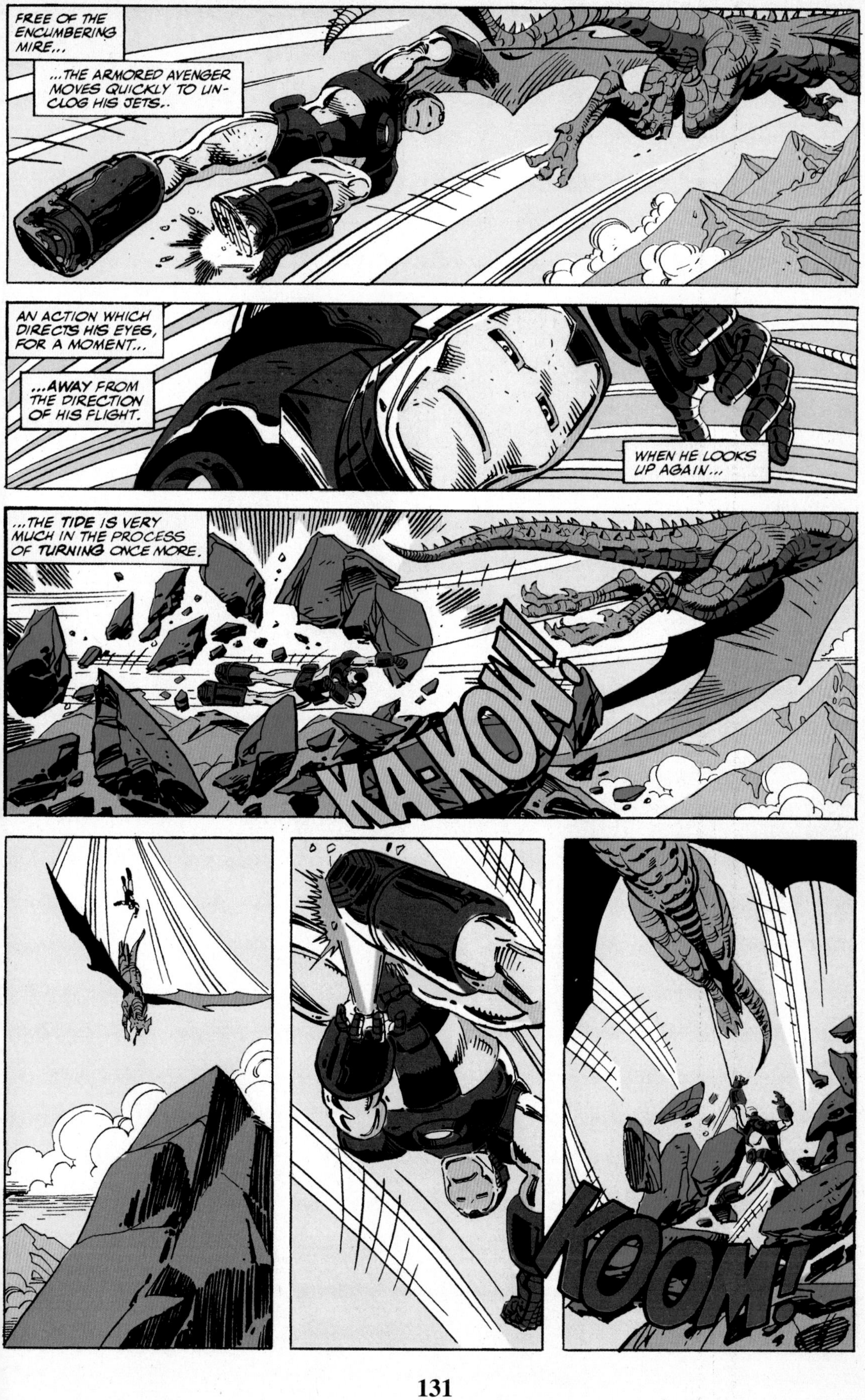
FREE OF THE ENCUMBERING MIRE...
...THE ARMORED AVENGER MOVES QUICKLY TO UN-CLOG HIS JETS..
AN ACTION WHICH DIRECTS HIS EYES, FOR A MOMENT...
...AWAY FROM THE DIRECTION OF HIS FLIGHT.
WHEN HE LOOKS UP AGAIN...
...THE TIDE IS VERY MUCH IN THE PROCESS OF TURNING ONCE MORE.
KAKOW!
KOOM!

THE SITUATION IS INCREASINGLY DESPERATE.

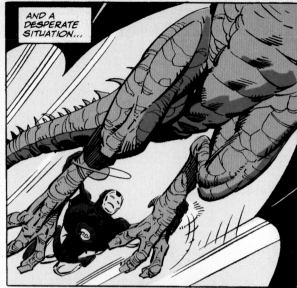

AND A DESPERATE SITUATION...

...MUST OFTEN LEAD...

...TO DESPERATE MEASURES!

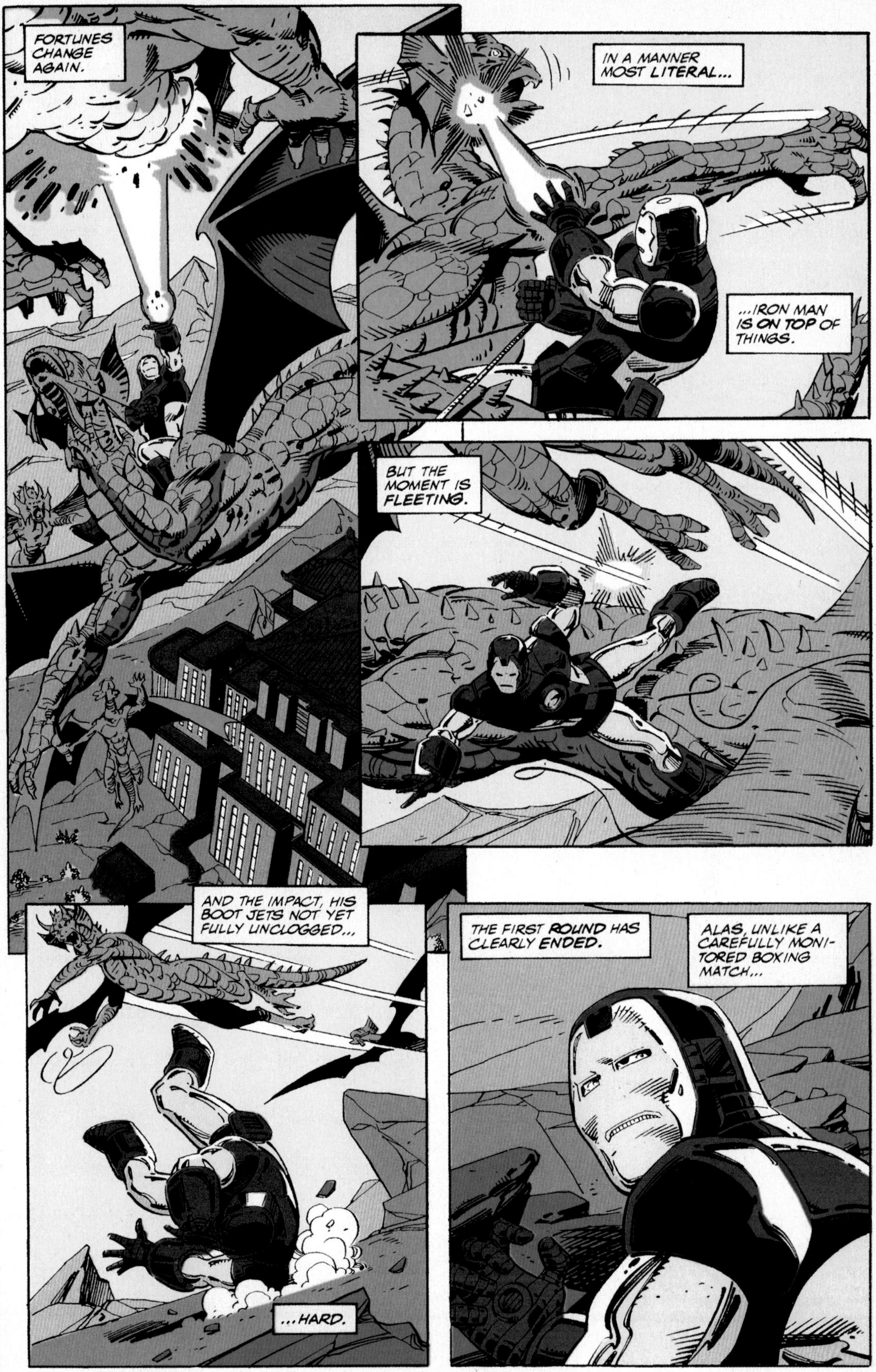
FORTUNES CHANGE AGAIN.
IN A MANNER MOST LITERAL...
...IRON MAN IS ON TOP OF THINGS.
BUT THE MOMENT IS FLEETING.
AND THE IMPACT, HIS BOOT JETS NOT YET FULLY UNCLOGGED...
...HARD.
THE FIRST ROUND HAS CLEARLY ENDED.
ALAS, UNLIKE A CAREFULLY MONI-TORED BOXING MATCH...

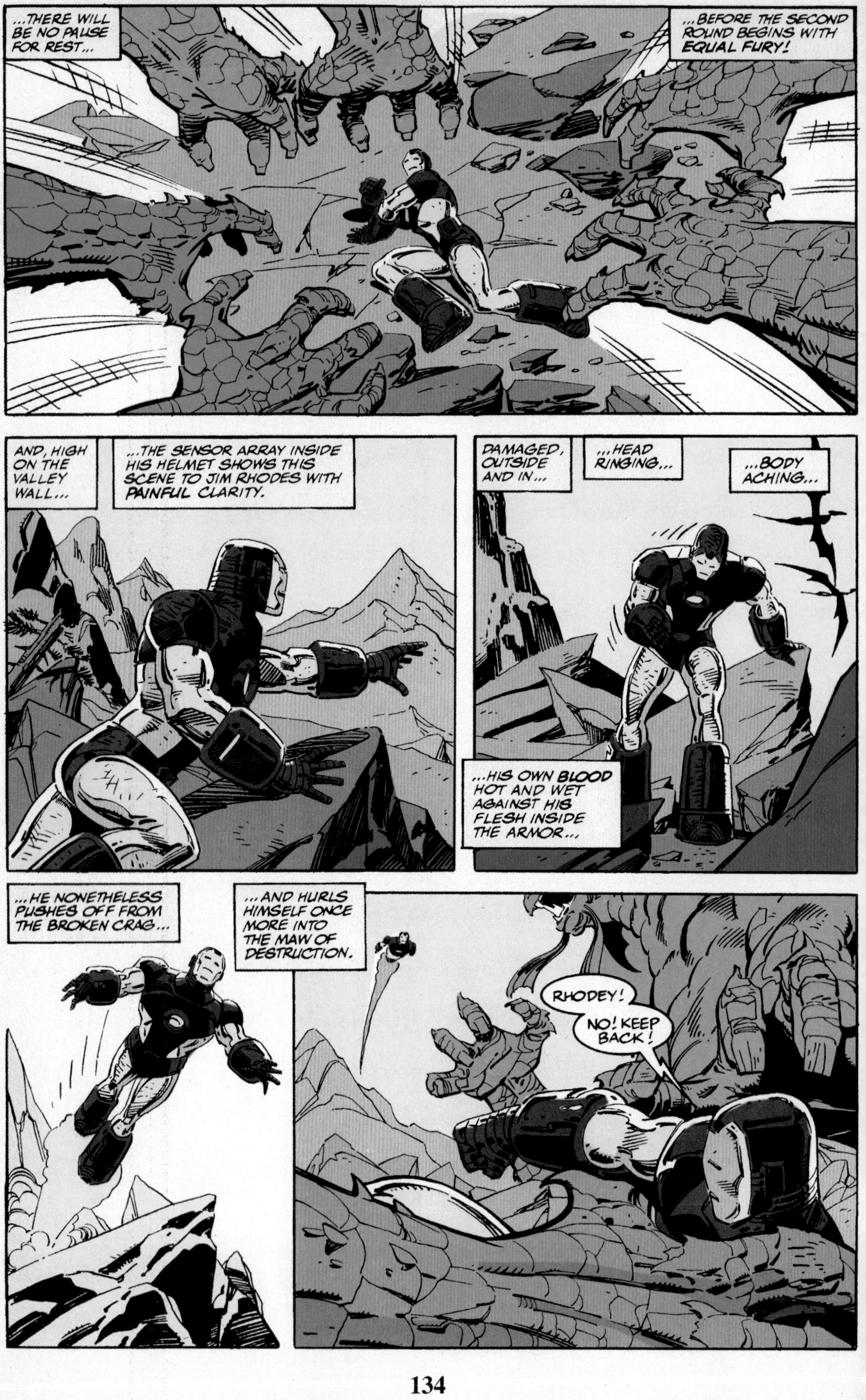
...THERE WILL BE NO PAUSE FOR REST...
...BEFORE THE SECOND ROUND BEGINS WITH EQUAL FURY!
AND, HIGH ON THE VALLEY WALL...
...THE SENSOR ARRAY INSIDE HIS HELMET SHOWS THIS SCENE TO JIM RHODES WITH PAINFUL CLARITY.
DAMAGED, OUTSIDE AND IN...
...HEAD RINGING...
...BODY ACHING...
...HIS OWN BLOOD HOT AND WET AGAINST HIS FLESH INSIDE THE ARMOR...
...HE NONETHELESS PUSHES OFF FROM THE BROKEN CRAG...
...AND HURLS HIMSELF ONCE MORE INTO THE MAW OF DESTRUCTION.
RHODEY!
NO! KEEP BACK!

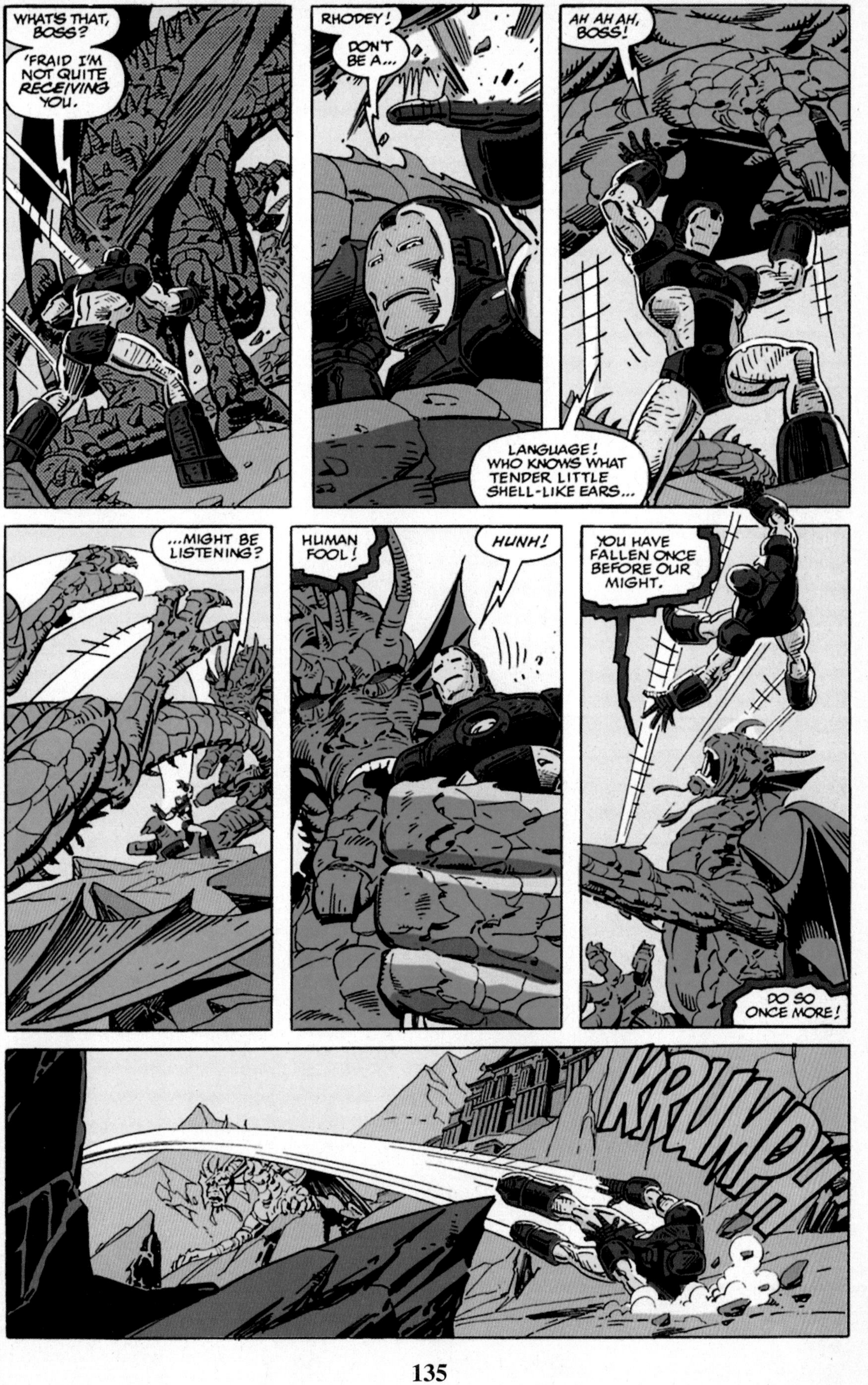
WHAT'S THAT, BOSS?
'FRAID I'M NOT QUITE RECEIVING YOU.
RHODEY!
DON'T BE A...
AH AH AH, BOSS!
LANGUAGE! WHO KNOWS WHAT TENDER LITTLE SHELL-LIKE EARS...
...MIGHT BE LISTENING?
HUMAN FOOL!
HUNH!
YOU HAVE FALLEN ONCE BEFORE OUR MIGHT.
DO SO ONCE MORE!
KRUMP!

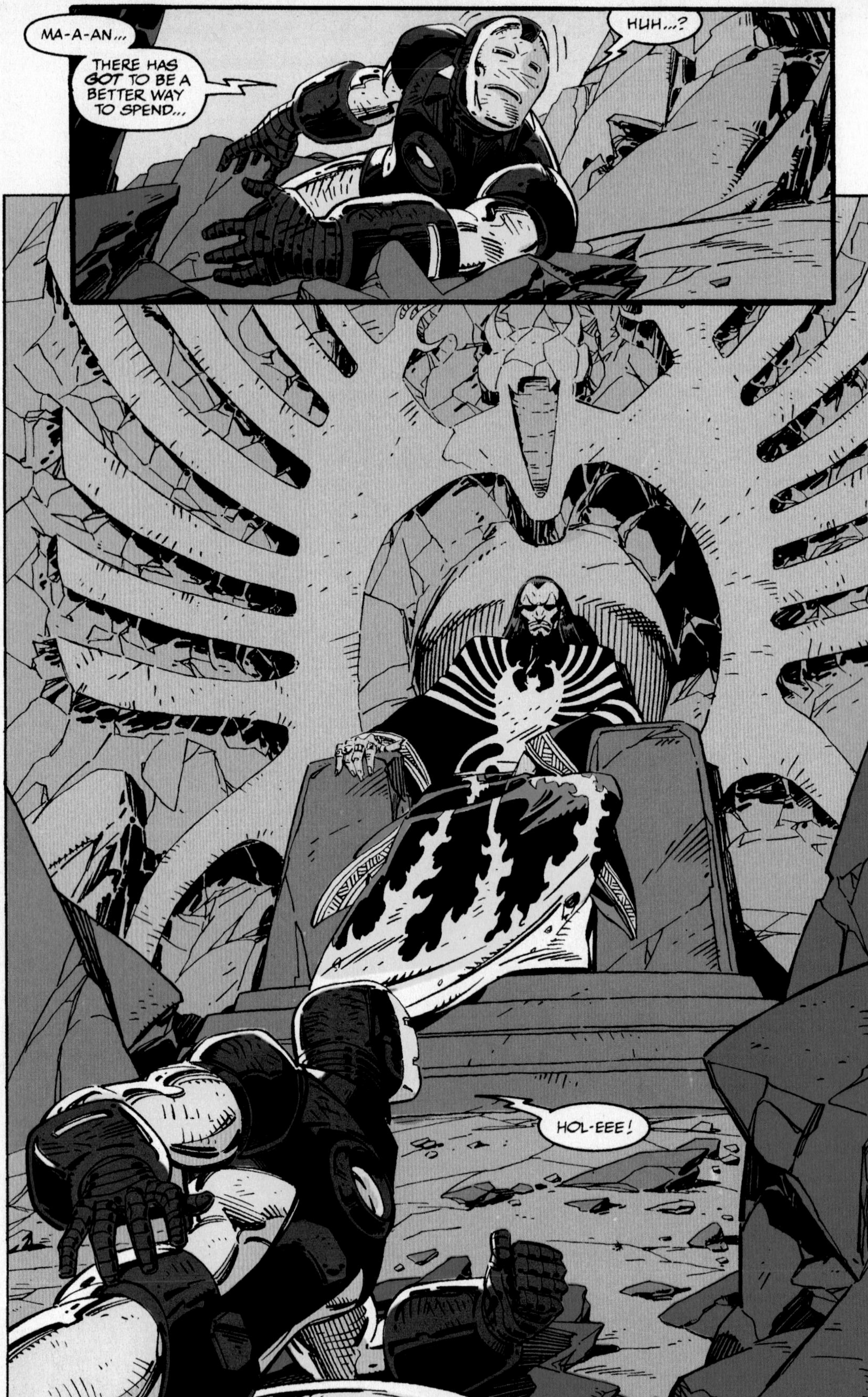
MA-A-AN...
THERE HAS GOT TO BE A BETTER WAY TO SPEND...
HUH...?
HOL-EEE!

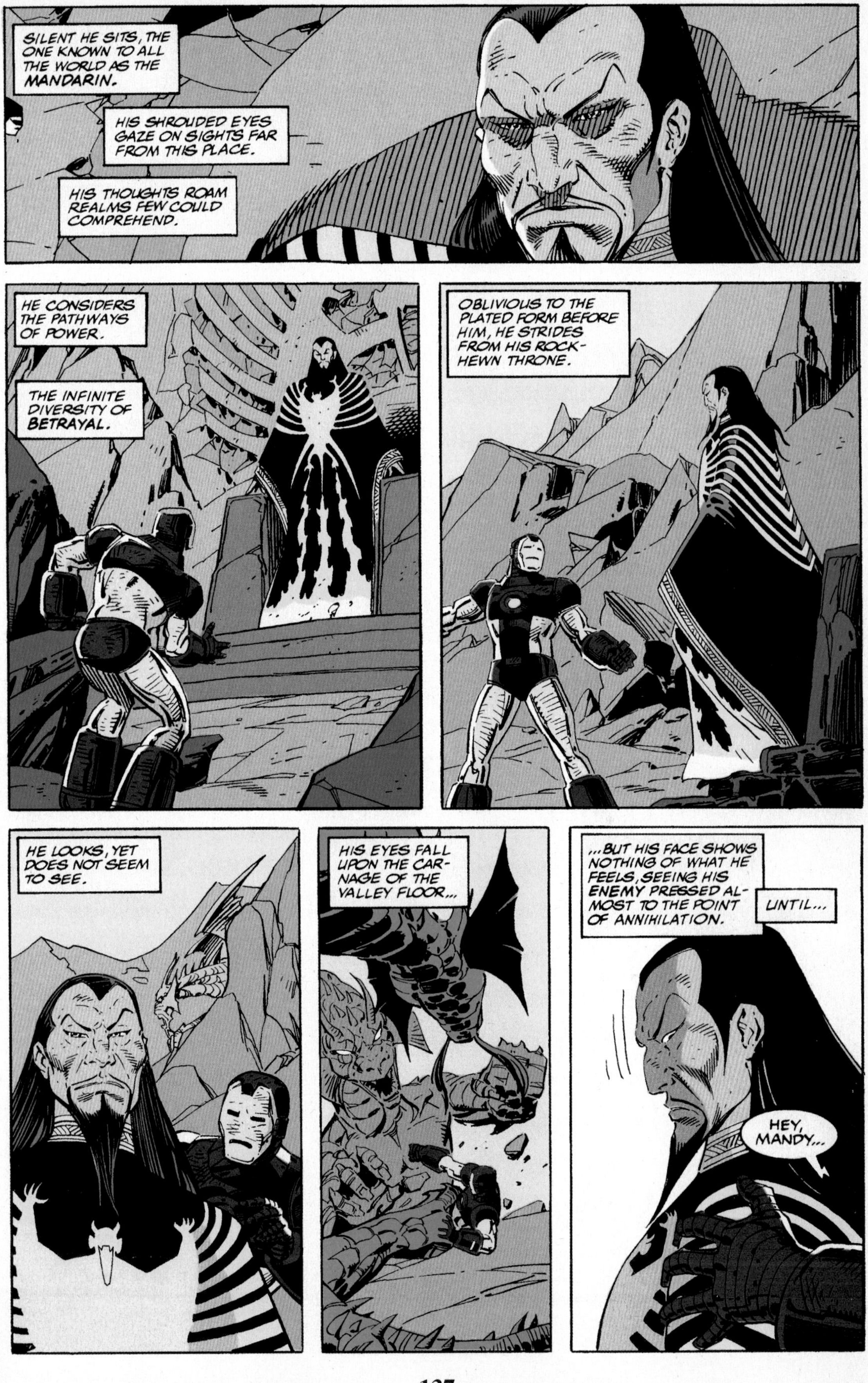
SILENT HE SITS, THE ONE KNOWN TO ALL THE WORLD AS THE MANDARIN.
HIS SHROUDED EYES GAZE ON SIGHTS FAR FROM THIS PLACE.
HIS THOUGHTS ROAM REALMS FEW COULD COMPREHEND.
HE CONSIDERS THE PATHWAYS OF POWER.
THE INFINITE DIVERSITY OF BETRAYAL.
OBLIVIOUS TO THE PLATED FORM BEFORE HIM, HE STRIDES FROM HIS ROCK-HEWN THRONE.
HE LOOKS, YET DOES NOT SEEM TO SEE.
HIS EYES FALL UPON THE CARNAGE OF THE VALLEY FLOOR...
...BUT HIS FACE SHOWS NOTHING OF WHAT HE FEELS, SEEING HIS ENEMY PRESSED ALMOST TO THE POINT OF ANNIHILATION.
UNTIL...
HEY, MANDY...

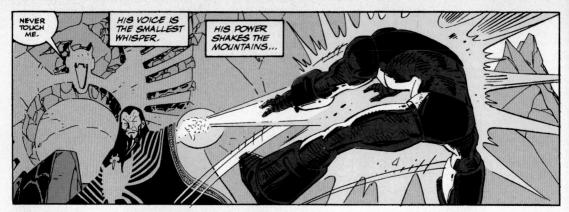

NEVER TOUCH ME.

HIS VOICE IS THE SMALLEST WHISPER.

HIS POWER SHAKES THE MOUNTAINS...

...AND JIM RHODES IS ONCE MORE HURLED FROM THE FIELD OF BATTLE.

THE FORCE OF HIS IMPACT REGISTERS ON SEISMOGRAPHS AS FAR AWAY AS CALIFORNIA...

...SEVEN THOUSAND MILES TO THE EAST.

AND HE DOES NOT STOP THERE.

RHODEY!

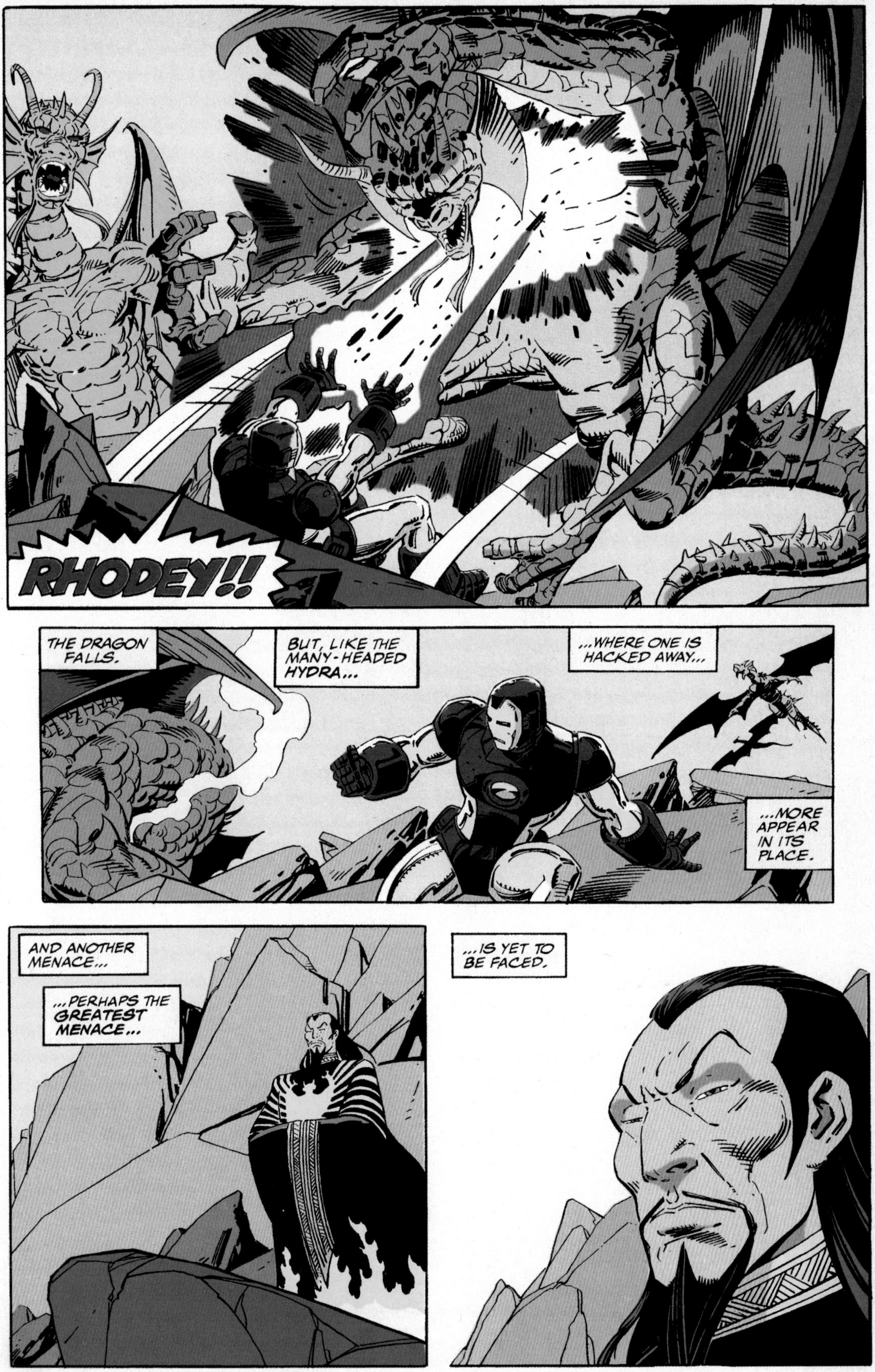
RHODEY!!
THE DRAGON FALLS.
BUT, LIKE THE MANY-HEADED HYDRA...
...WHERE ONE IS HACKED AWAY...
...MORE APPEAR IN ITS PLACE.
AND ANOTHER MENACE...
...PERHAPS THE GREATEST MENACE...
...IS YET TO BE FACED.

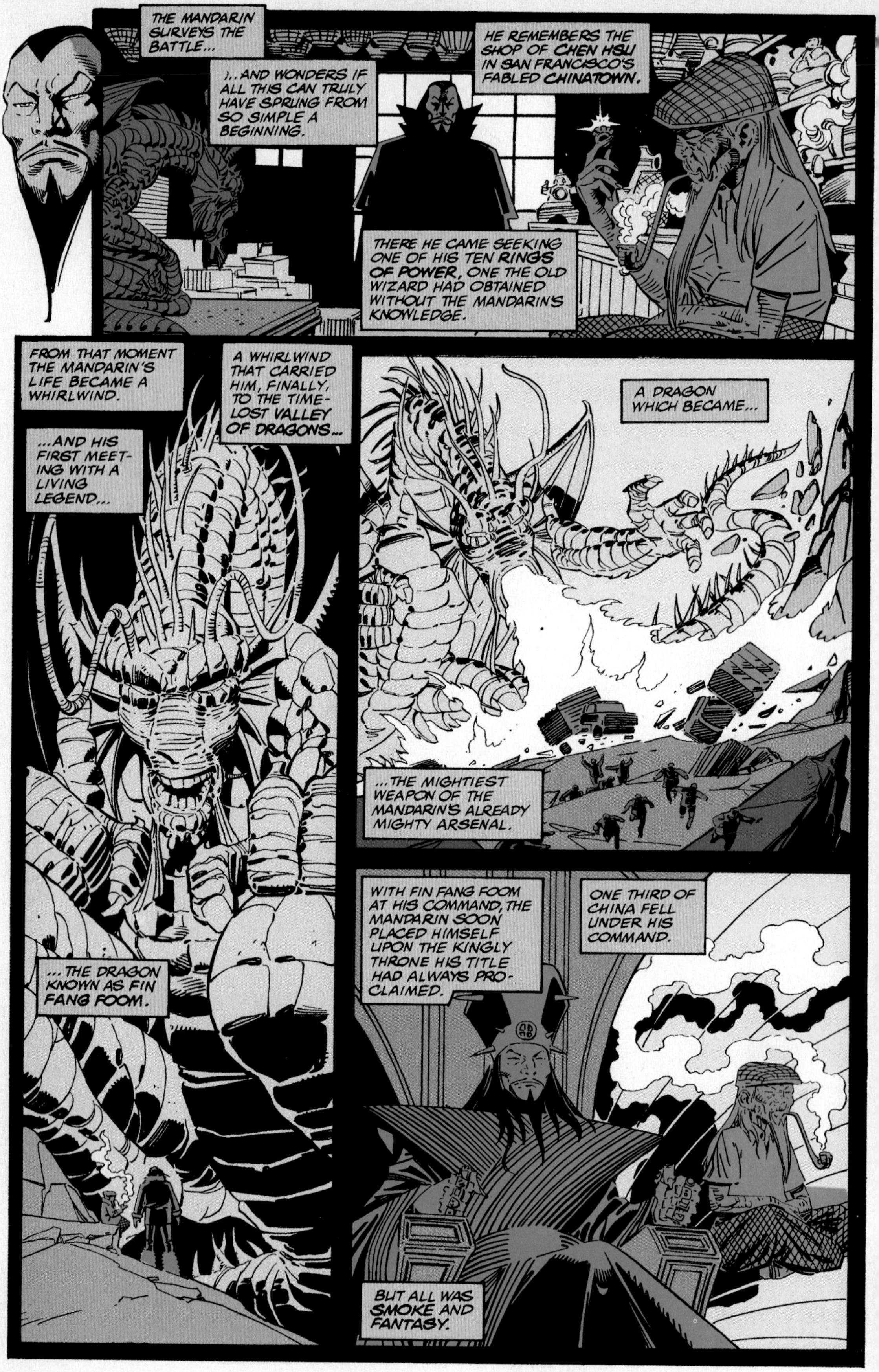
THE MANDARIN SURVEYS THE BATTLE...
...AND WONDERS IF ALL THIS CAN TRULY HAVE SPRUNG FROM SO SIMPLE A BEGINNING.
HE REMEMBERS THE SHOP OF CHEN HSU IN SAN FRANCISCO'S FABLED CHINATOWN.
THERE HE CAME SEEKING ONE OF HIS TEN RINGS OF POWER, ONE THE OLD WIZARD HAD OBTAINED WITHOUT THE MANDARIN'S KNOWLEDGE.
FROM THAT MOMENT THE MANDARIN'S LIFE BECAME A WHIRLWIND.
A WHIRLWIND THAT CARRIED HIM, FINALLY, TO THE TIME-LOST VALLEY OF DRAGONS...
...AND HIS FIRST MEETING WITH A LIVING LEGEND...
...THE DRAGON KNOWN AS FIN FANG FOOM.
A DRAGON WHICH BECAME...
...THE MIGHTIEST WEAPON OF THE MANDARIN'S ALREADY MIGHTY ARSENAL.
WITH FIN FANG FOOM AT HIS COMMAND, THE MANDARIN SOON PLACED HIMSELF UPON THE KINGLY THRONE HIS TITLE HAD ALWAYS PROCLAIMED.
ONE THIRD OF CHINA FELL UNDER HIS COMMAND.
BUT ALL WAS SMOKE AND FANTASY.

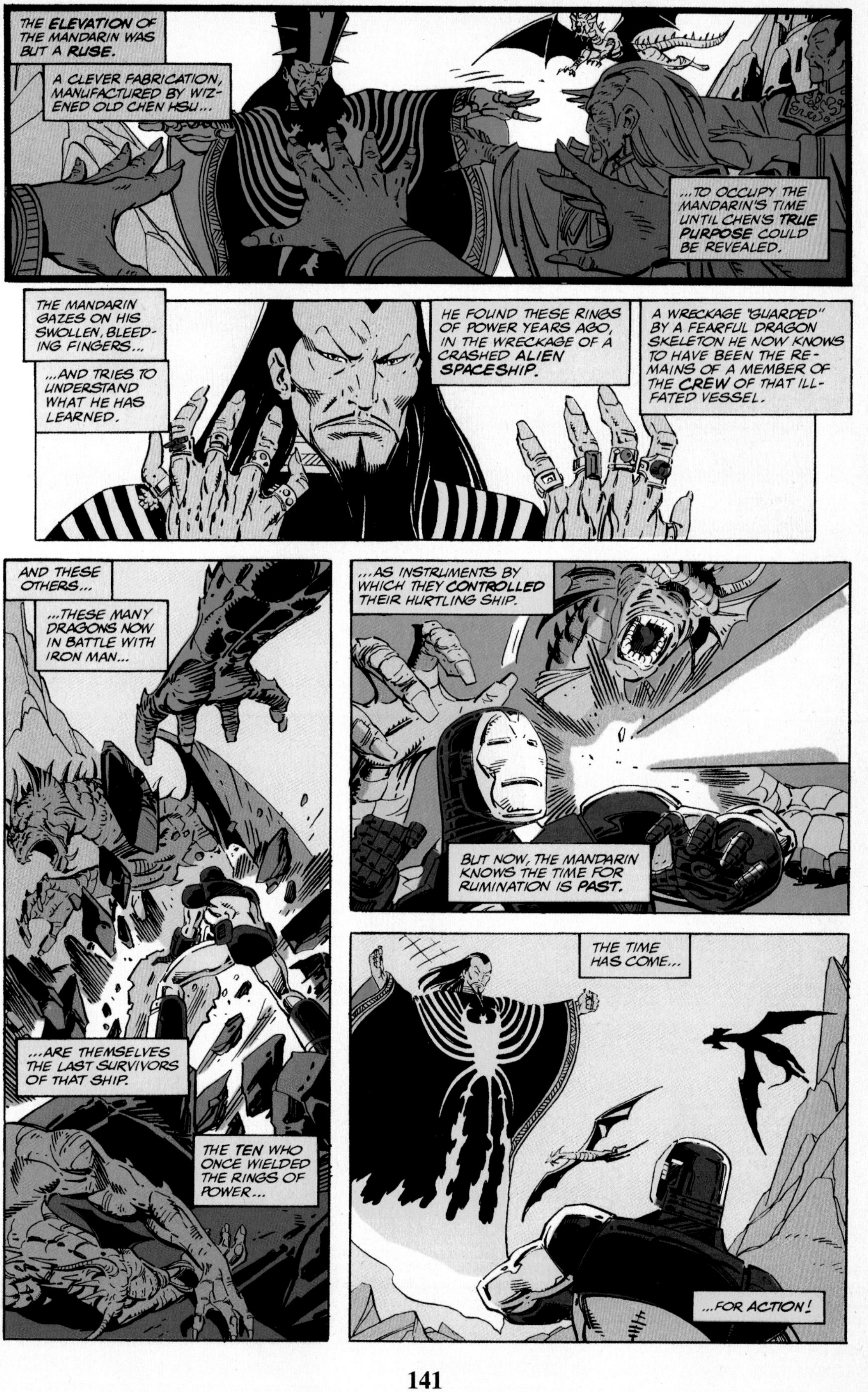
THE ELEVATION OF THE MANDARIN WAS BUT A RUSE.
A CLEVER FABRICATION, MANUFACTURED BY WIZENED OLD CHEN HSU...
...TO OCCUPY THE MANDARIN'S TIME UNTIL CHEN'S TRUE PURPOSE COULD BE REVEALED.
THE MANDARIN GAZES ON HIS SWOLLEN, BLEEDING FINGERS...
...AND TRIES TO UNDERSTAND WHAT HE HAS LEARNED.
HE FOUND THESE RINGS OF POWER YEARS AGO, IN THE WRECKAGE OF A CRASHED ALIEN SPACESHIP.
A WRECKAGE "GUARDED" BY A FEARFUL DRAGON SKELETON HE NOW KNOWS TO HAVE BEEN THE REMAINS OF A MEMBER OF THE CREW OF THAT ILL-FATED VESSEL.
AND THESE OTHERS...
...THESE MANY DRAGONS NOW IN BATTLE WITH IRON MAN...
...ARE THEMSELVES THE LAST SURVIVORS OF THAT SHIP.
THE TEN WHO ONCE WIELDED THE RINGS OF POWER...
...AS INSTRUMENTS BY WHICH THEY CONTROLLED THEIR HURTLING SHIP.
BUT NOW, THE MANDARIN KNOWS THE TIME FOR RUMINATION IS PAST.
THE TIME HAS COME...
...FOR ACTION!

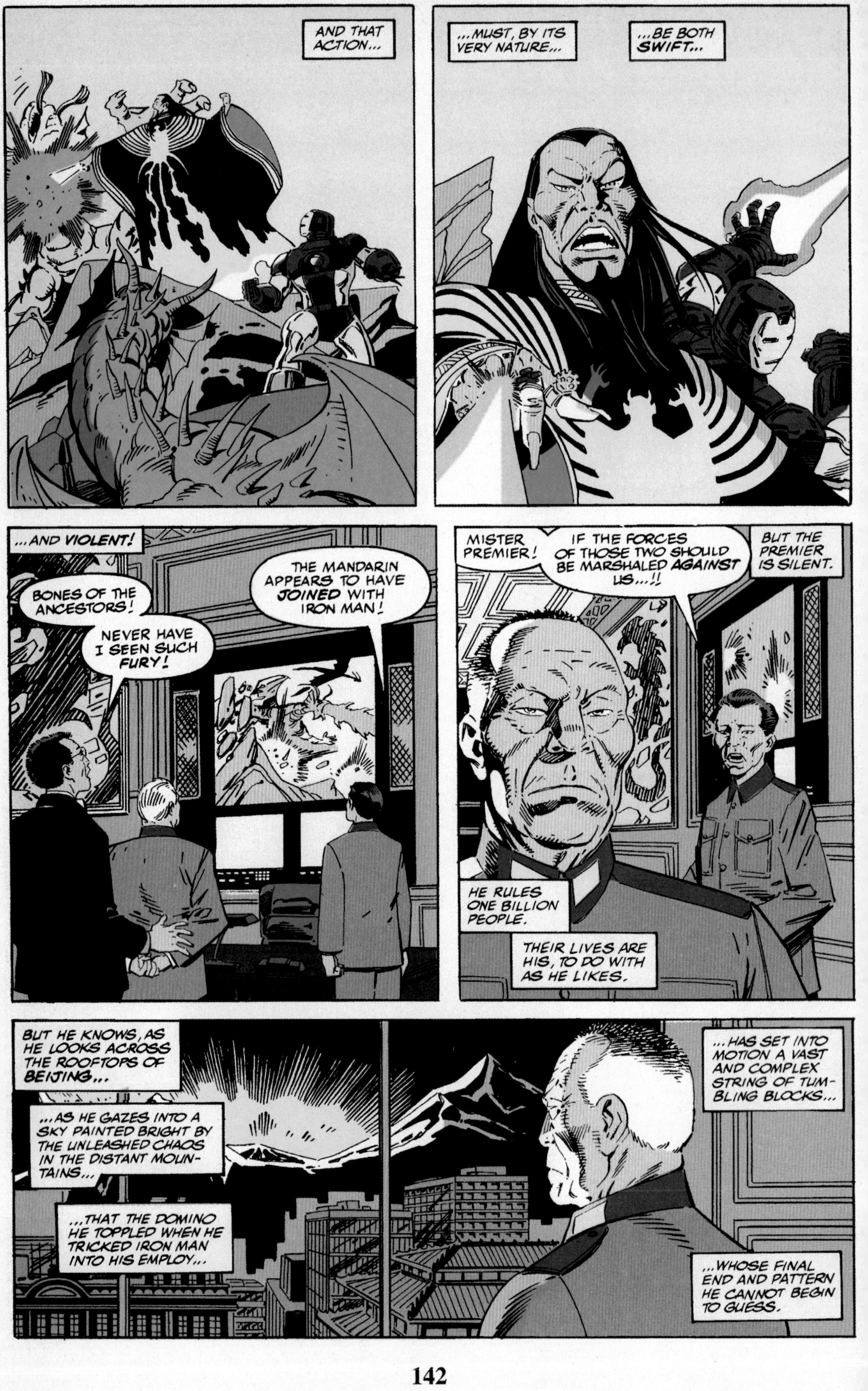
AND THAT ACTION...
...MUST, BY ITS VERY NATURE...
...BE BOTH SWIFT...
...AND VIOLENT!
BONES OF THE ANCESTORS!
NEVER HAVE I SEEN SUCH FURY!
THE MANDARIN APPEARS TO HAVE JOINED WITH IRON MAN!
MISTER PREMIER!
IF THE FORCES OF THOSE TWO SHOULD BE MARSHALED AGAINST US...!!
BUT THE PREMIER IS SILENT.
HE RULES ONE BILLION PEOPLE.
THEIR LIVES ARE HIS, TO DO WITH AS HE LIKES.
BUT HE KNOWS, AS HE LOOKS ACROSS THE ROOFTOPS OF BEIJING...
...AS HE GAZES INTO A SKY PAINTED BRIGHT BY THE UNLEASHED CHAOS IN THE DISTANT MOUNTAINS...
...THAT THE DOMINO HE TOPPLED WHEN HE TRICKED IRON MAN INTO HIS EMPLOY...
...HAS SET INTO MOTION A VAST AND COMPLEX STRING OF TUMBLING BLOCKS...
...WHOSE FINAL END AND PATTERN HE CANNOT BEGIN TO GUESS.

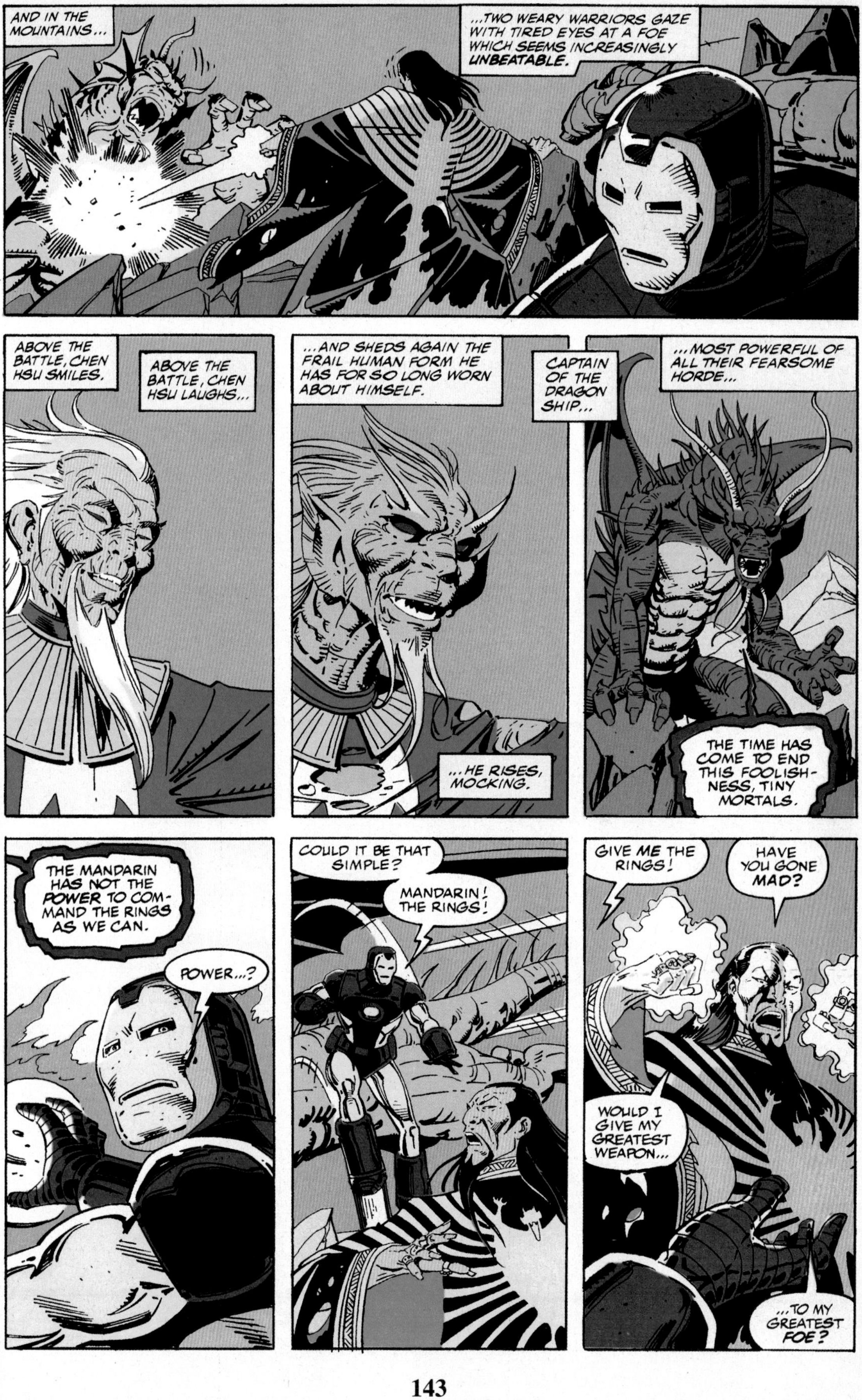
AND IN THE MOUNTAINS...
...TWO WEARY WARRIORS GAZE WITH TIRED EYES AT A FOE WHICH SEEMS INCREASINGLY UNBEATABLE.
ABOVE THE BATTLE, CHEN HSU SMILES.
ABOVE THE BATTLE, CHEN HSU LAUGHS...
...AND SHEDS AGAIN THE FRAIL HUMAN FORM HE HAS FOR SO LONG WORN ABOUT HIMSELF.
...HE RISES, MOCKING.
CAPTAIN OF THE DRAGON SHIP...
...MOST POWERFUL OF ALL THEIR FEARSOME HORDE...
THE TIME HAS COME TO END THIS FOOLISHNESS, TINY MORTALS.
THE MANDARIN HAS NOT THE POWER TO COMMAND THE RINGS AS WE CAN.
POWER...?
COULD IT BE THAT SIMPLE?
MANDARIN! THE RINGS!
GIVE ME THE RINGS!
HAVE YOU GONE MAD?
WOULD I GIVE MY GREATEST WEAPON...
...TO MY GREATEST FOE?

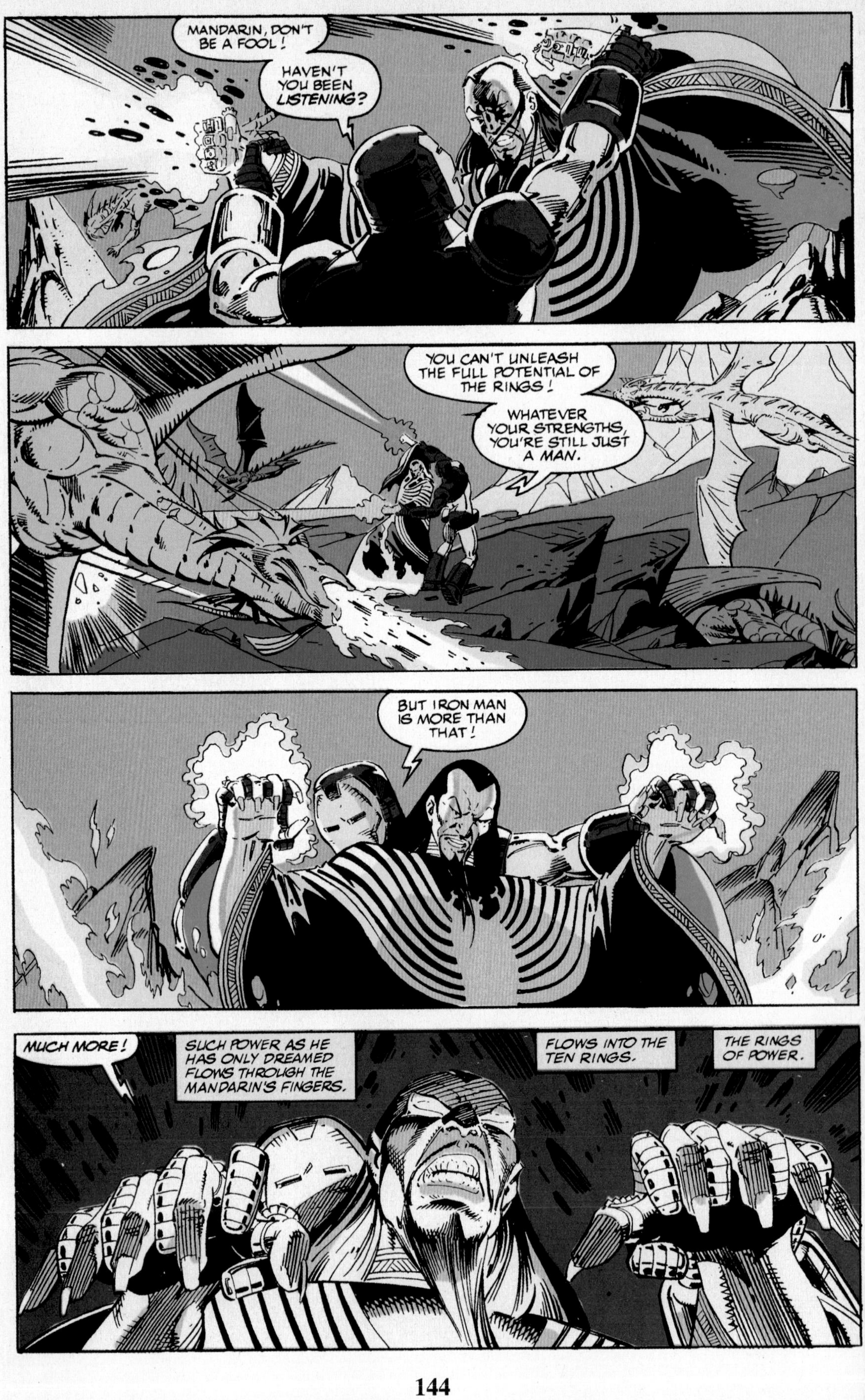
MANDARIN, DON'T BE A FOOL!
HAVEN'T YOU BEEN LISTENING?
YOU CAN'T UNLEASH THE FULL POTENTIAL OF THE RINGS!
WHATEVER YOUR STRENGTHS, YOU'RE STILL JUST A MAN.
BUT IRON MAN IS MORE THAN THAT!
MUCH MORE!
SUCH POWER AS HE HAS ONLY DREAMED FLOWS THROUGH THE MANDARIN'S FINGERS.
FLOWS INTO THE TEN RINGS.
THE RINGS OF POWER.

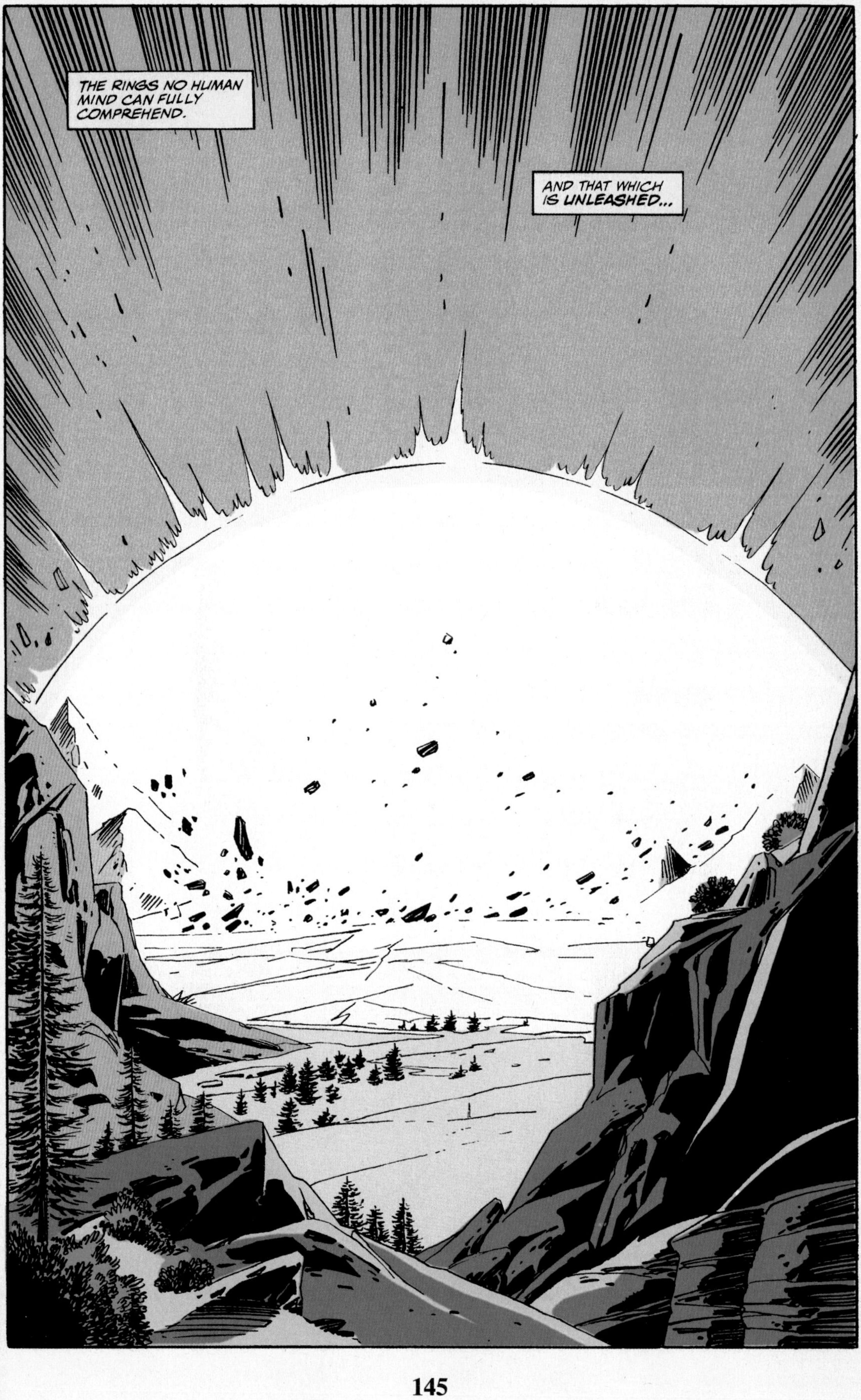
THE RINGS NO HUMAN MIND CAN FULLY COMPREHEND.
AND THAT WHICH IS UNLEASHED...

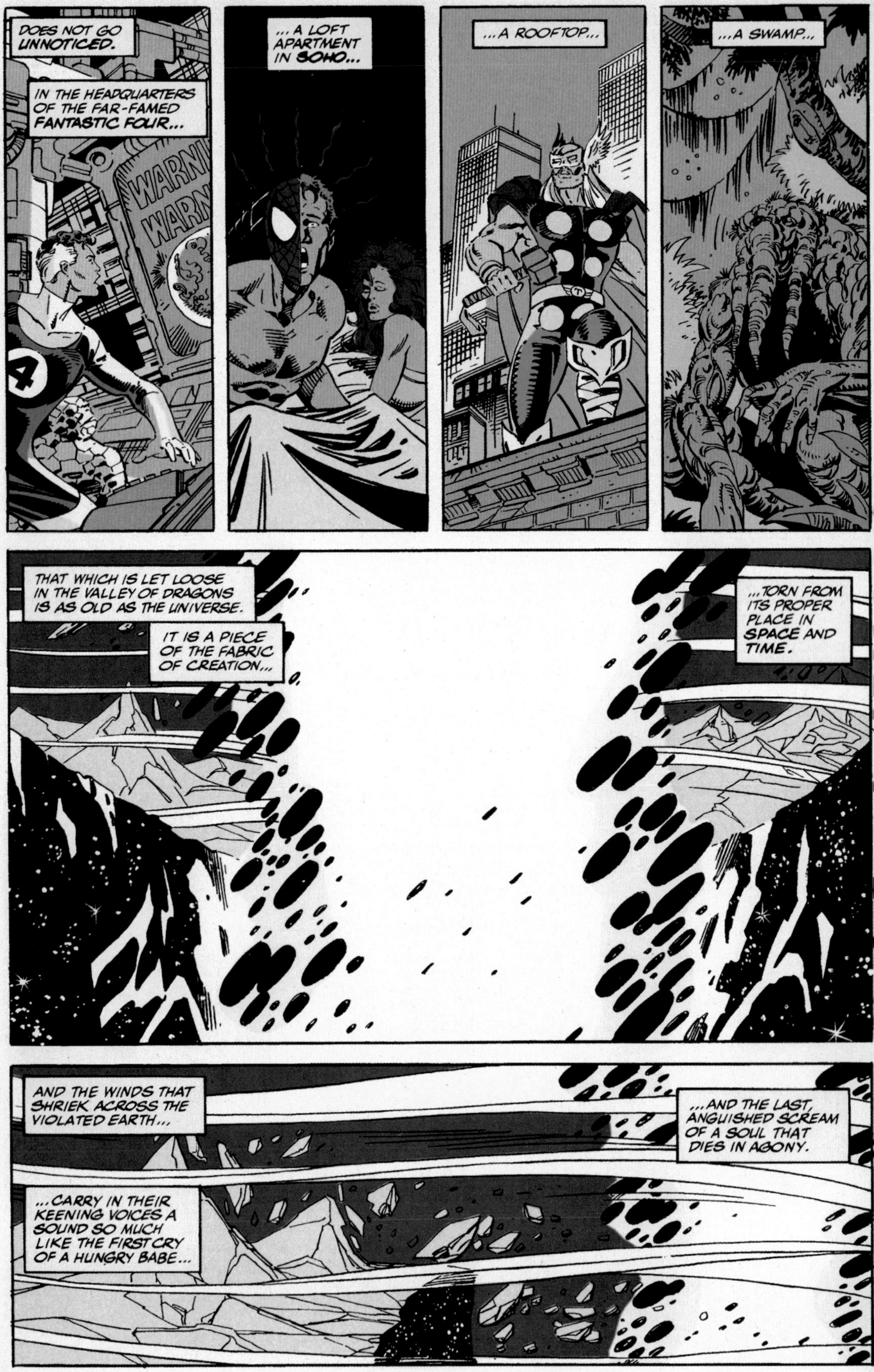
DOES NOT GO UNNOTICED.
IN THE HEADQUARTERS OF THE FAR-FAMED FANTASTIC FOUR...
WARN
WARN
...A LOFT APARTMENT IN SOHO...
...A ROOFTOP...
...A SWAMP...
THAT WHICH IS LET LOOSE IN THE VALLEY OF DRAGONS IS AS OLD AS THE UNIVERSE.
IT IS A PIECE OF THE FABRIC OF CREATION...
...TORN FROM ITS PROPER PLACE IN SPACE AND TIME.
AND THE WINDS THAT SHRIEK ACROSS THE VIOLATED EARTH...
...CARRY IN THEIR KEENING VOICES A SOUND SO MUCH LIKE THE FIRST CRY OF A HUNGRY BABE...
...AND THE LAST, ANGUISHED SCREAM OF A SOUL THAT DIES IN AGONY.

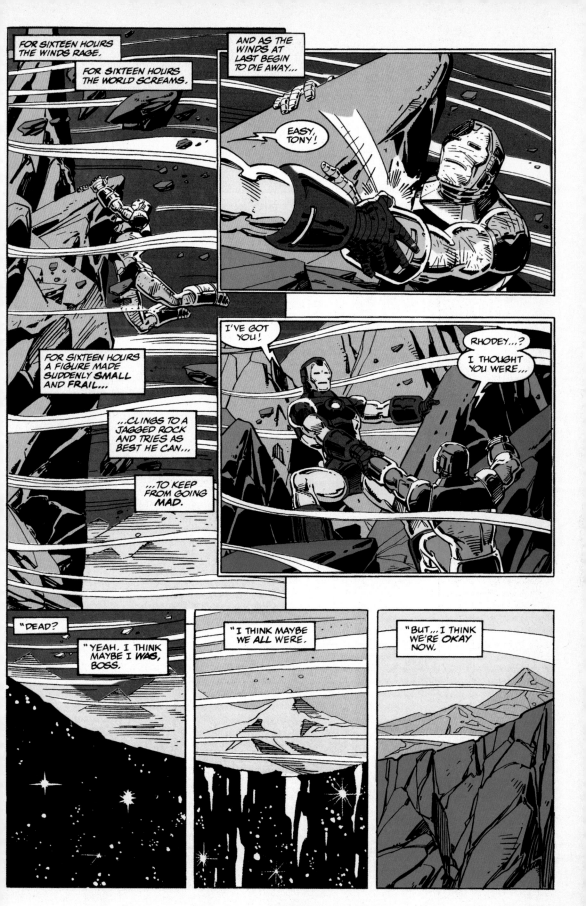

FOR SIXTEEN HOURS THE WINDS RAGE.

FOR SIXTEEN HOURS THE WORLD SCREAMS.

AND AS THE WINDS AT LAST BEGIN TO DIE AWAY...

EASY, TONY!

FOR SIXTEEN HOURS A FIGURE MADE SUDDENLY SMALL AND FRAIL...

...CLINGS TO A JAGGED ROCK AND TRIES AS BEST HE CAN...

...TO KEEP FROM GOING MAD.

I'VE GOT YOU!

RHODEY...? I THOUGHT YOU WERE...

"DEAD?

"YEAH. I THINK MAYBE I *WAS*, BOSS.

"I THINK MAYBE WE ALL WERE.

"BUT... I THINK WE'RE OKAY NOW.

147

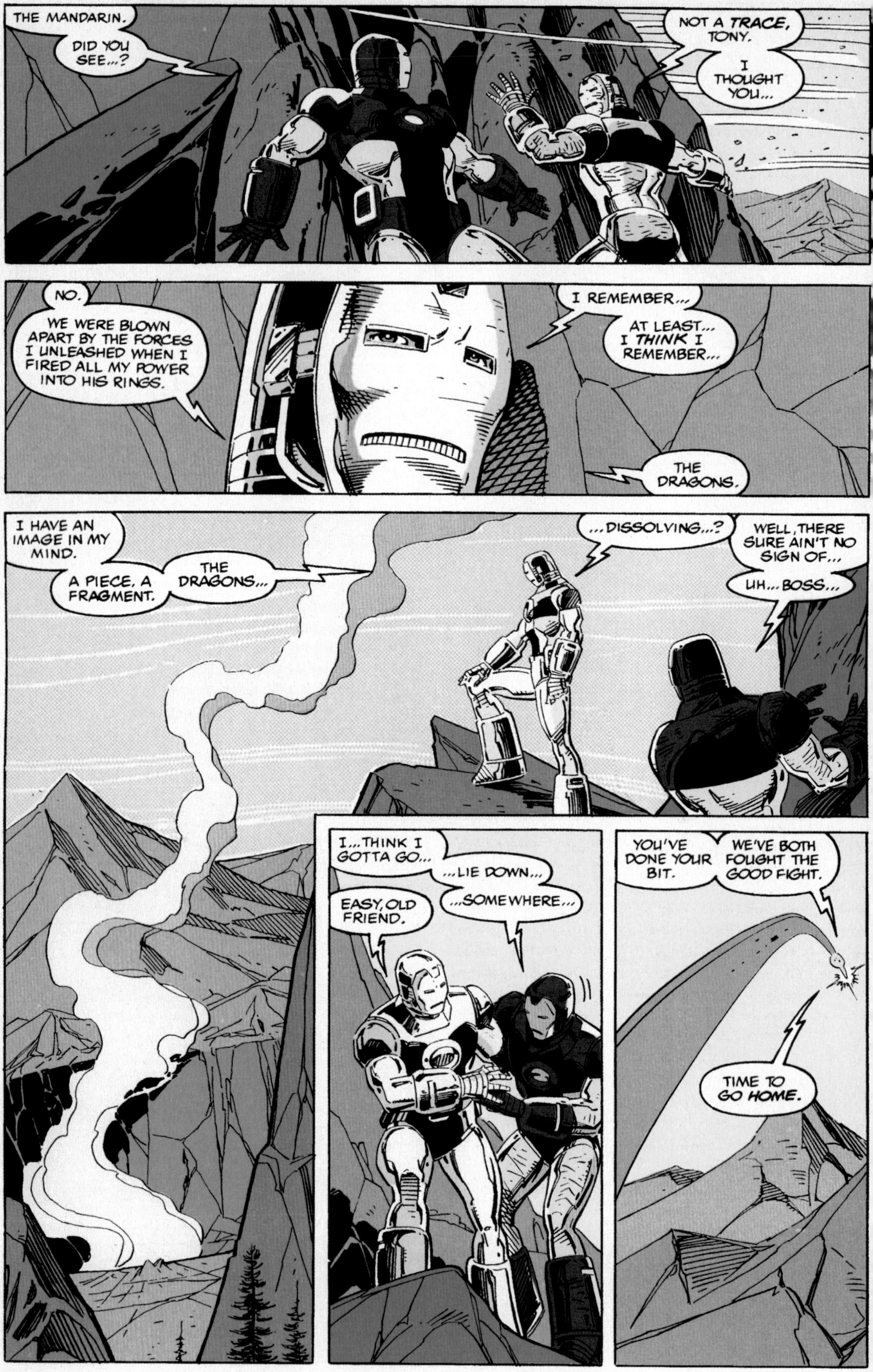
THE MANDARIN.
DID YOU SEE...?
NOT A TRACE, TONY.
I THOUGHT YOU...
NO.
WE WERE BLOWN APART BY THE FORCES I UNLEASHED WHEN I FIRED ALL MY POWER INTO HIS RINGS.
I REMEMBER...
AT LEAST... I THINK I REMEMBER...
THE DRAGONS.
I HAVE AN IMAGE IN MY MIND.
A PIECE. A FRAGMENT.
THE DRAGONS...
...DISSOLVING...?
WELL, THERE SURE AIN'T NO SIGN OF...
UH... BOSS...
I... THINK I GOTTA GO...
...LIE DOWN...
...SOMEWHERE...
EASY, OLD FRIEND.
YOU'VE DONE YOUR BIT.
WE'VE BOTH FOUGHT THE GOOD FIGHT.
TIME TO GO HOME.

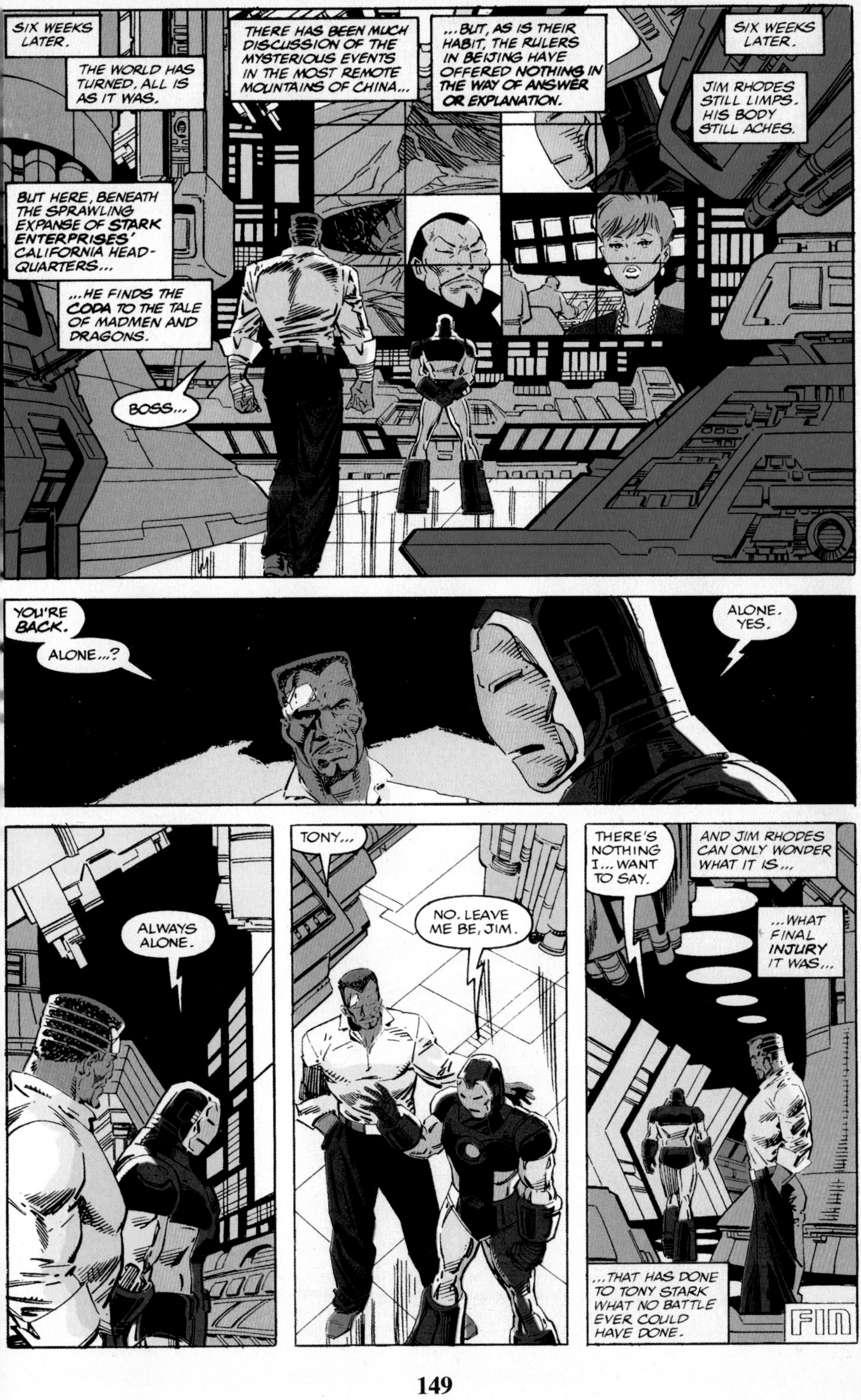
SIX WEEKS LATER.
THE WORLD HAS TURNED. ALL IS AS IT WAS.
THERE HAS BEEN MUCH DISCUSSION OF THE MYSTERIOUS EVENTS IN THE MOST REMOTE MOUNTAINS OF CHINA...
...BUT, AS IS THEIR HABIT, THE RULERS IN BEIJING HAVE OFFERED NOTHING IN THE WAY OF ANSWER OR EXPLANATION.
SIX WEEKS LATER.
JIM RHODES STILL LIMPS. HIS BODY STILL ACHES.
BUT HERE, BENEATH THE SPRAWLING EXPANSE OF STARK ENTERPRISES' CALIFORNIA HEAD-QUARTERS...
...HE FINDS THE CODA TO THE TALE OF MADMEN AND DRAGONS.
BOSS...
YOU'RE BACK.
ALONE...?
ALONE. YES.
ALWAYS ALONE.
TONY...
NO. LEAVE ME BE, JIM.
THERE'S NOTHING I... WANT TO SAY.
AND JIM RHODES CAN ONLY WONDER WHAT IT IS...
...WHAT FINAL INJURY IT WAS...
...THAT HAS DONE TO TONY STARK WHAT NO BATTLE EVER COULD HAVE DONE.
FIN

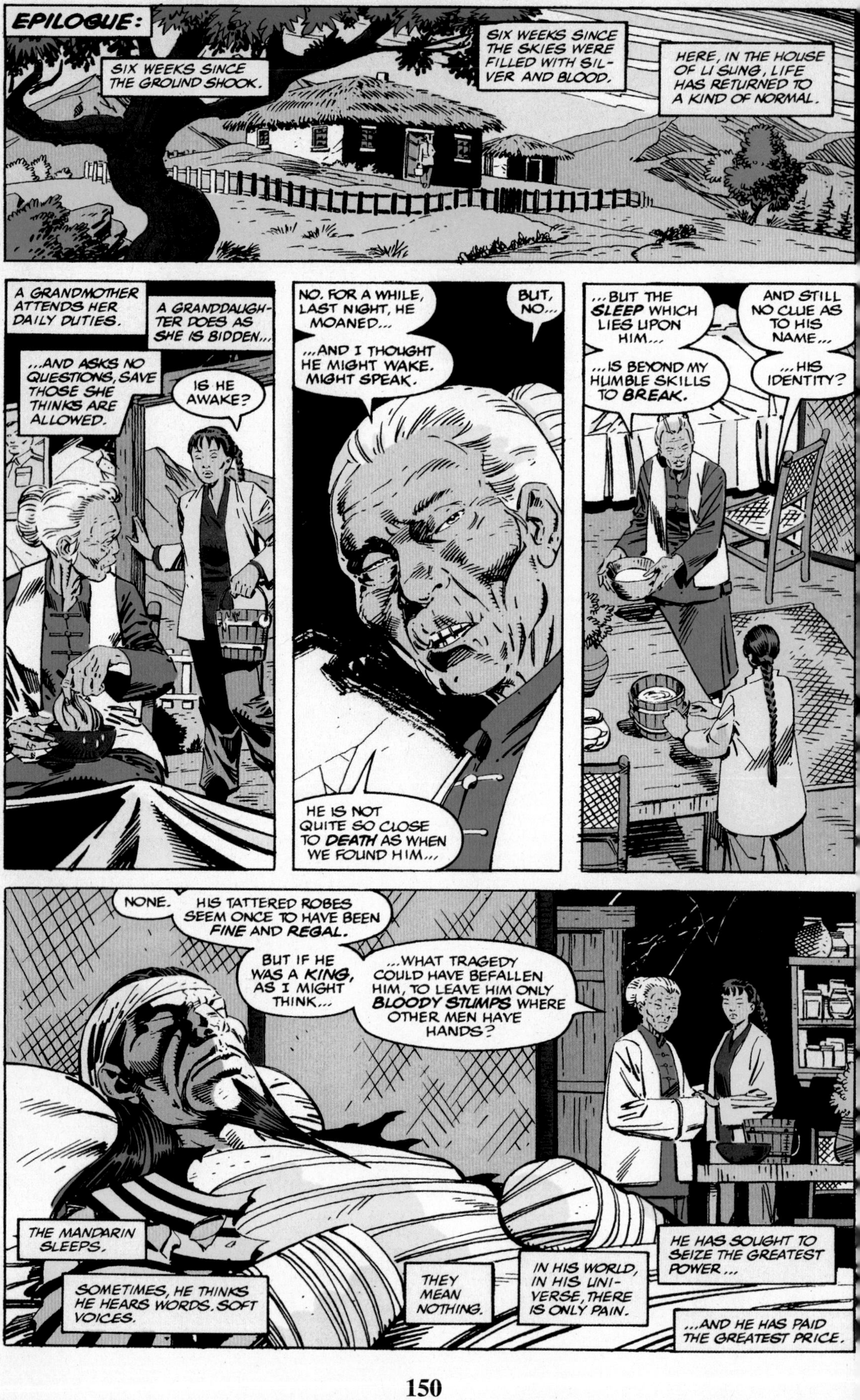
EPILOGUE:
SIX WEEKS SINCE THE GROUND SHOOK.
SIX WEEKS SINCE THE SKIES WERE FILLED WITH SIL-VER AND BLOOD.
HERE, IN THE HOUSE OF LI SUNG, LIFE HAS RETURNED TO A KIND OF NORMAL.
A GRANDMOTHER ATTENDS HER DAILY DUTIES.
A GRANDDAUGH-TER DOES AS SHE IS BIDDEN...
...AND ASKS NO QUESTIONS, SAVE THOSE SHE THINKS ARE ALLOWED.
IS HE AWAKE?
NO. FOR A WHILE, LAST NIGHT, HE MOANED...
...AND I THOUGHT HE MIGHT WAKE. MIGHT SPEAK.
BUT, NO...
HE IS NOT QUITE SO CLOSE TO DEATH AS WHEN WE FOUND HIM...
...BUT THE SLEEP WHICH LIES UPON HIM...
...IS BEYOND MY HUMBLE SKILLS TO BREAK.
AND STILL NO CLUE AS TO HIS NAME...
...HIS IDENTITY?
NONE.
HIS TATTERED ROBES SEEM ONCE TO HAVE BEEN FINE AND REGAL.
BUT IF HE WAS A KING, AS I MIGHT THINK...
...WHAT TRAGEDY COULD HAVE BEFALLEN HIM, TO LEAVE HIM ONLY BLOODY STUMPS WHERE OTHER MEN HAVE HANDS?
THE MANDARIN SLEEPS.
SOMETIMES, HE THINKS HE HEARS WORDS. SOFT VOICES.
THEY MEAN NOTHING.
IN HIS WORLD, IN HIS UNI-VERSE, THERE IS ONLY PAIN.
HE HAS SOUGHT TO SEIZE THE GREATEST POWER...
...AND HE HAS PAID THE GREATEST PRICE.

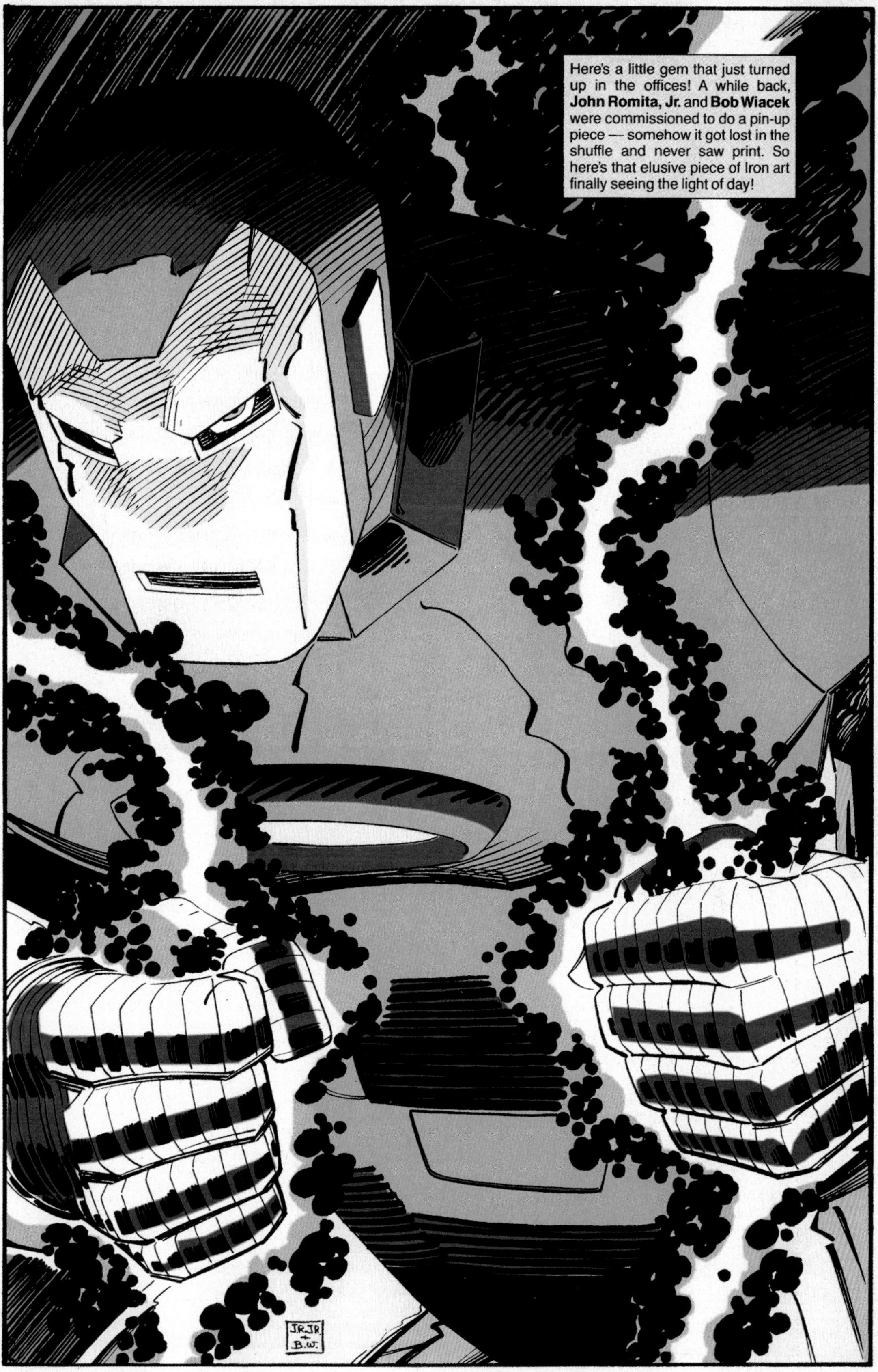
Here's a little gem that just turned up in the offices! A while back, **John Romita, Jr.** and **Bob Wiacek** were commissioned to do a pin-up piece — somehow it got lost in the shuffle and never saw print. So here's that elusive piece of Iron art finally seeing the light of day!

MOMENTS UNSEEN

TONY DeZUNIGA art - JOHN BYRNE story - JOHN COSTANZA letters - PAUL BECTON colors - NEL YOMTOV editor - TOM DeFALCO editor in chief

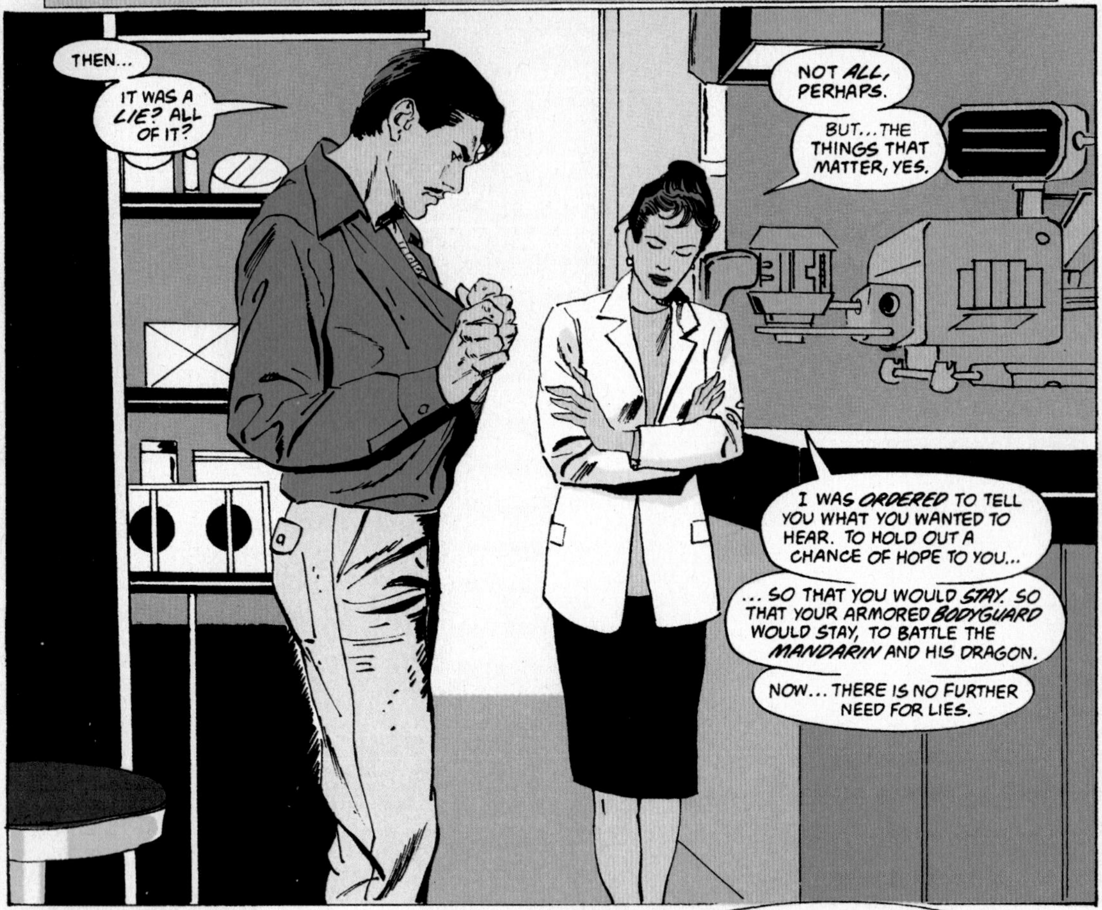

THEN...
IT WAS A LIE? ALL OF IT?
NOT ALL, PERHAPS.
BUT... THE THINGS THAT MATTER, YES.
I WAS ORDERED TO TELL YOU WHAT YOU WANTED TO HEAR. TO HOLD OUT A CHANCE OF HOPE TO YOU...
... SO THAT YOU WOULD STAY. SO THAT YOUR ARMORED BODYGUARD WOULD STAY, TO BATTLE THE MANDARIN AND HIS DRAGON.
NOW... THERE IS NO FURTHER NEED FOR LIES.

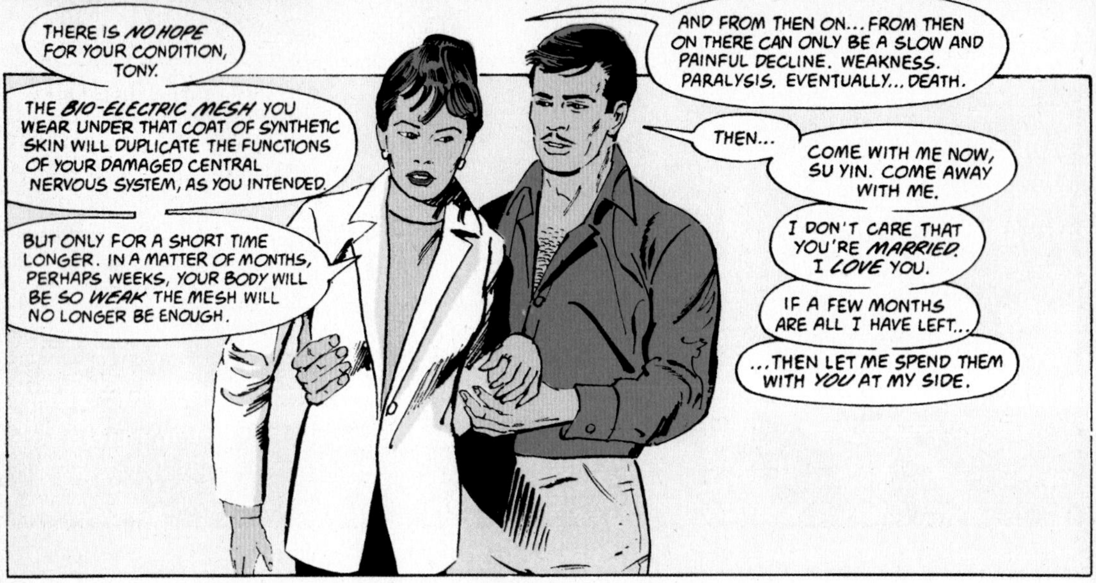

THERE IS NO HOPE FOR YOUR CONDITION, TONY.
THE BIO-ELECTRIC MESH YOU WEAR UNDER THAT COAT OF SYNTHETIC SKIN WILL DUPLICATE THE FUNCTIONS OF YOUR DAMAGED CENTRAL NERVOUS SYSTEM, AS YOU INTENDED.
BUT ONLY FOR A SHORT TIME LONGER. IN A MATTER OF MONTHS, PERHAPS WEEKS, YOUR BODY WILL BE SO WEAK THE MESH WILL NO LONGER BE ENOUGH.
AND FROM THEN ON... FROM THEN ON THERE CAN ONLY BE A SLOW AND PAINFUL DECLINE. WEAKNESS. PARALYSIS. EVENTUALLY... DEATH.
THEN...
COME WITH ME NOW, SU YIN. COME AWAY WITH ME.
I DON'T CARE THAT YOU'RE MARRIED. I LOVE YOU.
IF A FEW MONTHS ARE ALL I HAVE LEFT...
...THEN LET ME SPEND THEM WITH YOU AT MY SIDE.

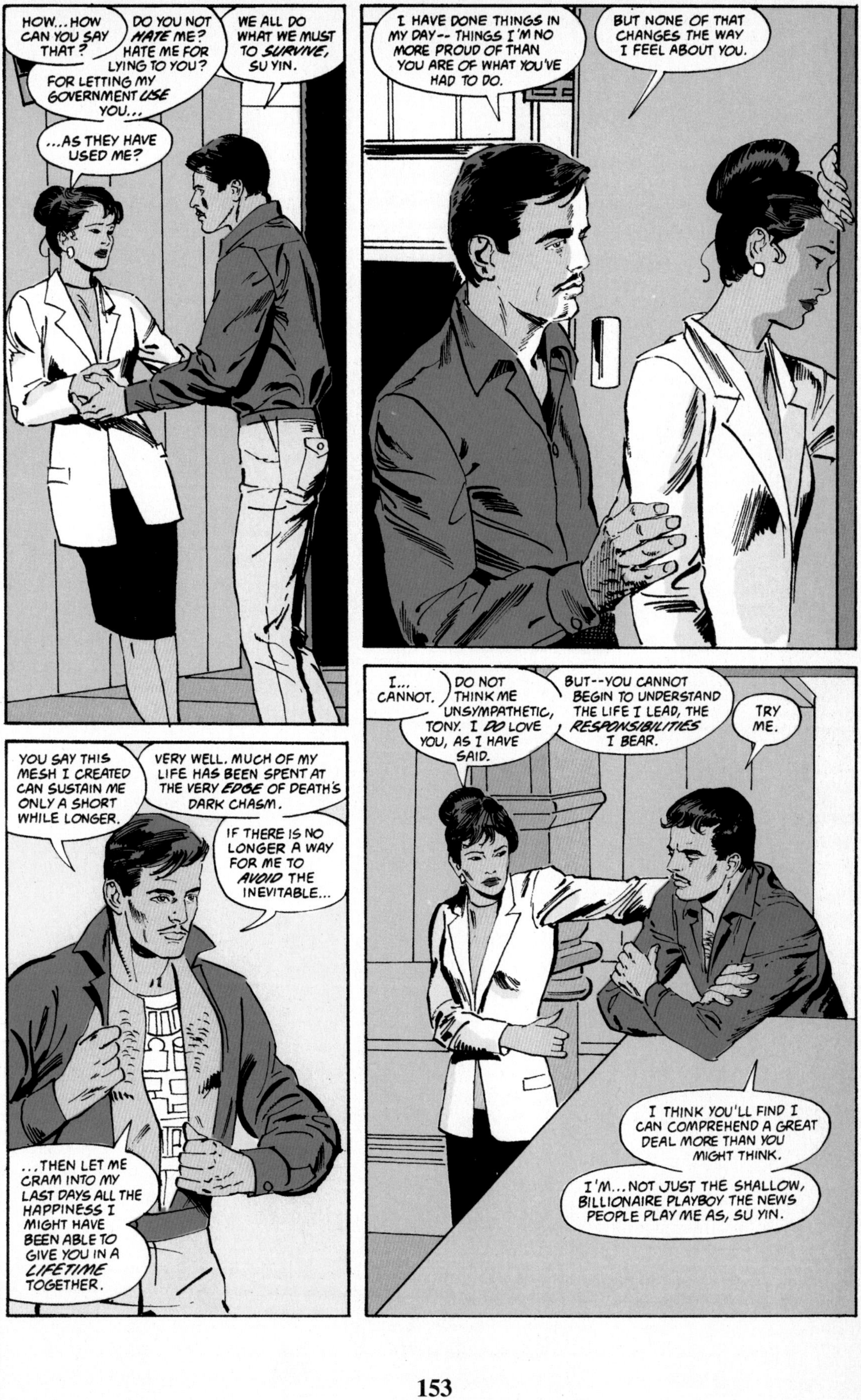
HOW...HOW CAN YOU SAY THAT?
DO YOU NOT HATE ME? HATE ME FOR LYING TO YOU? FOR LETTING MY GOVERNMENT USE YOU...
...AS THEY HAVE USED ME?
WE ALL DO WHAT WE MUST TO SURVIVE, SU YIN.
I HAVE DONE THINGS IN MY DAY-- THINGS I'M NO MORE PROUD OF THAN YOU ARE OF WHAT YOU'VE HAD TO DO.
BUT NONE OF THAT CHANGES THE WAY I FEEL ABOUT YOU.
YOU SAY THIS MESH I CREATED CAN SUSTAIN ME ONLY A SHORT WHILE LONGER.
VERY WELL. MUCH OF MY LIFE HAS BEEN SPENT AT THE VERY EDGE OF DEATH'S DARK CHASM.
IF THERE IS NO LONGER A WAY FOR ME TO AVOID THE INEVITABLE...
...THEN LET ME CRAM INTO MY LAST DAYS ALL THE HAPPINESS I MIGHT HAVE BEEN ABLE TO GIVE YOU IN A LIFETIME TOGETHER.
I... CANNOT.
DO NOT THINK ME UNSYMPATHETIC, TONY. I DO LOVE YOU, AS I HAVE SAID.
BUT--YOU CANNOT BEGIN TO UNDERSTAND THE LIFE I LEAD, THE RESPONSIBILITIES I BEAR.
TRY ME.
I THINK YOU'LL FIND I CAN COMPREHEND A GREAT DEAL MORE THAN YOU MIGHT THINK.
I'M...NOT JUST THE SHALLOW, BILLIONAIRE PLAYBOY THE NEWS PEOPLE PLAY ME AS, SU YIN.

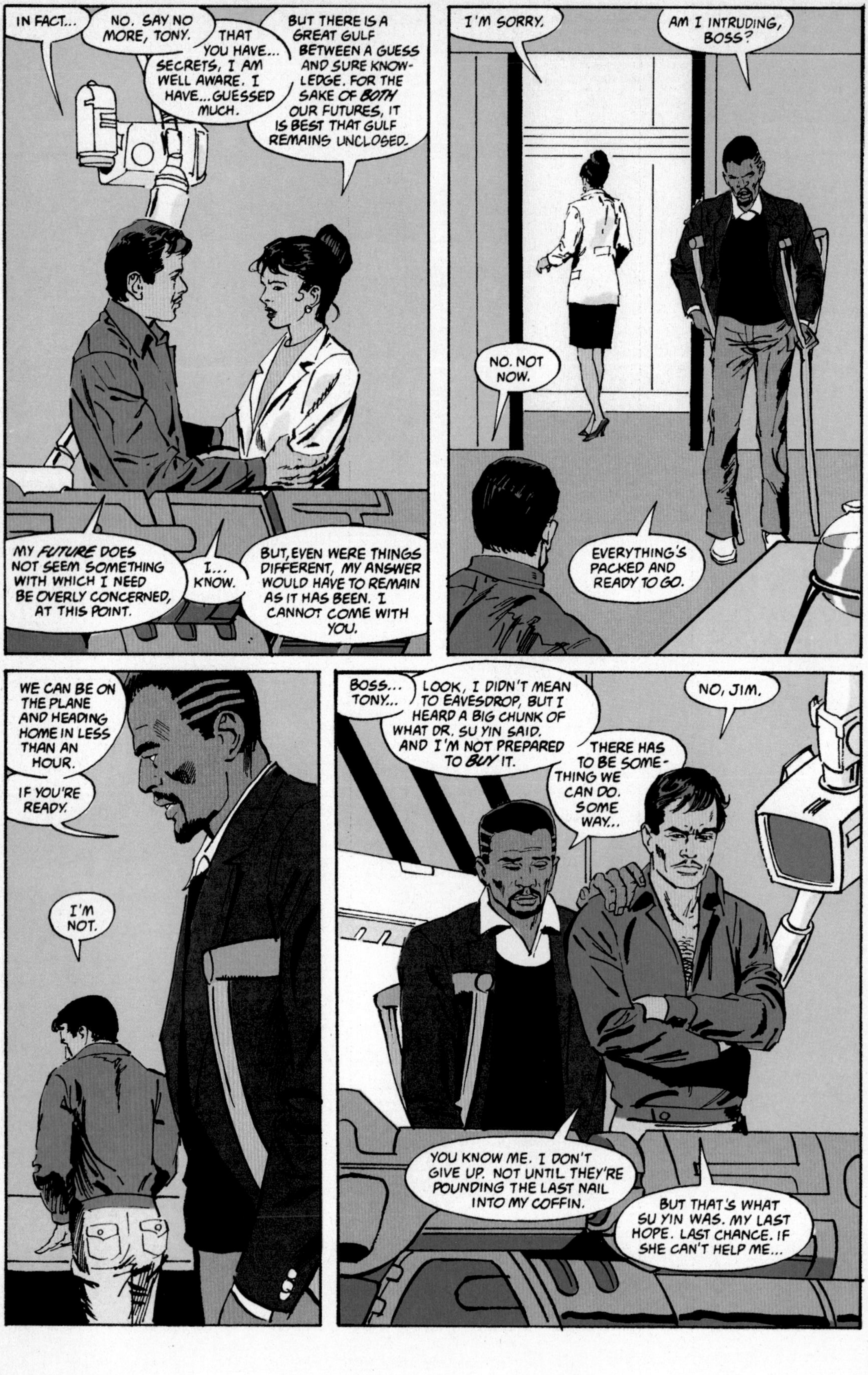

IN FACT...
NO. SAY NO MORE, TONY.
THAT YOU HAVE... SECRETS, I AM WELL AWARE. I HAVE...GUESSED MUCH.
BUT THERE IS A GREAT GULF BETWEEN A GUESS AND SURE KNOWLEDGE. FOR THE SAKE OF BOTH OUR FUTURES, IT IS BEST THAT GULF REMAINS UNCLOSED.
MY FUTURE DOES NOT SEEM SOMETHING WITH WHICH I NEED BE OVERLY CONCERNED, AT THIS POINT.
I... KNOW.
BUT, EVEN WERE THINGS DIFFERENT, MY ANSWER WOULD HAVE TO REMAIN AS IT HAS BEEN. I CANNOT COME WITH YOU.
I'M SORRY.
AM I INTRUDING, BOSS?
NO. NOT NOW.
EVERYTHING'S PACKED AND READY TO GO.
WE CAN BE ON THE PLANE AND HEADING HOME IN LESS THAN AN HOUR.
IF YOU'RE READY.
I'M NOT.
BOSS... TONY...
LOOK, I DIDN'T MEAN TO EAVESDROP, BUT I HEARD A BIG CHUNK OF WHAT DR. SU YIN SAID. AND I'M NOT PREPARED TO BUY IT.
NO, JIM.
THERE HAS TO BE SOMETHING WE CAN DO. SOME WAY...
YOU KNOW ME. I DON'T GIVE UP. NOT UNTIL THEY'RE POUNDING THE LAST NAIL INTO MY COFFIN.
BUT THAT'S WHAT SU YIN WAS. MY LAST HOPE. LAST CHANCE. IF SHE CAN'T HELP ME...

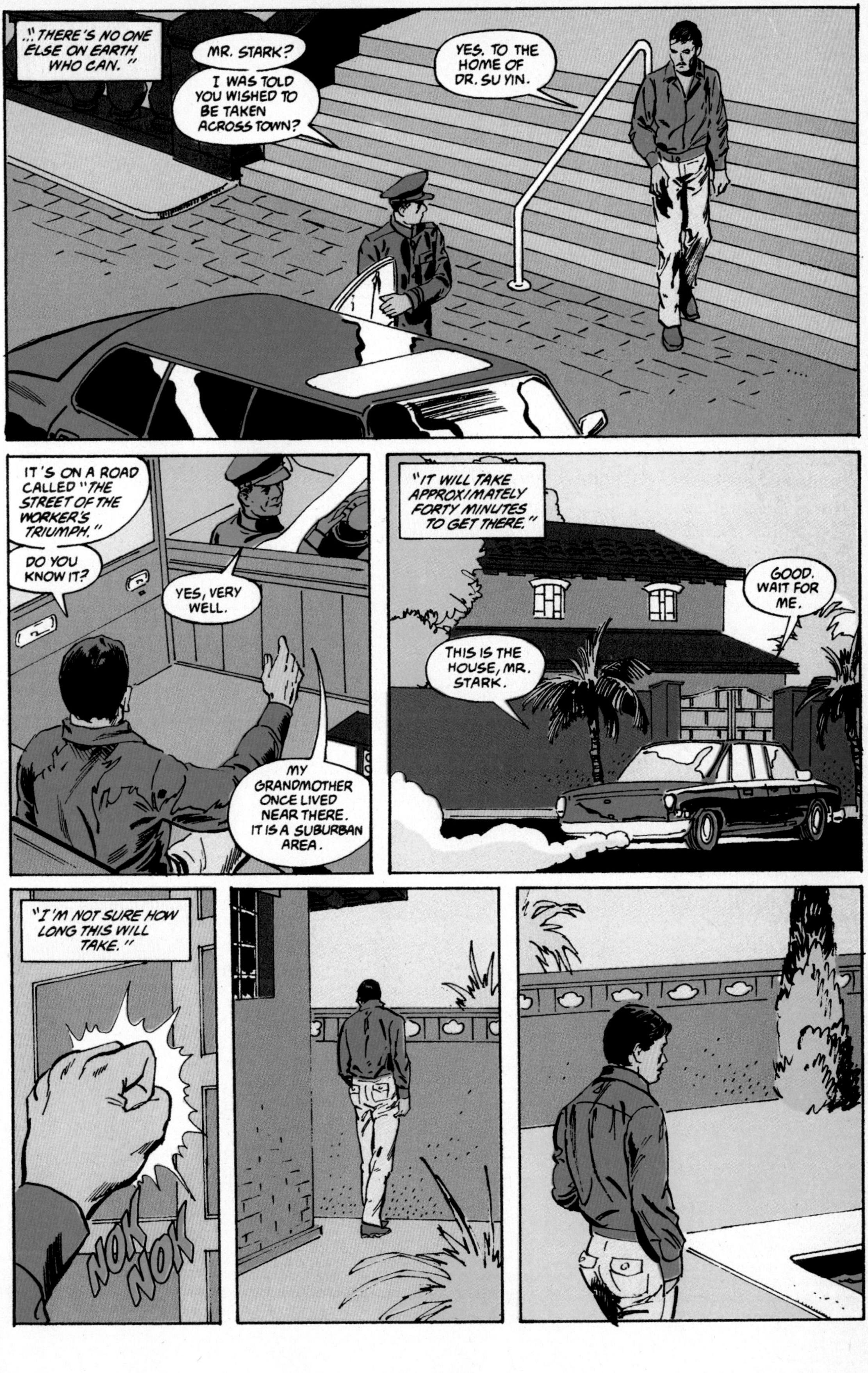

"...THERE'S NO ONE ELSE ON EARTH WHO CAN."
MR. STARK?
I WAS TOLD YOU WISHED TO BE TAKEN ACROSS TOWN?
YES. TO THE HOME OF DR. SU YIN.
IT'S ON A ROAD CALLED "THE STREET OF THE WORKER'S TRIUMPH."
DO YOU KNOW IT?
YES, VERY WELL.
MY GRANDMOTHER ONCE LIVED NEAR THERE. IT IS A SUBURBAN AREA.
"IT WILL TAKE APPROXIMATELY FORTY MINUTES TO GET THERE."
THIS IS THE HOUSE, MR. STARK.
GOOD. WAIT FOR ME.
"I'M NOT SURE HOW LONG THIS WILL TAKE."
NOK NOK

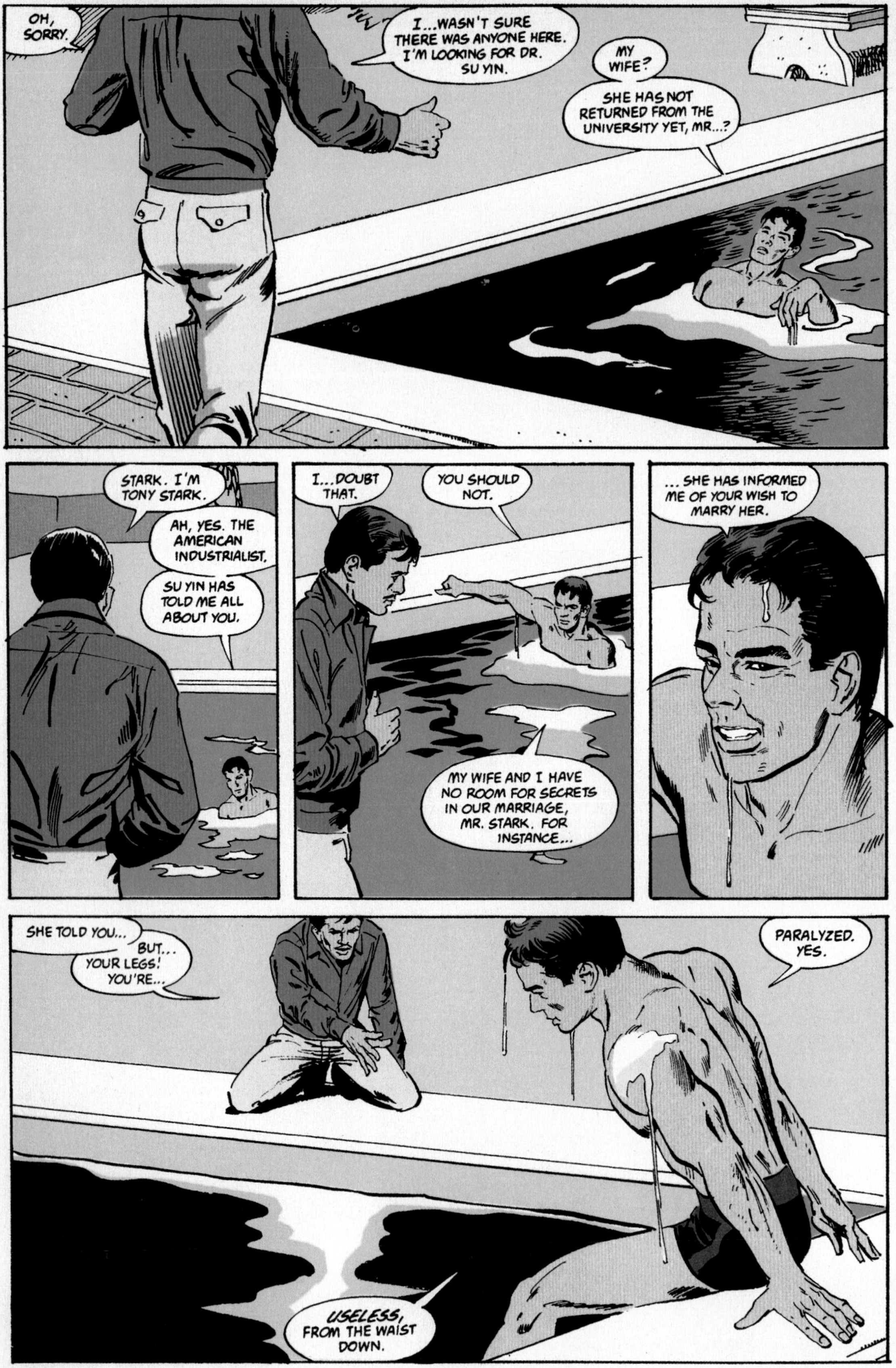
OH, SORRY.
I...WASN'T SURE THERE WAS ANYONE HERE. I'M LOOKING FOR DR. SU YIN.
MY WIFE?
SHE HAS NOT RETURNED FROM THE UNIVERSITY YET, MR...?
STARK. I'M TONY STARK.
AH, YES. THE AMERICAN INDUSTRIALIST.
SU YIN HAS TOLD ME ALL ABOUT YOU.
I...DOUBT THAT.
YOU SHOULD NOT.
MY WIFE AND I HAVE NO ROOM FOR SECRETS IN OUR MARRIAGE, MR. STARK. FOR INSTANCE...
... SHE HAS INFORMED ME OF YOUR WISH TO MARRY HER.
SHE TOLD YOU...
BUT... YOUR LEGS! YOU'RE...
PARALYZED. YES.
USELESS, FROM THE WAIST DOWN.

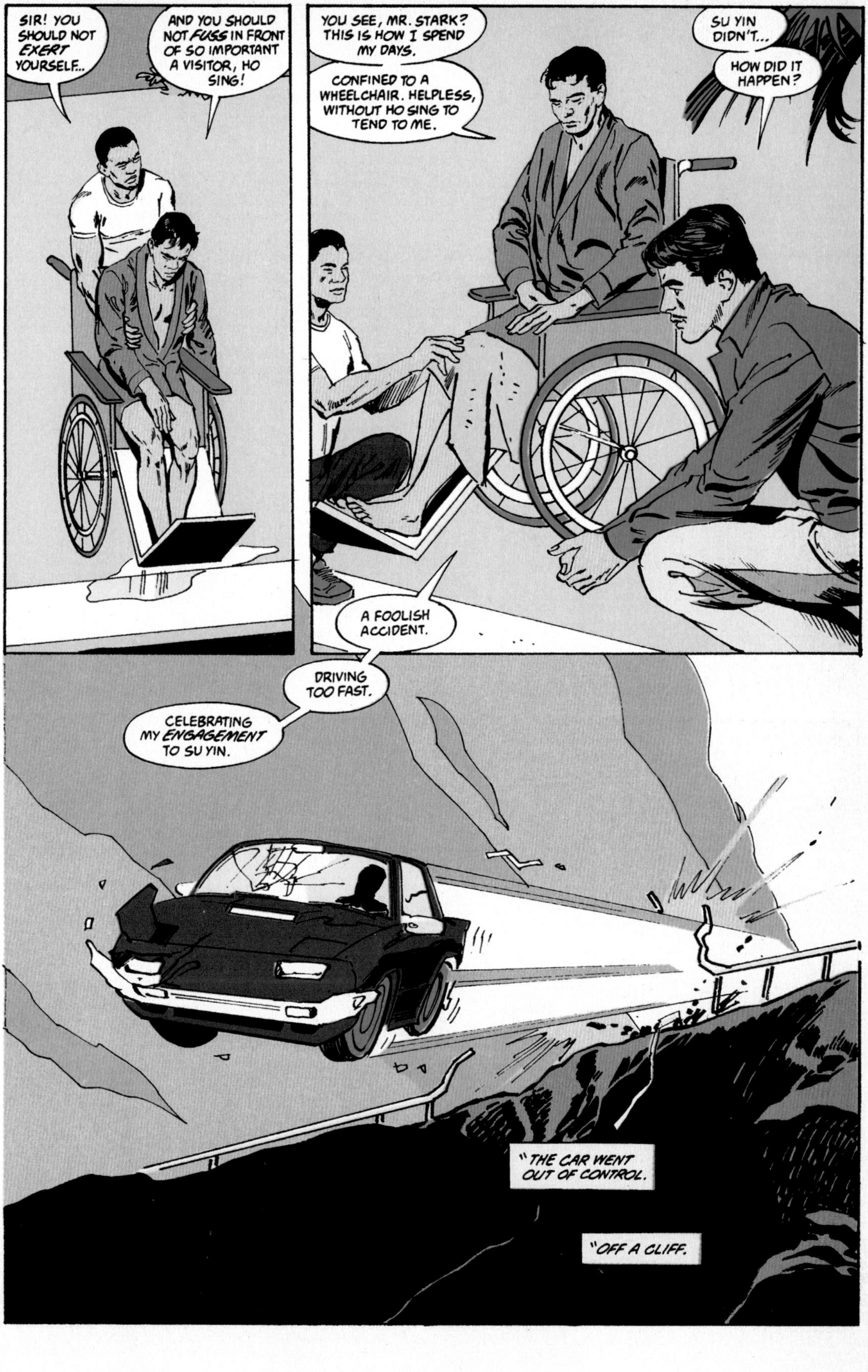
SIR! YOU SHOULD NOT *EXERT* YOURSELF..
AND YOU SHOULD NOT *FUSS* IN FRONT OF SO IMPORTANT A VISITOR, HO SING!
YOU SEE, MR. STARK? THIS IS HOW I SPEND MY DAYS.
CONFINED TO A WHEELCHAIR. HELPLESS, WITHOUT HO SING TO TEND TO ME.
SU YIN DIDN'T...
HOW DID IT HAPPEN?
A FOOLISH ACCIDENT.
DRIVING TOO FAST.
CELEBRATING MY *ENGAGEMENT* TO SU YIN.
"THE CAR WENT OUT OF CONTROL.
"OFF A CLIFF.

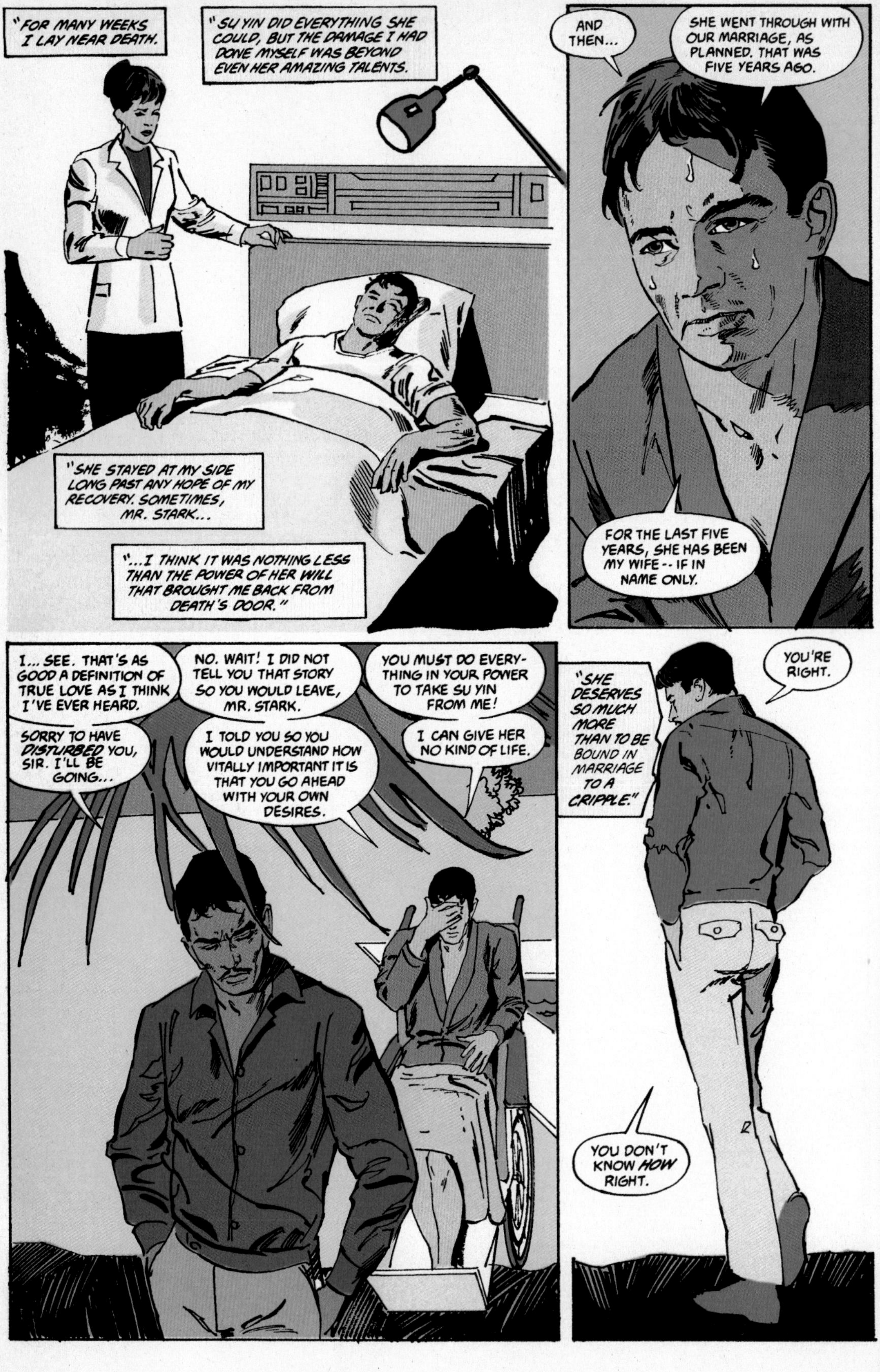
"FOR MANY WEEKS I LAY NEAR DEATH.
"SU YIN DID EVERYTHING SHE COULD, BUT THE DAMAGE I HAD DONE MYSELF WAS BEYOND EVEN HER AMAZING TALENTS.
"SHE STAYED AT MY SIDE LONG PAST ANY HOPE OF MY RECOVERY. SOMETIMES, MR. STARK...
"...I THINK IT WAS NOTHING LESS THAN THE POWER OF HER WILL THAT BROUGHT ME BACK FROM DEATH'S DOOR."
AND THEN...
SHE WENT THROUGH WITH OUR MARRIAGE, AS PLANNED. THAT WAS FIVE YEARS AGO.
FOR THE LAST FIVE YEARS, SHE HAS BEEN MY WIFE -- IF IN NAME ONLY.
I... SEE. THAT'S AS GOOD A DEFINITION OF TRUE LOVE AS I THINK I'VE EVER HEARD.
SORRY TO HAVE DISTURBED YOU, SIR. I'LL BE GOING...
NO. WAIT! I DID NOT TELL YOU THAT STORY SO YOU WOULD LEAVE, MR. STARK.
I TOLD YOU SO YOU WOULD UNDERSTAND HOW VITALLY IMPORTANT IT IS THAT YOU GO AHEAD WITH YOUR OWN DESIRES.
YOU MUST DO EVERYTHING IN YOUR POWER TO TAKE SU YIN FROM ME!
I CAN GIVE HER NO KIND OF LIFE.
"SHE DESERVES SO MUCH MORE THAN TO BE BOUND IN MARRIAGE TO A CRIPPLE."
YOU'RE RIGHT.
YOU DON'T KNOW HOW RIGHT.

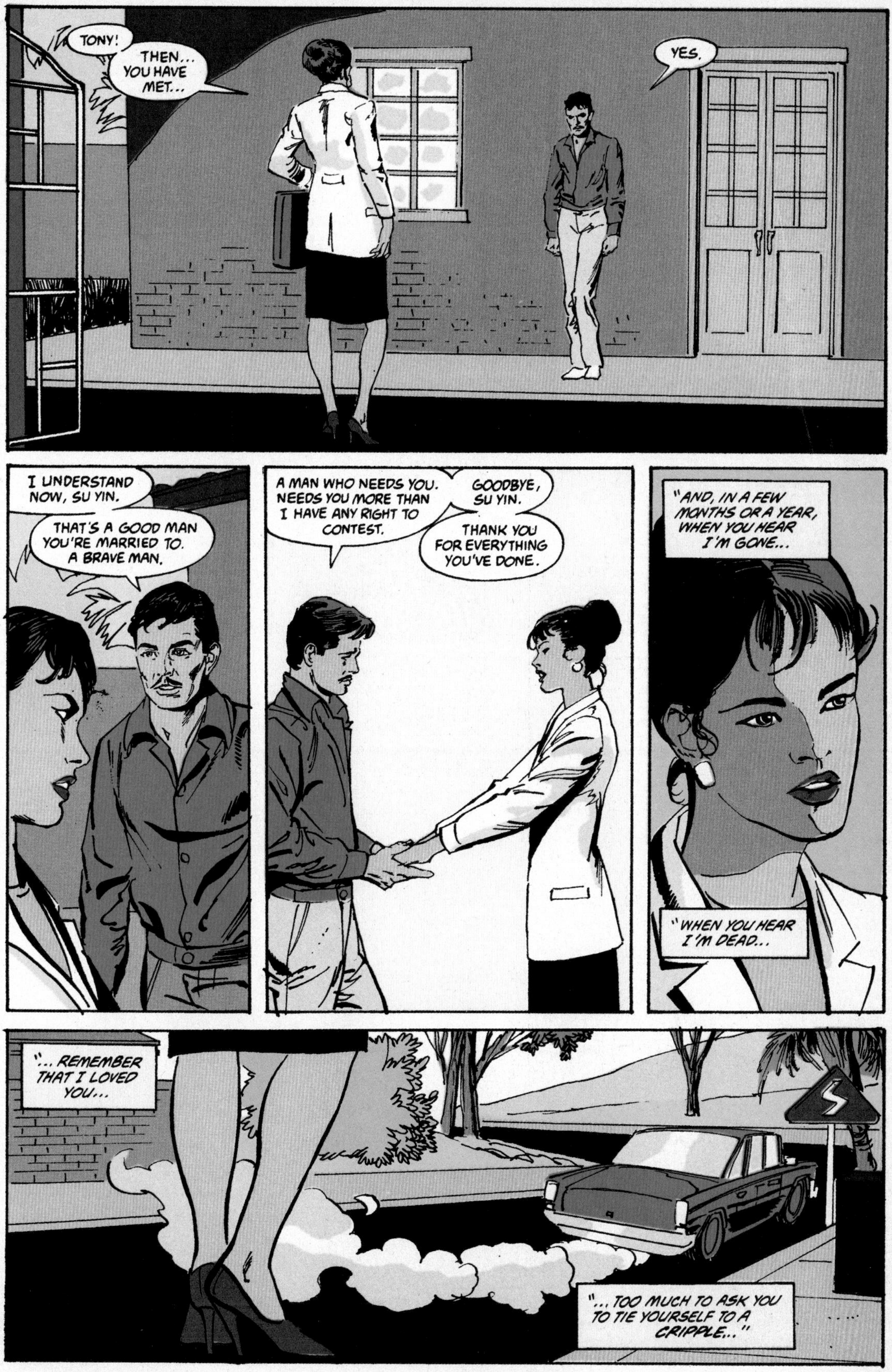
TONY!
THEN... YOU HAVE MET...
YES.
I UNDERSTAND NOW, SU YIN.
THAT'S A GOOD MAN YOU'RE MARRIED TO. A BRAVE MAN.
A MAN WHO NEEDS YOU. NEEDS YOU MORE THAN I HAVE ANY RIGHT TO CONTEST.
GOODBYE, SU YIN.
THANK YOU FOR EVERYTHING YOU'VE DONE.
"AND, IN A FEW MONTHS OR A YEAR, WHEN YOU HEAR I'M GONE...
"WHEN YOU HEAR I'M DEAD...
"...REMEMBER THAT I LOVED YOU...
"...TOO MUCH TO ASK YOU TO TIE YOURSELF TO A CRIPPLE..."